ROUSSEAU'S *SOCIAL CONTRACT*

An Introduction

If the greatness of a philosophical work can be measured by the volume and vehemence of the public response, there is little question that Rousseau's *Social Contract* stands out as a masterpiece. Within a week of its publication in 1762 it was banned in France. Soon thereafter, Rousseau fled to Geneva, where he saw the book burned in public. At the same time, many of his contemporaries, such as Kant, considered Rousseau to be "the Newton of the moral world," as he was the first philosopher to draw attention to the basic dignity of human nature. The *Social Contract* has never ceased to be read and debated in the 250 years since its publication. *Rousseau's* Social Contract*: An Introduction* offers a thorough and systematic tour of this notoriously paradoxical and challenging text. David Lay Williams offers a chapter-by-chapter reading of the *Social Contract*, squarely confronting its interpretive obstacles, leaving no stones unturned. The conclusion connects Rousseau's text to both his important influences and those who took inspiration and sometimes exception to his arguments. The book also features a special extended appendix dedicated to outlining his general will, which has been the object of controversy since the *Social Contract*'s publication.

DAVID LAY WILLIAMS is Associate Professor of Political Science at DePaul University and the author of *Rousseau's Platonic Enlightenment* (2007) and *The General Will: The Evolution of a Concept* (forthcoming from Cambridge University Press), as well as numerous articles in journals such as *History of Political Thought, Journal of the History of Ideas, The Journal of Politics*, the *American Journal of Political Science*, and *Polity*. He has twice held fellowships at the Institute for Research in the Humanities at the University of Wisconsin–Madison, as well as a fellowship at the DePaul Humanities Center. He was formerly Professor of Philosophy and Political Science at the University of Wisconsin–Stevens Point.

CAMBRIDGE INTRODUCTIONS TO KEY PHILOSOPHICAL TEXTS

This new series offers introductory textbooks on what are considered to be the most important texts of Western philosophy. Each book guides the reader through the main themes and arguments of the work in question, while also paying attention to its historical context and its philosophical legacy. No philosophical background knowledge is assumed, and the books will be well suited to introductory-level university courses.

Titles published in the series:

ROUSSEAU'S *SOCIAL CONTRACT*

An Introduction

DAVID LAY WILLIAMS
DePaul University

CAMBRIDGE
UNIVERSITY PRESS

CAMBRIDGE
UNIVERSITY PRESS

32 Avenue of the Americas, New York, NY 10013-2473, USA

Cambridge University Press is part of the University of Cambridge.

It furthers the University's mission by disseminating knowledge in the pursuit of
education, learning, and research at the highest international levels of excellence.

www.cambridge.org
Information on this title: www.cambridge.org/9780521124447

© David Lay Williams 2014

First published 2014

Printed in the United States of America

A catalog record for this publication is available from the British Library.

Library of Congress Cataloging in Publication data
Williams, David Lay, 1969–
Rousseau's social contract : an introduction / David Lay Williams, DePaul University.
pages cm. (Cambridge introductions to key philosophical texts)
Includes bibliographical references and index.
ISBN 978-0-521-19755-7 Hardback
ISBN 978-0-521-12444-7 Paperback
1. Rousseau, Jean-Jacques, 1712–1778. Du contrat social. I. Title.
JC179.R88W55 2014
320.1′1–dc23 CIP 2013008027

ISBN 978-0-521-19755-7 Hardback
ISBN 978-0-521-12444-7 Paperback

In Memory of Richard Taylor Williams, Sr.

Contents

Acknowledgments

One does not write a book like this without a good deal of assistance, and I have been fortunate to have received more than my fair share. I want to thank Nicholas Dent, Ryan Patrick Hanley, Christopher Kelly, Michael Locke McLendon, Ethan Putterman, Grace Roosevelt, Melissa Schwartzberg, and Matthew Simpson for sharing their expertise on Rousseau repeatedly in many unexpected and especially helpful ways. Daniel J. Kapust and Andrew Laird offered helpful insights on Roman politics, history, and culture when I was writing Chapter 4. A. P. Martinich patiently answered numerous inquiries on Thomas Hobbes. Nerissa Nelson and Alex Schmetzke were especially helpful and creative in assisting with various elements of this project at the University of Wisconsin–Stevens Point library. Jonathan Bloch, Alan J. Kellner, Matthew W. Maguire, Jonathan Marks, J. Rixey Ruffin, and an anonymous reader at Cambridge read this manuscript carefully, improving it significantly on myriad points. I would also like to thank Beatrice Rehl at Cambridge University Press for her confidence in and guidance on this project.

I also greatly benefited from the support of numerous friends and colleagues, including Ken Abrams, Dave Arnold, Michael and Carey Cairo, Darren Carlton, David Chan, Polo Chen, Jennifer Collins, James Farr, Doug Forbes, Karin Fry, Mark Hawley, Tracy Hofer, Anna Law, Brad and Megan Mapes-Martins, Ed Miller, Steven Nadler, Sean Phillips, James and Toni Sage, Greg Summers, Frank Thames, Mick Veum, and Scott Wallace. I also am grateful for administrative support from John Blakeman, Chris Cirmo, Susan Friedman, Wayne Steger, Chuck Suchar, and Dôna Warren. Along these lines, I want to thank the departments of Philosophy and Political Science at the University of Wisconsin–Stevens Point, the Institute for Research in the Humanities at the University of Wisconsin–Madison, the DePaul Humanities Center, and the Department of Political Science at DePaul University for providing academic homes during the past few years in which I developed and completed this project.

Since this book is intended to be accessible to students, I want to make a special point of thanking my own undergraduate political philosophy instructors, Gregg Franzwa, Richard Galvin, and Charles Lockhart, who introduced me to the field many years ago and patiently worked to polish a very rough stone. Along these lines, I also remain grateful to T. K. Seung and Patrick Riley, who continue to be sources of ideas and inspiration.

My family has been especially supportive and patient. My in-laws, Larry and Julia Weiser, Maggie Weiser, Ken Stevenson, and Michael and Emily Weiser, have generously included me in their clan, even at the risk of discussing Rousseau over Thanksgiving dinner. My mother, Julianne Williams, and my aunt, Carol Fletcher, have been regular sources of love and support. My wife, Jen Weiser, tolerates me for reasons that continue to escape me, but for which I remain very grateful; and our son, Benjamin Williams, has been a welcome distraction from work and a constant source of joy. Finally, I would like to dedicate this book to the memory of my father, Richard Taylor Williams, Sr., who passed away as I was completing the manuscript. It was only with that loss that I came to realize what first inclined me to study Rousseau. He was my original image of humanity's natural goodness, untouched by all corruption and entirely upright in his affairs. I will never understand why I should have been so lucky to have had him in my life, but I remain eternally grateful.

Frequently Cited Works

Citations in this book are, wherever possible, to existing English translations of Rousseau's works. For scholarly use, each citation is accompanied in brackets by a corresponding reference to the authoritative French edition to Rousseau's complete works. All references to the *Social Contract* are in text for easy access, including reference to Book, Chapter, and paragraph numbers, as can be found in Victor Gourevitch's edition for Cambridge Texts in the History of Political Thought series. All other citations are in footnotes. In the footnotes, the following terms stand in for full titles:

Confessions = *The Confessions and Correspondence, Including the Letters to Malesherbes*, ed. Christopher Kelly, Roger D. Masters, and Peter G. Stillman. Vol. 5 of *The Collected Writings of Rousseau*.

Corsica = *Plan for a Constitution for Corsica*, ed. Christopher Kelly. In *The Plan for Perpetual Peace, On the Government of Poland, and Other Writings on History and Politics*, Vol. 11 of *The Collected Writings of Rousseau*.

Dialogues = *Rousseau, Judge of Jean-Jacques: Dialogues*, ed. Roger D. Masters and Christopher Kelly. Vol. 1 of *The Collected Writings of Rousseau*.

Emile = *Emile, or On Education*. Trans. Allan Bloom. New York: Basic Books.

First Discourse = *Discourse on the Arts and Sciences*. In *The Discourses and Other Early Political Writings*, ed. Victor Gourevitch.

Government of Geneva = *History of the Government of Geneva*. In *Letter to Beaumont, Letters Written from the Mountain, and Related Writings*, ed. Christopher Kelly and Eve Grace. Vol. 9 of *The Collected Writings of Rousseau*.

Hero = *Discourse on This Question: What Is the Virtue a Hero Most Needs and Who Are the Heroes Who Have Lacked This Virtue?* In *The Discourses and Other Early Political Writings*, ed. Victor Gourevitch.

Judgment = *Judgment of the Plan for Perpetual Peace.* In *The Plan for Perpetual Peace, On the Government of Poland, and Other Writings on History and Politics*, ed. Christopher Kelly. In Vol. 11 of *The Collected Writings of Rousseau.*

Julie = *Julie; Or, the New Heloise: Letters of Two Lovers Who Live in a Small Town at the Foot of the Alps.* Trans. Philip Stewart and Jean Vaché. Vol. 6 of *The Collected Writings of Rousseau.*

"Last Reply" = "Last Reply by Jean-Jacques Rousseau of Geneva." In *The Discourses and Other Early Political Writings*, ed. Victor Gourevitch.

"Legal Profession" = "Response to the Anonymous Letter Written by Members of the Legal Profession." In *Letter to d'Alembert and Writings for the Theater*, ed. Allan Bloom, Charles Butterworth, and Christopher Kelly. Vol. 10 of *The Collected Writings of Rousseau.*

Letter to d'Alembert = *Letter to M. d'Alembert on the Theater*, trans. Allan Bloom. Ithaca, NY: Cornell University Press.

"Letter to Franquières" = "Letter from J. J. Rousseau to M. de Franquières, 25 March 1769." In *The Social Contract and Other Later Political Writings*, ed. Victor Gourevitch.

"Letter to Voltaire" = "Letter from J. J. Rousseau to M. de Voltaire, 18 August 1756." In *The Social Contract and Other Later Political Writings,* ed. Victor Gourevitch.

Mountain = *Letters Written from the Mountain.* In *Letter to Beaumont, Letters Written from the Mountain, and Related Writings*, ed. Christopher Kelly and Eve Grace. Vol. 9 of *The Collected Writings of Rousseau.*

"Narcissus" = "Preface to Narcissus." In *The Discourses and Other Early Political Writings*, ed. Victor Gourevitch.

"Observations" = "Observations by Jean-Jacques Rousseau of Geneva on the Answer Made to His Discourse." In *The Discourses and Other Early Political Writings*, ed. Victor Gourevitch.

Origin of Languages = *Essay on the Origin of Languages in Which Something Is Said About Melody and Musical Imitation.* In *The Discourses and Other Early Political Writings*, ed. Victor Gourevitch.

Poland = *Considerations on the Government of Poland.* In *The Social Contract and Other Later Political Writings*, ed. Victor Gourevitch.

Political Economy = *Discourse on Political Economy.* In *The Social Contract and Other Later Political Writings*, ed. Victor Gourevitch.

Reveries = Jean-Jacques Rousseau. *Reveries of the Solitary Walker.* Trans. Charles E. Butterworth.

SC = *Of the Social Contract*. Ed. Victor Gourevitch. Cambridge: Cambridge University Press.

Second Discourse = *Discourse on the Origin and the Foundations of Inequality Among Men*. In *The Discourses and Other Early Political Writings*, ed. Victor Gourevitch. Cambridge: Cambridge University Press.

"Theatrical Imitation" = "On Theatrical Imitation: An Essay Drawn from Plato's Dialogues." In *Essay on the Origin of Languages and Writings Related to Music*, ed. John T. Scott. Vol. 7 of *The Collected Writings of Rousseau*.

"Wealth" = "On Wealth and Fragments on Taste." In *The Plan for Perpetual Peace, On the Government of Poland, and Other Writings on History and Politics*, ed. Christopher Kelly. Vol. 11 of *The Collected Writings of Rousseau*.

Introduction

If the significance of a political treatise can be measured by the volume and vehemence of its commentators, then Jean-Jacques Rousseau's *Social Contract* easily stands out as among the most important works of its kind. Within weeks of its publication in 1762, it was banned in France. Less than a month thereafter, Rousseau found himself effectively banished. He sought refuge in his boyhood home of Geneva, only to find his book being burned in the public squares. Perhaps his best-known literary contemporary and interlocutor, Voltaire, would call the *Social Contract* the *"Unsocial Contract*, by the not very sociable Jean-Jacques Rousseau." He subsequently endorsed Rousseau's banishment from Geneva, remarking, "Let the Council punish him with the full severity of the laws … as a blasphemous subversive who blasphemes Jesus Christ while calling himself a Christian, and who wants to overturn his country while calling himself a citizen." Time did not mellow critics of the *Social Contract*. A generation later, Benjamin Constant argued that "the subtle metaphysics of the *Social Contract* can only serve today to supply weapons and pretexts to all kinds of tyranny, that of one man, that of several and that of all, to oppression either organized under legal forms or exercised through popular violence." Shortly thereafter, the nineteenth-century socialist Pierre-Joseph Proudhon would comment, "It is this [social] contract of hatred, this monument of incurable misanthropy, this coalition of the barons of property, commerce and industry against the disinherited lower class, this oath of social war indeed, which Rousseau calls *Social Contract*, with a presumption which I should call that of a scoundrel."[1]

In the twentieth century, in the wake of two horrific world wars, Rousseau became a favorite target of liberal intellectuals. Isaiah Berlin labeled him "the most sinister and most formidable enemy of liberty in the whole history of modern thought." Bertrand Russell warned that the

[1] Voltaire, quoted in Leo Damrosch 2005, 390; Constant [1814] 1988, 106; Proudhon [1851] 2007, 118.

Social Contract's "doctrine of the general will ... made possible the mystic identification of a leader with his people, which has no need of confirmation by so mundane an apparatus as the ballot-box." The philosopher of science, Karl Popper, would call Rousseau "one of the most pernicious influences in the history of social philosophy."[2]

Even today, Rousseau's doctrines articulated in the *Social Contract* continue to provoke hostility. Contemporary conservative commentators have identified Rousseau as laying the foundation for "all mob leaders, from Robespierre to Fidel Castro to the Democratic Party"; accused him of driving citizens away from God and family into the arms of "Beer, sports, television, movies, video games, iPods, the Internet, sex, [and] sleep"; found in him moral principles so flexible that they have produced "holocausts and gulags as easily as free dental plans and kindergartens"; and have even crowned him the "Dark Prince of the Enlightenment." At the same time he has remained threatening to the Left, having provoked Daniel Bell to remark, "The price of equality [in the *Social Contract*] is ... that 'an individual can no longer claim anything'; he has no individual rights; 'his person and his whole power' are dissolved into the general will. Equality is only possible in community through the eclipse of the self."[3]

Yet not all responses have been so viscerally negative. Among his contemporaries, Adam Smith was deeply stirred by Rousseau's critiques of the newly emerging commercial economy.[4] The French appropriated his concept of the general will and its associated values for its Declaration of the Rights of Man. James Madison described Rousseau as the "most distinguished" of philanthropists. Immanuel Kant found in Rousseau the "Newton of the moral world," the philosopher who for the first time drew attention to the basic dignity attached to human nature. Nearly two centuries later, this sentiment continued to echo in the writings of John Rawls, who identified both Rousseau and Kant as representing the "high point of the contractarian tradition," and the writings of Jürgen Habermas, who celebrates Rousseau for his championing of the democratic principles of liberty and equality.[5] Right, left, early modern, late modern, postmodern, analytic, or Continental – the ideas of the *Social Contract* have never failed to provoke, instigate, disgust, and inspire.

Of course, the widely divergent reactions to Rousseau and the *Social Contract* raise the question of *why* one text has lent itself to various and

[2] Berlin 2002, 49; Russell [1945] 1972, 700; Popper [1945] 1971, 257n20.
[3] Coulter 2011, 142; Wiker 2008, 52; Koons 2011, 136; Williamson 2011, 161; Bell 1976, 436.
[4] See Rasmussen 2008; Hanley 2008a; and Lomonaco 2002.
[5] Madison 1999, 505; Rawls 1971, 252; Habermas 1997, 44.

viscerally opposed readings. To be sure, readers always bring their own set of experiences, temperaments, backgrounds, and preferences with them. But this alone is inadequate to explain the contested readings of the *Social Contract*. Rousseau litters the treatise with juxtapositions, apparent paradoxes, puzzles, and ambiguities. He appropriates the modern device of the social contract to secure ancient values; he places sovereignty in the hands of those whom he labels ignorant; he condemns figures like Thomas Hobbes for the central tenets of his politics and metaphysics, yet praises his genius; he demands that his republic be held to sometimes impractical or even utopian standards, while at the same time providing counsel on how to proceed absent those conditions; he elevates the people to the level of sovereign and yet dismisses democratic governance as entirely impracticable; and, most (in)famously, he demands that republican subjects be forced to be free. Some of these tensions are resolved or at least understood easily enough with sufficient attention. Some of them will likely remain contentious and troublesome as long as readers continue to be drawn to the *Social Contract*. This book aims to understand and explain those tensions where possible and offer readers at least some capacity to make informed judgments on those elements of his political philosophy that continue to spark debate.

In order to make sense of Rousseau's political philosophy, however, it is necessary first to understand the context in which he wrote. The *Social Contract* is, after all, a solution to a set of social and political problems. Without grasping the problems it is meant to solve, readers will find the treatise elusive in important respects. These problems can be understood through consideration of the issues dominating Rousseau's Geneva, and then of his formulation of those problems in his first two *Discourses*: the *Discourse on the Sciences and the Arts* (1751) and the *Discourse on the Origins of Inequality* (1755).

I. THE GENEVAN CONTEXT

As he does with his first two *Discourses*, Rousseau identifies himself on the title page of the *Social Contract* as a "Citizen of Geneva." He was born and raised in the city-state, and it would remain a part of his political consciousness throughout his career. Geneva rests at the far west end of scenic Lake Geneva and within sight of the Alps. The city had at one time been a part of the Holy Roman Empire, but by the fifteenth century political power was officially shared between the local bishop and the citizens. As such, Geneva proudly defined itself as operating under a mixed constitution amidst a sea of monarchies. One of these monarchies, the House of Savoy, was a looming and persistent meddler – although Geneva had been generally successful in warding off its threats.

The Reformation introduced significant developments. The city embraced Luther's theology and officially rejected Catholicism in 1535, labeling the pope the Antichrist. To consolidate these changes Geneva invited the noted theologian, Jean Calvin, to establish a new code of civil and ecclesiastical laws. Calvin emphasized the importance of a religious education for children and established a consistory of pastors to ensure the conformity of civil laws to scripture. The overarching foundation of the law for Calvin was derived from his conception of God's moral law, which demands that citizens love one another "with unfeigned love," which he calls "the true and eternal rule of justice, laid down for all those in every age and of every nation who want to order their lives in accordance with the will of God."[6] In practice, his Genevan laws were stringent by today's standards and even those of the sixteenth century, including the regulation of drinking, dancing, sexuality, and swearing. And although these reforms would have their critics, Rousseau was at least partly an admirer, who expressed great appreciation for the "range of his [Calvin's] genius," especially in the "framing of our wise Edicts, in which he played a large part" (*SC*, 2.7.9n, 70n [III: 383n]).

In the years following Calvin, Geneva's deep religiosity and moralism slowly faded and more practical political dimensions took center stage. The city's constitution was officially mixed, with power shared between the citizens and a small group of elites. These two groups corresponded to the two "Councils" of the constitution. The General Council was an assembly of all citizens, who possessed in theory the power of legislation. On the one hand, placing legislative power in the hands of the citizens was a remarkably democratic device in the early eighteenth century, when monarchs still wielded enormous power in most neighboring lands. On the other hand, these democratic elements were moderated by somewhat predictable citizenship restrictions out of tune with our democratic standards. Of the nearly 25,000 inhabitants of Geneva, only approximately 1,500 qualified for citizenship by virtue of sex, moral uprightness, financial solvency, and residency status. The democratic dimensions of the constitution were further mitigated by the other major institution: the Small Council. The Small Council consisted of twenty members who were chosen by a committee of wealthy citizens – a committee itself selected by

[6] Calvin [1536] 1991, 67.

the Small Council. It is for this reason that James Miller has rejected the notion that Geneva was a democracy. It was rather, in his estimation, "a functioning oligarchy"[7] ruled by old money.

For many years, this division of power was accepted. But as the ruling elite became more ostentatious in displaying its wealth and wielding its power, the citizens demanded changes. In 1707, five years before Rousseau's birth, they found a sympathetic ear in Pierre Fatio, a member of the Small Council appointed to hear the grievances of the General Council. He accepted their complaints as largely valid and submitted a report to the Small Committee recommending several democratic reforms, including official recognition of the people as "sovereign." The Small Council responded by instituting ineffective and merely token reforms. After the citizens expressed their disappointment, the Small Council had Fatio arrested and shot. This silenced the movement for the short term, but the quest for a real popular sovereignty persisted and took on new life in the 1730s. Citizens raised the volume and frequency of their demands with a flurry of pamphlets asking, in the words of one, "To what will our freedom be reduced, if we cannot prescribe it for ourselves, if we cannot change the Laws and the Government as soon as a great number among us indicate the desire?"[8]

Two of the leading natural law theorists of the day, Jean Barbeyrac (1674–1744) and Jean-Jacques Burlamaqui (1698–1748), both with Genevan ties, lent their support to the Small Council.[9] Drawing largely from Thomas Hobbes's characterization of human nature as anti-social and violent, they argued that government's first responsibility is order and stability. Barbeyrac described the General Council as made up of "ignoramuses, trouble-makers, or people easily manipulated by the first demagogue who presents himself," and proceeded on those lines to conclude that popular sovereignty could only result in "a perpetual theater of disorder, sedition, trouble, and injustice." And although he admired liberty, he was an even greater believer in peace and tranquility, which requires that "a few things must be sacrificed for it."[10]

These political tensions came to a head in 1734–38 when armed militia members joined the popular movement and took to the streets. With Rousseau in town on August 21, 1737, the citizens overwhelmed a mercenary garrison, killed their captain, and seized control of Geneva. Realizing

[7] Miller 1984, 15.
[8] Anonymous pamphlet, quoted in Miller 1984, 16.
[9] See Rosenblatt 1997, 101–2.
[10] Barbeyrace, quoted in Rosenblatt 1997, 130.

it had no other choice, the Small Council agreed to a compromise acknowledging the General Council as "sovereign" and granting it the right to protest the abuses of the Small Council. While some members of the uprising were concerned that the compromise failed to secure greater rights for the citizens, the majority, weary of unrest and eager to restore some degree of normalcy, struck a truce.

Parallel to these explicitly political events in Geneva were economic and social developments. The slow shift from feudalism to capitalism was accompanied by significant growing pains. The emerging bourgeois class generated abundant wealth, to be sure. This included the manufacturing of luxury goods and a robust industry of international banking. Yet this wealth was not broadly shared. The bankers and merchants effectively controlled the government and hence public policy, which only exacerbated existing economic inequalities. As the well-to-do demanded the dismantling of free trade restrictions, workers' wages declined. The wealthy congregated in fashionable new sections of town and constructed opulent estates, which only fed the workers' envy. There were intellectuals of roughly this period, such as Bernard Mandeville, Jean-François Melon, Baron de Montesquieu, and David Hume, who had predicted in a new doctrine known as *doux commerce* that this increased commerce would result in greater social harmony.[11] Yet much of the Genevan citizenry remained unconvinced. Georges-Louis Le Sage (1676–1769), for example, condemned the "monstrous subordination that ambition, wealth, and luxury have introduced amongst" the merchants. In a similar spirit, Micheli du Crest lamented that the increased riches of the wealthy merely "cause them to *abandon themselves to arrogance* and to the ambition they have of *increasing their power* beyond the prescribed bounds."[12]

As scholars have previously noted, this Genevan background would manifest itself throughout Rousseau's works. His insistence that an austere yet virtuous people can hold off the threats of imposing neighbors reflects Geneva's own success in holding off the Savoy threat. His insistence that a people have strong morals reflects something of Calvin's rigorous moralism. The political instability flowing from economic inequalities between Genevan patricians and citizens is reflected in his frequent calls for more equitable distributions of wealth and explicit dismissals of *doux commerce*. His continual complaints about Hobbesianism reflect his rejection of Barbeyrac's and Burlamaqui's defense of the Small Council.

---

[11] See Rosenblatt 1997, 20–1, 53–60.
[12] Le Sage, quoted in Rosenblatt 1997, 63; Crest, quoted in Rosenblatt 1997, 64.

Most obviously, Rousseau would dedicate his *Second Discourse* to the "Magnificent, Most Honored, and Sovereign Lords" of the Genevan republic, namely, the General Council, and to express his desire to live in a land where the "People and the Sovereign are one and the same." But perhaps the greatest and most persistent legacy of the political debates in Geneva can be found in the requirement of his theory of the "general will" that the law emanate from the people themselves; this requirement echoes the repeated demands of the Genevans for popular sovereignty via their General Council.

2. FIRST DISCOURSE: DISCOURSE ON THE SCIENCES AND THE ARTS

As a relative youth, Rousseau did not set out to offer solutions to the great political problems of his day, much less those that have proved to be perennially vexing.[13] He had originally moved to Paris in 1741 at the age of twenty-nine with fifteen silver louis in his pocket, driven by the ambition to be a musical innovator and a man of letters.[14] It took him the better part of a decade, however, to arrive at the discipline on which the bulk of his reputation would ultimately rest: politics. Between 1742 and 1751, he found himself completely immersed in the inner circles of the most radical and original thinkers in Europe. Identified as an immense talent by the French literati, Rousseau was quickly ushered into Parisian salon culture, which was rapidly becoming host to the *Philosophes*, including figures such as Baron d'Holbach and Rousseau's close friend (and eventual enemy) Denis Diderot. While not a defined club or organization, the *Philosophes* were largely a group of tight-knit thinkers excited by the rapid pace of natural science to win over converts on the basis of its obvious capacity to improve human affairs. At the same time, however, they were frustrated by the inability of respectable society to get behind a similar revolution taking place in the realms of metaphysics, theology, politics, and morality.[15] Most notably and notoriously, an influential subset of them aspired to advance

---

[13] I do not offer here a biographical account of Rousseau's compelling life. This has been done effectively elsewhere by others – both in abbreviated and extended versions – so as to render yet another account superfluous here. Excellent brief biographies in English can be found in Wokler 2001, Bertram 2004, and Simpson 2007. The best recent one-volume biography in English is Leo Damrosch 2005. And the most comprehensive account of Rousseau's life is Maurice Cranston's three-volume study. While some discussion of Rousseau's life will on occasion be necessary in this volume, I direct readers to these other works for more systematic and detailed narratives.

[14] *Confessions*, 237 [I: 282].

[15] Israel 2011, 56–82.

the ideas of materialism, atheism, and a politics advancing a proto-utilitarianism. At their sessions – customarily held in the drawing rooms of sympathetic aristocrats – they would discuss developments in the natural sciences and humanities, share their own thoughts, and plot to bring what they viewed as greater enlightenment to the broader world.

Coming from a modest background by comparison, Rousseau was deeply flattered to be invited into the inner circles of Paris's most elite intellectual coterie. For their own part, the *Philosophes* were impressed by Rousseau's natural brilliance and perhaps a bit amused by his rustic manners.[16] The more time he spent in their presence, however, the more disgusted he became by the nature and implications of their doctrines. As he understood them, they sought to embrace privilege, and to advance precisely those elements of modernity that he viewed as a threat to civilization itself: the celebration of the individual above the community, praise above probity, talent and vanity above virtue, and money above modesty. Rousseau's task in the first two *Discourses* is to diagnose these maladies and to spell out their immanent dangers.

The core of the *Philosophes'* moral and political philosophy was a thoroughgoing embrace of egoism. As Mark Hulliung has observed, Holbach's motto for the Enlightenment might as well have been, "Dare to love Thyself." This underlying and fundamental egoism must be understood as a consciously chosen diversion from the path of the ancient and Medieval philosophers, who clung in vain, these *Philosophes* held, to the notion that one could reasonably expect citizens to privilege the community over the self. The long Christian experiment of promoting love of neighbor had peaked not so much in fraternal love as in the tyranny of the Church over its unwitting congregants. As Hulliung has summarized, "Their championing of self-love and justification of self-interest were natural outgrowths of a larger campaign to reclaim human nature" from the Church. Only "by accepting and relishing our [selfish] nature can we be at home, whole and complete."[17]

Rousseau would spell out his frustrations with this trending egoism and self-love late in his career. In his autobiographical *Dialogues*, he describes his contemporaries, such as the *Philosophes,* as aware

only of the advantages relative to their own little selves, and letting no opportunity escape, they are constantly busy, with a success that is hardly surprising, disparaging their rivals, scattering their competitors, shining in society, excelling

---

[16] Cranston 1982, 161. See also McLendon 2009, 507–9.
[17] Hulliung 1994, 10.

in letters, and depreciating everything that is not connected to their wagon. It is no miracle that such men are wicked and evil-doing; but that they experience any passion other than the egoism that dominates them, that they have true sensitivity, that they are capable of attachment, of friendship, even of love, is what I deny. They don't even know how to love themselves; they only know how to hate what is not themselves.[18]

This autobiographical reflection, however, is really only a continuation of the thoughts he began formulating in the early 1750s, beginning with the *Discourse on the Sciences and Arts* (or *First Discourse*).

The *First Discourse* offers a multipronged attack on modernity. Rousseau's choice of targets – including the natural sciences, the arts, philosophy, and commerce – is, if anything, more perplexing to readers today than it was to his contemporary audience. The natural sciences represented the first – and in some obvious respects the greatest – success story of modernity. After some initial resistance from the Church, Europeans soon embraced the science of figures like Copernicus, Kepler, Galileo, and Newton as a welcome departure from centuries of determined ignorance and an opportunity, in the words of Francis Bacon, to introduce "an improvement in man's estate, and an enlargement of his power over nature."[19] By the time Rousseau was writing in the mid-eighteenth century, it was virtually an article of faith in the intellectual class that the natural sciences were not only freeing humankind from obdurate ignorance, but also substantively improving the quality of life across the continent.

Similar enthusiasm for the arts and letters soon followed. Modernity brought an end to the hegemonic reign of the sacred in music. Composers were liberated from exclusively religious themes, as well as from the constraints of liturgical musical forms. They were free to explore the themes of everyday life – such as nature, love, eating, and drinking – and began rapidly exploiting new harmonic possibilities. In this context, early modernity gave birth to opera, among myriad other genres. Early modern literature likewise found itself liberated from earlier constraints – and was particularly empowered by the invention of the printing press. New literary forms, such as the novel, were born – and found their way into households. Further, philosophy was largely freed from the shackles imposed by centuries of strict adherence to the medieval dogma that it must be the "handmaiden" of theology. Soon enough, it gave rise to figures such as Descartes, Spinoza, Leibniz, Hobbes, and Locke.

---

[18] *Dialogues*, 157 [I: 863].
[19] Bacon [1620] 1999, 189.

Rousseau never disputes the brilliance, power, and appeal of these achievements. In his *Observations*, he notes, "Science in itself is very good, that is obvious; and one would have to have taken leave of good sense, to maintain the contrary." He comments on how science makes life more convenient, promotes a greater understanding of the divine creation, and in the abstract, "deserves all our admiration."[20]

Likewise, Rousseau admits a deep affection for philosophy and the arts. He reflects in his *Essay on the Origin of Languages* that "all men in the universe will take pleasure in listening to beautiful sounds." He writes on another occasion of Italian operas, "I devour them every day with a new eagerness and I do not believe that there is a man on earth so little sensitive to beautiful sounds as to be able to hear without pleasure those who make this admirable music heard."[21] And he would praise the achievements of the early modern philosophers, such as Descartes, Leibniz, and Malebranche.

Furthermore, Rousseau would not simply admire these developments – he would actively participate in them. Within the natural sciences, while he eschewed geology, since it offers "nothing lovely or attractive," and zoology as he had no use for "stinking corpses, slavering and livid flesh, blood, disgusting intestines, dreadful skeletons, [and] pestilential fumes,"[22] he was in his last years an enthusiastic and relatively sophisticated botanist.

He was even more renowned as an author, composer, and music theorist. He would devise an entirely novel mode of music notation that made his contemporaries take serious notice. His opera, *The Village Soothsayer*, was among the most popular of the eighteenth century. Likewise, he wrote a novel, *Julie, or the New Heloise*, that similarly attained status as one of the most popular and influential contributions to its literary genre. He would also try his hand at the theater, drafting several plays, and even having one, *Narcissus*, produced in 1752. And, of course, he would become arguably the most famous philosopher of the eighteenth century – writing on not only politics, but ethics, metaphysics, epistemology, linguistics, and economics.

Given his artistic and intellectual ambitions, Rousseau's *Discourse on the Sciences and Arts* came as a great surprise. His *Discourse* represents his answer to a question, posed by the Academy of Dijon, he had encountered quite haphazardly: *Has the progress of the sciences and arts tended to corrupt*

---

[20] *Observations*, 32 [III: 36]; *Narcissus*, 97 [II: 965].
[21] *Origin of Languages*, 286 [V: 415]; "Letter on Italian and French Opera," 102 [V: 253].
[22] *Reveries* 96, 97 [I: 1067, 1068].

or purify morals?[23] Despite the virtues of the arts and sciences he himself acknowledged, and despite his own contributions to them, Rousseau answered that they had done far more to corrupt than to purify the morals of his time.

Rousseau's core argument against the arts and sciences can be found in Part II of the *First Discourse*. The fundamental problem with privileging the arts and sciences is that they represent a great waste of human energy and distraction from what ought to be the top priority, pursuing virtue:

> While the cultivation of the sciences is harmful to the martial qualities, it is even more so to the moral qualities. From our very first years a senseless education adorns our mind and corrupts our judgment. Everywhere I see huge establishments, in which young people are brought up at great expense to learn everything except their duties. Your children will not know their own language, but will speak others that are nowhere in use: they will know how to write Verses they will hardly be able to understand: without being able to distinguish error from truth, they will possess the art of making them unrecognizable to others by specious arguments: but they will not know the meaning of the words magnanimity, equity, temperance, humanity, courage; the sweet name of the Fatherland will never strike their ear; and if they hear God spoken of at all, it will be less to be in awe than to be in fear of him.[24]

The more time and energy citizens invest in these other tasks, the less they can dedicate to their civic duties.

But the problem of the arts and sciences goes deeper than being a mere distraction. In the eighteenth century, citizens' very sense of self-worth was wrapped up in their intellectual achievements. Whereas in the glory days of Rome and Sparta, on Rousseau's account, citizens were valued according to their contributions to the common good, by the 1750s they were valued by the glitter of their prose, the complexity of their harmonies, or the abstruseness of their philosophies. As Rousseau comments, "Every artist wants to be applauded. His contemporaries' praise is the most precious portion of his reward."[25] This principle can be broadened to apply to all intellectual endeavors: People pursue them to win social esteem. This provides a perverse incentive, by Rousseau's standards. In order to win public approval, citizens must abandon the pursuit of virtue in order to be celebrated as artists, musicians, poets, scientists, or philosophers.

Rousseau acknowledges that most lack the requisite talent to make genuine insights into or contributions in these endeavors: "These truly

[23] *Confessions*, 294 [I: 351].
[24] *First Discourse*, 22 [III: 24].
[25] *First Discourse*, 19 [III: 21].

Learned men are few in number, I admit."²⁶ The result is an existentially depressed citizenry, bad art in profusion, and a withered republic. These problems are well captured in an anecdote from Rousseau's own life. One afternoon in 1754, the *Philosophes* had gathered for their regular salon at Baron d'Holbach's home in Paris. As Maurice Cranston narrates,

> Diderot had been introduced some months before to a country parson from Normandy named the Abbé Petit, who turned out to be an unpublished author who wanted Diderot to read a madrigal of seven hundred stanzas he had written. Diderot side-stepped the demand by urging the *curé* to write a tragedy, and when Petit took him at his word and pestered him again for an opinion, Diderot, as a joke, invited him to read his play aloud at Mme d'Holbach's salon. Rousseau was present with Holbach, Diderot, Marmontel, Raynal, Saint-Lambert and others when the reading took place. Everyone else enjoyed … [making] a show of mock admiration for the wretched author's tragedy, but Rousseau could not stand the pretense: after some time, according to the story attributed to Holbach, "Jean-Jacques rose from his chair like a madman, and springing towards the *curé* seized his manuscript, threw it on the floor and exclaimed to the horrified author: 'Your play is worthless.… All these gentlemen are laughing at you. Go away from here; go back to your parish duties in the country.'"²⁷

The moral of this story is already present in the *First Discourse*. Living in a corrupt age, the Abbé was operating on the assumption that the only way he could win social esteem was with his intellectual talents. So, despite his meager talents, he set aside countless other worthy duties – to his congregants and fellow citizens – in order to write an awful play. In the end, he produced terrible art, was made to feel lowly, and neglected his duties as a clergyman and citizen. The only ones to gain any pleasure from this incident were those members of the salon who took a twisted pleasure in mocking him. Such are the fruits of a society that elevates the arts and sciences above all else, according to Rousseau.

The core vice fueling the arts and sciences was what he here calls "pride" or "vanity." As Rousseau spells out at the conclusion of Part I of the *First Discourse*, in order to get to the bottom of the problem, "one need only examine closely the vanity and vacuousness of those proud titles which dazzle us." In other words, the root problem is the pervasive egoism born of modernity itself. The reason the arts and sciences in the eighteenth century tend to corrupt is that they draw fuel from the engine of self-love. Modern citizens largely practice the arts and sciences in order to win their neighbors' praises – not for any inherent value in wisdom or beauty. In

²⁶ "Observations," 35 [III: 39].
²⁷ Cranston 1982, 313. This is discussed in McLendon 2009, 511–12.

illustrating this point toward the end of his life, he laments that most botanists "no longer find any true pleasure in their study. We no longer want to know, but to show that we know."²⁸ Ultimately, the arts and sciences are themselves defeated by this disposition. Scientific, artistic, and even moral truths become secondary to winning popular applause. The point is not discovering the truth – the point becomes being lauded for being perceived as doing so. So cleverness and crowd-pleasing become the muses of science, philosophy, and the arts. Such priorities are ultimately fated to produce inferior contributions in the very arenas that are purportedly most valued.

Egoism's role as the root cause explains why Rousseau can condemn the practice of the arts and sciences in his milieu without necessarily condemning the arts and sciences as a whole. If pursued for the right motives, art and science may be worthy of esteem. This is why Rousseau admires Virgil, Plutarch, Socrates, and Plato, insofar as he reads them as pursuing their crafts not primarily as a means of seeking public applause but rather to contribute to the causes of justice and virtue. He muses in this spirit, "My veneration for Socrates would greatly diminish if I believed that he had had the silly vanity of wishing to be the leader of a sect."²⁹

Rousseau understands his own contributions to the arts and sciences in this light, even as he acknowledges "the accusation that I cultivate letters while despising them." He steadfastly denies that he attacks all the arts and sciences, and, indeed, to characterize him as such is to set up a a straw man.³⁰ In truth, Rousseau tolerates, or even celebrates, those achievements in the arts and sciences satisfying one of two standards. First, they are to be pursued by the talented, good, and virtuous for virtuous (or at least benign) ends. This is his primary standard for producing his artistic and philosophical works in any age. Rousseau strives to attain it himself in his own works, such as in his novel and opera. The second standard justifying the arts and sciences is contextual: in societies where virtue has long been dead, the warnings about the effects of the arts and sciences are largely moot, "since a vicious people never returns to virtue." Under such conditions, literature, music, the theater, and philosophy can be practiced since "it would still be preferable to live among scoundrels than among bandits."³¹

---

²⁸ *First Discourse*, 14 [III: 16]; *Reveries*, 99 [I: 1069].
²⁹ "Last Reply," 83 [III: 94].
³⁰ *Narcissus*, 95 [II: 963]; *Narcissus*, 96 [II: 963–94].
³¹ *Narcissus*, 103, 104 [II: 972].

The evidence is mixed on whether or not Rousseau thought early modern Europe was beyond salvation. By his standards, Paris had already travelled quite far down the "vicious" path, and was unlikely ever to recover. Paris, therefore, might as well maintain its academies of learning since it diverted citizens from more scandalous and outright violent behavior. But other corners of Europe, such as his native Geneva, were still potentially redeemable, if they could resist the powerful lures of high culture. In this context, Rousseau concludes his assault on modernity's love affair with learning with a modest appeal:

O virtue! Sublime science of simple souls, are so many efforts and so much equipment really required to know you? Are not your principles engraved in all hearts, and is it not enough in order to learn your Law to return into oneself and to listen to the voice of one's conscience in the silence of the passions? That is genuine Philosophy, let us know how to rest content with it; and without envying the glory of those famous men who render themselves immortal in the Republic of Letters, let us try to place between them and ourselves the glorious distinction formerly seen between two great Peoples; that the one knew how to speak well, and the other, to act well.[32]

For Rousseau, "genuine Philosophy" is neither synonymous with cleverness nor intellectual weight. "Genuine Philosophy" represents nothing more than the simple principles of the conscience, written on the heart. This is where true human dignity resides. And it is only when citizens are rewarded and esteemed for fidelity to this conscience and its principles of virtue and justice that a society can truly thrive.

3. SECOND DISCOURSE: DISCOURSE ON THE ORIGIN AND FOUNDATIONS OF INEQUALITY AMONG MEN

Rousseau had occasion to revisit these matters of society, politics, and morality again in 1753 and 1754 when the Academy of Dijon announced another essay contest, this time on the question: "What is the origin of inequality among men, and whether it is authorized by the natural Law?" Years of sparring with his critics over the merits of his *First Discourse* had considerably sharpened his insights, and he was able to clarify issues only vaguely suggested in the earlier work, while extending his critique beyond the arts and sciences into deeper questions of human nature, economics, and political society. In particular, Rousseau develops far greater sophistication in his understanding of what he called "pride" and "vanity" in the *First Discourse* – with a sharper framing of its threats to civil society.

---

[32] *First Discourse*, 28 [III: 30].

Like the *First Discourse*, the *Second Discourse* is divided into halves. He dedicates the first half to the question of human nature. In doing so, he engages the state of nature tradition commonly found in seventeenth- and eighteenth-century political thought, exemplified in Thomas Hobbes, Samuel Pufendorf, John Locke, and others. In employing this thought experiment, philosophers ask the question: what were people like before they were shaped by social and political institutions? This device means to answer two fundamental questions: (1) what is human nature? and (2) what were the original purposes of government? In finding an answer to the latter, it was supposed by thinkers like Locke, one could reasonably hold contemporary governments accountable to clear standards.

Rousseau eagerly engages this tradition in his *Second Discourse*, though he makes explicit in its *Exordium* that his reflections should "not be taken for historical truths, but only for hypothetical and conditional reasonings; better suited to elucidate the Nature of things than to show their genuine origin." To be sure, however, he intends for this "hypothetical" account to reveal the genuine "Nature of things."[33]

Part I of the *Second Discourse* is itself informally divided into two halves, each dedicated to refuting the influential deductions of other notable philosophers. The first several pages address what Rousseau finds to be the flawed reasoning of Samuel Pufendorf and Jean-Jacques Burlamaqui. The second half is an explicit refutation of Thomas Hobbes, a figure particularly influential among the *Philosophes*.

Samuel Pufendorf argues that it was the natural weakness and timidity of humankind that compelled them to join with others to form political society. Pufendorf reflects that natural man in the state of nature "would straight away die without help from others." Closer to Rousseau's own times and milieu, the Genevan philosopher Jean-Jacques Burlamaqui similarly posits that without the benefit of political society, "man would undoubtedly be the most miserable of all animals. We should discover nothing in him but weakness, savageness, and ignorance; scarce would he be able to satisfy the wants of his body, exposed, poor wretch, to perish with hunger or cold, or by the ravenous teeth of wild beasts."[34] Rousseau aggressively challenges this received wisdom, noting that whatever advantages the beasts might have in strength, man is more than compensated in skill and cleverness. Natural men, "armed with stones, and a good stick," quickly level the playing field against the other animals in the state of nature and soon shed the kind of fear that Pufendorf and

---

[33] *Second Discourse*, 132 [III: 133].
[34] Pufendorf [1673] 1991, 115 [2.1.4]; Burlamaqui [1747] 2006, 59 [1.4.4].

Burlamaqui assume must drive them quickly into the arms of a sovereign. Furthermore, Rousseau asserts that many of the physical ailments associated with humanity are themselves the function of social life itself. Modern peoples, burdened by idleness, poor diets, and wealth inequality, offer a poor facsimile for natural ones. In fact, this combination of idleness and poor diet (both the unhealthy delicacies of the wealthy and malnourishment of the destitute) conspires "to inflict upon ourselves more ills than Medicine can provide Remedies." So his seventeenth- and eighteenth-century contemporaries have followed a fundamentally false indicator in drawing conclusions about natural man from the socialized human beings they encounter in their actual lives. They have failed to grasp that what they view is predominantly artificial, when they mean to describe what is natural. Removing this layer of artificiality, then, Rousseau finds "an animal less strong than some, less agile than others, but, all things considered, the most advantageously organized of all."[35]

Rousseau's next target, Thomas Hobbes, receives much the same treatment. Hobbes infamously portrays natural man not so much as timid, but rather quite the opposite – aggressive and fearsomely violent. He argues that in the state of nature humankind is characterized by a broad equality among individuals that gives rise, successively, to competition, diffidence, glory, and ultimately war. Perhaps more than any figure of early modernity, Hobbes posits and then relies on a conception of human nature that is egoistic. As he comments in his *Leviathan*, the object of every man's voluntary acts "is some *good to himself.*" It is simply inconceivable, on his view, that natural human beings would act altruistically or out of a genuine sense of pity for one another. He deduces confidently from this premise that the state of nature itself is synonymous with the state of war wherein the "life of man [is] solitary, poor, nasty, brutish, and short."[36] This is ultimately the foundation for his solution – that in order to avoid this outcome, all residents of the state of nature must transfer their natural rights to do as they please to an absolute sovereign, or Leviathan, who wields all power and whose commands have the force of law.

As does Pufendorf, Hobbes confuses modern social man with natural man. He improperly assumes, according to Rousseau, faculties that simply were absent in the earliest times – such as language and abstract thought. Language and abstract thought, it turns out, are required for human beings to compare themselves with one another and pursue desires

[35] *Second Discourse*, 136 [III: 136]; *Second Discourse*, 137 [III: 138]; *Second Discourse*, 134 [III: 134–5].
[36] Hobbes [1651] 2002, 100 [14.8]; see also 113 [15.16]; Hobbes [1651] 2002, 96 [13.9].

like glory. As such, Hobbes falsely includes "in Savage man's care for his preservation the need to satisfy a multitude of passions that are the product of Society and have made Laws necessary."[37]

Beyond this, Hobbes entirely neglects the native faculty of pity [*pitié*], which Rousseau describes as "pure movement of Nature" that "carries us without reflection to the assistance of those we see suffer." As Rousseau asks in his *Emile*, "who does not pity the unhappy man whom he sees suffering? Who would not want to deliver him from his ills if it only cost a wish for that?"[38] It is this sentiment of pity, Rousseau submits, that takes the place of the "more perfect" principle of justice in the state of nature. It softens relations between individuals and makes human relations in that condition largely peaceful and amiable.[39]

By characterizing natural human beings as both capable and sensitive, Rousseau gave birth to what has since been called the "Noble Savage." In their natural conditions, people are exceptionally robust – yet not ones who employ their skills to manipulate or harm others. Inasmuch as they are truly natural, reasons Rousseau, they seek to satisfy what he calls *amour de soi-même*, or self-love, which he defines as "a natural sentiment which inclines every animal to attend to its self-preservation, and which, guided in man by reason and modified by pity, produces humanity and virtue." Some, such as Voltaire, read Rousseau's embrace of *amour de soi-même* to echo the Hobbesian Mandevillian call to egoism. But, unlike Hobbesian egoism, Rousseau's self-love as *amour de soi-même* fosters mere self-preservation, not hostility. This form of self-love leads people to brush their teeth, not to plot against others. Natural humans do not view one another as competitors and so do not approach others with suspicion. Self-love is in nature a largely benign force. This leads Rousseau to the bold proposition in the *Second Discourse* that "man is naturally good."[40] This natural goodness persists so long as human beings exist in nature – that is, outside of any kind of organized society. But once they come together, other forces come to dominate human nature. These are detailed in Part II of the *Second Discourse*.

[37] *Second Discourse*, 151 [III: 153].
[38] *Second Discourse*, 152 [III: 155]; *Second Discourse*, 154 [III: 156]; *Emile*, 221 [IV: 503–4].
[39] Some have argued that pity or compassion forms the foundation of Rousseau's moral and political thought. See, for example, Strauss [1953] 1965, 270 and Inston 2010, 92–5. For an opposing view, see Boyd 2004; see also Maguire 2006, 85.
[40] *Second Discourse*, 218n.xv [III: 219n.xv]; *Second Discourse*, 197n.ix [III: 202n.ix]. Rousseau draws an important distinction in his philosophy between human goodness and virtue. Goodness is largely a natural disposition. Virtue requires thought and even moral effort. So the individual who instinctually jumps into the pool to save a drowning baby is good. The individual who overcomes a fear of water to do the same is virtuous.

Once Rousseau has established what he takes to be natural human beings, he observes that various hardships, such as droughts, harsh winters, and natural disasters, ultimately push otherwise solitary individuals into cooperation out of necessity. Over time, peoples in particular regions working together for survival inevitably come to be "united in morals and character." They acquire natural bonds without yet the benefit of rules and laws. At the same time, however, their close proximity fosters a sense of preference: "They grow accustomed to attend to different objects and to make comparisons; imperceptibly they acquire ideas of merit and beauty which produce sentiments of preference."[41] Whereas in the state of nature, everyone was perfectly equal in the eyes of others, civilization fosters attention to that which distinguishes one person from another. It did not matter in the state of nature, for example, that one might have been taller or stronger, since it carried no real consequences. Everyone ate and lived equally well. But in a world where people live in close proximity and begin to rely on their respective skills, people acquire distinction for their relative assets. As Rousseau speculates,

Everyone began to look at everyone else and to wish to be looked at himself, and public esteem acquired a price. The one who sang or danced the best; the handsomest, the strongest, the most skillful, or the most eloquent came to be the most highly regarded, and this was the first step at once toward inequality and vice: from these first preferences arose vanity and contempt on the one hand, shame and envy on the other; and the fermentation caused by these new leavens eventually produced compounds fatal to happiness and innocence.[42]

This is the birth of the final component of Rousseau's basic moral psychology. Human beings are motivated by self-love [*amour de soi-même*] and pity [*pitié*] in the state of nature. Once social, they are now further motivated by what he calls *amour propre*, which can also be translated as "self-love" but means something quite different from *amour de soi-même*. He defines this in his notes as "only a relative sentiment, factitious, and born in society, which inclines every individual to set greater store by himself than by anyone else, inspires men with all the evils they do to one another, and is the genuine source of honor."[43] Rousseau had employed this concept in his *First Discourse* without yet having defined it, much less given it a name. But in its malicious form it is the egoism that drives individuals to seek distinction without regard to higher standards or care for others.

---

[41] *Second Discourse*, 165 [III: 169].
[42] *Second Discourse*, 166 [III: 169–70].
[43] *Second Discourse*, 218n.xv [III: 219n.xv].

It is the force that drives artists to seek the audience's applause with cheap devices; it is what drives scientists to fudge data to win awards; it is what drives philosophers to such abstraction as to be speaking nonsense, just so that others might think them clever. Further, *amour propre* and social esteem are a zero-sum game. If social esteem were granted to everyone, it would mean nothing. It is valuable only insofar as it is scarce. One can advance in this game in one of two fashions: through personal actions and accomplishments, or by the public failure of others competing for the same esteem. Both have an effect on the social hierarchy that inspires *amour propre*.

All of this is still far from its historical origins, however, as Rousseau paints the transition from the state of nature to political society. Although *amour propre* is born in the earliest human civilizations, it takes some time to ferment and become sour. Before this happens, members of such societies "lived free, healthy, good, and happy" lives. This is why he considers this moment "between the indolence of the primitive state and the petulant activity of our *amour propre*" to be "the happiest and the most lasting epoch."[44]

Rousseau's narrative obviously does not end here. The more time spent in one another's company, the more the differences become pronounced – and further, the more some are able to exploit their natural talents to gain advantages over others. Over time, natural inequalities that were of little consequence in the state of nature fuel a very real social inequality. Someone born with great potential as an engineer can do nothing with this capacity in a world with no need for engineers, such as the state of nature. But in a society where such skills are valued, both monetarily and in social esteem, these talents are quickly developed, refined, and implemented. Such is the case in early societies, where individuals capitalize on their natural talents and begin amassing great wealth. These wealth inequalities only become exacerbated over time with inheritance, and eventually society is bifurcated into two classes: rich and poor.

By this time, the wealthy are further transformed by *amour propre*. Because *amour propre* is fueled by the drive to ascend the social hierarchy, the wealthy eventually discover their greatest pleasure: the pleasure of domination. As Rousseau describes it,

The rich, for their part, had scarcely become acquainted with the pleasure of domination than they disdained all other pleasures, and using their old Slaves

---

[44] *Second Discourse*, 167 [III: 171]. See Jonathan Marks 2005 for a persuasive account of why Rousseau views this as the best stage of human history (60–5).

to subject new ones, they thought only of subjugating and enslaving their neighbors; like those ravenous wolves which once they have tasted human flesh scorn all other food, and from then on want to devour only men.[45]

The great "pleasure" of subjugation comes from not only exercising one's own power, but simultaneously exercising that power to control and lord over all others. This is the ultimate drug of the wealthy class, as Rousseau conceives it, since it fuels both sides of the *amour propre* equation – the celebration of the self and the denigration of others.

Driven by the desire for domination, the wealthy exercise "a kind of right" to usurp the poor's property. The victims respond violently, resulting in a state of war where the rich steal from the poor and the poor steal from the rich; natural pity and a nascent sense of justice are stifled, and most everyone is "greedy, ambitious, and wicked."[46]

The poor have little to lose in this conflict, as they have little or no property. The wealthy, however, have a great deal at stake. All of their great property holdings rest on the war's outcome. Further, they quickly realize a system of property based in usurpation renders their holdings tenuous at best. They have what is theirs only until someone stronger or wealthier comes along. This leads them to what Rousseau calls, with the kind of admiration or awe one reserves for monsters, "the most well-conceived project ever to enter the human mind."[47] They develop a plan that ends the violence and simultaneously secures property against further theft and insecurity. To this end, a representative of their interests approaches the poor with a proposal:

"Let us unite," he told them, "to protect the weak from oppression, restrain the ambitious, and secure for everyone the possession of what belongs to him: Let us institute rules of Justice and peace to which all are obliged to conform, which favor no one, and which in a way make up for the vagaries of fortune by subjecting the powerful and weak alike to mutual duties. In a word, instead of turning our forces against one another, let us gather them into a supreme power that might govern us according to wise Laws, protect and defend all the members of the association, repulse common enemies, and preserve us in everlasting concord."[48]

This was the proposal. And given their relative simplicity and their desperation to put an end to the miseries associated with constant warfare, the poor and weak signed on the dotted line. As Rousseau memorably

[45] *Second Discourse*, 171 [III: 175–6].
[46] *Second Discourse*, 171 [III: 176].
[47] *Second Discourse*, 172 [III: 177].
[48] *Second Discourse*, 173 [III: 177].

phrases it, "All ran toward their chains in the belief they were securing their freedom.... Such was, or must have been, the origin of Society and of Laws, which gave the weak new fetters and the rich new forces."[49] Such was, in fact, the social contract.

This ushers in the last stage of political history, as Rousseau envisions it. It is characterized by a broad system of despotism or slavery (these terms are largely synonymous for Rousseau), where the wealthy have instituted laws and rights specifically designed to secure their own possessions. At the same time, they keep the poor in their place as, more or less, slaves. This system works largely because the slaves are unaware of their status as slaves. Subjects believe they have acquired freedom, security, equality, justice, and the rule of law when in fact they have secured their servitude, inequality, and injustice. To achieve this, the new official ruling class draws on the forces of the subjects' own *amour propre*, letting citizens "be oppressed only so far as they are swept up by blind ambition and, looking below more than above themselves, come to hold Domination dearer than independence, and consent to bear chains in turn."[50]

In the end, all subjects are reduced to slavery, since they have no real will of their own. "Blind obedience," he writes, "is the only virtue left to Slaves." In the end, all return full circle to equality:

Here all private individuals again become equal because they are nothing and, since the Subjects have no other Law left than the will of the Master, and the Master no rule than his passions, the notions of the good and the principles of justice again vanish. Here everything reverts to the sole Law of the stronger and consequently to a new State of Nature, different from that with which we began in that the first was the state of Nature in his purity, whereas this last is the fruit of an excess of corruption.[51]

Everyone is equal since all are slaves. In fact, the rulers are as much slaves as the subjects since they are slaves to their own passions, unable to exercise their free wills against their own inclinations.

Rousseau's account of political history in the *Second Discourse* is strikingly dismal on the whole, and readers might be inclined to assume that it leaves very little room for constructive solutions or aspirations. This is undoubtedly true of the general tenor of the essay. To take this view, however, is to overlook the work's important Epistle Dedicatory, which Rousseau dedicates to the General Council of the Genevan Republic. In

---

[49] *Second Discourse*, 173 [III: 177–8].
[50] *Second Discourse*, 183 [III: 188].
[51] *Second Discourse*, 185–86 [III: 191].

it, Rousseau cursorily outlines the features of a republic he would choose for a homeland, should he have been given a choice of his birthplace. He specifies here that it should be relatively small, so that all citizens know one another. It should cultivate a love of fatherland and fellow citizens. It would place sovereignty in the people, and grant citizens the right to legislative collectively. It would consequently be governed by that rule of law. It would cultivate an ethos of freedom. It would be neither rich nor poor. Of course, none of these are to be found in the state depicted in Part II of the *Second Discourse*. Yet, as it turns out, these are all goals of the *Social Contract*. So, although the former presents a model of failure, it also provides a set of substantive goals to be achieved in the latter. And it is quite possibly for this reason that he later reflected in his *Confessions* that "Everything that is bold in *The Social Contract* was previously in the *Discourse on Inequality*."[52]

4. BIRTH OF THE *SOCIAL CONTRACT*

Rousseau had always intended to write a much larger book on politics than the relatively compact *Social Contract*. This was to be called *Political Institutions*, and he describes its origins as grounded in his personal experiences working from 1743 to 1744 as a secretary for Pierre-François-Auguste, Comte de Montaigu, the French ambassador to the republic of Venice:

Of the various writings I had in progress [in 1756], the one which I meditated about for the longest time, which I attended to with the most relish, which I wanted to work on for my whole life, and which in my opinion ought to be the seal on my reputation was my *Political Institutions*. I had conceived its first idea thirteen or fourteen years before, when – being at Venice – I had had some occasion to notice the flaws of that so vaunted Government. Since then, my views have been much more extended by means of historical study of morality. I had seen that everything depends radically on politics, and that, from whatever aspect one considers it, no people ever would be anything other than what it was made into by the nature of its Government; thus this great question of the best possible Government appeared to me to be reduced to this one. What is the nature of Government suited to forming a people that was the most virtuous, most enlightened, most wise, in sum, the best, taking this word in its most extended sense. I had believed that I had seen that this question depended very closely on this other one, if it even differs from it. What is the Government which by its nature keeps itself closest to the law? From that, what is law? and a chain of questions of that importance. I saw that all this was leading me to great truths, useful to the

---

[52] *Second Discourse*, 114–23 [III: 111–21]; *Confessions*, 342 [I: 407].

happiness of the human race, but above all to that of my fatherland, where on the trip I had just made I had not found them forming what I thought to be sufficiently precise and clear concepts about the laws and freedom and I had believed that this indirect way of giving them these concepts was the one most suited for sparing the amour-propre of its members, and for getting myself pardoned for having been able to see a little farther than they could.[53]

Rousseau developed this project for an estimated five or six years in secret before abandoning it for a lack of courage and ultimately burning it. He did not burn the entire draft, however. Before setting it ablaze, Rousseau removed the four books that would comprise the *Social Contract*.

In the description of his plan for *Political Institutions*, Rousseau suggests that politics stands at the center of his conception of the moral universe. This is true in at least two respects. First, it is true in the sense suggested in the *Second Discourse* that there is no genuine morality prior to fully formed free human beings living together. Second, political institutions play a role in shaping the moral lives of their citizens. Leo Damrosch speculates that this was Rousseau's great insight in Venice – that a corrupted nobility sought to retain power and forestall unrest by promoting gambling, prostitution, and pleasure-seeking.[54] This had the effect of corrupting the population at large. By contrast, Rousseau might have wondered, what would happen to a people governed by uncorrupted and wise institutions?

This suggests a crucial and sometimes underemphasized theme of the *Social Contract*. A fundamental goal in his constructive political philosophy is a virtuous citizenry. It animates nearly the entire work – sometimes suggesting that a virtuous citizenry is required to set its institutional forces in motion, sometimes suggesting that its institutions must vigorously pursue all measures necessary to produce that same virtuous citizenry. Rousseau's ideal vision for political institutions described in the *Social Contract* is to create something of a self-perpetuating machine (once established by a lawgiver). The more virtuous citizens it creates, the greater success it will have in governing justly, and, in turn, the better it will do in producing more virtuous citizens. This is Rousseau's ideal vision, and in many respects it is derived from his affection for ancient models of politics found in Rome, Sparta, and the Platonic dialogues.

At the same time, however, Rousseau is sensitive to the looming dangers of *amour propre* in all its manifestations – and the likelihood that it

---

[53] *Confessions*, 339–40 [I: 404–5].
[54] Damrosch 2005, 180.

can never be entirely extinguished. For this reason, one finds passages in the *Social Contract* that reflect somewhat "fallen" citizens operating in his republic. Presumably, for example, truly wise and virtuous citizens would not require mechanisms such as checks and balances. They would simply all pursue the common good as a matter of principle.

The *Social Contract* therefore appears simultaneously to pursue two ambitions. It sets out the goal of cultivating virtuous citizens, who in turn legislate for and govern virtuously for the common good. At the same time, however, it occasionally and somewhat tacitly acknowledges the quixotic nature of this ambition and lays out measures to approach the common good with flawed citizens and governments. One finds precisely this kind of strategy, for example, in his treatment of the problem of factions at 2.3. He first insists that no factions should be permitted. Yet "if there are partial societies," he concedes, "their number must be multiplied, and inequality among them prevented, as was done by Solon, Numa, and Servius" (*SC*, 2.3.4, 60 [III: 372]).

Ultimately, however, the heart of Rousseau's program outlined in the *Social Contract* is his general will. He introduces it as soon as he begins to articulate his positive political vision at 1.6.9, and it animates everything that follows thereafter. The problem for readers, however, is that he never offers a singular, comprehensive definition of his most important concept. Instead, he describes it piecemeal, as he thinks necessary to address whatever controversy he engages at the moment. For this reason, this book includes an appendix that offers a more comprehensive statement on the general will than one can find in any particular discussion throughout Rousseau's own works. For now, however, it is essential to understand that the general will aims to solve the problems of modernity – the sovereign individual and its associated egoism and *amour propre*. Whereas the sovereign individual makes autonomous choices to serve self-interest, Rousseau's citizen under the general will makes autonomous choices to serve the common good. Whereas egoists prioritize themselves, Rousseauean citizens prioritize the community. And whereas those driven by unsocial *amour propre* love themselves, true citizens love their communal fellows. Rousseau thus aims with the general will – insofar as such a thing is possible – to tame those forces that make the individual the center of the moral universe, and replace them with a love for fellow citizens in service to the common good. Or, as Rousseau's Savoyard Vicar observes in the *Emile*, "the good man orders himself in relation to the whole, and wicked one orders the whole in relation to himself. The latter makes himself the center of all things." The point of the general will is to make a "good man" by this measure – to make citizens order themselves for the whole, rather than precisely the opposite. One might suggest that Rousseau can only achieve this by slaying *amour propre*; but almost all scholars today believe he channels the very forces of *amour propre* into support for the common good.[55] It is clear enough from the text that while it is a generally dangerous and socially divisive force, Rousseau at least occasionally seeks to channel it into forces he finds supportive of the general will, such as fraternity and nationalism. Whether or not such devices solve their respective problems adequately, without bequeathing equal or greater difficulties, is a matter to be resolved elsewhere. Yet his general will remains an admirably ambitious attempt to halt or at least channel the encroachments of forces that had already demonstrated their capacity to divide modern citizens against one another.

---

[55] *Emile*, 292 [IV: 602]; Frederick Neuhouser has written most extensively on this matter in Neuhouser 2008. See also O'Hagan 1999, 166–72, Cooper 1999, 122–30, and Dent 1988, 21–31.

CHAPTER I

Book I

TITLE PAGE AND "NOTICE"

The *Social Contract* was initially issued with two similar, yet distinct, title pages. Each version includes the title, a statement of his Genevan citizenship, a quotation from Virgil's *Aeneid*, and a sketch with many of the same symbols. Rousseau had made it clear to his publisher, Marc-Michel Rey, that he wanted to use the same images found on the title page of his *Second Discourse*. He was mostly happy with that illustration and requested that it be repeated on the title page for the *Social Contract*, with one important alteration. He feared that the depiction of Lady Liberty in the *Second Discourse* rendered her chubby and hence "ignoble." So he requested that she appear more slender in the *Social Contract*. Rey commissioned Benjamin Samuel Bolomey to draw two images and Charles-Ange Boily to engrave them for the book.[1]

TITLE PAGE: THE IMAGE(S)

The first title page image includes several symbols, some more obvious than others. At the center is the image of an apparently Roman woman with the scales of justice in her right hand and a pike in her left. Most immediately, the scales evoke associations with Lady Justice, the Roman god of Justice (*Justitia*), who is always portrayed with the scales, a symbol of justice and equality. As will become evident in reading the text, equality is one of the preeminent values of the *Social Contract*. The social contract, as Rousseau asserts in his conclusion to Book I, establishes a "moral and legitimate equality" (*SC*, 1.9.8, 56 [III: 367]), such that "all commit themselves under the same conditions and must enjoy all the same rights" (*SC*, 2.4.8, 61 [III: 374]).

[1] Bibliographic details can be found in Theophile Dufour 1925, 117–21; see also Derathé 1964 notes in *OC* III: 1868–9. My thanks to Christopher Kelly for his assistance in tracking down these sources and sharing his insights into the circumstances surrounding Rousseau's desires for his title page.

D U

CONTRACT SOCIAL;

O U,

P R I N C I P E S

D U

DROIT POLITIQUE.

P À R J. J. R O U S S E A U,

C I T O Y E N D E G E N E V E.

Dicamus leges.

—— *fœderis æquas*

Æneid. XI.

A AMSTERDAM,

Chez M A R C M I C H E L R E Y.

M D C C L X I I.

Image reprinted from R. A. Leigh's *Correspondance complète de Jean Jacques Rousseau, vol. 10* (Madison: University of Wisconsin Press, 1969). Original, created in 1762 by Benjamin Samuel Bolomey (1739–1819), appeared in *Le Contrat social*. Heinemann Collection, New York.

The woman holds in her left hand a hat atop a pole. This has a specific iconographic meaning. The eighteenth century saw a rise in the popularity of "liberty poles," often held by the Roman goddess of Liberty rather than Justice. This goddess, *Libertas*, was most often depicted holding a wand in one hand and a cap in the other.[2] According to David Hackett Fischer, both the wand and cap were Roman symbols of emancipation, since a *praetor* would touch Roman slaves upon release from bondage with his wand and offer them a cap "as a token of their liberty." This image was popular at the founding of the Netherlands in 1626, during the Glorious English Revolution of 1688, and even in the revolutionary days of America.[3]

One striking departure from the standard liberty pole in this image, however, is the bottom end, which consists of a sharp pike. It is typical, of course, for political theories to authorize and even to mandate the use of force when necessary. Indeed, one of Rousseau's main interlocutors and targets in the *Social Contract*, Thomas Hobbes, depicts on the frontispiece of his *Leviathan* an outsized man wielding a massive sword over a community.[4] In Rousseau's case, however, the combining of the pike with the liberty pole is unique. It is quite possibly an allusion to Rousseau's association in the *Social Contract* of liberty with force. He announces in Book I that citizens must be "forced to be free" (*SC*, 1.7.8, 53 [III: 364]). This is perhaps the most paradoxical and bewildering claim in a book well known for such turns of phrase. It is also one of the most crucial elements of his political philosophy generally. Much of the *Social Contract* hinges upon understanding this paradox in its full complexity. There can be no freedom without force; there can be no just use of force if not in service of freedom.

At the foot of the goddess is a cat. This is a more difficult symbol to read, depending on whether the cat is viewed more in a Roman or Christian tradition. For the Romans, the cat is a friend of the goddess of liberty and sits by her feet. It is therefore in this tradition a symbol of freedom. If this is the case, then the cat potentially represents a commitment to liberty, simultaneous to prizing equality – paralleling Rousseau's

---

[2] It is worth observing that many of the symbols here are also present on the title page image from the first edition of his *Discourse on the Origins of Inequality*, including the wand, hat, cat, and bird.

[3] Fischer 2004, 41, 37–49. Indeed, one also finds a striking parallel image on the Idaho State flag today, with *Libertas* holding scales in the right hand and the liberty pole in the left. My thanks to Jonathan Marks and Matthew Simpson for their assistance in interpreting these symbols.

[4] While the *Leviathan's* cover image depicts this massive image standing over the city, it is only fair to add that this figure is made up of the hundreds or thousands of subjects that authorized its very existence.

declaration that "the greatest good … comes down to these two principal objects, *freedom* and *equality*" (*SC*, 2.11.1, 78 [III: 391]). But for Christians, the cat is a much darker symbol, representing Satan, darkness, and sometimes lust. As such, the cat potentially represents the many threats to a just and equal republic, such as demagogues, self-love, and opinion. In short, the cat could represent all those forces of the private will, countervailing and threatening the general will. Given Rousseau's personal affection for cats and explicit association of them with freedom, however, it seems that the Roman reading is more likely correct. James Boswell once recorded a conversation he and Rousseau had about cats on December 15, 1764:

ROUSSEAU: "Do you like cats?" BOSWELL: "No." ROUSSEAU: "I was sure of that. It is my test of character. There you have the despotic instinct of men. They do not like cats because the cat is free and will never consent to be a slave. He will do nothing to your order, as the other animals do." BOSWELL: "Nor a hen, either." ROUSSEAU: "A hen would obey your orders if you could make her understand them. But a cat will understand you perfectly and not obey them." BOSWELL: "But a cat is treacherous." ROUSSEAU: "No. That's untrue. A cat is an animal that can be very much attached to you; he will do anything you please out of friendship. I have a cat here. He has been brought up with my dog; they play together. The cat will give the dog a blow with his tail, and the dog will offer him his paw."[5]

The cat hence complements the Liberty pole as a symbol of freedom.

The bird is a significant symbol. It has traditionally been associated with transcendence, the soul, and an ability to communicate with the gods. All of these readings have potential meaning in the context of the *Social Contract*, which emphasizes that "all justice comes from God," indeed a "universal justice," as he emphasizes (*SC*, 2.6.2, 66 [III: 378]). Yet at the same time, he acknowledges the difficulty in receiving this message. So while there is a transcendent justice for Rousseau, it is an eternal and vigilant struggle to establish and maintain it in a republic. Beyond this, however, is the simple observation that by virtue of its power of flight a bird is free and unconstrained. It is another symbol of freedom. This reading might be confirmed by a parallel image on the title page of Rousseau's *Discourse on the Origins of Inequality*, where a birdcage sits in the background, its door ajar, and a bird is seen fleeing its former prison. Here on the *Social Contract* image, the bird is seen with a string dangling beneath it, not yet far separated from another string blowing in the wind and attached

---

[5] Boswell 1953, 261.

to the pike. In each instance, the bird appears to be yet another symbol of the freedom and independence so central to the *Social Contract.*

Finally, the setting itself is telling. The entire scene takes place in nature, with the goddess surrounded by trees. Yet readers can see the city in the background. This suggests yet another important theme in Rousseau's work: the necessity of escaping the city in order to be free from corrupting forces and also to make sound determinations about what is just and truly equal. As Rousseau remarks in Book IV, it is "[w]hen … troops of peasants are seen attending to affairs of State under an oak tree" that they can deliberate wisely about the true needs of that state and the common good" (*SC*, 4.1.1, 121 [III: 437]). Rousseau emphasizes throughout his literary career the need to flee the distractions of urban life in order to think. As he wrote earlier in his "Letter to d'Alembert," "Solitude calms the soul and appeases the passions born of the disorder of the world. Far from the vices which irritate us, we speak of them with less indignation; far from the ills which touch us, our hearts are less moved by them." It is in this solitude that he is able to "substitute the love of justice … for the love of vengeance."[6] This solitude, therefore, seems conducive to that mode of reasoning that facilitates proper thought on justice and equality.

The first image was used for the first printings, but it was quickly supplanted by the second, as Rousseau was concerned that the initial title page was too busy.[7] The second image is different in modest ways from the first. In this case, the woman is clearly *Libertas*, not *Justitia*, as she has no scales. She likewise wields a Liberty pole, although in this version, she holds the hat in her right hand rather than resting it atop the pole. The cat and the bird also appear as likely symbols of freedom. And finally, the relationship of country and city remains, although this time she appears surrounded by towering classical columns, with the country as the backdrop. Rousseau never suggested that he preferred one illustration to another. Although the first one appears to embrace more of the themes of the *Social Contract*, the second appears more consistent with his request that the image recapture the themes of the *Second Discourse*.

TITLE PAGE: *FOEDERIS AEQUAS DICAMUS LEGES*

This passage, which Gourevitch translates as "Let us declare the fair laws of a compact," is drawn from Book XI of Virgil's *Aeneid*. As Christopher Kelly and Roger Masters have observed, Rousseau always chooses his literary

---

[6] *Letter to d'Alembert*, 256 [V: 7].
[7] Rousseau did not complain about the first illustration – only the layout of the page in its totality.

dd. Le *Contrat social*, titre de la première édition in-8⁰, variante montrant
la vignette de la Liberté assise, au lieu de la Justice debout;
exemplaire ayant appartenu à Rousseau
(Bibliothèque de Neuchâtel).

Image reprinted from R. A. Leigh's *Correspondance complète de Jean Jacques Rousseau, vol. II*
(Madison: University of Wisconsin Press, 1970). Original, created in 1762 by Benjamin Samuel
Bolomey (1739–1819), appeared in *Le Contrat social*. Bibliothèque de la Ville, Neuchâtel.

allusions carefully.[8] In the most obvious respect, the quoted passage suggests the very object of the *Social Contract* – a broad agreement to conform to just terms. Immediately after the quoted passage in the *Aeneid*, the text continues to compare the alternative to living according to the terms of a just compact. One might instead prefer to militarize and conquer other territories, which only leads to more strife. Politics through conquering is

---

[8] Kelly and Masters 1994, 241–42n.3.

a manifestation of "might makes right," and Rousseau will identify and condemn this flawed doctrine early in Book I of the *Social Contract* (*SC*, 1.3). Finally, it is also worth noting that Rousseau also cites the *Aeneid* in his *Emile*, published in the same year as the *Social Contract*, but in an apparently very different context. Rousseau here is writing in the voice of a Savoyard Vicar, who is laboring to demonstrate the shortcomings of the materialist philosophy associated with the *Philosophes*. Specifically, he wants to argue that the world is orderly because it was designed as such. He asks Emile to imagine that someone has a hat full of letters. Now imagine that he were to throw them to the ground. How likely is it that they would all fall to the ground and spell out Virgil's epic poem, the *Aeneid*? The Vicar suggests this is inconceivable. Now ask how likely it is that one would simply stumble upon letters on the ground that *already* spell out the *Aeneid*. What are the odds that these letters were laid out by an intelligent creature? "I can give odds of infinity to one," responds the Vicar.[9] The same is true of the universe, he posits by analogy. What is the more likely cause of the incredible structure and order of the universe? Random chance or an intelligent design? Reason certainly suggests the latter, says the Vicar. To be sure, matters of intelligent design extend beyond matters most central to the *Social Contract*. But the broader association with order is potentially significant, if one takes the simultaneous references to the *Aeneid* to be relevant to the interpretation of these two texts. In the *Emile*, he associates the *Aeneid* with the establishment of physical order. In the *Social Contract*, he associates the *Aeneid* with the establishment of the political order.

TITLE PAGE: "CITIZEN OF GENEVA"

Since Rousseau was living in Paris while writing the *Social Contract*, one might reasonably wonder why he signed it "citizen of Geneva." In the most immediate sense, Geneva was Rousseau's birthplace and site of his formative years. But Geneva also represents something more for Rousseau. Despite many unhappy childhood memories, the city always retained a certain romantic appeal, as well as a constant source of ideas for Rousseau's proposed political reforms. As suggested in the introduction to this book, Helena Rosenblatt has drawn careful attention not only to the development of Rousseau's political thought and its relationship to Genevan institutions and controversies, but also to how these are worked out in the *Social Contract*, including and especially his thoughts on civil

---

[9] *Emile*, 276 [IV: 579].

religion. Although Rousseau technically had lost his Genevan citizenship after fleeing the city as an adolescent, it was reestablished in 1754 during a four-month stay. In a letter written during this visit, he remarked, "This city seems to me one of the most charming in the world, and its inhabitants the wisest and happiest that I know. Liberty is well established, the government is peaceful, and the citizens are enlightened, steady, and modest." He was particularly impressed by the dignity in which the working classes labored. Unlike Parisians, Genevan workers were free from oppressive taxation, and also benefited from price controls on food, a modest welfare state, and a generous public educational system.[10]

TITLE PAGE: "NOTICE"

The *Social Contract*'s title page is followed by a brief "NOTICE" [*AVERTISSEMENT*], in which Rousseau explains that the existing material constituting the book is in fact drawn from a much larger work he eventually had to abandon. This larger work, to the best of present knowledge, consisted of twelve parts: (1) size of nations, (2) government, (3) laws, (4) religion, (5) honor, (6) "f," (7) commerce, (8) travel, (9) types of food, (10) abuses of society, (11) cultivation of the sciences, and (12) an examination of Plato's *Republic*.[11] In fact, many of these themes are addressed in the *Social Contract*, including the size of nations, government, laws, and religion. Some of the remaining themes are addressed elsewhere in his works, including honor, the abuses of society, and the cultivation of science. But he would never synthesize all of these in one work, such as his ambitions might have once desired.

BOOK I: OVERVIEW

Book I explores the possible foundations for a political state. In doing so, he engages a longstanding, time-honored tradition in political philosophy. In Plato's *Republic*, the state stands on the foundations of eternal ideas accessible to a wise few. In Aristotle, the state is grounded in standards given by nature. Saint Thomas Aquinas draws the principles of his state from the eternal law of a Christian God. By the seventeenth and eighteenth

---

[10] Damrosch 2005, 244–49; Letter to Mme Dupin, quoted in Damrosch 2005, 248; Cranston 1982, 340.

[11] The "f" in question is possibly finances, the French, or Women [*femmes*]. See Kelly and Masters 1994, 232. Regarding travel, Rousseau did address the matter in his *Emile* (*Emile*, 450–71 [IV: 826–55]). This list is drawn from his "Political Fragments," 16 [III: 473]. It is worth noting here that recently much recent attention has been devoted to Rousseau's interest in Plato and the *Republic*, including Millet 1967, Silverthorne 1973, Trachtenberg 2001, Cooper 2002, Williams 2007a, and Kelly 2010, esp. xx–xxiii.

centuries, however, this question is refined a bit more. As Rousseau himself phrases it, "what is the foundation of this obligation [of subjects to the laws of the State]?"[12] This word, "obligation," is an especially modern term. As Patrick Riley has observed, in the ancient world, "Politics being the highest end of man, obligation was not the real problem, and the task of the great legislator was not to show why men ought to obey but merely in what way."[13] For early modern philosophers, such as Thomas Hobbes, Hugo Grotius, John Locke, Samuel Pufendorf, and others, the assumption was that subjects needed *reasons* for obeying the law.

Rousseau understands the tradition and the modern adaptations of this tradition well. And in Book I of the *Social Contract*, he bifurcates the choices into two types of foundations – those by *nature* and those by *agreement* or *convention*. These terms require some explication. "Nature" here does not imply "natural law" in the moral sense. It is to be taken here in its most literal sense – such as force, power, and family. Convention explicitly means agreement or consent. It becomes clear in these early chapters that this is his preferred route. But although Rousseau rejects "nature" as a foundation, this does not imply that any kind of convention will suffice. This much is perfectly apparent in the story depicted in Part II of the *Second Discourse*, where the poor are duped into agreeing to a government that ultimately promises their own enslavement. There are better and worse conventions, and Rousseau is careful to spell out the difference in Chapters Four to Eight. The legitimate state, the one that truly obligates subjects to obey the laws, is that in which all agree to place themselves under the authority of the general will (*SC*, 1.6.10, 50 [III: 361]). Although Rousseau does not define this crucial term here in Book I,[14] its importance to his overall project is perfectly obvious. There can be no legitimate political obligations in the absence of the general will. Book I thus explains why all the other options fail, and why a general will is required. The subsequent books of the *Social Contract* detail how the general will is established, maintained, and safeguarded.

BOOK I: PROEMIUM

Before embarking on Chapter One, Rousseau first introduces his themes in three brief paragraphs. He opens by insisting on "taking men as they

---

[12] *Mountain*, 231 [III: 806].

[13] Riley 1982, 3.

[14] Rousseau never offers a single, systematic, and thorough account of the general will. See Appendix A at the end of this book for an attempt to provide one.

are, and the laws as they can be" (*SC*, 1.Intro, 41 [III: 351]). He has no intention of trying to change human nature.¹⁵ This suggests a departure from certain ancient and Christian traditions that attempt to re-mold human nature into something more than it is in raw nature. Aristotle, for example, wants to re-mold human beings to make them more virtuous. One finds an early modern example in Thomas More's *Utopia*, which argues that we can abolish private property, work a mere six hours a day, pursue virtue and learning in our spare time, and so on. But by the seventeenth and eighteenth centuries, modernity is largely backing off from this trend. This is apparent in Thomas Hobbes (1588–1679), though he does not expressly state it. Others do expressly state it – such as Machiavelli, Spinoza, Vico, and Hume. Machiavelli writes, "I thought it sensible to go straight to a discussion of how things are in real life and not waste time with a discussion of an imaginary world." Spinoza likewise laments, "For they [philosophers] conceive of men, not as they are, but as they themselves would like them to be. Whence it comes to pass that, instead of ethics, they have generally written satire, and that they have never conceived a theory of politics, which could be turned to use, but such as might be taken for chimera, or might have been formed in Utopia, or in that golden age of the poets when, to be sure, there was least need of it." Vico echoes, "Philosophy considers people as they should be, and hence is useful only to the very few who want to live in the republic of Plato, rather than to sink into the dregs of Romulus." And finally, Rousseau's contemporary and one-time close friend, David Hume, writes, "Sovereigns must take mankind as they find them, and cannot pretend to introduce any violent change in their principles and ways of thinking."¹⁶

So the trend of much of the early modern tradition is clear in its rejection of Utopianism and firm in its commitment to working with rather than against human nature. Nevertheless, while Rousseau speaks in line with these radicals, there is an undertone of the traditionalist in his work. In the *Political Economy*, for example, he suggests something very different from his words in the *Social Contract*: "While it is good to know how to use men as they are, it is much better still to make them what one needs them to be; the most absolute authority is that which penetrates to man's inmost being, and affects his will no less than it does his actions."¹⁷

---

¹⁵ He apparently changes his mind about this in *SC*, 2.7.
¹⁶ These cites come from Gourevitch 1997, 297; *Machiavelli [1513] 1995, 47–48,; corrected}*; Spinoza 2000, Ch. 1, §1; Vico [1725] 2000, 1.2.6; David Hume [1752a] 1994, 98.
¹⁷ *Political Economy*, 12 [III: 251].

Rousseau continues in this first paragraph to remark, "I shall try always to combine what right permits with what interest prescribes" (1.Proemium, 41 [III: 351]). This is consistent with his goal of taking men as they are, to be sure. This also reveals much about what follows. The question is, "How do we get people to want what is right?" Rousseau here responds to Diderot's essay on *Natural Right*.[18] Diderot suggests that natural man – that is, man in the state of nature – is a perfectly rational creature who will freely choose what is good for the community, that is the general will. Rousseau will counter that it is not that simple.

1.1. *Subject of this First Book*

Rousseau stands out among the great philosophers for his ability to open with extraordinary flair. His *Emile* opens with the declaration, "Everything is good as it leaves the hands of the Author of things; everything degenerates in the hands of man." His *Reveries of the Solitary Walker* embarks with the sad confession, "I am now alone on earth, no longer having any brother, neighbor, friend, or society other than myself."[19] But surely his most famous opening line remains that from Chapter One of the *Social Contract*: "Man is born free, and everywhere he is in chains" (*SC*, 1.1.1, 41 [III: 351]). Rousseau is referencing the natural freedom of man discussed in his *Second Discourse*. Early human beings were perfectly free in the sense that they had no rules or external governance of any kind. They were free of all constraints. Yet, following the narrative of the *Second Discourse* to its dark conclusion, readers know from Part II of that work that everyone who was born free ends up in the chains of despotism, fooled by a sham social contract. This is what Rousseau has in mind in carefully constructing this passage.[20]

It is worth noting here what might strike some readers as either contradictory or disingenuous in these opening lines. He asks in this first paragraph, "How did this change [from freedom to chains] come about?" only to answer, "I do not know" (*SC*, 1.1.1, 41 [III: 351]). The problem seems to be generated by the fact that Rousseau provides an elaborate account of how those chains came about in his *Discourse on Inequality* – and hence has a very good idea of the origin of chains burdening subjects at the opening of the *Social Contract*. But it is important to bear in mind

---

[18] Diderot 1992, 17–21.

[19] *Emile*, 37 [IV: 245]; *Reveries*, 1 [I: 995].

[20] For an extensive discussion of the metaphor of the chain in Rousseau's political thought, see my *Rousseau's Platonic Enlightenment*, 129–55.

that Rousseau proposes his *Second Discourse* account as "conjectures" or a "hypothetical account." Later in the *Social Contract*, when discussing Roman history, he confesses that the founding of nations is always poorly documented and posterity is left with "scarcely anything but conjectures" (*SC*, 4.4.1, 127 [III: 444]). In the end, one is left more with "fables" (*SC*, 4.4.1, 127 [III: 444]) than with historical accurate records. He subsequently defines fables as fictions with a "moral purpose."[21]

Nevertheless, whereas the *Second Discourse* concludes with citizens converted into slaves, the *Social Contract* takes a more optimistic route. He asks, "What can make it [the chains] legitimate? I believe I can solve this problem" (*SC*, 1.1.1, 41 [III: 351]). This is a striking claim, since the normal reaction to chains is to break them. Plato's prisoner in the Cave is freed from his chains. Marx encourages laborers to sever the chains to the capitalist system as a whole. Yet Rousseau does not follow this pattern. He rather makes a subtle distinction between legitimate and illegitimate chains. Chains themselves are inevitable – but differ widely in character. In the *Emile*, the pupil declares at the end of an intensive education, "What course have I chosen! To remain what you have made me and voluntarily to add no other chain to the one with which nature and the laws burden me." He continues, "the eternal laws of nature and order do exist. For the wise man, they take the place of positive law. They are written in the depth of his heart by conscience and reason. It is to these that he ought to enslave himself in order to be free."[22] So the point is not to be free from chains, but to find the right ones. It is clear from the *Discourses* that the chains of opinion, tyrants, and *amour propre* are the wrong kind. The aim of the *Social Contract* is to find and employ the right ones.

Rousseau already hints at his solution in the second paragraph of Chapter One. He insists that the right chains do not exist in nature, leaving convention as the only viable alternative. The dichotomy of nature and convention goes back to the ancient Greeks in their distinction between *phusis* (nature) and *nomos* (law or convention). For the early Greeks, as well as the ancient Jews, laws [*nomos*] were accepted as coming from the gods. But as the Greeks became less theocentric, *phusis* gained in its appeal.[23] It was this *phusis*-based ethic advocated by Plato's character of Polus in the *Gorgias* that Socrates challenges, turning politics back to *nomos*.[24]

---

[21] *Second Discourse*, 125, 128 [III: 123, 127]; *Reveries*, 48 [I: 1029].
[22] *Emile*, 471 [IV: 855], 473 [IV: 857]
[23] See Seung 1996, 9–10, for details on this transition.
[24] *Gorgias*, 282e–283d.

Rousseau addresses the nature-based approaches to politics advanced by Aristotle, Grotius, Filmer, and Hobbes in Chapters Two through Four.

1.2. *Of the First Societies*

Rousseau opens Chapter Two by exploring the most natural society: the family.[25] The argument for political authority resting on the natural authority of the family had been made especially popular in the work of the English philosopher, Robert Filmer. Filmer argues, "creation made man prince of his posterity. And indeed not only Adam but the succeeding patriarchs had, by right of fatherhood, royal authority over their children.... This lordship which Adam by creation had over the whole world, and by right descending from him to the partriarchs did enjoy, was as large and ample as the absolutist dominion of any monarch which hath been seen since the creation."[26] In other words, Filmer posits that all authority comes from God. And since God set up Adam as an absolute sovereign of Eden, it is safe to say that God's will is that authority emanates from this patriarchal model, passed down through a hereditary line of succession of eldest sons.

Rousseau had previously explored this parallel between paternal and political power in his *Discourse on Political Economy*.[27] In this essay, he observes that fathers acquire their power by nature. They are simply stronger than their children and the children are so weak that they are utterly dependent. Further, because of the reliable natural feelings or sentiments fathers have for their children, they are highly trustworthy in making just use of their authority. But just as Rousseau seems to be building the case for natural authority on the model of the family, he concludes that these considerations are entirely irrelevant to politics. This is because "Far from the chief's having a natural interest in the happiness of private individuals, it is not uncommon for him to seek his own happiness in their misery." The important difference between familial societies and political ones is that parents actually love their children – rulers do not naturally love their subjects in the same way. Instead, they have a love or pleasure of commanding others. And whereas for Rousseau a father cannot but

---

[25] Rousseau provides a condensed version of this account in his *Emile*, 459 [IV: 838]. It is worth adding that with his treatment of the family here through his critiques of slavery, the right of conquest, and despotism in *SC*, 1.4, he is actually following familiar arguments already spelled out in Part II of the *Second Discourse*.

[26] Filmer [1680] 1991, 6, 7.

[27] *Political Economy*, 3–6 [III: 241–4]. See also *Political Fragments*, 26 [III: 487].

grieve at harm done to his children, a ruler can benefit immeasurably from inflicting harm. So the analogy between family and state fails, which leads to Rousseau's rejection of Filmer's "odious system."[28] His argument against Filmer in the *Social Contract* is less developed and mostly takes on a mocking tone. He succinctly echoes his assessment that while fathers naturally love their children, monarchs have no such natural inclination (*SC*, 1.2.3, 42 [III: 352]) and then speculates, "since I am a direct descendant from these Princes [Noah's sons, Shem, Ham, and Japheth],[29] and perhaps from the elder branch, for all I know, I might, upon verification of titles, find I am the legitimate King of humankind" (*SC*, 1.2.9, 43 [III: 354]).

In resurrecting his arguments against Filmer, however, Rousseau also inflicts collateral damage on Grotius, Hobbes, and Aristotle. These arguments are broadly related to Filmer's insofar as they take nature to be the source of political legitimacy. The first of these is the Dutch philosopher, Hugo Grotius (1583–1645). As a young man, Rousseau had read and admired Grotius,[30] but by the time he fleshed out his own political philosophy he had lowered his assessment.[31] The source of Grotius' problems, according to Rousseau, resides in two assumptions. First, he derives rights from empirical facts. That is, he fails to distinguish *is* from *ought*. Second is his denial that "all human power is established for the sake of the governed" (*SC*, 1.2.4, 42 [III: 352–53]).[32] Rousseau apparently has in mind the *Rights of War and Peace*, where Grotius condemns the view that "all Government was ordained for the Sake of the Governed, not of the Governor." Grotius continues, "for some Power are of themselves established for the Sake of the Governor, as that of a Master over his Slave: For there the Benefit of the Slave is extrinsical and accidental."[33]

---

[28] *Political Economy*, 4 [III: 243], 5 [III: 244].

[29] Filmer reasons that since Noah and his sons are the only male survivors of the Flood, there is no reason to trace royal lineage past them back to Adam.

[30] See Cranston 1982, 148, 206. In the "Epistle Dedicatory" to his *Second Discourse*, Rousseau praises his own father, remarking, "I see Tacitus, Plutarch, and Grotius before him amidst the tools of his trade. I see at his side a beloved son receiving with too little profit the tender teachings of the best of Father" (*Second Discourse*, 120 [III: 118]).

[31] In the *Emile*, in speaking of Emile's political education, he writes, "Grotius, the master of all our learned men in this matter, is only a child and, what is worse, a child of bad faith" (*Emile*, 458 [IV: 836]).

[32] This may be an apt description of Jean-Jacques Burlamaqui's politics, which holds that "As for what concerns the sovereign, the ends he aims at for himself, by giving laws to his subjects, is the satisfaction and glory arising from the execution of the wise designs he proposes" (Burlamaqui [1747] 2006, 104 [1.10.2]). He later says that in passing laws, the sovereign is to "consult his own satisfaction and glory" ... but "by rendering his subjects happy" (105 [1.10.4]). So while the sovereign is to seek his own glory, he is supposed to achieve this by making his subjects rational and happy. This is worth noting since Burlamaqui was a Genevan with some influence on Genevan politics. Rousseau was familiar with his work, as established in Rosenblatt 1997.

[33] Grotius [1625] 2005, 272, 273 [1.3.8.2].

Rousseau finds much the same reasoning in Thomas Hobbes, who similarly places no legal conditions on the right of a sovereign to rule other than its ability to master its subjects and keep them in its awe. By sharply distinguishing sovereign and subjects, he effectively divides humankind "into herds of cattle, each with its chief who tends to devour it" (*SC*, 1.3, 43 [III: 353]). Lumping Hobbes and Grotius together,[34] Rousseau finds no special distinction between their influential philosophies and that practiced by the notorious Roman despot Caligula. It is a short step from establishing the superiority of rulers by natural fact to granting them despotic power. As Rousseau paraphrases his targets, "As a shepherd is of a nature superior to his flock's, so too are the shepherds of men, who are their chiefs, of a nature superior to their peoples'" (*SC*, 1.2.6, 43 [III: 353]). Such reasoning, Rousseau concludes, leads to the inevitable deduction that subjects are indistinguishable from slaves.[35]

Along these lines, Rousseau here offers a brief but effective critique of Aristotle's doctrine of natural slaves. Aristotle had reasoned in his *Politics* that some are slaves by nature.[36] That is, their minds are of a naturally inferior capacity so that their natural social role is to serve as slaves to more capable individuals. Rousseau does not deny that there are many under such circumstances who give this impression. But he scolds Aristotle for mistaking the effect for the cause. It is only because their nature has been so twisted by ill-conceived conventions that they appear naturally deficient. Slavery has this effect: "Slaves lose everything in their chains, even the desire to be rid of them" (*SC*, 1.2.8, 43 [III: 353]). So while it appears to Aristotle that slaves are fit for their lot in life, one should not mistake appearances for nature.

To be sure, in Book 1, Chapter xix of the *Politics*, Aristotle acknowledges the existence of slaves by convention as much as by nature. He describes the practice of prisoners of war being converted to slaves as this kind of

---

[34] In his *Emile*, Rousseau writes of Hobbes and Grotius, "The truth is that their principles are exactly alike. They only differ in their manner of expression. They also differ in method. Hobbes bases everything on sophisms, and Grotius on poets. They have everything else in common" (*Emile*, 458 [IV: 836]).

[35] I note here that Rousseau's treatment of slavery here and in Chapter 4 largely considers "slavery" as a moral or political relation rather than specifically the pervasive chattel slavery that characterized the Americas in this period. As Jimmy Casas Klausen observes, however, Rousseau was perfectly aware of this mode of slavery as well, including in his *Julie*, where St. Preux comments on "those vast and unfortunate countries that seem destined only to cover the earth with herds of slaves. At their lowly appearance I turned aside my eyes in contempt, horror, and pity, and seeing the fourth part of my equals turned into beasts for the service of others, I rued being a man" (*Julie*, 340 [II: 414]). See Klausen 2014, chapter 2.

[36] Aristotle, *Politics*, Book I, chapters 5–6.

slavery by convention. This practice, however, still carries with it a natural dimension for Aristotle. Those who lose wars lose because of their inferior virtue. That is, they are naturally inferior. So they are still, in a sense, natural slaves. Beyond this, when they agree to continue living as slaves, Aristotle's arguments come to resemble those of Grotius, condemned earlier in this chapter by Rousseau. That is, for Rousseau, one cannot agree to live in slavery.

Of course, this discussion of Aristotle has far broader implications beyond a critique of the eighteenth-century system of slavery. The term "slave" can equally apply to subjects of a despot. By reading Rousseau's discussion in this light, it is clear that he means to shake citizens free from their illegitimate chains. Slave-subjects may not wear chains in the literal sense as those victims of chattel slavery in North America, but these chains for Rousseau are no less real and threatening. Slave-subjects, like their chattel slave counterparts, have been beaten down so thoroughly by a system of oppression that they have lost the will to break free. In the end, naturally, despotic systems thrive on precisely this disposition on behalf of their subjects.

1.3. *The Right of the Strongest*

This chapter repeats a sentiment that occurs with great frequency in Rousseau's writings – a rejection of the supposed right of the strongest.[37] The supposed "right of the strongest" has a long history in Western thought, stemming back to the Platonic characters of Callicles in the *Gorgias* and Thrasymachus in the *Republic*. Callicles, for example, posits that nature teaches precisely the opposite of Socrates and his ilk: "nature itself reveals that it's a just thing for the better man and the more capable man to have a greater share." This is true amongst the "other animals" and it is true among human beings as well. To deviate from this is to deviate from *natural* justice, as Callicles understands it. Indeed, to take power from their hands and place it in the hands of the many or the weak is to "subdue them [the powerful] into slavery."[38] The point, as Callicles sees it, is to foster the ascent of the powerful, where nature would shine. Rousseau sees this argument as no doubt lingering in his own day. Indeed, the spirit of Thrasymachus' arguments is reintroduced by Spinoza, who

---

[37] See: *Julie*, 474 [*OC*, II: 579]; *Second Discourse*, 186 [III:191]; *Mountain*, 239 [III: 815]; "State of War," 162 [III: 609]; *Government of Geneva*, 203 [V: 499]. See *Emile*, 459 [IV: 838] for a condensed account of his arguments in this chapter.

[38] Plato, *Gorgias*, 483cd, 483e–484a.

argues, "the right of the state or of the sovereign is nothing more than the right of Nature itself and is determined by ... power."[39] Rousseau identifies a similar conception of right operating in the "horrible system of Hobbes," where "Justice and trust have to be bent to the interest of the most powerful: such is the rule."[40]

The nature of this kind of natural right, however, is ephemeral, according to Rousseau. Right can only be sustained so long as one actually possesses power. The moment a stronger force asserts itself is the moment power is transferred and natural "right" is changed – from being the will of the first powerful force to the will of the second. Rousseau asks that we consider what this entails: "For once force makes right, the effect changes together with the cause; every force that overcomes the first, inherits the right. Once one can disobey with impunity, one can do so legitimately, and since the stronger is always right, one need only make sure to be stronger" (*SC*, 1.3.2, 44 [III: 354]). This means that the doctrine, "might makes right," is tautological and meaningless. If the two terms move in absolute parallel, it adds nothing to the term "might" to add "right." Might is simply might.

He further adds that there is no morality in force: "force is a physical power; I fail to see what morality can result from its effects. To yield to force is an act of necessity, not of will; at most it is any act of prudence. In what sense can it become a duty?" (*SC*, 1.3.1, 44 [III: 354]). This brief passage reveals much about Rousseau's moral thought generally, if one accepts the so-called Kantian reading of his work.[41] On this reading, virtue itself is for Rousseau contingent upon the existence and efforts of a free will. One can act from an inclination to do good, but it is *not* virtue, strictly speaking. If it is in one's *nature* to feed the poor, one has done a good deed, but is not virtuous. This is because virtue requires an exercise of freedom – of the free will – against one's passions or inclinations.[42] Consider two examples. First, imagine the good-natured person who works with the mentally handicapped in her spare time. She likes the people she helps, and actually enjoys herself. Now consider the misanthrope who does the same. He hates people and most of all the handicapped, who make him feel positively uncomfortable. The first person has performed a *good* deed,

---

[39] Spinoza 2000, 3.2. Christopher Bertram also finds it in Bossuet and Pascal (Bertram 2004, 62). Bossuet speaks of a "right of conquest" ([1709] 1990, 52).

[40] *State of War*, 163, 162 [III: 610, 609].

[41] The most notable works of this type are Cassirer [1945] 1963 and [1954] 1963, as well as Levine 1976.

[42] Immanuel Kant (1724–1804), who identifies Rousseau as the Newton of the moral world, takes this as foundational in his moral philosophy.

but is not necessarily virtuous. There was minimal exercise of the will. She would have done it whether or not it was the right thing to do. The second person, however, has done a good deed *and is virtuous*. What is the difference? He would not do good deeds without this strength of will. He struggled against his nature. He made himself do it because it was the right thing to do. That is the nature of virtue. As Rousseau elsewhere observes, "This word virtuous means *force*."[43] The will is that force that is enacted against nature itself. Individuals are virtuous when they combat nature to do the good. They commit a vice when failing to overcome nature to the detriment of the good.

What the "right of the stronger" doctrine fails to consider, then, is the faculty of the will. Again, as Rousseau observes, "To yield to force is an act of necessity, not of will." For this reason, while it may often be true that the stronger force legislates, this does not mean that it has any moral authority. This fact is confirmed in the narrative of his *Second Discourse*, where the strong, in the form of the clever propertied class, dupe the weak into signing a sham social contract. Here the strong sway "crude, easily seduced men" into political arrangements that guarantee their own subjection. They are not in a position to grant their consent in a meaningful way, either because they are too crude to know what is in their interest or because the strong have carefully concealed the true consequences of the contract. So there is no genuine exercise of will and hence the resulting society is utterly absent of moral content and obligation. It consists of mere relationships of force.

There is one final component worth addressing in Chapter Three, which is its actual opening: "The stronger is never strong enough to be forever master, unless he transforms his force into right, and obedience into duty." This speaks again to the ephemeral nature of might as right. But it also strikingly claims that power can be sustained, if it is quickly joined with right and duty. Although there is no evidence to

---

[43] "Letter to Franquières," 281. Support for reading Rousseau in this fashion can be found in his two final autobiographical works. In the *Reveries*, he writes, there is no virtue in "following our inclinations and in giving ourselves the pleasure of doing good when they lead us to do so. But virtue consists in overcoming them when duty commands in order to do what duty prescribes" (*Reveries*, 77 [I: 1053]). See also the *Dialogues*, 140 [I: 841–42]), *Emile*, 444–45 [IV: 817], and *Julie*, 560 [II: 682]. Timothy O'Hagan has objected to making too much of the Kantian reading insofar as Rousseau's conscience is "a kind of feeling. So, even when he is apparently furthest from the morality of the senses, and closest to the morality of virtue and duty, he does not establish the same clear distinction between the two as Kant and later deontologist would do" (O'Hagan 1999, 28). An alternative non-Kantian reading of this (*SC*, 1.3.1, 44 [III: 354]) and similar passages is that when one is struggling against nature, one is struggling against *amour-propre* insofar as it is a self-assertive impulse. So on this reading, virtue generally resides in various modes of self-denial.

suggest that Rousseau had read David Hume on this point, it nevertheless speaks to Hume's challenge to social contract theory from 1748.
Critiquing the likes of John Locke, Hume argues, "Almost all the governments, which exist at present, or of which there remains any record in
history, have been founded originally, either on usurpation or conquest,
or both, without any pretence of a fair consent, or voluntary subjection
of the people."[44] While Rousseau does not grant that such governments
are legitimate, he concedes that their power will endure far longer than
where right and duty are ignored.[45] As he concludes Chapter Three, "one
is only obliged to obey legitimate powers" (*SC*, 1.3.4, 44 [III: 355]). So
far, he has established that there can be no legitimate power originating
in nature.

1.4. *Of Slavery*

Chapters Two and Three were dedicated to demonstrating that political
authority cannot be established by nature – whether by the principles of
Callicles, Thrasymachus, Aristotle, Filmer, or Caligula. There is no natural
principle, strictly speaking. So Rousseau turns to convention – "conventions therefore remain as the basis of all legitimate authority among men"
(*SC*, 1.4.1, 44 [III: 355]). This is simply a reminder of what he posited earlier (*SC*, 1.1.2, 41 [III: 352]). Rousseau emphasizes this strategy again in his
Letters Written from the Mountain:

> But what is the foundation of this obligation? That is what Authors are divided
> upon. According to some, it is force, according to others, paternal authority;
> according to others, the will of God. Each establishes his principle and attacks
> that of the others: I have not done otherwise myself, and following the soundest
> portion of those who have discussed these matters, I posited as a foundation of
> the body politic [in the *Social Contract*] the convention of its members, I refuted
> the principles different from my own.[46]

The mere fact of convention, however, is obviously insufficient to create
a political obligation. There is a difference between good and bad convention. As he makes evident in Chapter Four, enslaving agreements are
bad. Good agreements or conventions will come later. Also keep in mind
in Chapter Four that the sham social contract of the *Second Discourse*
is a convention or agreement. But obviously, it is a bad one. So mere

---

[44] Hume [1748] 1994, 189–90.
[45] Wingrove 2000 has argued that Rousseau endorses precisely this approach in his *Lévite d'Ephraïm*,
ch. 6. This has been contested in Morgenstern 2008.
[46] *Mountain*, 231 [III: 806]). See Williams 2007b, 482–83.

agreement or convention is insufficient to generate legitimate political obligation.

Rousseau here again targets Grotius. According to Rousseau, Grotius draws an analogy between individuals who sell themselves into servitude and subjects who submit to a king/tyrant. Since individuals have a right to do this, so should peoples.[47] Keep in mind that this is precisely what Rousseau describes happening in the *Second Discourse* – so this is not a diversion from his purposes. Before Rousseau can sketch a good contract or good convention, he must lay out an invalid one. He offers several arguments aimed at debunking Grotius.

The first argument he identifies for slavery might be called the "argument from tranquility." Some argue that agreeing to live under a despot is worth the cost insofar as the despot brings tranquility.[48] Recall that in the *Second Discourse*, the subjects run into the arms of the rich because it brings an end to the state of war. And even more specifically relevant, he comments there, "I know that enslaved peoples do nothing but boast of the peace and tranquility they enjoy in their chains."[49] In the *Social Contract*, he reminds readers that tranquility is no sure measure of justice. A tranquil life is also had in dungeons (*SC*, 1.4.3, 45 [III: 355]). He observes that the Cyclops' cave in the *Odyssey* was likewise tranquil. A cyclops only uses this apparent tranquility as bait to lure in his unsuspecting prey.[50] So is also the case with tyrants, reasons Rousseau. They may promise tranquility, but in the end they deliver tyranny.

For Rousseau, to surrender one's freedom amounts to surrendering one's reason or sanity. A populace can submit to a tyrant only if it has no wits about it. To imagine a people submitting itself this way is "to suppose a populace [is] composed of madmen" (*SC*, 1.4.4, 45 [III: 356]). They are simply not in the right frame of mind if they make this agreement. As madmen, they have no right to contract with the tyrant and the agreement is "illegitimate and null" (*SC*, 1.4.4, 45 [III: 356]). This is

---

[47] Grotius [1625] 2005, 1.3.8.1. A condensed version of this critique of Grotius can be found in the *Emile*, 460 [IV: 838]. Grotius offers several accounts of how this sovereignty may be granted by the people to a king. They may be on the "brink of ruin" (262), they have no other means to save themselves (262), they may be in great want (262), some people are natural slaves, as Aristotle suggests (264), people can live "happily under an arbitrary Government" (264). Grotius attempts to meet all counterarguments – arguments for popular sovereignty – at 272–6.

[48] Again, we find Rousseau citing one of Grotius' arguments. Grotius says, "Moreover, the Examples of other Nations, who for many Ages, lived happily under an arbitrary Government" (Grotius [1625] 2005, 264 [1.3.8]).

[49] *Second Discourse*, 70 [III: 177–8]; *Second Discourse*, 72 [III: 181].

[50] Also see Rousseau's "State of War," in which he likewise describes the predatory Cyclops, who lures unsuspecting prey with overtures of tranquility (162 [IV: 609]).

a strong statement – but not entirely surprising. Locke likewise excludes madmen from the full rights of citizenship.[51] Rousseau's innovation is to extend this principle to people otherwise thought to be sane. The very fact of their consent to a certain kind of contract, however, is sufficient to declare them "mad." This madness then invalidates the contract, the same way as if they had been children.

Likewise, it is illegitimate to assign slave status to children on the basis of social institutions or parental decisions. Here again, Rousseau has Grotius in mind, who comments, "If there were indeed no other Way of maintaining their Children, Parents might with themselves bring their future Progeny into Slavery: Because upon the very same Account, Parents may even sell their free-born Children."[52] Rousseau concedes that parents have many rights over their children insofar as they exercise these for their preservation and well-being, as Grotius directs, but these do not extend to surrendering their children into slavery. Such a gesture "exceeds the rights of paternity" (*SC*, 1.4.5, 45 [III: 356]).

Rousseau immediately extends the metaphor of slavery to that of an arbitrary government: can one generation's explicit consent to an arbitrary government obligate subsequent generations to the same arbitrary government? His answer is a firm "no." This is because, in the first place, each generation would have to make its own decisions. But in the second place, if a people were truly consenting, the government would by definition no longer be arbitrary. So any assent by previous generations to live under despotic governments is not obligatory for descendent generations under the same despotism. One might ask whether Rousseau is backtracking here and making room for an argument he has just rejected: namely, consenting to be a slave-subject. This is unlikely. What is more probable is that Rousseau speaks of the accepting or rejecting of a state in a normative sense. That is, if they are capable of assenting to a state, it could not be despotic, by definition.

His next argument against slavery may be called the *argument from human dignity*. He writes, "To renounce one's freedom is to renounce one's quality as a man, the rights of humanity, and even its duties" (*SC*, 1.4.6, 45 [III: 356]). The argument itself is simple. The dignity of man stems from his freedom. Submitting to slavery through despotism is surrendering one's freedom. Therefore, submitting to slavery through despotism

[51] John Locke [1690] 1988, §60.
[52] Grotius [1625] 2005, 2.5.30.

is the renouncing of one's dignity. The implied premise is that our freedom permits us to be moral. There can be no morality without freedom.
Therefore, the denial of freedom through submission to a tyrant is tantamount to the denial of our very humanity – or human dignity. It is worth
emphasizing that this notion of an inherent human dignity is taken for
granted in much of the world today. But there is good reason to believe
that at least the modern strain of it stems precisely from Rousseau. No less
figure than Immanuel Kant wrote, "*Rousseau* brought me around. This
blinding superiority disappeared, I learned to honor human beings."[53]

The last set of arguments pertains to the acquisition of slaves through
warfare and conquest. Some thinkers argue that slavery or despotism is
implied by the rules of warfare. That is, the victor has the right to convert
the vanquished into slaves. This has been the argument of many, including Grotius and Burlamaqui.[54] Their argument runs roughly as follows:

1. The victor has a right to kill the vanquished.
2. The right to kill implies all lesser rights.
3. Slavery is one such lesser right.
4. Therefore, the victor has the right to enslave the vanquished.

The fundamental problem with this argument, according to Rousseau,
is that while parties have a right to kill each other during warfare, no one
has the right to kill another party that has laid down its arms (*SC*, 1.4.10,
47 [III: 357]). Once soldiers have laid down their arms [as they always do
when the war ends], they return to being merely individuals – and their
right to live must be respected. So premise (1) is rejected, which unravels
the rest of the argument.

For good measure, Rousseau adds a second argument against contracts
for slavery here. Suppose that some parties were to make a contract for the
enslavement of one to the other. This would be nothing less than a continuation of war, just as Locke suggests.[55] As such, there are no obligations,
and the agreement is invalid. In the end, all arguments of this sort are
fated to fail, and are indeed "absurd and meaningless"(*SC*, 1.4.13, 48 [III:
358]). The words "slavery" and "right" cannot be used meaningfully in the
same sentence. The point of this chapter has really boiled down to this:
while convention of some kind is required, it cannot be an unjust convention. It must be the right sort of agreement.

[53] Kant [1765] 2005, 7.
[54] See Grotius [1625] 2005, 3.7.1–3; Locke [1690] 1988, §24; Burlamaqui [1747] 2006, 4.7.29–30.
[55] Locke [1690] 1988, §24.

1.5. *That One Always Has to Go Back to a First Convention*

Rousseau has two separate tasks in Chapter Five: (1) to reaffirm the arguments of Chapter Four against instituting despotism, and (2) to establish the "people" as an independent entity. In furthering his argument against despotism, he holds that even if one were to grant all the flawed arguments dismissed in Chapter Four, one would not have a society. One merely has masters and slaves. There is an "aggregation" but not "association." There is no public good – merely a private will. So such an aggregation could never be a legitimate society. In this brief argument, he conveys an important premise: a political society must be ruled for the benefit of its people, the common good. It cannot be ruled on the basis of the ruler's private interest. This is an essential consideration in developing his conception of the general will.

Second, Rousseau works to establish the "people" as an independent entity. Grotius had argued, Rousseau observes, that the people hand themselves over to a king – but this presupposes that the people already exist as an entity. That is to say, the people already have an independent status from its government and some decision-making capacity. This fact, Rousseau suggests, implies at least one moment in time where there was unanimity – unanimity in forming a unity.

The final paragraph of Chapter Five raises a possible tension in Rousseau's thinking, where he suggests the submission of the people to a "master" (*SC*, 1.5.3, 49 [III: 359]). The tension is this: why would Rousseau, who has just argued that individuals cannot alienate their freedom at all (*SC*, 1.4.4–6, 45–46 [III: 356]), suggest here that they can do just that – that is, alienate their freedom to a "master"? Melissa Schwartzberg has argued that his intention was actually to draw attention to a tension in Grotius' thought. Grotius had suggested that "it is certainly to be presumed, that those who enter into a Society are willing that there should be some Method Fixed of deciding Affairs; but it is altogether unreasonable, that a greater Number should be governed by a less; and therefore, tho' there were no Contracts or Laws that regulate the Manner of determining Affairs, the Majority would naturally have the Right and Authority of the Whole." According to Schwartzberg, Rousseau is observing that his move to majority rule would have to presuppose a prior establishment that this rule was permissible: "In Rousseau's view, once a people possessed a will, such a will could not be alienated: he had thus demonstrated that the existence of majority rule signified the prior existence of a popular will and that the choice to subject such a will was incoherent."[56]

1.6. *Of the Social Pact*

This chapter takes readers to the very heart of the book in the most obvious sense, since it addresses the book's very title. Rousseau has just spent the better parts of Chapters Four and Five dismissing the wrongheaded conventions of slavery and despotism. Now he commences the task of sketching a correct or appropriate contract – that is, a legitimate convention. He begins the chapter by acknowledging the necessity of a political solution. In doing so, he suggests that the state of nature, as presented in the *Second Discourse*, is impossible to sustain indefinitely. He points there specifically to the role of natural disasters and the vicissitudes of climate in forcing natural men together where they would find society.[57] So as pleasant as the golden days of natural society might have been, it will eventually meet enough obstacles to necessitate political life. Indeed, human life depends on it: "humankind would perish if it did not change its way of being" (*SC*, 1.6.1, 49 [III: 360]).[58]

In forging a social contract, however, Rousseau insists that individuals must work with existing materials: "men cannot engender new forces, but only unite and direct those that exist" (*SC*, 1.6.2, 49 [III: 360]). This indicates that he is sticking with his introductory assumption that he is taking "men as they are" (*SC*, 1.Intro, 41 [III: 351]). These natural resources amount to "each man's force and freedom" (*SC*, 1.6.3, 49 [III: 360]).[59] As others have acknowledged,[60] Rousseau wrote the *Social Contract* without discussing its ideas with Diderot. This might be because he was challenging some of Diderot's ideas from his essay, *Natural Right*. Such is the case here. Diderot believed that people were rational enough to sign on to the general will in the state of nature simply by appealing to their reason. But Rousseau casts doubt on this narrative. One must work with the existing

---

[56] Grotius [1625] 2005, 2.5.17; Schwartzberg 2008, 408.

[57] This includes floods and earthquakes (*SD*, 165 [III: 168–9]). See also his *Essay on the Origin of Human Languages*, where Rousseau adds volcanic eruptions and fires (274 [III: 402–3]).

[58] Rousseau was scarcely alone in this opinion. Just three years prior to the publication of the *Social Contract*, for example, Adam Smith wrote that man "can subsist only in society" (Smith [1759] 2009, 2.2.3). This was received wisdom in the tradition going back to Aristotle's *Politics*. In fact, Rousseau's *Second Discourse* is generally understood as the greatest challenge to this assumption.

[59] Rousseau points to freedom as a natural faculty of humanity in his *Second Discourse* (140 [III: 141]).

[60] See Simpson 2007, 80. See *Confessions*, 340 [I: 405].

passions – and somehow bring them into accord with the general will. This is the controversial theme of 2.7.

This brings Rousseau to the "fundamental problem" of the social contract:

> To find a form of association which defends and protects with all common forces the persons and goods of each associate, and by means of which each one, while uniting with all, nevertheless obeys only himself and remains as free as before. (*SC*, 1.6.4, 49 [III: 360)

This statement holds immense meaning for the nature of Rousseau's political program and is worth careful parsing. He expresses at least four important concepts here in one sentence: the protection of each, the uniting of all, obeying only oneself, and remaining as free as before. The uniting of all is a prevalent theme throughout the *Social Contract*. It is a central point of politics to unite with others and become part of a larger whole. But since this is the theme of the general will, it is discussed more substantially later.

Regarding the protection of each, it is the government's job to protect everyone. This apparently includes the protection of property, which is indicated by the protection of "persons and goods" – thus defusing the misconception some have from the *Second Discourse* that Rousseau wants to abolish private property. Clearly, he does not. This will be amplified in *SC*, 1.9.

It is trickier to clarify what Rousseau means by "obey[ing] only himself," and at the same time it is absolutely crucial to understanding his political project. It is tricky because in becoming part of a political association, it seems that most decisions are out of the hands of individuals. That is, they trade individual autonomy for the benefits provided by heteronomy, or the authority of others. Rousseau wants a political system in which citizens still determine their own lives – through politics. Again, this will be elaborated on substantially in the coming pages. But the general point here is that citizens obey themselves insofar as the government dictates follow their own will.

Finally, readers must confront the notion that somehow in joining political society, each member "remains as free as before." This is especially important to Rousseau. People are perfectly free in the state of nature. So how do they retain that freedom in political society? Hobbes will say this is impossible – that we surrender our freedom to gain the protection and advantages of society; but we certainly lose freedom. Rousseau wants to say that we should remain just as free as we were before. Isaiah Berlin has written that liberty is an "absolute value" for Rousseau that he will not sacrifice for anything. Berlin also thinks that Rousseau cannot pull this off without defining liberty in a most unusual way – by saying that liberty and authority are two sides of the same coin, a notion that strikes him as "lunatic" and "insane."[61] We will consider these charges in due course.

Closely upon the heals of the social contract, Rousseau introduces the general will, which Judith Shklar once called, "Rousseau's most famous metaphor. It conveys everything he most wanted to say."[62] Chapter Six, however, does little to elucidate this concept. But he does say the following: *"Each of us places his general person and all his power in common under the supreme direction of the general will; and as one we receive each member as an indivisible part of the whole"* (*SC*, 1.6.9, 50 [III: 361]). It is this entire submission of individuals to the general will that has disturbed many of Rousseau's readers. But the point here is submission to the general will, whatever that might be. Citizens must give themselves to it – and it will help carry out the goals stated earlier in this chapter of submitting to government and remaining as free as they were before. In other words, this magic can only be carried off through the general will. So it is clear why Shklar thought this so important to Rousseau's philosophy. Again, however, this is merely the introduction of a concept. Rousseau returns to it over and over, each time adding layers of complexity.

Rousseau concludes Chapter Six with a series of definitions. As he employs these terms throughout the *Social Contract*, it is especially important to grasp their meaning. These include:

Republic [*République*] – This is the name of a collective body living under the direction of the general will. Bear in mind the resemblance of this term to Plato's *Republic*. Also keep in mind the initial subtitle of the first draft of this work: *Essay about the Form of the Republic*.[63] So a republic is not merely a descriptive term, but a normative one – it must uphold certain ideals embodied in the general will.

---

[61] Berlin 2002, 31, 37, 43.

[62] Shklar 1969, 184. This constitutes Rousseau's introduction to the general will. At no point does he offer an analytic or systemic account of this central element in his political thought, either in the *Social Contract* or anywhere else. Throughout Chapters 1–4 of this book, I address the general will in the specific contexts that Rousseau chooses to place his own discussions of its various attributes. In Appendix B, however, I have assembled a more systemic account of the general will. Readers are free to examine the appendix before pressing forward with Rousseau's arguments, or they may choose to study it only after first engaging it as Rousseau himself presented his case.

[63] Roger D. Masters comments on the resemblance of this title to Plato's *Republic*. Masters points out that in the *Geneva Manuscript* – the first draft of the *Social Contract* – Rousseau describes the general will as the "idea of the civil state" (*Geneva Manuscript*, 1.4), "thus reminding us that his

State [*État*] – A state is a republic when it is passive – that is, not legislating.

Sovereign [*Souverain*] – A sovereign is a republic when it is active – that is, legislating.

People [*peuple*] – The people are the members of the republic.

Citizens [*Citoyens*] – Citizens are the people when they are participating in the sovereign, that is, legislating.

Subjects [*Sujects*] – Subjects are the people when they are passive, that is, when they are following the laws or suffering the consequences of not following the laws. In other words, subjects are the people when they are not legislating.

Finally, Rousseau is adamant in Chapter Six that violations of the *Social Contract* return its parties to their "natural freedom" (*SC*, 1.6.5, 50 [III: 360]). That means, no one is obligated to obey the contract if one party signs on in bad faith.[64] So surely, any government that engages in the social contract on fair terms but then goes on to rule tyrannically violates the contract. This is surely the implied theme of the *Second Discourse*, where the wealthy promise peace, justice, and wise laws aimed at protecting each participant of the social contract,[65] while in reality delivering only despotism.[66] There can be no question that this is the archetype of the illegitimate contract Rousseau condemns here.

Of course, Rousseau's words here in Chapter Six leave open a more dangerous possibility. Since he does not specify which party "slightly modif[ies]" the contract, rendering it void, careful readers might ask what happens when individual citizens do the same. This would happen when, for example, a citizen violates a law. Would this, then, dissolve the entire contract? That seems extremely unlikely, as it would render the entire republic too fragile to be taken seriously.

1.7. *Of the Sovereign*

Chapter Six's definition of sovereign of a republic when it is active is skeletal. Rousseau has a great deal more to say about sovereignty in Chapter

---

principles are a modern equivalent of the Plato "Ideas" or "Forms" (Masters 1978, 19). It is also useful to recall that Rousseau's intention in the larger version of this work was to include a chapter on Plato's *Republic*.

[64] Keep in mind that Rousseau refers to Grotius as a man of "bad faith" (*Emile*, 458 [IV: 836]).

[65] *Second Discourse*, 173 [III: 177].

[66] Although Rousseau does not speak of rendering this contract "null and void" in the *Second Discourse*, again the title page image provides suggestive imagery. As with the title page of the *Social Contract*, one finds a bird fleeing (in this case from an open birdcage). And further, a set of broken manacles can be found at the feet of the goddess of Liberty.

Seven, both formally and substantively. Formally, he insists that it is "contrary to the nature of the body politic for the Sovereign to impose on itself a law which it cannot break" (*SC*, 1.8.2, 52 [III: 362]). This speaks to the absolute authority of the sovereign in Rousseau's republic. It is the nature of a sovereign that it cannot be constrained by previous holdings and conventions. This is specifically because a sovereign, formally speaking, is a legislative body. It is not a subject. Hence in a technical sense, it cannot be subject to legislation. But there is a substantive reason for maintaining this position, as well. As will become evident in Book III, because circumstances change over time, laws will have to be adjusted to meet emerging challenges. It would make little sense for a sovereign to constrain itself in a changing world[67] where artificial conventions cannot be changed to promote the public good.

A second feature of sovereignty is that it cannot be alienated. That is, sovereignty cannot be transferred from one body to another. The most natural sense in which this might occur would be for a sovereign to hand itself over to another nation. John Locke had condemned "The delivery … of the People into the subjection of a Foreign Power" as a firm indicator that the government had dissolved.[68] For Rousseau, the transferring of sovereign power to another land violates the "sanctity" of the social contract itself. The contract involves particular parties. Transferring sovereignty in effect changes the parties *ex post facto* and therefore effectively dissolves the contract itself. No subject would be bound to the legislation of any other sovereign than the one designated by the contract itself.

A third feature of sovereignty is that "one cannot injure one of the members without attacking the body, and still less can one injure the body without the members being affected" (*SC*, 1.7.4, 52 [III: 363]). Rousseau speaks here to the intimate relationship he is forging between individuals and the state. Strikingly, although Rousseau is often accused of anti-liberal sentiments, this element of sovereignty suggests a vigilant protection of individual rights. Harming a citizen, whether by a foreigner in an act anticipating war or even by a fellow subject, amounts to an insult against the whole state. For this reason, it can be deduced, a state is fully justified in responding either with criminal proceedings on the one hand or potentially war in an extreme version of the other. At the same time, Rousseau insists that all subjects are likewise affected by an insult or injury to the state. This is because the state has in the social pact been charged with

[67] It is worth noting here that for Rousseau, "Everything is in continual flux on earth. Nothing on it retains constant and static form" (*Reveries*, 68 [I: 1046]).
[68] Locke [1690] 1988, §217.

defending and protecting each individual. Insofar as it has been injured, its capacity to tend to its subjects has been compromised.

Rousseau adds that in the context of the social contract, "duty and interest alike obligate contracting parties to help one another" (*SC*, 1.7.4, 52 [III: 363]). The terms "duty" and "interest" are of special significance here, since they suggest how Rousseau is still working with individuals "as they are" (*SC*, 1.Proemium), but at the same time adding a layer of moral obligation. He observes here that it is in the simple interest, stemming from *amour de soi*, that the state looks after its subjects and subjects care for the state. Neither could survive without the other. But at the same time, after the contract has been established, both parties also have a moral obligation to tend to the other's preservation.

Whereas the first three elements of sovereignty in Chapter Seven are relatively straightforward and intuitively agreeable, the fourth element is striking and potentially alarming: the sovereign cannot err. "The Sovereign, by the mere fact that it is, is always everything it ought to be" (*SC*, 1.7.5, 52 [III: 363]). He explains that this is because, as it consists of the individuals who constitute it, it cannot possibly have any interests contrary to theirs. In other words, popular sovereignty provides an assurance against bad or tyrannical laws. This may seem exceptionally sanguine. Students of history are well aware of the many occasions on which popular legislatures have run amok. This is not what Rousseau endorses here. His denial of sovereign error is tightly linked to his normative conception of sovereignty. Sovereignty is not merely the people in their legislative function. In order for sovereignty to exist, it must conform to a normative idea. Although Rousseau does not spell this out in Chapter Seven, this is the normative idea of the general will. He expands this theme substantially in *SC*, 2.3.

The final paragraph of Chapter Seven is indisputably the most controversial. Indeed, it includes one of the most infamous passages in the history of political thought. He sets this up in the penultimate paragraph of the chapter with his distinction between an individual's common interest and private interest. The common interest, he suggests, is the general will of the citizen and looks to the interest of the entire community. But each individual also possesses a particular interest, which is quite distinct and often opposed to the common interest or general will. This particular interest "may lead him to look upon what he owes to the common cause as a gratuitous contribution, the loss of which will harm others less than its payment burdens him" (*SC*, 1.7.7, 53 [III: 363]). Individuals, for example, may well come to the conclusion that it is in their particular interest not to report their taxes, insofar as those taxes may represent a personal burden. Rousseau understands this inclination. Yet at the same time, he asserts this cannot be permitted since this kind of decision is "an injustice, the progress of which would cause the ruin of the body politic" (*SC*, 1.7.7, 53 [III: 363]).

Of course, this is a problem for any political philosopher, not just Rousseau. But Rousseau's solution is arguably far more radical than most:

> Hence for the social compact not to be an empty formula, it tacitly includes the following engagement which alone can give force to the rest, that whoever refuses to obey the general will shall be constrained to do so by the entire body: which means nothing other than that he shall be forced to be free; for this is the condition which by giving each Citizen to the Fatherland, guarantees him against all personal dependence; the condition which is the device and makes for the operation of the political machine, and alone renders legitimate civil engagements which would otherwise be absurd, tyrannical, and liable to the most enormous abuses (*SC*, 1.7.8, 53 [III: 364]).

It is not merely that the government will force subjects to obey the law; it is that the government will *force them to be free*. This has long struck interpreters as a dubious and indeed dangerous paradox. Isaiah Berlin went so far as to call it both a "monstrous" and "sinister" paradox – one that would be employed by the likes of the Jacobins, Robespierre, Hitler, Mussolini, and the Communists,[69] where an arbitrary tyrant would decide what is best for subjects and implement it willy-nilly.

Setting aside such evaluations, it seems that Rousseau is concerned with addressing at least two problems in this often-maligned passage. Frederick Neuhouser has called these the (1) "freedom-through-personal-independence" and (2) "social autonomy" or "moral freedom" problems. The former is largely a question of how one can be free in the context of living socially with others – namely, it focuses on Rousseau's concern that those "forced to be free" are at the same time freed from "all personal dependence." The latter is fundamentally a matter of individual moral or metaphysical freedom – namely, is it possible for individual citizens to exercise free will in a social context? As Neuhouser correctly insists, both elements are essential to grasp the full impact of this passage.[70]

The freedom-through-personal-independence reading of Rousseau's "forced to be free" passage, as suggested, emphasizes his attention to the problem of personal dependence. In this section of Chapter Seven – and indeed throughout his corpus – Rousseau is concerned that individuals not find themselves in a position where their wills are subject to arbitrary whims of others without appeal. This is largely the condition of the political world as Rousseau knew it in eighteenth-century Europe, including France. The laws were imposed on subjects by a relatively elite few, who were more or less exempt from them. These subjects, thus, experienced all the burdens of residence with none of the independence. They paid all of the taxes, for example, but were often denied the benefits purchased with those funds. By contrast, the ruling class enjoyed all the benefits of the state, including legal protection, the use of public lands, and even housing, without the burden of taxation.

Of course, the existence of "laws" that promote the interests of one class over that of others is a poor excuse for law and is, to Rousseau's mind, no law at all. A genuine law replaces the dependence of subjects on others to a dependence on the republic as a whole. That is, one must replace *personal* dependence with *communal* dependence. This is clear when he subsequently observes that in the social contract "every Citizen [should] be perfectly independent of all the others, and excessively dependent on the City" (*SC*, 2.12.3, 80 [III: 393]).

But what exactly does he mean by replacing personal dependence with communal dependence? This draws attention to the overwhelming importance of the rule of law in Rousseau's republic. In the *Emile*, he observes that the only way to overcome a dependence on men is "to substitute law for man and arm the general wills with a real strength superior to the action of every particular will."[71] The rule of law effectively evens the playing field such that no one individual is subject to the whim of any other individual. Timothy O'Hagan has effectively related Rousseau's appeal to the rule of law to the free-rider problem, an association that is raised by Rousseau himself. A free-rider may "look upon what he owes to the common cause as a gratuitous contribution, the loss of which will harm others less than its payment burdens him." Consider, for example, a community dog park where citizens take their dogs for much-needed off-leash exercise. In an established community park, most citizens follow the guidelines to dispose of their dogs' waste – so that others will be spared the burden of doing it for them. If this is true, so the free-rider logic goes, then why should I trouble myself to clean up after my own dog so long as I escape detection? The other community members are taking care of this. The park is clean. My dog is getting her exercise. Insofar as other park

---

[71] *Emile*, 85 [IV: 310].

members are left with the burden of my dog's mess, then, they are subject to the whims of my will. When the rule of law is enforced, however, and I am compelled to pick up the waste, others are no longer subject to my will. That is, they are no longer subject to personal dependence. This is replaced by the communal dependence related to the rule of law.[72]

The rule of law as a solution to the free-rider problem has broad implications for Rousseau's constructive political theory. This is because, as he notes, the rule of law itself requires a deep commitment to the principle of equality, if it is to be the rule of law in a genuine sense rather than a ruse. A rule of law in the context of significant social and economic inequalities, for example, is almost certainly mere pretense. The more social and economic inequality, the more those at the top of the hierarchy can shape laws advancing their private or personal wills. As already discussed, this was roughly the predicament burdening much of eighteenth-century Europe. Those with the most were able to write the laws in such a way as to continue promoting their personal interests. There was a "rule of law" in the technical sense – but without social and economic equality, it remained technical indeed.

While the "freedom-through-personal-independence" mode of reading this passage of Chapter Eight is crucial, it does not capture everything that Rousseau meant to convey in insisting that subjects must be "forced to be free." Whereas that mode focuses on Rousseau's attention to the problem of dependence on other individuals, the "social autonomy" or "moral freedom" reading takes seriously Rousseau's emphasis here on freedom more personally. That is, the social autonomy or moral freedom model understands Rousseau as solving a slightly different problem from the freedom-through-personal-independence model. While both models seek to free individuals from dependence on the wills of others, the social autonomy or moral freedom model also seeks to protect individuals from themselves.

What does it mean to be protected against oneself? Consider the following example. My doctor has recommended that I lose twenty pounds. I think this is a good idea, too, but I am concerned that I lack sufficient willpower to follow through. So I go home, put a lock on the refrigerator, and hand the key over to my wife. I plead with her, "Do not under any circumstances give me this key, unless it is to get an apple or broccoli. Even if I beg you. And if you see me attempting to pick the lock at night,

---

[72] See O'Hagan 1999, 98–9, 125–30, Trachtenberg 1993, 61–73, Dagger 1981, 364, and Braybrooke 2001, 62.

you reserve the right – and even have the obligation, if you agree – to kick me as hard as you can in the shins." She agrees. A week later, she catches me attempting to pick the lock and then kicks me in the shins. Am I free? Paradoxically, yes! This is because she is only doing that which I authorized her to do for my own best interest. I knew when I authorized her that it would be difficult for me to do what is right – and that force might be involved to keep me faithful to my will. In fact, I was *not* free when attempting to pick that lock because I was a slave to my appetite. But my freedom was restored in the kick to the shin. I was reminded of my own best interest, as determined by me.

More subtle examples of this occur all the time in the lives of individuals. Students, for example, presumably want an education when they enroll at a college or university. They know at some level that they will not receive an education if they do not study. They are thus in a sense authorizing faculty members to fail them if they fail to do their work. This goes doubly for students guilty of plagiarism. The student suspended for academic dishonesty is forced to be free, insofar as the student is aware of the policy upon registration and is aware that this policy is for his own good.

The logic of the individuals here can be expanded to the political level that ultimately matters most here to Rousseau. All citizens have, as he suggests in these pages (e.g., *SC*, 1.8.7, 52 [III: 363]), both an individual will and a general will. Generally speaking, it takes very little prompting for most people to act in accordance with what they understand to be in their individual or private wills. It does not take the full apparatus of political institutions, for example, to inspire me to brush my teeth. The natural consequences of not doing so are sufficiently evident to compel me. But the forces are less obvious when it comes to my general will. For sheer natural force over the individual, "the general will is always the weakest" and the particular will is always the strongest (*SC*, 3.2.7, 87 [III: 401]). So the law, then, gives actual force to that will that is naturally weak in each citizen. And since the general will is my actual will, in such instances subjects are "forced to be free." They want what the general will demands of them. They are simply too weak, distracted, or manipulated by other forces to hold to it reliably without external enforcement. So the law in this respect is not only a way of confronting free-riders. It is a means by which I may perform what I will in the sense of my having a general will.

1.8. *Of the Civil State*

In Chapter Eight, Rousseau pauses to consider the implications of the proceeding pages for the psychic developments in human nature. In the move from the state of nature to civil society, Rousseau observes a "remarkable change in man" (*SC*, 1.8.1, 53 [III: 364]). This includes many important features. In the state of nature, people act according to instinct. In the *Second Discourse*, Rousseau describes savage man as acting primarily according to the faculties of *amour de soi-même* and *pitié*. But he also notes that these instincts – especially pity – are "much less perfect" than justice.[73] Indeed, in Rousseau's state of nature, there is no conception of justice, which is inapplicable without social relations and furthermore beyond the intellectual capacities of *l'homme sauvage*. This is consistent with his thoughts in Chapter Eight, where justice is substituted for instinct. Acting according to justice gives human beings a "moral quality" previously lacking in humanity – and this is undeniably an improvement in the human condition. Individuals cannot be moral merely in acting according to inclinations.[74] So duty replaces appetite and inclination. This ultimately effects the transition from "a stupid and bounded animal ... [to] an intelligent being and a man" (*SC*, 1.8.1, 53 [III: 364]).[75] It ennobles and elevates the soul.

Rousseau records here a second striking transition in humankind. In the social contract, they exchange natural liberty for civil liberty. Their natural liberty consists in "an unlimited right to everything" (1.8.2, 54 [III: 364]). This is, in essence, a Hobbesian "right of nature" – a rule of natural force.[76] In return, they get civil liberty, which is defined here merely as being "limited by the general will" (1.8.2, 54 [III: 365]). This includes, among other things, the right to hold property. This is something like the liberty celebrated in contemporary liberal societies – the rights of property, conscience, speech, religion, association, etc.[77] The important limitation

---

[73] *Second Discourse*, 154 [III: 156].

[74] See, for example, his *Reveries*: "[T]here is none [no virtue] at all in following our inclinations and in giving ourselves the pleasure of doing good when they lead us to do so. But virtue consists in overcoming them when duty commands in order to do what duty prescribes" (*Reveries*, 77 [I: 1053]).

[75] Bear in mind what Rousseau says in the *Second Discourse* regarding the distinction between human beings and animals. He says there that human beings are distinct by virtue of their free will and perfectibility (*Second Discourse*, 44–5 [III: 141–2]). The morality man receives in civil society builds on our capacity for free will, since free will is manifested in acting contrary to appetite, instinct, or inclination.

[76] For Hobbes, in the state of nature, "every man has a right to everything, even to one another's body" (Hobbes [1651] 2002, 14.4).

[77] Matthew Simpson indeed interprets Rousseau's conception of "civil liberty" as being "what we would today call a liberal interpretation of his philosophy. On this view, the highest political good is the creation and preservation of a sphere of free choice within which individual citizens can determine for themselves the contours of their lives, especially regarding basic rights such as conscience, expression, movement, and association" (Simpson 2006b, 2). Simpson draws attention to a footnote at *SC*, 4.8, where he quotes d'Argenson as saying, "*In the Republic ... everyone is perfectly free with respect to what does not harm others. That is the invariable boundary; it cannot be drawn more accurately*" (*SC*, 4.8.31, 150 [III: 467]).

here, again, is the general will. Subjects are free to do as they choose, *so long as they do not violate the general will.* But as the general will remains to this point undefined and ambiguous, its implications are unclear.

Rousseau finally addresses another form of liberty in Chapter Eight: moral liberty. This is also newly acquired in the civil state. This is what he elsewhere calls free will. And its importance is emphasized here: it "alone makes man truly the master of himself; for the impulsion of mere appetite is slavery" (*SC*, 1.8.3, 54 [III: 365]). This is one reason that the state must be republican rather than despotic, since subjects have no opportunity to develop their moral liberty under the latter. They are treated as animals, acting only according to fear and inclination, as Rousseau outlines in the latter stages of his *Second Discourse.* It is this moral liberty that makes morality itself possible for Rousseau, so it must be carefully cultivated in civil society.[78] The importance of this change for Rousseau is not to be underestimated. His entire moral theory rests on the premise of this moral liberty. And since moral liberty in turn rests on the social contract, it is not unreasonable to conclude that for Rousseau, morality is impossible without politics.

1.9. *Of Real Property*

As Christopher Bertram has observed, it is striking that immediately after establishing civil liberty, Rousseau dedicates a chapter to "real property."[79] His interest in protecting private property is at least partly consistent with his claim in his *Political Economy* that "property is the most sacred of all the rights of citizens" and is, in fact, "the true foundation of civil society." He posits this because the possession of property puts something of each citizen at stake. They will want society to flourish, since its success will protect their property. At the same time, however, the sacred character of this right does not imply its inalienability. This includes the fair imposition of taxation for upkeep, which should fall especially to the wealthy, since their abundant holdings require more government resources to protect.[80]

---

[78] Toward the conclusion of the *Second Discourse*, he writes, "in the end everything would be swallowed up by the Monster [despot]; and Peoples would no longer have Chiefs or Laws, but only Tyrants. From that moment on there would also no longer be any question of morals or virtue; for wherever Despotism rules, *where honesty offers no hope*, it suffers no other master; as soon as it speaks, there is no consulting probity or duty, and the blindest obedience is the only virtue left to Slaves" (*Second Discourse*, 185 [III: 191]).

[79] The French here is *"du domaine réel."* As the editors of the *OC* have observed, "Domain is synonymous with property" (*OC*, IV: 1450).

[80] *Political Economy*, 23 [III: 263], 31 [III: 271–2]. See also *Emile*, 461 [IV: 841]).

Rousseau emphasizes at the outset of Chapter Nine that the social contract involves total alienation of one's natural self, including all the goods in one's possession. This immediately suggests an alternative to Locke, for whom the government's primary task – at least as occasionally described – is to protect that property acquired prior to the contract.[81] Rousseau entertains two possible modes of acquiring property in the state of nature: (1) force, and (2) the right of first occupant. He has already dismissed in *SC*, 1.3 any rights that might come via force. But he is certainly open to the right of first occupant, which suggests some commonalities with Locke. Rousseau's right of first occupant makes four important assumptions:

a. Everyone has a right by nature to what they need.
b. Property may not be previously occupied by anyone else.
c. No one may occupy more than what is necessary to subsist.
d. One takes possession by working and cultivating that property.

This account bears some resemblance to Locke's account of property, which is also essentially the right of first occupant. Both place limits on property acquisition – and both suggest that property is acquired by virtue of working and cultivating the land. But there are at least a couple of important differences, as noted by Christopher Bertram.[82] First, Locke's property rights are fully fledged before the social contract. And second, Locke's limitations on property holdings fade quickly after the introduction of money. Rousseau maintains strict limitations on property holdings without qualification or exceptions. These will be considered shortly.

In moving from the state of nature to political society, property becomes "legitimate possession, chang[ing] usurpation into a true right, and use into property" (*SC*, 1.9.6, 56 [III: 367]). This means that property will be protected by the state. Others seeking to usurp this property will be excluded by the force of the state. Rousseau also adds that private property owners "are considered trustees of the public good" (*SC*, 1.9.6, 56 [III: 367]), which suggests something of the opposite spirit – that they are not the true owners of the land so much as the stewards or guardians of the land that truly belongs to the sovereign. This is notably different from the arrangement in the social contract of the *Second Discourse*, wherein the purpose of the agreement is to "secure for everyone the possession of what

---

[81] In comparing the two, Bertrand Russell remarks, "Rousseau has not that profound respect for private property that characterizes Locke and his disciples" ([1945] 1972], 697).
[82] Bertram 2004, 91.

belongs to him,"[83] suggesting a clear difference on the role of property in the two contracts.

Rousseau reminds his readers that "the right every individual has over his own land is always subordinate to the right the community has over everyone, without which there would be neither solidarity in the social bond, nor real force in the exercise of sovereignty" (*SC*, 1.9.7, 56 [III: 367]). So private property is *not* an absolute right here, as is the case with Locke. This pushes him a few steps in the direction of Hobbes, who says that all property is at the disposal of the sovereign.[84] Without this, the sovereign power really amounts to little. As Bertram has noted, Rousseau elaborates on this in the *Emile*, with an important caveat: "[T]he sovereign has no right to touch the possessions of one or more individuals. But it can legitimately seize the possessions of all, as was done at Sparta in the time of Lycurgus; the abolition of debts by Solon, on the other hand, was an illegitimate act."[85] So the sovereign cannot take property willy-nilly. Indeed, it can only take the property of all at once. There can be no one singled out for property seizure. This is also consistent with his demand that the dictates of the sovereign be *general* rather than specific, which certainly limits the rights of the sovereign considerably in comparing Rousseau's theory of property to Hobbes's.

In this context, Rousseau closes this chapter and Book I with a few remarks on equality. He emphasizes that the social contract does not destroy natural equality so much as it substitutes for it a "moral and legitimate equality" (*SC*, 1.9.8, 56 [III: 367]). The word "legitimate" is an important caveat, since the *Second Discourse* outlines the replacing of natural equality with a social illegitimate inequality. The most important dimension of this new equality is that "all become equal by convention and by right" – which is really to say, they possess equality under the law. No one is to be singled out for preferences by the law. Why is Rousseau emphasizing equality here in his chapter on property? It may be because he views property and economic inequalities as serious threats to the public good. In this respect, it is very much worth examining the concluding footnote of Book I:

---

[83] *Second Discourse*, 173 [III: 177].

[84] Hobbes [1651] 2002, 24.5–6. This also suggests a right of eminent domain. One possible source for Rousseau here is Samuel Pufendorf, who writes, "in a national emergency, sovereigns may seize and apply to public use the property of any subject which the crisis particularly requires, even if the property seized far exceeds the amount which had been fixed his normal obligatory contribution to the country's expenses" (Pufendorf [1673] 1991, [2.15.4]).

[85] Bertram 2004, 94; *Emile*, 461–2 [IV: 841]).

Under bad governments this equality is only apparent and illusory.[86] It serves only to maintain the poor man in his misery and the rich in his usurpation. In fact, the laws are always useful to those who possess something and harmful to those who have nothing: Whence it follows that the social state is advantageous for men only insofar as all have something and none has too much of anything. (*SC*, 1.9.8, 56 [III: 367])

The last sentence is especially important. If there are great economic inequalities, everything else crumbles, and individuals are returned to Part II of the *Second Discourse* – where the laws merely serve as the tools of despotism.[87] As he observes in his "Letter to d'Alembert," "Never in a Monarchy can the opulence of an individual put him above the Prince; but, in a republic, it can easily put him above the laws. Then the government no longer has force, and the rich are always the true sovereign."[88] The excessive concentration of wealth is simply inconsistent with maintaining the rule of law central to Rousseau's conception of a republic. While maintaining the importance of property rights, he is also serious about economic equality.

In this spirit, it is especially important to recall that the illegitimate contract of the *Second Discourse* proceeds in a context of substantial property and economic inequalities. These inequalities provide precisely the climate necessary for both parties to make the worst possible decision when establishing their political society. The wealthy are blinded to the just claims of others by virtue of their desire to secure and enhance their riches. The poor are so desperate that they will agree to almost anything that offers a possibility of eating and getting on at the most basic level. Given this, it is fair to say that economic equality represents a kind of epistemic requirement for both parties to make sound decisions about the social contract and society that it establishes.

[86] See the *Emile*: "Those specious names, justice and order, will always serve as instruments of violence and as arms of iniquity" (236 [IV: 524]); and also the *State of War*: "Justice and truth have to be bent to the interest of the most powerful: such is the rule" (162 [III: 609]).

[87] Rousseau later remarks, "freedom cannot subsist without it [equality]" (*SC*, 2.11.1, 78 [III: 391]). I address some of the parallels between Rousseau's emphasis on economic equality and Plato's in Williams 2007a, 174–6. See also Vaughan 2008, 63–81, and Neuhouser 1993, 387–8.

[88] "Letter to d'Alembert," 115 [V: 105]).

CHAPTER 2

Book II

OVERVIEW

Whereas Book I is largely dedicated to the mission of demonstrating the need for a social contract and the general will, Book II addresses the nature of the general will and how it might animate the foundation of a republic. In the first four chapters here, Rousseau establishes the tight relationship between sovereignty and the general will. In doing so, he establishes his unique brand of popular sovereignty – namely, that the people are sovereign insofar as their will corresponds to the general will. If their will deviates from the general will, the result is merely an aggregation of particular wills or a "will of all."

The remainder of Book II is largely directed to the problem of constitutional or founding law. That is, once the people have unanimously agreed to be governed by the general will, how does that general will animate the founding of constitutional laws? This matter is considerably complicated by the fact that a "blind multitude" of people "often does not know what it wills because it rarely knows what is good for it" (*SC*, 2.6.10, 68 [III: 380]). Into this broad ignorance, Rousseau introduces the character of the lawgiver, a figure of "superior intelligence" (*SC*, 2.7.1, 68 [III: 381]) and "a great soul" (*SC*, 2.7.11, 71 [III: 384]). The lawgiver must have both great art and great technical talents. He must artfully rally the still raw citizens to support a new constitution of his own design by virtue of a surprising appeal to divine authority. At the same time, the lawgiver must have exceptional technical skills and empirical knowledge about governments, laws, institutions, and especially knowledge of the people for whom he is to legislate. Rousseau dedicates three chapters here specifically to the problem of understanding a people before designing institutions for them and insists that although the idea of justice is itself universal, the constitution for each country must be adapted to local conditions and the idiosyncratic nature of each people.

2.1. *That Sovereignty Is Inalienable*

Rousseau earlier introduced the sovereign in Book I, Chapter Six of the *SC*, defining it as the members of the state when active (*SC*, 1.6.10, 51 [III: 362]). He developed it considerably in the next chapter, positing its inalienability and infallibility. These attributes have puzzled many readers, but his observations in Book II, Chapter One offer some clarity. Here he outlines the intimate relationship of sovereignty with the general will. Specifically, he posits, "sovereignty ... is nothing but the exercise of the general will" (*SC*, 2.1.2, 57 [III: 368]). It is thus fair to read sovereignty and the general will almost synonymously throughout the *Social Contract*, even as each term stresses its essence slightly differently.[1] So the key to understanding sovereignty is unraveling the riddle of the general will.

In this spirit of understanding sovereignty as the general will, Rousseau opens Chapter One with a declaration that the "general will alone can direct the forces of the State," adding that they must be directed "according to the end of its institution, which is the common good" (*SC*, 2.1.1, 57 [III: 368]). He had already implied this at *SC*, 1.5.1, in noting that despotism ignores the common good. But now the point is explicit and clearly essential. For Rousseau, there can be no legitimate political society without orientation to the common good or common interest.[2]

He expands on his commitment to the common good by distinguishing the general will from a particular will. Rousseau has to this point only broadly sketched this distinction (*SC*, 1.7), suggesting that the two wills are often opposed to one another – and that the private will inclines against the common interest. Here he adds a bit more. Specifically, he is concerned with the question of when the particular will and general will might coincide. But it is important first to take note of what he attributes to each will. The particular will tends toward *partiality*, whereas the general will tends to privilege *equality* (*SC*, 2.1.3, 57 [III: 368]). This commitment to equality is not fleeting for Rousseau. Subsequently, in his *Plan for a Constitution for Corsica*, he insists, "the fundamental law of your foundation ought to be equality. Everything ought to be related to it, even authority itself which is established only to defend it. All ought

---

[1] Rousseau emphasizes, "the essence of sovereignty consists in the general will" (*Emile*, 462 [IV: 842]). The subtle difference is suggested by the word "exercise" (*l'exercice*). The general will is what the people express they want. Sovereignty is the people acting on this will through legislation. This is further clarified at *SC*, 4.6. See Appendix A, A.5.

[2] Rousseau employs both terms common good (*bien commun*]) and common interest (*intérêt commun*) in *SC*, 2.1.1. They are apparently employed synonymously here.

to be equal by right of birth. The state ought not to grant distinctions except to merit, to virtues, to services rendered to the fatherland."[3] The reason for this emphasis on equality is that the particular will privileges a portion or fraction of the whole, whereas the general will privileges the whole.[4] According to Rousseau, the private and general will *can* agree. But it resembles the occasion of the planets lining up – it is rare and fleeting. And, worse than the planets, their coinciding is entirely random or arbitrary. There will be moments when they do match one another. But one can never *count* on them coinciding.

In this context, Rousseau specifies that a people can never simply agree to obey the existing authority. Obedience is owed only to the general will. If a people were to agree to obey only a particular person or body of persons, this would amount to obeying a particular will. It may sometimes be the case that this authority wills the general will. But as he repeatedly insists, all particular wills are inevitably informed by partial rather than general interests. The stakes here are high for Rousseau: "If, then, the people promises simply to obey, it dissolves itself by this very act, it loses its quality of being a people; as soon as there is a master, there is no more sovereign, and the body politic is destroyed forthwith" (*SC*, 2.1.3, 57 [III: 369]). As he remarks in his *Second Discourse*, "the blindest obedience is the only virtue left to Slaves." It is worth comparing Rousseau here with Thomas Hobbes and Benedict Spinoza,[5] both of whom counsel obedience as among the highest political virtues. In his *State of War*, Rousseau refers to Hobbes as advocating "passive obedience."[6] Although he does not elaborate, he appears to imply it is a doctrine of blind obedience, obedience for the sake of obedience without regard to the content of the sovereign's command. It is an unthinking, reflexive obedience.

And, to be certain, obedience is important in Rousseau's state. But for him it holds no independent value. It is only contingently good. Obedience is good only when it is given in the context of a state founded on and governed according to the general will. When it deviates from the general will, it is more likely to be the tool of a tyrant than the marker of a just order. As he elaborates in his *Letters Written from the Mountain*, "A free people obeys, but it does not serve; it has leaders and not masters; it

---

[3] *Corsica*, 130 (III: 909–10).

[4] Rousseau presumably employs the word "equality" (*l'égalité*) to stand for the equal consideration of every member of the political community, as specified earlier at *SC*, 1.6.6 and 1.7.4.

[5] *Second Discourse*, 185 [III: 191]; Hobbes [1651] 2002, 30.7; *Theological-Political Treatise*, ch. 2, 418; ch. 16, 530.

[6] *State of War*, 164 [IV: 611].

obeys the laws, but it only obeys the laws and it is from the force of laws that it does not obey men."[7] Since for Rousseau valid law is a normative concept required to express the general will (*SC*, 2.6.5, 67 [III: 379]), this amounts to asserting that obedience is only required to the general will. It is never to be given to particular wills. We might, then, call this "active obedience," in contrast with the "passive obedience" he associates with Hobbes and Spinoza. It is active insofar as it calls on the subject to reflect on the command's sympathy with the general will. In this way, subjects are at least ideally always reaffirming the general will with their lawful behavior.

In this spirit, Rousseau elsewhere cautions against teaching obedience too early to children: "let him [the child] not know what obedience is." He elaborates, "In trying to persuade your children of the duty of obedience, you unite promises and threats to persuasion; therefore constrained by force they pretend to be convinced." Teaching children obedience as an independent virtue, according to Rousseau, is ultimately counterproductive insofar as "it is the law of obedience that produces the necessity of lying, because since obedience is irksome, it is secretly dispensed with as much as possible, and the present interest in avoiding punishment or reproach wins out over the distant interest of revealing the truth about facts." Beyond this, teaching children obedience as an independent virtue renders them vulnerable to manipulation. Rousseau warns against resorting to "because-I-told-you-so" appeals. "With all these fine speeches that you make to him now in order to get him to be obedient, you are preparing the success of those speeches which will be made to him one day by a visionary, an alchemist, a charlatan, a cheat, or any kind of madman in order to catch your pupil in his trap or to get him to adopt his madness."[8] In other words, teaching children obedience results in passive, docile subjects, ripe for despotic manipulation. Unconditional obedience is precisely the opposite of Rousseau's celebrated value of liberty, as he reminds readers in his *Letters Written from the Mountain*: "liberty consists less in doing one's own will than in not being subject to someone else's."[9] So while obedience to just laws is an essential component of a thriving republic, it lacks independent value, and can even work against the very citizens it is supposed to protect.

---

[7] *Mountain*, 261 [IV: 842].
[8] *Emile*, 85 [IV: 311]; *Favre Manuscript of Emile*, 35 [IV: 94]; *Emile*, 101 [IV: 335]; *Emile*, 178 [IV: 445].
[9] *Mountain*, 260 [III: 841].

2.2. *That Sovereignty Is Indivisible*

Not only is sovereignty inalienable, according to Rousseau; it is also indivisible. This is so in two respects. First, it is indivisible insofar as it is derived from the entire body of citizens. This is an important component of the general will for Rousseau, which is largely synonymous with sovereignty. To say that it is derived from the entire body of citizens, however, is not the same as to require unanimity. As he clarifies in a footnote, "For a will to be general, it is not always necessary that it be unanimous, but it is necessary that all votes be counted; any formal exclusion destroys generality" (*SC*, 2.2.1.fn, 58 [III: 369]). This is a crucial element of Rousseau's conception of sovereign and the general will. And it is specifically a formal element, as contrasted with the earlier substantive requirement that it serve the common good. It must be derived from an accounting of *all* citizens, not simply a portion.

It is worth commenting briefly on the fact that Rousseau adds the caveat that any "formal exclusion" destroys the general will. In the most obvious sense, no class of citizens can be excluded from the process of deriving the general will. A truly general will cannot exclude the wills of the poor, unemployed, the ill, the undereducated, or for that matter the rich and privileged. They must be formally included in any calculus of the general will or exercise of sovereignty. Yet the phrase "formal exclusion" concedes the inevitable fact that not all citizens will actually contribute. Some will presumably be unable due to temporary ailments, travel, and other circumstances. Rousseau apparently accepts this practical reality, so long as no one is *formally* excluded.

A second dimension of the argument is more complex. Sovereignty is indivisible insofar as it cannot be divided among different branches of government. As Robert Derathé has observed, many commentators have taken this to be a critique of Montesquieu's separation of powers, as outlined in the *Spirit of the Laws*.[10] One such example is Lester G. Crocker, who argues that *SC*, 2.2 prohibits the separation of powers into legislative, executive, and judicial functions.[11] Yet it is perfectly evident here and in the subsequent pages of the *Social Contract* that separate powers do in fact exist (e.g., *SC*, 3.7.4, 99 [III: 413–14]). This does not, however, represent a division of the *sovereign* power. Rather, as Rousseau himself remarks, "the rights which one takes for parts of this sovereignty [in the

---

[10] Montesquieu, *Spirit of the Laws*, 1.11.6. See Derathé 1970, 281 and Cobban 1968, 81–91.
[11] Crocker 1968, 69. See also Grimsley 1972, 108.

form of different branches] are all subordinate to it, and always presuppose supreme wills which these rights simply implement" (*SC*, 2.2.4, 59 [III: 370]). As Derathé notes, Rousseau is largely in line with the likes of Pufendorf and Hobbes in asserting that an indivisible sovereign exercises different powers,[12] in rejecting the philosophies of Grotius and Jean-Jacques Burlamaqui. Grotius apparently desires a unitary sovereign, but ultimately concedes that it is sometimes "divided" as a "Partition of Sovereignty" – either between different territories or between king and people. Likewise, Burlamaqui permits the "exercise of the different parts of the supreme power to different persons or bodies."[13]

For Rousseau, the likes of Grotius and Burlamaqui confuse powers deriving from sovereignty with sovereignty itself. He clarifies with an example concerning the powers of declaring war and peace. Declarations of war and peace are not, according to Rousseau, exercises of sovereignty. They are merely applications of sovereign law. The law presumably sets the guidelines for when war and peace might be declared and further authorizes a power for making these decisions. But it is not a law itself, and hence not an exercise of sovereignty. Likewise, the prosecution of Enron executives, for Rousseau, would not be an exercise of sovereignty. The exercise of sovereignty would be the enacting of the laws that (1) prohibit specific forms of corporate corruption, and (2) authorize the executive branch to enforce those prohibitions. As such, this is not a division of sovereignty. It is rather a distribution of tasks derivative from and accountable to the sovereign.

2.3. *Whether the General Will Can Err*

Chapter Three asks whether the general will can err. It answers that it cannot. This connects back to Rousseau's claim in Book I that "The Sovereign, by the mere fact that it is, is always everything it ought to be" (*SC*, 1.7.5, 52, [III: 363]). When reading sovereignty and the general will as synonymous, this follows with deductive simplicity. Many casual readers of Rousseau take this as evidence to support the argument that the *Social Contract* facilitates tyrannical regimes. The notion of an infallible power

---

[12] Pufendorf remarks, "Even though supreme civil authority is in itself something one and undivided, it is nonetheless commonly understood to have many parts" (Pufendorf [1673] 1991, 7.4.1). Thomas Hobbes: "the doctrine that *sovereign power can be divided* is absolutely fatal to commonwealths" (Hobbes, *On the Citizen*, 12.5). See Derathé 1970, 280–94 generally and Derathé's *OC* note, III: 1455.

[13] Grotius [1625] 2005, 1.3.17 (Derathé 1970, 286); Burlamaqui [1747] 2006, 2.1.19; (Derathé 1970, 287).

can indeed be threatening. But it is important to keep Rousseau's meaning in mind before rushing to such conclusions. The general will is *not* simply the commands of the president, prime minister, chancellor, king, or queen. He has recently emphasized that he is not counseling blind obedience to the government (*SC*, 2.1.3). He has also stipulated that the general will must take all of the people into account (*SC*, 2.2.1). And finally, he has insisted that the general will is ordained to the common good, rather than to any particular subset of citizens (*SC*, 2.1.1). In saying that the general will does not err, therefore, the furthest thing from Rousseau's mind is to provide the philosophical justification of infallible partial dictators. Rather, the general will's incapacity for error is virtually tautological. The general will represents a kind of idea. And the same way that the idea of beauty cannot in itself err, neither can the idea of the general will.

This background facilitates greater understanding of Rousseau's otherwise puzzling opening paragraph to Chapter Three. "From the preceding it follows that the general will is always upright and always tends to the public utility: but it does not follow from it that the people's deliberations are always equally upright" (*SC*, 2.3.1, 59 [III: 371]). The general will is always upright because of its intimate relationship to an idea. Some have suggested that the general will is largely a voluntaristic conception.[14] That is to say, the general will takes whatever substantive content to which the citizens themselves have agreed. This reading, however, ignores that the individuals of Part II in the *Second Discourse* agreed to a society Rousseau condemns as despotic. It is certainly not the general will. This much is clear in what he says in Chapter Three: "One always wants what is good, but one does not always see it: one can never corrupt the people, but one can often cause it to be mistaken, and only when it is, does it appear to want what is bad" (*SC*, 2.3.1, 59 [III: 371]).

Rousseau importantly emphasizes that it is the people, and not the general will, that can be corrupted. The people – though always intending the good – can fall from it in countless ways. One of the most obvious and threatening is to fall prey to the charms of demagogues. He raises this threat in his *Discourse on Political Economy*, where he warns the people not to be "seduced by private interests which some few skillful men succeed by their reputation and eloquence to substitute for the people's own interest. Then the public deliberation will be one thing, and the general will another thing entirely." To some degree here Rousseau amplifies a warning issued in the "Epistle Dedicatory" of his *Second Discourse*, where he cautions his readers against "sinister interpretations and venomous discourses."

[14] E.g., Roger Masters 1968 and Arthur Melzer 1983, 1990.

He repeats this concern in his *Letters Written from the Mountain*, where he remarks, "In the majority of States internal troubles come from a brutalized and stupid populace, at first inflamed by unbearable vexations, then stirred up in secret by skillful troublemakers, invested with some authority they want to extend."[15] Such is the most immediate cause of the failed contract of the *Second Discourse*, where an eloquent wealthy class persuades the poor and desperate to agree to a set of rules fundamentally aimed at depriving them of any future hope of equal or just consideration in future deliberations. As the wealthy promote their own particular will, they are fundamentally antithetical to the general will, even as all give their assent. So the general will is something quite different from simple consent, even though that consent is itself required.[16]

Rousseau further advances this conception of the general will as independent of simple convention or agreement by distinguishing it from what he calls the "will of all." This comes in the second paragraph of Chapter Three, which is worth quoting in full:

There is often a considerable difference between the will of all and the general will: the latter looks only to the common interest, the former looks to private interest, and is nothing but the sum of particular wills; but if, from these same wills, one takes away the plusses and minuses which cancel each other out, what is left as the sum of the differences is the general will. (*SC*, 2.3.2, 60 [III: 371])

Rousseau gives similar expression to the general will in quasi-mathematical terms in his *Government of Poland*:

Now, the law, which is but the expression of the general will, is indeed the resultant of all the particular interests combined and in balance by virtue of their large number. But corporate interests, because of their excessive weight, would upset the balance, and should not be included in it collectively. Each individual should have his vote, no [corporate] body whatsoever should have one.[17]

This parsing of the general will has invited much scholarly commentary. Lester Crocker, for example, has observed that this distinction "contains difficulties." John Plamenatz has described it as "sheer nonsense." He formulates his objection thus:

What can the "pluses" and "minuses" of particular wills be except what is peculiar to each of them. Let John's will be $x + a$, Richard's $x + b$, and Thomas's $x + c$, x being what is common to them all, and a, b, and c, what is peculiar to each. If the

---

[15] *Political Economy*, 8 [III: 246]; *Second Discourse*, 119 [III: 117]; *Mountain*, 299 [IV: 889].

[16] As Patrick Riley has emphasized, "though 'that which is good and conformable to order is such by the nature of things, independent of human conventions,' those conventions are yet required" (Riley 1970, 91).

[17] *Poland*, 206 [III: 984]; see O'Hagan 1999, 115.

general will is what remains after the "pluses" and "minuses" have cancelled each other out, it is x; but if it is the sum of the differences it is $a + b + c$. Whichever it is, it cannot be both; and the second alternative is too absurd to be considered. Beware of political philosophers who use mathematics, not matter how simple, to illustrate their meaning! God will forgive them, for they know what they do, but we shall not understand them.[18]

Taken literally, insofar as Rousseau means $a + b + c$ to constitute the "sum of the differences," Plamenatz is probably correct. But Richard Dagger suggests that Plamenatz has likely taken Rousseau too literally in this specific passage.[19] That is, Rousseau means the "sum of the differences" to be what Plamenatz calls x. In defending Rousseau, Dagger points to two other passages in Chapter Three:

(1) If, when an adequately informed people deliberates, the Citizens had no communication among themselves, the general will would always result from the large number of small differences, and the deliberation would always be good (*SC*, 2.3.3, 60 [III: 371]).
(2) The agreement between all interests is formed by opposition to each one's interest. If there were no different interests, the common interest would scarcely be sensible since it would never encounter obstacles (*SC*, 2.3.2n, 60n [III: 371n]).

What these two additional passages suggest is that the general will represents the "sum of the differences" insofar as multiple small differences point citizens toward a common interest. Put slightly differently, a few large differences – as occasion factions – have the ability to mislead citizens, thinking that factional or partial interests are in fact the general will. But many small differences have the opposite effect.

Consider the following example. Tom Jones might desire a personal income tax exemption on the basis of his individual charms. Such might also be the private will of many other citizens. Yet it is easy enough, Rousseau thinks, for others to recognize that such private wills are not the general will. The many clashes of these individual interests make it obvious that none of them speak for the interests of all. This is true even if everyone's private will mirrors Mr. Jones's – since taxes clearly must be raised. But discerning this might be trickier if powerful factions combine private interests into larger groups. So whereas it is easy enough to recognize that no individual should have a personal tax exemption on the basis

---

[18] Crocker 1968, 70; Plamenatz 1992, 155.
[19] See Dagger 1981, 365–6.

of his or her charms, it is murkier when it comes to larger groups. A class of wealthy citizens, for example, might argue that it merits tax exemptions insofar as it creates jobs for others. Because there are fewer such clashes, it is more difficult for the average citizen to know whether this is a private interest of a class of citizens or something genuinely aimed at the general will. The relative absence of clashing interests makes a group or corporate interest appear as if it were the general will.

So, to return to Rousseau's nomenclature, the will of all represents the sum of the many different private interests, where those interests differ from the common interest. By contrast, Rousseau specifies that the general will "looks only to the common interest." This is a significant departure from the will of all, which accepts private and selfish wills as perfectly legitimate.

How does this work in practice? Consider that in voting, each citizen has a set of interests, including both private and general wills. Most private interests are never so widely shared that they could naturally generate majority consensus. Tom Jones's interest in a personal tax exemption is one such example. So would be the desire of a private business owner to be exempted from workplace or environmental regulations. It is more likely that citizens' interests overlap where those interests are in fact common or general. For example, most citizens share a common interest in drinking clean water or breathing clean air. Most citizens benefit from well-maintained schools and infrastructure. Most citizens benefit from the presence of public parks and community festivals. This is the remaining ground when "one takes away the plusses and minuses which cancel each other out."

As already suggested, however, there is still room here for concern. And this is suggested by Rousseau's formulation of the general will in *Poland* cited previously. Corporate interests – which do not specifically mean corporate interests in the contemporary sense of large business interests, though they might pose a considerable threat to generating the general will – represent factions within the larger society seeking to satisfy their private interests at the expense of the general will, or as he puts it, the prioritization of "small associations at the expense of the large association" (*SC*, 2.3.3, 60 [III: 371]).[20] This is among the perennial problems in the history of political thought. The first systematic political philosopher in Western history, Plato, warned, "whoever makes the city subject to faction, and does all this through violence and the stirring up of civil strife against

---

[20] For an account of Rousseau's problematization of factions, see O'Hagan 1999, 114–18.

the law, this man must be regarded as the greatest enemy of all to the whole city."[21] "Faction" is simply giving a name to what has concerned Rousseau all along – private interests. The best way to prevent factions from corrupting public discourse and guiding legislation, according to Rousseau, is to eliminate communication among citizens while deliberating public policy. This is striking and somewhat counterintuitive. Democracy and public deliberation in much Anglo-American twentieth- and early twenty-first-century political philosophy are thought to be inseparable. The point of democracy is to deliberate the issues; and deliberation means an extended conversation between citizens about those issues. The theory is that as the conversation expands, information is disseminated, and policy becomes informed and more effective. Rousseau embraces the notion that legislation requires deliberation. He clarifies what he means by "deliberate" [*Délibérer*] in his *Letters Written from the Mountain*: "*To Deliberate* is to weigh the pro and con."[22] He expressly requires that the people be "adequately informed" (*SC*, 2.3.3, 60 [III: 371]). Where he differs from most contemporary theorists is on the role of conversation and discussion. He specifies that deliberation requires that "Citizens ha[ve] no communication among themselves" (*SC*, 2.3.3, 60 [III: 371]).[23] His reason for this striking constraint is simple. Conversation and discussion are the vectors for the pestilence of factions.[24] Communication does not lead to the dissemination of information and wisdom so much as it does the encroachments of *amour propre*[25] and misinformation. In the first place, simply being with others means that *amour propre* has an opportunity to seize deliberative sovereignty. That is, when in groups, individuals are more inclined to dazzle others more so than to seek justice and the common good. This is likely one reason why Rousseau makes an explicit call for solitude in his later autobiographical works. As he remarks in his *Dialogues*, "Amour-propre, the principle of all wickedness, is revived and thrives in society, which caused it to be born and where one is forced to compare oneself at each instant. It languishes and dies for want of nourishment in solitude."[26]

---

[21] Plato, *Laws*, 856b; see also *Republic*, 351d, 551de.

[22] *Mountain*, 253n [IV: 833n]. He there contrasts deliberation with giving an opinion ("to state one's advice and give reasons for it") and voting ("when nothing is left to do but to collect the votes").

[23] It is reasonable to ask at this juncture how citizens might acquire the information they need to be "adequately informed," if they are to be barred from communication with others. Rousseau does not anticipate this question. We might only imagine that it might be permissible to read books or materials prepared by those without a stake in the debate – such as the wisdom of ancient philosophers and historians, or perhaps from foreigners.

[24] A version of this argument can be found in Cohen 2010, 76.

[25] See Chapter 1, §3 of this book or *Second Discourse*, 218 [III: 219–20].

[26] *Dialogues*, 100 [I: 789–90].

Further, conversation facilitates the rise of demagogues who would take advantage of the opportunity to mislead citizens about what is and is not the common good. They could falsify data, appeal to the latent *amour propre* of citizens with flattery, or whip them into an impassioned frenzy, among other routes to faction formation. But for Rousseau, the result is almost inevitably the same. Citizens would lose sight of the general will and be led into the hands of one or another private will. Such reflections might well have been born of his own experiences in Baron d'Holbach's salon, where upon his arrival, all "conversation ceased to be general. They [the *Philosophes*] assembled in little clusters, they whispered in each others' ears, and I remained alone without knowing with whom to speak."[27] The ability to deliberate secretly in small groups in this way worked against the general interest – presumably one in which Rousseau might himself have been treated more fairly. Deliberation as Rousseau understands the term, then, takes place as an internal discussion – in consulting one's conscience, the purest, least-corrupted part of the self. As he remarks in the *Emile*, the "conscience never deceives; it is man's true guide. It is to the soul what instinct is to the body; he who follows conscience does not fear being led astray."[28] This is not to be done hastily, one might add. In Book IV, Rousseau cites Roman practices that provide ample time for individual reflection on weighty issues, so that citizens "might vote only once they could do so knowledgeably" (*SC*, 4.4.31, 134 [III: 451]).

All this being noted, later in the *Social Contract* Rousseau insists that the inalienable rights of citizens as sovereign include "voicing opinions, proposing, dividing, [and] discussing [motions]" (*SC*, 4.1.7, 122 [IV: 439]). This passage suggests either that his constraints on public deliberation are more limited than suggested here in Book II, Chapter Three, or he is simply contradicting himself. Assuming that he does not intend to contradict himself here, Rousseau can be understood to embrace some degree of public deliberation, although he provides no specific guidance on how it might operate. In fact, he explicitly dodges this question: "this important matter would require a separate treatise, and I cannot say everything in this one" (*SC*, 4.1.7, 122 [IV: 439]). But in this vein, Frederick Neuhouser has argued that after a round of public deliberation, citizens

---

[27] *Confessions*, 324 [I: 386]. In this respect, Rousseau finds that French politics have completely failed generally. "The French have no personal existence. They think and act only in groups; each one of them by himself is nothing. Now there is never any disinterested love of justice in these collective bodies. Nature engraved it only in the hearts of individuals where it is soon extinguished by the spirit of conspiracy" (*Dialogues*, 237–8 [I: 965]).

[28] *Emile*, 286–7 [IV: 595].

are then charged with the responsibility of deliberating personally in the absence of further communication with others before casting a vote in order to determine whether a bill "conforms or not to the general will that is theirs" (*SC*, 4.2.7, 124 [IV: 440]).[29]

Rousseau's solution to the problem of faction can be fruitfully contrasted with a near-contemporaneous approach embraced by the American Founders, as articulated in Federalist No. 10 and No. 51. James Madison is likewise deeply troubled by the looming threat of factions when advocating the yet un-ratified Constitution. His solutions, however, are different. First, he is optimistic that the large size of the American republic will make it difficult for any one faction to gain majority assent. This differs considerably from Rousseau's requirement that a republic should be small enough that "every citizen can easily know all the rest" (*SC*, 3.4.5, 91 [III: 405]). Second, instead of seeking to close off the formation of factions, as Rousseau does in shutting down debate, Madison accepts them as inevitable. He then suggests they should be allowed to flourish, expecting that the prevalence of numerous factions will ultimately lead to their mutual diminution before they can seize control of public policy and legislation. Madison's solution is a liberal one – in its faith that greater political liberty will solve the problem and its indifference to the motives of citizens. Rousseau's preference for personal or inner deliberation is communitarian or republican – in its compromising of personal liberties and its insistence that the motives for legislation must be upright from the start.

This being stated, it is especially striking to observe that Rousseau concedes something to the liberal approach in his conclusion to Chapter Three. He restates his preference that no factions should be permitted, as Lycurgus succeeded in effecting in ancient Sparta. Yet "if there are partial societies," he concedes, "their number must be multiplied, and inequality among them prevented, as was done by Solon, Numa, and Servius" (*SC*, 2.3.4, 60 [III: 372]).[30] That is, there might very well be factions, despite the best efforts of the lawgiver. If this occurs, then the strategy is roughly Madisonian – to encourage many such factions of equal size and power to arise, where they might cancel each other out, as suggested earlier.[31] But it

---

[29] Neuhouser 2008, 203.

[30] Rousseau specifically develops this in *SC*, 4.4 on the Roman Comitia, which he attributes to Servius. The Roman institutions, while taking pains to cultivate civic virtue, also on Rousseau's account gave institutional voices to each distinct class or faction. To the degree they counterbalance one another, the outcome would "ensure that the general will is always enlightened, and that the people make no mistakes" (*SC*, 2.3.4, 60 [III: 372]).

[31] It is possible that both Rousseau and Madison found a common inspiration for this view in Hume [1741] 1994, 33–9. This view can also be found in Immanuel Kant: "nature comes to the aid of the

is clear from his overall remarks throughout the *Social Contract* that this is a second-best solution. The best solution is to foster a mutual love among fellow citizens that renders such selfishness relatively rare.

2.4. *Of the Limits of Sovereign Power*

Rousseau has just stated in *SC*, 2.3 that the general will is always right – but this does not mean that the sovereign has the power to act arbitrarily. Indeed, his purpose in Chapter Four is to specify the limits of sovereign power. What can it *not* do? He offers two specific limits here on sovereign power. The first limit is that the sovereign cannot require people to do things that are useless to the community (*SC*, 2.4.4, 61 [III: 373]). It cannot waste citizens' time for pointless tasks. Anything asked of us must have a communal purpose.

A second limit on sovereign power is that "the general will, to be really such, must be so in its object as well as in its essence" (*SC*, 2.4.5, 62 [III: 373]).[32] This appears to rule out anything like bills of attainder[33] – laws written pertaining to single individuals or groups.[34] Laws must instead apply to the entire populace. This is a natural extension of Rousseau's antipathy for factions. To issue a bill of attainder, for example, would amount to the codification of factious interests. It is also possible to read the generality of object more broadly. According to Tracy Strong, the generality of object speaks to a shared commonality among citizens. It is a kind of solidarity

---

general will grounded in reason, revered but impotent in practice, and does so precisely through those self-seeking inclinations, so that it is a matter only of a good organization of a state (which is certainly within the capacity of human beings), of arranging those forces of nature in opposition to one another in such a way that one checks the destructive effect of the other or cancels it, so that the result for reason turns out as if neither of them existed at all and the human being is constrained to become a good citizen even if not a morally good human being" (*Perpetual Peace*, 335).

[32] This also likely relates to the general will's character as *law*. Consider, for example, his remark in the *Letters Written from the Mountain*: "Law, by its nature, may not have a particular and individual object" (III: 808).

[33] As bills of attainder were common tools of tyrants and despots, the U.S. Constitution, written only fifteen years after the publication of the *Social Contract*, likewise prohibits them in Article I, §9. It is quite possible that this was raised as an issue for Rousseau in his reading of Montesquieu's *Spirit of the Laws*, which notes, "There are, in the states where one sets the most store by liberty, laws that violate it for a single person in order to keep it for all. Such are what are called *bills of attainder* in England." Montesquieu goes on to trace this to its ancient Greek and Roman origins: "They are related to those laws of Athens that were enacted against an individual provided they were made by the vote of six thousand citizens. They are related to those laws made in Rome against individual citizens, which were called *privileges*. They were made only in the great estates of the people. But, however the people made them, Cicero wanted them abolished, because the force of the law consists only in its being enacted for everyone" (Montesquieu [1748] 1989, 12.19; see also Cicero's *On the Laws*, 3.19–44).

[34] See also *SC*, 2.6.6, 67 [III: 379].

that expresses a deeply shared reciprocal identity – as Strong says, "the actuality of *my* existence as yours (and yours as mine)."[35]

In his treatment of limits on sovereign power, Rousseau expands on his conception of the general will. One such observation pertains to its derivation and application. A general will must "issue from all in order to apply to all" (*SC*, 2.4.5, 62 [III: 373]).[36] This is an important and concise restatement of principles already suggested[37] in the *Social Contract*. For Rousseau, the generality of the general will applies at both the stages of derivation and application. This is not shared by all advocates of the general will. Immanuel Kant, for example, suggests that the general will need not be derived from all the people, so long as it applies to all. For Rousseau, the term "general" is meant in both senses. It cannot be a general will if not derived from the general body of citizens and applied to the general interests of all.

A second elaboration on the general will pertains to its substantive content. Rousseau describes the general will as an "admirable accord between interest and justice" (*SC*, 2.4.7, 62 [III: 374]). This is important for at least two reasons. First, it demonstrates beyond a reasonable doubt that the general will is connected to Rousseau's conception of justice – which is disputed by some of his interpreters.[38] This connection is confirmed in the *Political Economy*, where he remarks, "one need only be just in order to be sure of following the general will."[39] Second, Rousseau explains that the general will combines justice with interest – that is, we *want* what is just when we arrive at the general will.[40] We must desire justice as much as we do our own good. This fusion of interest and justice is suggested in the first draft of the *Social Contract*, known as the *Geneva Manuscript*, where Rousseau describes the socialization process of a "violent interlocutor" into a citizen, who eventually harmonizes justice

---

[35] Strong [1994] 2002, 34; see also 81–3.

[36] He elaborates a bit later, "[T]he general will changes in nature when it has a particular object, and it cannot, being general, pronounce judgment on a particular man or fact" (*SC*, 2.4.6, 62 [III: 374]). Matthew Simpson has taken this to be a sticking point in Rousseau's purported system of checks and balances (Simpson 2006b).

[37] The general will's requirement of general derivation is stated at *SC*, 2.2.1; its general application is stated numerous times throughout the work, including 1.7.7, 2.1.1, 2.3.3, and especially, 2.6.5.

[38] Notably, see the work of Arthur M. Melzer, who writes, "If Rousseau favors the general will, then, it is most certainly *not* as the *embodiment* of justice but rather as a hardheaded and practical *replacement* for it" (Melzer 1990, 157); see also Melzer 1983. I address this in Williams 2007a, 113.

[39] *Political Economy*, 12 [III: 251].

[40] In this regard, Rousseau is anticipating Hegel's desire to fuse our subjective will (*für sich*) with the objective will (*an sich*). For Hegel, this can only occur at the end of history. For Rousseau, it must happen to forge a legitimate state. See the conclusion (5.5) for a contrast of Rousseau and Hegel on this point.

and happiness when he learns "to prefer to his apparent interest his interest rightly understood." By "interest rightly understood" Rousseau means the citizen will adopt a notion of happiness that means sharing it with others.[41]

Finally, Chapter Four also elaborates on another important dimension of the general will – its emphasis on equality. The social contract establishes an equality among citizens, specifically, an equality of rights.[42] Acts of sovereignty should favor no one class of citizens any more than it would favor another.[43] This is a formal rather than a substantive equality. The general will does not guarantee substantively similar economic conditions, for example – though he implies elsewhere that this formal equality is made a mockery by substantial economic inequalities. The final footnote in Book I is authoritative here:

> Under bad governments this equality is only apparent and illusory; it serves only to maintain the poor man in his misery and the rich in his usurpation. In fact, laws are always useful to those who possess something and harmful to those who have nothing: Whence it follows that the social state is advantageous to men only insofar as they all have something and none has too much of anything. (*SC*, 1.9.8n, 56n [III: 367n])

So for formal equality to be legitimate, it must be supported by an underlying economic equality. Indeed, it is likely that this is what he means when he says that "all commit themselves under the same conditions" (*SC*, 2.4.8, 63 [III: 374]). One cannot expect equal treatment by the law under conditions of radical economic inequality. It was this kind of inequality that led to the disastrous social contract of the *Second Discourse*. As John Rawls has aptly summarized Rousseau on this matter, "the first social contract was, in effect, fraudulent, the rich dominating and deceiving the poor. The central evil was economic inequality, with the rich having assured possessions, the poor having little or nothing. But the poor, not foreseeing the consequences, were ready to acquiesce in law and political

---

[41] *Geneva Manuscript*, 159 [III: 288–9]. Interestingly, Rousseau attributes the spread of this doctrine throughout the West to Christianity (*Geneva Manuscript*, 158 [III: 287]). This is striking due to his subsequent problems with the political applications of Christianity discussed at *SC*, 4.8.

[42] "One ought rather to presume that the particular will will often be contrary to the general will, for private interest always tends to preferences, and the public interest always tends to equality" (*Emile*, 462 [IV: 842]).

[43] There is textual evidence in the *Letters Written from the Mountain* that Rousseau perceived justice and the general will to be precisely the same in this substantive respect: "The first and greatest public interest is always justice. All wish the conditions to be equal for all, and justice is nothing but this equality" (*Mountain*, 301 [III: 891]). This again suggests that Melzer et al. are mistaken to suggest that the general will operates completely independently of justice.

authority as a remedy for the conflict and insecurity of an agricultural society without government."[44]

He concludes Chapter Four by noting the obvious benefits of this society over the state of nature. This is especially important since many casual readers of and commentators on Rousseau mistakenly advance the view that he naïvely prefers the state of nature over political society. This is patently false. He makes this perfectly clear here where he portrays the state of nature as characterized by great peril and the waging of "inevitable fights" among individuals (*SC*, 2.4.10, 63 [III: 375]). It is especially important to recall that although Rousseau's state of nature starts out peacefully, circumstances prompt its inevitable decline into a Hobbesian state of war.

2.5. *Of the Right of Life and Death*

Rousseau wants to create room for the possibility of a death penalty in Chapter Five. But in doing so, he must admittedly overcome an apparently substantial obstacle. It seems paradoxical for the sovereign to possess a power over life and death of the subjects. This is because the sovereign consists of the citizens, who join the state in part only so that their lives would be protected (via their *amour de soi*, presumably). So *how* can individuals will their own death? This is the big question to be confronted in this chapter.

Rousseau gives a general and specific answer to that question. His general answer is that "Whoever wills the end [the common good] also wills the means [in this case, death of enemies of the state]" (*SC*, 2.5.2, 64 [III: 376]). So if citizens really want the common good, they must grant to the state the power of putting down those who threaten it.

More specifically, there is a technical issue here that allows the state to execute criminals. By virtue of a law-breaking act, the criminal "ceases to be a member of it [the political society], and he even enters war with it" (2.5.4, 64 [III: 376]). At this point, the sovereign may rightfully regard the criminal as an enemy of the state, who may be killed, just as any other opponent in open warfare.

This raises an important question stemming from the fact that Rousseau does not make any kind of distinction here between murderers and petty thieves. A petty thief has violated the law, formally speaking, just as much as the murderer. So, does Rousseau's sovereign retain the power to kill an

---

[44] Rawls 2007, 202–3.

individual who steals a turnip from another's farm? He offers no answer to this question. The best answer to this is to appeal to the general will, and since Rousseau posits, "one need only be just in order to be sure of following the general will,"[45] it really becomes a question of justice. By this standard, it seems difficult to consider the murderer and the turnip thief – though equally violators of the law – equal offenders deserving equal punishments. One might pose another question here of Rousseau. When examining the rules of just war earlier, Rousseau says anyone who puts down his arms cannot be killed (*SC*, 1.4.10, 47 [III: 357]). So does the state really have the right to kill a criminal, at least if he puts down his arms? He does not anticipate this problem, but I think he could conceivably accommodate it. One might argue that the criminal cannot be killed once he puts down his arms, and may only be restrained in prison, like prisoners of war. Or he might argue that the unarmed subject criminal is somehow more deserving of a stronger penalty by virtue of his violating the sanctity of the social contract. This is suggested by a remark he makes toward the end of the *Social Contract* that subjects who are "incapable of sincerely loving the laws [and] justice" can be punished with death (*SC*, 4.8.32, 150 [III: 468]).

Rousseau warns, however, "frequent harsh punishments are always a sign of weakness or laziness in the Government" (*SC*, 2.5.6, 65 [III: 377]). Here again he seems to be borrowing from Montesquieu, who wrote, "Severity in penalties suits despotic government, whose principle is terror, better than monarchies and republics, which have honor and virtue for their spring." Despotic governments are lazy, presumably, because they fail to invest the energy necessary on the front end to shape citizens who would not think of committing crimes such as might result in the death penalty.[46] So the more common the death penalty in a given state, the less likely subjects are to be invested in the good of their fellow citizens/subjects, and the less likely one is to find there a general will.

He concludes Chapter Five with a few remarks on the pardoning power, which he describes as belonging exclusively to the sovereign. He notably describes the sovereign here as the "one which is above judge and law" (*SC*, 2.5.7, 65 [III: 377]). This is important for Rousseau because both executive and judicial functions of the state are to work scrupulously according to the rule of law as determined by the legislature. As a

---

[45] *Political Economy*, 12 [III: 251].
[46] As Montesquieu says, "a good legislator will insist less on punishing crimes than on preventing them" (*Spirit of the Laws*, 6.9).

pardon is in essence the temporary suspension of the law in a particular case, this can only be carried out by the law-making body of the state – the sovereign. Rousseau concedes that this power is "not altogether clear" and specifies that "the occasions to exercise it are very rare" (*SC*, 2.5.7, 65 [III: 377]). And if one finds this power employed with great frequency, it can only mean that the republic is soon coming to an end. On the one hand, this power raises a problem for Rousseau, insofar as a pardon appears to violate the principle of generality required of all sovereign actions. A pardon in its very nature is particular – exempting a particular individual from the consequences associated with a criminal action. On the other hand, it might be necessary if the sovereign sees that its will is not being carried out effectively in particular instances by its delegates in the executive or judicial branches (e.g., as when the innocent have been condemned). So it may not be a form of retroactive legislation so much as a means by which to prevent a factious partial prosecution and condemnation of innocent subjects.

2.6. *Of Law*

In many ways, Chapter Six addresses some of the most important issues in Rousseau's political thought, as well as issues central to political theory itself. In broad terms, it marks the transition of his inquiry from the social contract itself to legislation. And as regards that legislation, Rousseau lays out the very foundation of the laws. He does so in an especially significant paragraph. Since this paragraph is the subject of much scholarly scrutiny and disagreement, it is worth reproducing in its entirety.

What is good and conformable to order is so by the nature of things and independently of human conventions. All justice comes from God, he alone is its source; but if we were capable of receiving it from so high, we would need neither government nor laws. No doubt there is a universal justice emanating from reason alone; but this justice, to be admitted among us, has to be reciprocal. Considering things in human terms, the laws of justice are vain among men for want of natural sanctions; they only bring good to the wicked and evil to the just when he observes them toward everyone while no one observes them toward him. Conventions and laws are therefore necessary to combine rights with duties and to bring justice back to its object. In the state of nature, where everything is common, I owe nothing to those to whom I have promised nothing. I recognize as another's only what is of no use myself. It is not so in the civil state where all rights are fixed by law. (*SC*, 2.6.2, 66 [III: 378])

This paragraph demands careful attention, one sentence at a time.

"What is good and conformable to order is so by the nature of things and independently of human conventions."[47] Rousseau here affirms the position that natural goodness is independent of convention. Whatever is good, it is not so simply because people agree to it. There can be no question that Rousseau is rejecting the conception of justice articulated in Hobbes and Grotius – that justice is simply a matter of upholding agreement. This is only logical, as so much of Book I was directed against these two. This is also consistent with his rejection of the social contract in Part II of the *Second Discourse*. We find more of the same here. Whatever justice and goodness are, they are not simply the outcomes of human agreement. They have a higher foundation than that.

"All justice comes from God, he alone is its source; but if we were capable of receiving it from so high, we would need neither government nor laws." The second sentence makes two independent claims. The first is that justice comes from God.[48] It is important here to identify some background in understanding what Rousseau means by this claim. He declares his faith in God frequently and forcefully throughout his career. Though he acknowledges his arguments for God are far from airtight, he affirmed in his "Letter to Voltaire," for example, "I believe in God just as strongly as I believe any other truth."[49] It is especially important not to read into this that Rousseau's understanding of Christianity corresponds with dominant contemporary strains of the religion that stress a personal relationship with God and the immanent divinity of Christ. Although Rousseau claimed to be a Christian in the very broad sense of agreeing with its moral teachings, his religion is more specifically Deistic. While he finds the Gospels promoting important moral truths, they are also "full of unbelievable things, of things repugnant to reason and impossible for any sensible man to conceive or accept." Rousseau's God is a creator of both the physical and moral universe – the one imparting order to the natural and moral worlds.[50] Beyond this, his God is largely disengaged, not inclined in any way to intervene in human affairs after creation. But that establishment of order most emphatically includes the origins of justice. And this is crucial

---

[47] This phrasing notably resembles that of Montesquieu's Usbek in the *Persian Letters*: "justice is eternal and independent of human conventions" (*Persian Letters*, 140).

[48] Rousseau confirms this view in his *Emile*, where he writes, the duties of humankind are "like an innate principle ... graven in our hearts by the Author of all justice" (*Emile*, 100n [IV: 334n]). See also *Emile*, 284 [IV: 591], where he describes God again as the "Author of all justice."

[49] "Letter to Voltaire," 242 [IV: 1070]. See Grimsley 1968, 52–8; Williams 2007a, 65–6.

[50] *Emile*, 308 [IV: 627]; as Rousseau opens his *Emile*, "Everything is good as it leaves the hands of the Author of things" (*Emile*, 37 [IV: 245]).

for Rousseau's political theory insofar as he has already posited that the general will is intimately connected with his concept of justice.

While it is comforting in some sense to know that justice comes from what Rousseau regards as probably *the* most reliable source, the second half of this sentence threatens to dash all hopes. He concedes here that although justice comes from a high source, human beings possess at best imperfect knowledge of it. Indeed, if they did have such knowledge, there would be no need for laws or government. People would know justice and then rule according to its substantive content. This resembles Plato's story of the Age of Cronus, described in the *Laws* (713b–14a) and *Statesman* (271d–2b), where divine rulers had no need of positive or written laws by virtue of their comprehensive and intuitive knowledge of the highest laws.[51] Rousseau has already conceded, however, that the people can often be mistaken about what justice or the general will is. That is, the people are epistemically fallible. Some scholars have taken this to imply that Rousseau despairs entirely of any role for justice in his politics. Therefore, they argue, Rousseau sharply distinguishes the general will from anything having to do with justice. Roger D. Masters has called this doctrine the "detachability thesis,"[52] whereby Rousseau allegedly detaches his political theory from his grander metaphysical commitments. But it is far from clear that Rousseau means to make any such sweeping statements. What the text itself suggests is that, given the people's inevitable epistemic failings, it is unreasonable simply to expect them to know justice and then act accordingly. That is, no solution to the social problem can be resolved without government or laws.

"*No doubt there is a universal justice emanating from reason alone; but this justice, to be admitted among us, has to be reciprocal.*" This sentence likewise includes two very different, yet highly significant, parts. The first half includes both epistemic and substantive elements. Substantively, Rousseau insists that this conception of justice is universal. That is, like the general will, it is not partial. There is no one justice for one set of persons and another justice for another group. There is one justice with the same standards for all. This sense of justice is repeated in the *Emile*, where he speaks of an "eternal justice" and of "eternal laws of nature and order"[53] that inform the properly educated citizen – that is, the uncorrupted

---

[51] Of course, Plato rejects this in favor of the rule of law (*Laws*, 715d) – and so does Rousseau later in this paragraph under examination here.

[52] Masters 1968, 73–89; see also Bertram 2004, 116–18. This has been challenged in O'Hagan 2004, Williams 2007a, 106–14, and Williams 2010a, 534.

[53] *Emile*, 292 [IV: 603], 473 [IV: 857]; see also *Emile*, 259 [IV: 556].

citizen, the one who is free from evil. This premise is a corollary of his earlier assertion that justice is independent of convention. Its content is fixed and beyond any possibility of change. The epistemic message in the first half of this sentence is that justice is knowable through reason and reason alone. Rousseau has a mixed relationship with reason. On some occasions he can be found praising it; on others he seems to be flatly condemning it. This is because it is a tool that can be put to the service of many different masters. Insofar as it serves *amour propre* and the private interests of segments within the community, it deserves condemnation. This is why Rousseau can be found so frequently condemning the "reason" of the *Philosophes*. By contrast, however, reason can also be employed to good purposes – such as for knowing goodness and justice. As Rousseau says in the *Emile*, "Reason alone teaches us to know good and bad. Conscience, which makes us love the former and hate the latter, although independent of reason, cannot therefore be developed without it."[54] So reason is an epistemic tool for knowing justice, according to Rousseau.

The second half of the sentence speaks to an important rule pertaining to the application of justice. The "universal justice" he cites in this paragraph only applies when all are held accountable to it. Rousseau elaborates in the next sentence.

"*Considering things in human terms, the laws of justice are vain among men for want of natural sanctions; they only bring good to the wicked and evil to the just when he observes them toward everyone while no one observes them toward him.*" Setting aside considerations of divine rewards and sanctions, Rousseau explores what happens to the just and the wicked in the absence of laws and sanctions. He notes that "universal justice" has no real natural sanctions.[55] That is to say, nature does not necessarily punish those who violate its laws.[56] In the real world, so long as no one is willing to enforce the laws of justice, violators will go unpunished. This is what Hobbes says about the state of nature – that the laws of nature, lacking sanction in the state of nature, would be followed only by those seeking to be taken advantage of.[57] Indeed, so long as this is the case, the wicked will prosper,

---

[54] *Emile*, 67 [IV: 288].

[55] In making this claim, he tacitly rejects a claim by Spinoza and others that there are natural sanctions for unjust behavior.

[56] This raises the question of whether Rousseau's God is willing to step in and provide sanctions against the violations of His law. As Ronald Grimsley has argued, however, "Rousseau has no firm doctrine of hell" (1968, 123). Indeed, Rousseau is dubious that an all-good creature could condemn someone to eternal torment.

[57] Hobbes [1651] 2002, 15.36. Arthur Melzer (1983, 640, 642–3) observes these similarities and draws the conclusion that there is little separating Hobbes and Rousseau substantively.

just as the only honest player in an otherwise fixed poker game is almost certain to lose. This is why Rousseau asks elsewhere, "Of what use is justice with tyrants"?[58] This is because presumably the tyrant refuses to play according to the rules of justice (*SC*, 3.10.9, 108 [III: 423]). When one party is exempted from the rules, the rules primarily serve the exempted party's interests. Furthermore, Rousseau suggests in the *Emile* that this is precisely the condition characterizing Europe as he knew it in the eighteenth century: "considering the present state of things: the wicked man prospers, and the just man remains oppressed."[59] Any serious act of legislation requires universal compliance to the rules of justice so that the just prosper and the wicked suffer the consequences of their deeds.

"Conventions and laws are therefore necessary to combine rights with duties and to bring justice back to its object." It is because justice is not self-enforcing that laws are required. The laws, as Rousseau says, "bring justice back to its object." Arthur M. Melzer has argued on the basis of the paragraph in question that "Rousseau's political doctrine, rather than flowing from some higher moral imperative [as implied by a *'universal justice'*], is made possible precisely by virtue of its conscious and radical liberation from all transcendent foundations."[60] This reading, however, fails to take seriously Rousseau's insistence that justice be brought "back to its object." In bringing justice back to its object, Rousseau means that the laws give teeth to that universal justice, which has no natural teeth of its own. Consider an analogy. Performance-enhancing drugs have been an epidemic in professional sports for many years now. These drugs are generally illegal when taken for reasons not approved by physicians. Yet not all players took them. Some did, and some did not. Clearly, everything else being equal, those on the performance-enhancing drugs were profiting at the expense of the law-abiding athletes. Quoting Rousseau again, "the laws of justice are vain among men for want of natural sanctions; they only bring good to the wicked and evil to the just when he observes them toward everyone while no one observes them toward him." As a consequence, many athletic organizations and player unions have agreed to institute strict rules against the consumption of these drugs, along with significant penalties. The point of these agreements is not to dispense with the moral intuition that it is unfair for some to profit at the expense of others by taking dangerous and illegal drugs. The point is rather the opposite: to give teeth to

---

[58] *Hero*, 316 [II: 1274].
[59] *Emile*, 282 [IV: 589].
[60] Melzer 1990, 155.

those moral intuitions – in the words of Rousseau, "to bring justice back
to its object."

*"In the state of nature, where everything is common, I owe nothing to those
to whom I have promised nothing. I recognize as another's only what is of no
use myself. It is not so in the civil state where all rights are fixed by law."* The
final three sentences of this crucial paragraph speak to the importance of
these rules being agreed upon. This follows from what has already been
said. Without gaining the agreement of all to follow the rules of justice,
heeding justice is counterproductive in many relevant ways. So the rules
of justice are conditionally obligatory.[61] While the rules of justice always
exist as ideas, individuals can only be held accountable to them when they
have consented to obey those ideas in the form of laws. This is the point
of the general will. While the general will is substantively tied to the idea
of justice,[62] it does not truly come into existence as an agent of force until
it has met with the community's consent.

This still leaves open questions about the substantive content of justice. Rousseau offers at least some guidance in his *Letters Written from the
Mountain*, published in 1764 as a defense of his *Social Contract*: "The first
and greatest public interest is always justice. All wish the conditions to be
equal for all, and justice is nothing but this equality."[63] This equality has
two broad components. First, it includes institutional or legal equality,
consisting of equality before the law or equality as subjects (*SC*, 1.6.10 and
2.4.8), equality as members of the collective sovereign or legislator (*SC*,
2.4.5), and equality in political participation (including identical rights of
citizens to participate in assembly, vote, and stand for office).[64] But second,
this institutional and legal equality requires a degree of economic equality (*SC*, 1.9.8, 56 [III: 367]).[65] Rousseau makes this perfectly clear in the
context of this passage from the *Letters Written from the Mountain*: "Is it
in these two extremes [of economic inequality], the one made to buy, the

---

[61] See Noone 1972.

[62] "[O]ne need only be just in order to be sure of following the general will" (*Political Economy*,
12 [III: 251]).

[63] *Mountain*, 301 [III: 891].

[64] These are addressed in Neuhouser 2008, 166–71. It is also likely that Rousseau understands this to
imply what more contemporary philosophers would call "equality of opportunity." This is because
Rousseau explicitly embraces this principle elsewhere. In his *Corsica*, he specifies, "A plowman must
not be inferior by birth to anyone, he must see above him only the laws and the magistrates and he
must be capable of becoming a magistrate himself if he is worthy of it from his enlightenment or
from his probity" (*Corsica*, 132 [III: 911]).

[65] The spirit of Rousseau's logic was subsequently employed in Franklin Roosevelt's speech before the
1936 Democratic National Convention, where he remarked that political equality is "meaningless
in the face of economic inequality" (quoted in Sandel 1996, 256).

other to sell itself, that one should look for love of justice and the laws? It is by means of them that the State always degenerates: the rich man holds the Law in his purse, and the poor prefers bread to liberty."[66] This two-pronged conception of equality is thus at the heart of his understandings of law and justice – themselves at the heart of the *Social Contract*. Law is meant to enforce justice; justice means equal treatment and consideration under the law; equal treatment requires a relative (though undefined) economic equality.

While the second paragraph is the most significant in Chapter Six, the remaining paragraphs are not without interest. He defines two important terms: law and republic. A "law" [*une loi*] amounts to this: "when the people enacts statutes for the whole people considers only itself, and if a relation is then formed, it is between the entire object from one point of view and the entire object from another point of view, with no division of the whole. Then the matter with regard to which the statute is being enacted is general, as the enacting will" (*SC*, 2.6.5, 67 [III: 379]). Rousseau here emphasizes familiar themes – the general derivation and the general application of a will. In raising these themes previously, he associated them with the general will. And he is clearly suggesting the general will here again. But here he calls it a "law." This has at least two consequences. First, Rousseau is suggesting that "law" is a normative concept – and not merely in the sense that it establishes norms to which subjects will be held accountable. Beyond this, in order for a law to be called a "law" in his lexicon, it must conform to those standards informing the substantive content of the general will. This kind of association of positive law to substantive ideas is traditionally associated with the natural law school of jurisprudence. Second, Rousseau is suggesting that the law is really the legislative manifestation of the general will. When the general will is legislated, it is "law."

Rousseau's definition of "Republic" [*République*] that follows is derived from his definition of *loi* and follows the same pattern of built-in normativity. A republic is "any State ruled by laws, whatever may be the form of administration" (*SC*, 2.6.9, 67 [III: 379]). This is consistent with the definition he offered in *SC*, 1.6.10 that a republic is a collective body living under the direction of the general will, since an act of legislation can only be called a "law" when it is consistent with the general will. So like his definition of a law, a republic is a normative concept, not merely a descriptive one. He elaborates here that republics are the only legitimate governments. So either a government is governed by the general will, or else it is illegitimate.

---

[66] *Mountain*, 300 [IV: 890].

Rousseau reserves an immensely important claim for his final paragraph of Chapter Six: "The People subject to the laws ought to be their author" (*SC*, 2.6.10, 68 [III: 380]). This is nothing less than the doctrine of popular sovereignty. The people are sovereign for Rousseau. In the context of eighteenth-century French politics, dominated by aristocrats, clergy, and a monarch, this is radical.[67] But, of course, this must also be read in the context of his normative definitions. As was made clear in his distinction between the general will and the will of all (*SC*, 2.3.2, 60 [III: 371]), not any aggregation of popular will suffices for sovereignty. The people must agree to what is actually just. He clarifies this by continuing, "By itself the people always wills the good, but by itself does not always see it. The general will is always upright [*droite*], but the judgment which guides it is not always enlightened [*éclairé*]" (*SC*, 2.6.10, 68 [III: 380]). Indeed, earlier in the paragraph, Rousseau sounds even less optimistic, asking, "How will a blind multitude, which often does not know what it wills because it rarely knows what is good for it, carry out an undertaking as great, as difficult as a system of legislation?" (*SC*, 2.6.10, 68 [III: 380]). So in one and the same paragraph, Rousseau asserts the sovereignty of the people, and then expresses great skepticism about their ability to do their job well. It is for such juxtapositions or paradoxes that Rousseau is rightfully known. Complicating this matter, he reintroduces into this mix those who know what the good is, but nevertheless seek to seduce the people into bad, partial choices in public policy. This raises the question of how can one effect a "smooth cooperation of the parts" from this combination of manipulative parties and ignorance (*SC*, 2.6.10, 68 [III: 380])? He offers an answer in Chapter Seven.

2.7. *Of the Lawgiver [Législateur]*

It becomes clear in Chapter Seven that the form of legislation Rousseau has been addressing in Book II is fundamentally constitutional design – that is, laying out the principles that should inform constitutional authors. And he makes it perfectly evident in the opening sentence that this task is well beyond the skills of ordinary citizens:

To discover the best rules of society suited to each Nation would require a superior intelligence who saw all of man's passions and experienced none of them, who had no relation to our nature yet know it thoroughly, whose happiness was independent of us and who was nevertheless willing to care for ours; finally, one

---

[67] This was not always the case for Rousseau, who cites the peak of the Roman Republic as illustrative of this kind of sovereignty, where "no Citizen was excluded from the right to vote, and that the Roman People was [hence] genuinely Sovereign both by right and in fact" (*SC*, 4.4.21, 132 [III: 449]).

who, preparing his distant glory in the progress of times, could work in one century and enjoy reward in another. It would require gods give men laws. (*SC*, 2.7.1, 68–9 [III: 381])

In other words, Rousseau makes it appear here that his political project is contingent upon the impossible – that god-like[68] individuals, with near-omniscience and omni-benevolence, wrote the constitutions of republics.

The lawgiver's tasks can be divided into its formal and informal elements.[69] Formally speaking, the lawgiver must construct a constitution. Informally, the lawgiver is to change human beings from asocial savages into citizens and also to make those citizens embrace those laws and one another. Both the formal and informal tasks require great skill. The formal task requires "superior intelligence" in the science of politics – namely an ability to match a people and their circumstances with the laws that align most closely with justice. This is a technical intelligence – akin to the skills of the great natural scientists of his age. Some have taken this for a superior moral intelligence, but this does not appear supported by the text. Rousseau explicitly refers to the lawgiver as having a technical expertise: "He is the mechanic who invents the machine" (*SC*, 2.7.2, 69 [III: 381]).

The informal tasks of the legislator represent an even greater challenge. One may be gifted in choosing the right set of laws for a people; but if that people cannot be persuaded to adopt those laws and embrace one another, the legislative science is worthless. A great obstacle facing the legislator is that the people do not share this mastery of political science. Nor do they share in anything like the sophistication that would make it possible to communicate the principles underlying the choice of regime types and fundamental laws. Rousseau expresses the apprehension that "The wise who would speak to the vulgar in their own rather than in the vulgar language will not be understood by them. Yet there are a thousand kinds of ideas which it is impossible to translate into the language of the people"

---

[68] Judith Shklar comments, "the Great Legislator is a god" (1969, 155). To be sure, one might worry in Rousseau's scheme that such geniuses run the risk of being excessively vain. Yet he does not make this association himself. In fact, in his *Emile* he claims precisely the opposite: "Great men are not deceived about their superiority; they see it, feel it, and are no less modest because of it. The more they have, the more they know all that they lack. They are less vain about being raised about us than they are humbled by the sentiment of their poverty" (*Emile*, 245 [IV: 537]). This is presumably why he does not express concern about the likes of Newton and Descartes in his *First Discourse*. The truly wise and great have a Socratic humility and are not inflamed by *amour propre*. It is only the pretenders to that throne that pose a genuine threat. To be sure, Rousseau presupposes his lawgiver here resembles the "great men" described in this passage from the *Emile*.

[69] Although many translations use the more literal English of "legislator," Gourevitch's "Lawgiver" appropriately distinguishes this unique office from common legislation or policies, which the people undertake themselves.

(*SC*, 2.7.9, 70 [III: 383]). The capacity to grasp the principles of legislation lies beyond the intellectual reach of most citizens, the same way that the finer points of most natural sciences would do the same.

The informal task has a second component, equally challenging. Rousseau operates under no illusions in approaching the problem:

> Anyone who dares to institute a people must feel capable of, so to speak, changing human nature; of transforming each individual who by himself is a perfect and solitary whole into part of a larger whole from which that individual would as it were receive his life and his being; of weakening man's constitution in order to strengthen it; of substituting a partial and moral existence for the independent and physical existence we have all received from nature. (*SC*, 2.7.3, 69 [III: 381])

More succinctly, Christopher Kelly has described it as the ability to convert "an asocial multitude into the specific condition of citizenship."[70] Prior to legislation, individuals resemble the *l'homme sauvage* of the *Second Discourse* insofar as they are largely selfish. Natural human beings may not be vicious, on Rousseau's account, but neither are they inclined to weigh the needs of others in their actions, much less considerations of justice and goodness. The legislator's aim is radical: "So that when each Citizen is nothing and can do nothing except with all the others … the legislation may be said to be at the highest pitch of perfection" (*SC*, 2.7.3, 69 [III: 382]). Rousseau elaborates in the *Government of Poland* that the goal of the legislator, as was the case with Moses, Lycurgus, and Numa, is to foster "bonds that might attach the Citizens to the fatherland and to one another," suggesting a somewhat more moderate and attainable goal than what is suggested by the *Social Contract* here. This was the great genius of the ancient constitutions lacking in his own day. Modern constitutions have abandoned the ancient task of fostering fraternal love in favor of simple commands – aimed more at calculated self-interest than at the heart: "If the moderns have laws, it is solely in order to teach them to obey their masters well, not to pick pockets, and to give public scoundrels a great deal of money."[71]

Rousseau's means for effecting both informal tasks – that of changing the nature of citizens and persuading them to adopt the constitution of the legislator – is an appeal to the gods. This is because the technical knowledge of the legislator transcends the understanding of most citizens, just as most citizens today likewise fail to grasp the technical details of academic articles published on physics. As he pleads, "This sublime reason [of

---

[70] Kelly 1987, 326.
[71] *Poland*, 181, 182 [III: 958]. For the "moderate" reading of Rousseau's lawgiver, see Hanley 2008b, 226–30.

how the lawgiver's constitution serves the general will] which rises beyond
the reach of vulgar men it is whose decision the lawgiver places in the
mouth of the immortals, in order to rally by divine authority those whom
human prudence could not move" (*SC*, 2.7.10, 71 [III: 383–4]). This move
is necessitated by at least three factors. First, the people must be brought
to embrace their constitution in one fashion or another. Second, the people are insufficiently sophisticated to understand and accept a rational justification of the constitution on the terms of the lawgiver. Third, whereas
violence as a means of persuasion might be an option for some, it is unacceptable for Rousseau. In this spirit, Rousseau insists that the lawgiver
must "have recourse to an authority of a different order, which might be
able to rally without violence and to persuade without convincing" (*SC*,
2.7.9, 71 [III: 383]).[72]

Persuading without convincing involves accessing the hearts of citizens,
less so their reason. The lawgiver does this by invoking the divine authority of the gods. In other words, the lawgiver suggests that the constitution
is divinely inspired. This appeal to deities accomplishes something that,
Rousseau says, reason cannot: reaching the hearts of individuals, binding
them together as fellow citizens, and engendering a profound respect for
the laws.

Rousseau explains that the appeal to the gods is a time-honored tradition in political thought. Of particular note, he cites the authority of
Machiavelli, who likewise observes, "truly there was never any orderer
of extraordinary laws for a people who did not have recourse to God,
because otherwise they would not have been accepted. For a prudent individual knows many goods that do not have in themselves evident reasons
with which one can persuade others. Thus wise men who wish to take
away this difficulty have recourse to God."[73] Machiavelli cites the success
of Lycurgus, Solon, and Numa[74] in this regard. It is this appeal to divine

---

[72] As Christopher Kelly (1987, 327–31) observes, Rousseau first employs this phrase, "persuading without convincing," in the *Essay on the Origins of Language* (256 [V: 383]).

[73] Machiavelli, *Discourses*, ii.i. For another version of civil religion, see Spinoza's *Theological-Political
Treatise*, chapter 14. For a comparison of Rousseau and Spinoza on civil religion, see Williams
2010b, 350. Immanuel Kant subsequently confronts the same problem only to say that citizens
should not even contemplate the origin of their laws – in essence implying their divinity. Indeed,
Kant further adds, the law must be considered not as coming "from human beings but from some
highest, flawless lawgiver; and that is what the saying 'All authority comes from God' means"
([1797] 1996, 462).

[74] As Plutarch observes, Lycurgus derived his divine wisdom from Apollo at Delphi (Plutarch, I: 56).
Plutarch does not report, however, that Lycurgus emphasized this source when legislating to the
Spartans. Plutarch says little to suggest a role for the gods in Solon's act of legislation. Plutarch's
account of Numa is rich in references to the Roman legislator's piety (e.g., I: 83, 85) and his actual

authority, according to Machiavelli and Rousseau, that reaches the heart where reason is impotent. "This sublime reason which rises beyond the reach of vulgar men it is whose decisions the lawgiver places in the mouth of the immortals, in order to rally by divine authority those whom human prudence could not move" (*SC*, 2.7.11, 71 [III: 383–4]).

All this raises obvious and important questions – and it has been subject to much scholarly scrutiny. Among these questions is whether or not Rousseau conceives of the lawgiver's appeal to divine authority as a grand, or noble lie. Plato proposes in his *Republic* that there are occasions on which constitutional designers and even rulers must lie to their subjects.[75] This would be surprising, given Rousseau's repeated professions of his commitment to truth. In fact, he made the phrase, *vitam impendere vero* [to consecrate one's life to the truth], his personal motto.[76] Yet several Rousseau interpreters find the appeal to the gods here analogous to Plato's proposal – that Rousseau requires a major act of deception to establish his republic. As Matthew W. Maguire has commented, "The idea of the legislator is a troubling concept." Further, others, such as Patrick Riley, have argued that Rousseau's deception here fundamentally undermines the notion of a will that is the fundamental underpinning of the entire *Social Contract*, hence rendering the entire project a spectacular failure. That is, in a political theory that places so much emphasis on the free agreement of its citizens, it seems odd that they should be led with stories and lies.[77]

If these claims are true, at the very least they raise serious questions. Yet there are at least a few reasons not to rush to this conclusion. First, the argument that Rousseau advocates lying here presumes that Rousseau himself does not believe in the existence of gods or, if they did exist, that they are not in any way relevant to his politics. If this were true, one would have to explain, then, why Rousseau professes a strong faith in the existence of God, and further, why he attributes the origin of justice to

interactions with the gods. Plutarch speculates that Numa's piety and close association with the gods played some role in maintaining order in Rome (Plutarch, I: 99).

[75] Plato, *Republic*, 414d–15c.

[76] *Letter to d'Alembert* (121 [V: 132]); *Emile* (260 [IV: 558]), *Mountain* (131 [III: 683]), and *Reveries* (43 [I: 1024]).

[77] Those concerned about the perceived deception here include Butterworth 1992, 188, Gourevitch 1994, 95–96, and Grant 1997, 125–29; Maguire 2006, 99; Riley 1982. This point is also made directly by Matthew Simpson, who asks, "what kind of civil liberty exists when people must in some sense be brainwashed into being good citizens before they can live in a society that creates these civil liberties" (2006a, 67). By contrast, John Rawls finds in the lawgiver largely a "fictional figure" who poses "no problems for the unity and coherence of Rousseau's view, as is sometimes alleged" (2007, 241).

that God.[78] Second, Rousseau might here be speaking of something he subsequently calls a "fable," rather than an attempt at deception. In his *Reveries*, he defines fables as follows: "Fictions which have a moral purpose are called allegories or fables; and as their purpose is or must be only to wrap useful truths in easily perceived and pleasing forms, in such cases we hardly care about hiding the *de facto* lie, which is only the cloak of truth; and he who merely sets forth a fable as a fable in no way lies."[79] In this case, it is unclear that he is attempting to deceive so much as connect important moral truths to a pleasing story that might inspire citizens to action.

A third response is potentially grounded in the argument that Rousseau really does not require this lawgiver as much as some have presumed. Nicholas Dent, for example, questions whether the *Social Contract* even needs a lawgiver, noting that the rest of the *Social Contract* outside of 2.7 makes no appeals to the lawgiver or the conditions the discussion seems to require.[80] Dent's argument is sophisticated and worth engaging insofar as it forces readers to think through Rousseau's text and the role of the lawgiver. He draws attention to Rousseau's claim that the lawgiver's most important task is that of binding citizens to one another. That is, citizens should feel themselves as members of an association rather than an aggregation. In this spirit, he points to *SC*, 2.10, where Rousseau spells out the conditions necessary for establishing a republic. One can only legislate, in this sense, to a people "already bound together by some union of origin, interest, or convention, [and] has not yet borne the true yoke of laws ... one which combines the stability of an ancient people with the docility of a new people" (*SC*, 2.10.5, 77–8 [III: 390–1]). In this, Dent observes that Rousseau assumes before legislation the lawgiver's most important work is already accomplished by the historical circumstances of the people in question.

Dent's thesis is at first blush persuasive with regard to the lawgiver's "informal" task of creating an association. He astutely observes that Rousseau already presumes that an association precedes the arrival of the lawgiver. But this argument still must confront the lawgiver's other duties. This specifically includes the technical and formal task of writing

---

[78] Regarding God's existence: "I believe in God just as strongly as I believe in any other truth" ("Letter to Voltaire," 242 [IV: 1070]). Rousseau's God, however, is not standard among those who would identify as "Christians." See section 4.8 of Chapter 4. On attributing the origin of the laws to God, see *SC*, 2.6.2.

[79] *Reveries*, 48 [I: 1029].

[80] Dent 1988, 213–18 and Dent 2005, 140–2.

a constitution and the informal task of convincing subjects to obey its laws. Those duties remain with the lawgiver, which is perhaps one reason why Rousseau does not subsequently abandon the office of lawgiver in his subsequent constitutional proposal for Poland. But Rousseau also emphasizes in that later work that a central task of the lawgiver remains seeking a "bond that might attach the Citizens to the fatherland and to one another."[81] So even if he thought the lawgiver's associational tasks were largely satisfied before legislation in the *Social Contract*, in his later work he sees that dimension of the lawgiver's task as central.

Rousseau concludes Chapter Seven remarking, "One should not from all this conclude with Warburton that among us politics and religion have a common object, but rather at the origin of nations the one serves as the instrument of the other" (*SC*, 2.7.12, 72 [III: 384]). William Warburton was a bishop from Gloucester, England, who in his *Alliance between Church and State* (1736) and *Divine Legation of Moses* (1738) argues along with Rousseau that religion is necessary to politics. But for Rousseau, Warburton mistakenly unifies the aims of Christianity and the state.[82] For Rousseau, there can be no confusion – religion is to be a servant to politics. He elaborates on this principle considerably in his chapter on "Civil Religion" (*SC*, 4.8).

Assuming the Lawgiver can accomplish the legislative task, Rousseau adds one final component: he should ideally leave. "This office which gives the republic its constitution has no place in its constitution" and if he were to remain as a public figure, "the laws, as ministers to his passions, would often only perpetuate his injustices, and he could never avoid having particular views vitiate the sanctity of his work" (*SC*, 2.7.4, 69–70 [III: 382]). Designing one's own constitution offers powerful incentives to the particular will. Knowing that he would live under laws of his own making, the wealthy man, for example, would be sorely tempted to shape laws that favor his own interests. This is, after all, precisely what happens in the *Second Discourse*, where wealthy individuals write a constitution from which they will directly benefit. In this spirit, Rousseau praises the ancient Greek custom of importing foreign lawgivers. Bringing in a foreigner to

---

[81] *Poland*, 181 [III: 958].

[82] It is unclear that Rousseau is being fair to Warburton, who clearly distinguishes the aims of the state, "SECURITY TO THE TEMPORARY LIBERTY AND PROPERTY OF MAN" (*Divine Legation of Moses*, 2.5, p. 341; uppercase in original) from those of Christianity, "the SALVATION OF SOULS (*Legation*, 2.5, p. 342; uppercase in original). As he states a bit later, "*the care of the civil Society extends only to the body, and its concerns; and the care of the religious Society only to the soul*" (*Legation*, 2.5, p. 343; italics in original). See Book II, §5 and 6 generally for Warburton's arguments pertaining to the proper relationship between church and state.

write those rules removes those incentives that so deeply corrupted the regime of the *Second Discourse*.

2.8. *Of the People*

Chapters Eight through Ten all concern the people in one fashion or another. Chapter Eight concerns the timing of legislation. Chapter Nine concerns the size of a state. Chapter Ten addresses size again as well as the general suitability of people for a constitution. It is in these pages that we see the depth of influence that Montesquieu exercises over Rousseau.

Regarding the timing of legislation, a people cannot be given laws – even good ones – without first attaining a certain level of virtue. Rousseau compares this to the architect who must survey the foundation before construction. A weak foundation will not support even the grandest and most beautiful of structures. Likewise, "the wise institutor [*instituteur*] does not begin by drawing up laws good in themselves, but first examines whether the people for whom he intends them is fit to bear them" (*SC*, 2.8.1, 72 [III: 384–5]). This is why, Rousseau says, Plato refused to give laws to the Arcadians and Cyrenians. Vicious peoples cannot be governed by laws – even the best of them. They are fated to live despotically.

One might ask how these people Rousseau has just labeled "vulgar" (*SC*, 2.7.9, 70 [III: 383]) could satisfy this criterion. The reason they do is because there is a great difference between philosophic or scientific sophistication and virtue. The people may very well be ignorant about astronomy, physics, and politics – but so long as they have not yet been corrupted by factions, orators, flattery, and *amour propre* generally, they should be well-suited to issue ordinary legislation.

For Rousseau, populations are really only capable of receiving laws in their youth. As they age, they already have prejudices that become impossible to uproot. They will be unable to take on new laws and new ways of life. In this respect, Rousseau says, they are much like individual persons. We can shape children greatly through an upbringing. But once they are grown, it is nearly impossible to alter them. One must instead work with their flaws; however, this is always a second-best solution. The best and most reliable way to achieve one's aims is to start from the beginning with a flexible clay mold, as it were. This does not mean that it is impossible to work with settled clay. Rousseau allows that each people has the capacity to be re-founded *once* (*SC*, 2.8.3–4, 71–3 [III: 385]). It can happen only when they have been severely decimated and are sufficiently desperate to try anything to regain their lost glory. When it is done well, it is like a Phoenix rising from the ashes. This is how Sparta was re-formed by Lycurgus. But it can only happen *once*. If a society collapses again after the second founding, it needs a master more than a liberator. This raises many provocative questions. Is Rousseau suggesting here that there might be a time and a place for despotism? Are there certain peoples who can be ruled in no other fashion? He certainly does not lay out any prescriptions for ruling despotically, as one finds in Montesquieu, for example. Nor is he any kind of aficionado of tyrants. One cannot forget his rants against tyranny throughout Book I. But this admission raises curious possibilities.

So one must have impeccable timing in lawgiving. And the timing will vary from people to people. Some will be ripe for laws early on. Others will not be ripe for laws until after ten centuries. Along these lines, Rousseau is convinced that Russia is doomed to failure by virtue of the fact that Peter attempted to give them laws too early.[83] This will result, he concludes, in "The Russian Empire ... try[ing] to subjugate Europe, and will itself be subjugated" (*SC*, 2.8.5, 73 [III: 386]).

2.9. *The People (Continued)*

This chapter tackles the technical problem of state size. What is the appropriate size of a territory for a people? The particular focus of this chapter is the problems of territories that are too large. His clear preference is for small states wherever possible. Large states are burdened by their plodding character. Administering over vast territories is simply cumbersome. Rousseau provides a helpful analogy: "administration grows more difficult at great distances just as a weight grows heavier at the end of a larger lever" (*SC*, 2.9.2, 74 [III: 387]). The number of administrative levels multiplies, and the required supreme administration is unwieldy.[84]

The more significant social problem from Rousseau's perspective is the decreasing affection a widely spread populace has for their leader and for one another.[85] This is a substantial stumbling block in sustaining the general will, which thrives on fraternity – a widely shared love among citizens. The more citizens know one another, the greater their bonds. And

---

[83] Peter the Great (1672–1725) was Czar of Russia from 1682 to 1725. He introduced numerous reforms to modernize Russia, so that it might more closely resemble Western Europe than its own medieval past. For Rousseau, he committed the sin of making them something they were not – Frenchmen, Germans, Englishmen. He should have made them Russians. Rousseau will take this point very seriously in his *Government of Poland*.

[84] This was identified by Montesquieu as one of the problems that ultimately led to the fall of the Roman Empire. See Montesquieu [1734] 1999.

[85] See de Jouvenel 1972.

the more they love each other, the more they keep each other's interests in mind when legislating. This is a crucial component of sustaining the fundamental character of the general will. In large territories, the vast majority of fellow citizens are strangers. They have varying customs, live in different climates, and cannot even be ruled by the same kind of government. Furthermore, "Talents are hidden; virtues unknown; vices unpunished" (*SC*, 2.9.3, 74 [III: 387]). This is to say, it is easy to hide in the masses. Virtuous deeds fail to get the praise they merit; anti-social behavior fails to be condemned. The concealment of both is detrimental to the republic. The virtues could promote the thriving of the community; the vices could bring it to an end. And both are carefully and systematically concealed in large states.

2.10. *The People (Continued)*

The final of three chapters on the people continues Rousseau's thoughts on the size of a state and also elaborates something close to a final theory on what kind of people are most suited to laws – that is, which people can live without the benefit of a tyrant. The primary concern here is how to balance the size of a territory with population. Specifically, how does the Lawgiver ensure a state's self-sufficiency? Self-sufficiency is a serious matter for Rousseau. A state lacking in this regard will be forced either into a dependency on its neighbors or into aggressive militarism. At the same time, however, a state must not be *too* productive. This was not a common concern among Rousseau's contemporaries, but his reasoning is worth considering. He argues that a state with too many resources is subject to the invasion of others, who are envious or needy themselves. He stresses that he has no mathematical formula to determine the right balance of people and land – it depends on a multitude of factors, including the characteristics of the terrain, the degree of its fertility, the nature of its crops, the climate, the temperament of its citizens (e.g., how hard are they able/willing to work? And how much do they eat?), the fertility of its women, the abundance of seafood, the proximity to the ocean, the presence of rocks near the shore, and similar considerations. In short, "there are a thousand occasions when particular accidental features require or permit taking up more land than appears needed" (169 [III: 389]).

This then takes Rousseau to the discussion's denouement, where he outlines the features of a people most suited to a constitutional founding. This list of features includes (*SC*, 2.10.5, 77–8 [III: 390–1]):

a. No deeply rooted customs or superstitions.
b. No immediate fear of being overrun by neighbors. And if this danger exists, the citizens should be able to handle this threat easily.
c. Each citizen should be capable of being known to all.
d. There is no need to place impossible burdens on citizens.
e. It is self-sufficient – and at the same time not an attractive target for foreign invasions.
f. There is neither wealth[86] nor poverty – and everyone is capable of self-sufficiency within the republic.
g. It combines the stability of ancient peoples with the docility of a new one.

Rousseau concedes that this is not an easy list to satisfy – "It is true that it is difficult to find all these conditions together" (2.10.5, 78 [III: 391]). The only place, in fact, where he thinks all these *might* be found in Europe is on the small island of Corsica.[87] Rousseau would subsequently be asked to write a constitutional proposal for Corsica – in effect, they wanted him to be their lawgiver.

It is easy to see the appeal of many of his criteria. But combining all of them is, as Rousseau concedes, nearly impossible. Indeed, he subsequently asks in his discussion of democracy, "how many things difficult to combine does this Government not presuppose?" (*SC,* 3.4.5, 91 [III: 405]). If this is the case, we might very plausibly ask how practical are Rousseau's own recommendations? In one respect, they are not practical at all – especially if Corsica is the only conceivable pupil for these lessons. But it is doubtful that Rousseau meant his principles to have such narrow applications. Evidence of flexibility on these points is present throughout *Government of Poland*, a constitutional proposal for Poland he wrote in 1772, which he acknowledges has failed to meet all these criteria. Poland was neither sufficiently small – nor lacking in bordering enemies. Nevertheless, he argued that these deficits could be overcome enough to enable meaningful legislation. As regards the size problem, Rousseau advocated federalism, which shrinks the state in a real sense, while retaining large national boundaries. Second, regarding the external threats, he argues for the development of a

---

[86] John P. McCormick has argued that Rousseau maintains a distinction between classes in the *Social Contract*, and further that his institutions and processes are "biased toward the wealthiest citizens" (2007, 4). I think this interpretation assumes a greater wealth disparity than Rousseau himself is likely to endorse, given his general admonitions against wealth and poverty.

[87] The notion that once freedom has been lost it is nearly impossible to recover or re-found a republic is present in Machiavelli's *Discourses*, 1.17.

strong army to repel invaders, as well as a deep patriotism built on a genuine love of Poland, which he thought could repel Russia and Prussia. It is
certainly worth pondering these subsequent developments to see if they
adequately overcome the limitations apparent in these few chapters.

2.11. *Of the Various Systems of Legislation*

This chapter addresses two important issues: (1) the purpose of the laws,
and (2) the question of how to realize this purpose in varying contexts.
Both issues are of enormous importance to Rousseau and political theory
generally. Rousseau says that the purpose of every system of legislation
comes down to two ideas: freedom (*liberté*) and equality (*egalité*). Both
terms deserve careful examination.

Freedom is obviously of great importance to Rousseau. As Matthew
Simpson has noted, there are at least four types of freedom operating in
the *Social Contract*: (1) natural, (2) civil, (3) democratic, and (4) moral.[88]
The question is: which of these gets priority here? It appears that by liberty here he specifically means "civil" freedom. This is because Rousseau
notes, "I have already said what civil freedom is" (2.11.2, 78 [III: 391]).[89]
So Rousseau appears to place a very high priority indeed on the personal
liberty of individuals to shape their own lives, including and especially
the right to property discussed at *SC*, 1.9. Rousseau's high priority on civil
freedom is often missed by his interpreters, such as Bertrand Russell and
Isaiah Berlin,[90] who read him as largely indifferent or even hostile to civil
liberties. These interpreters fail to take into account his insistence on the
importance of those liberties and the limits of the state's ability to interfere with them, as outlined in *SC*, 2.4.

Beyond this, Rousseau links his prioritization of freedom here to the
problem of personal dependence: "any personal dependence is that much
force taken away from the State" (*SC*, 2.11.1, 78 [III: 391]). This recalls
his earlier attention to the same issue during his discussion of subjects
being "forced to be free" (*SC*, 1.7.8, 53 [III: 364]). He is concerned in both
instances with enabling citizens to lead their lives without being at the

---

[88] See Simpson 2006a generally, but especially pages 1–3 for an effective summary.

[89] He dedicates *SC*, 2.8 to discussing the importance of civil liberty, which is gained in exchange for
natural liberty in the initial social contract.

[90] Russell [1945] 1972, 694–701; Berlin 2002, 31–8, 48–9. Even a more sympathetic reader of Rousseau,
Matthew Simpson, confesses, "while Rousseau's defense of civil liberty is very strong on one side
it seems weak on the other. Its strength is that it shows how individual rights would be protected
both from outside dangers and from the members of one's own society. But, on the other hand, it
seems to offer no protection against the government itself" (Simpson 2006b, 53).

service of other particular individuals. Insofar as I depend on another citizen, my own will is weakened. Therefore – and this is the important additional point in Chapter Eleven – the state itself is weakened. It is weakened insofar as the voices contributing to the legislative process are not in fact a true representation of *all* the people. If I am fearful, for example, that my boss might fire me for voting contrary to his private interests, then I am in an important sense dependent on him. This weakens the state against the force of private wills and empowers those wills against the general will.

Having elaborated a little on freedom here, Rousseau moves quickly to equality. He divides equality into two dimensions here: wealth and power. Although he insists that there should not be absolute equality between citizens on either dimension, it is important to maintain a degree of equality in both. Regarding power, inequality should "stop short of all violence and never be exercised except by virtue of rank and laws" (*SC*, 2.11.2, 78 [III: 391]). So no private citizen should ever have the right to harm another – to do so would be to exercise an improper and unauthorized power. Violence can only be delivered legitimately by those with rank and according to the law. Namely, only a legitimate government can punish individuals for violation of the laws. All other violence is prohibited.

Regarding wealth, Rousseau insists, "no citizen [should] be so very rich that he can buy another, and none so poor that he is compelled to sell himself" (*SC*, 2.11.2, 78 [III: 391–2]). Rousseau's words here recall ancient Athens, when extreme differences in wealth resulted in parents selling themselves and their children into slavery.[91] The resulting chaos necessitated abandoning its old constitution entirely and starting over again with an appeal to their great legislator, Solon. Rousseau clearly identifies this as a growing menace in his own age, with the growth of the merchant class. But as the widening gap between rich and poor inevitably results in a concomitant gap in power, he is especially keen to keep this under control. Indeed, this must also be read in the context of his *Second Discourse*, where the wealthy establish a despotism of absolute power over the indigent. And in his *Government of Poland*, he adds that of all the selfish interests,

---

[91] According to Plutarch: "All the people were indebted to the rich; and either they tilled their land for their creditors, paying them a sixth part of the increase, and were, therefore, called Hectemorii and Thetes, or else they engaged their body for debt, and might be seized, and either sent into slavery at home, or sold to strangers; some (for no law forbade it) were forced to sell their children, or fly their country to avoid the cruelty of their creditors; but the most part and the bravest of them began to combine together and encourage one another to stand to it, to choose a leader, to liberate the condemned debtors, divide the land, and change the government" (Plutarch 2001, I: 114). It is almost certainly with this history in mind that Plato abolishes wealth and poverty from his Kallipolis (*Republic*, 421c–3c).

"the pecuniary interest is the worst of all, the vilest, the most liable to corruption."[92] It therefore represents perhaps the single greatest threat to the general will in the form of a partial interest or faction. In this context, Rousseau makes his case for economic equality: "Do you, then, want to give the State stability? bring the extremes as close together as possible; tolerate neither very rich nor beggars. These two states, which are naturally inseparable, are equally fatal to the common good; from one come the abettors of tyranny, and from the other tyrant; it is always between these two that there is trafficking in public freedom; one buys it, the other sells it" (*SC*, 2.11.2, fn, 78 [III: 392]). This is entirely consistent with his earlier position staked in the *Discourse on Political Economy*:

It is … one of the most important tasks of government to prevent extreme inequality of fortunes, not by taking treasures away from those who possess them, but by depriving everyone of the means to accumulate treasures, nor by building poorhouses, but by shielding citizens from becoming poor.[93]

Rousseau concedes that such equality is difficult to enforce in practice, but nevertheless insists, "if abuse is inevitable, does it not follow that it should not at least be regulated?" (*SC*, 2.11.3, 79 [III: 392]). He does not elaborate here on how this might occur. His *Political Economy* and *Government of Poland*, however, both suggest that much of this would be regulated through taxation. In the *Political Economy*, he stipulates that the tax system must be guided by the general will, with a particular emphasis on taxing luxuries and excess wealth. In his *Fragments* from the *Plan for a Constitution for Corsica*, he proposes an inheritance tax, which tends "to bring things back to equality so that each might have something and no one have anything in excess." Another solution suggested in the *Political Economy* is more preemptive – preventing desires for luxuries and other useless commodities for which people accumulate fortunes.[94] At any rate, it is clear enough that Rousseau is firmly committed to a large degree of economic equality – though not absolute equality – because it makes freedom possible and is consistent with the general will. So all laws must be passed with the thought of how they will protect and promote both liberty and equality.

Rousseau dedicates the remainder of Chapter Eleven to the question of how to fit legislation to particular peoples. He strongly cautions against

---

[92] *Poland*, 226 [III: 1005]. He later adds, "Nowhere will you find a great moral or political evil in which money is not involved" (*Poland*, 227 [III: 1006]).

[93] *Political Economy* (19 [III: 258].

[94] *Poland*, 231–32 [III: 1011–12]; *Political Economy*, 30–1 [III: 270–1]; *Separate Fragments* from *Corsica*, 160 [III: 945]; *Political Economy*, 27 [III: 267–8].

a one-size-fits-all solution to legislation. We cannot say for certain just how much liberty and equality are to work in all lands. There is no way to do so a priori, or independent of empirical knowledge. This is necessarily a principle that can only be spelled out on a case-by-case basis because every territory and people will differ in relevant ways. We must consider the "local conditions" and the "character of the inhabitants" (*SC*, 2.11.4, 79 [III: 392]). There are no institutions that can be guaranteed to work for all conditions. As Rousseau observes, "it is on the basis of these relations [local situations and peoples] that each people has to be assigned a particular system of institutions which is the best, not, perhaps, in itself, but for the State for which it is intended" (*SC*, 2.11.4, 79 [III: 392]). Among these conditions are the quality of the soil and the nature of the coast-lines.[95] Therefore, he concludes, "there is within each People some cause which orders these maxims in a particular manner and makes its legislation suited for itself alone" (*SC*, 2.11.4, 79 [III: 393]).

2.12. *Classification of the Laws*

Rousseau wraps up Book II with a simple classification of the laws. This includes political, civil, and criminal laws, in addition to another category he calls "morals" (*mœurs*) or "customs" (*coutumes*). Rousseau defines these different laws according to their formal relationships of one group or institution to another, in addition to their social functions. Political laws are the laws of political institutions. In other words, they are in essence constitutional laws. These concern the relationship of the sovereign to the state. Political laws set out the rights and duties of the state, as determined by the sovereign. Rousseau also calls these "fundamental laws" (*loix fondementales*) – though they only merit this additional title if they are conceived wisely, namely, they are consistent with morality and justice (*SC*, 2.12.2, 80 [III: 393]).[96] Political laws poorly conceived would not merit the title of fundamental laws. He notes that the people always have the power to change their laws, even for the worse: "for if it pleases it to harm itself, who has the right to prevent it from doing so?" (*SC*, 2.12.2, 80 [III: 384]). This is a particularly tricky passage, since Rousseau has already placed careful limits on sovereign power – especially that the sovereign can never violate the general will (*SC*, 2.4). So it seems that he is contradicting himself here. But before jumping to this conclusion, it is worth giving careful

---

[95] As Rousseau himself notes, he draws these points in large part from Montesquieu's *Spirit of the Laws*.

[96] For more on Rousseau's treatment of "fundamental law" see Schwartzberg 2003.

attention to Rousseau's choice of words. He does not say that a sovereign can harm itself. He says that a "people" (*peuple*) can choose to harm itself. The difference between a sovereign and people makes all the difference here. Rousseau states earlier, "sovereignty ... is nothing but the exercise of the general will" (*SC*, 2.1.2, 57 [III: 368]). So by definition, a people choosing to harm itself is not sovereign. It is merely a people, a conglomeration. It is the will of all, not the general will. Further, when Rousseau rhetorically asks, "who has the right to prevent it [the people] from doing so [harming themselves]?" he speaks of "right" (*droit*) in a technical sense, as well. There is a tradition in modern philosophy of associating the word right with power, stemming back to Hobbes and Spinoza.[97] In this tradition, the word right has no normative force. It is simply a force of nature. It is quite possible that Rousseau means right in this sense. It is important to recall what he says about such models of right in Book I, however: "Force is a physical power; I fail to see what morality can result from its effects" (*SC*, 1.3.1, 44 [III: 354]). On this reading, to say that the people have the "right" to harm themselves is not to say it constitutes a sovereign act or that it is in any way morally permissible in Rousseau's sense.

The second mode of law is civil law. In contemporary Anglo-American law, this refers to the class of laws that includes torts, property, wills, and contracts. What unites these categories is that civil law pits citizens against one another, as opposed to the state. Further, civil law typically does not result in prison sentences but in damages awarded to the plaintiff or offended party. Broadly speaking, these regulate citizens such that they treat one another fairly. It is partly for the benefit of these civil laws that we are "forced to be free," as Rousseau boldly asserted in Book I (*SC*, 1.7.8, 53 [III: 364]). In joining the social contract, I know I will sometimes lack sufficient willpower to do what I know is right. For example, I might sign a contract to pay for a car, knowing full well that I will not be able to make the payments. By signing the contract, I authorize the state to make and enforce civil laws that hold me to my better will – the general will. So the civil law extracts the car from my possession and returns it to the original owner, along with damages. Rousseau remarks that insofar as the laws regulate the treatment of one another, they should be minimal.[98] Citizens who genuinely embrace the general will should need relatively

---

[97] Hobbes: "every man has a right to everything, even to one another's body" ([1651] 2002, 14.4; see also 14.1); Spinoza: "it is by sovereign natural right that fish inhabit the water, and the big ones eat the smaller ones" (*Theological-Political Treatise*, 527).

[98] Plato likewise counsels keeping the number of laws to a minimum – *Republic*, 425b.

little guidance from civil laws, as their hearts or consciences should tend toward justice.

The third category consists of criminal laws, which pertains to the relationship of man and the law, according to Rousseau. Whereas the civil law regulates behavior of citizens toward other citizens, the criminal law pertains to the relationship of citizens to the state. This is why in criminal law the state is typically listed as the plaintiff. These are perhaps the most visible of all laws. They establish the definition of "crimes" and the associated penalties. Further, these penalties differ from civil penalties, which are damages awarded to a plaintiff. Penalties are paid directly to the state, either in fines, prison terms, or in extreme cases, with the defendant's life. Criminal law is typically associated with violent deeds, though this is not exclusively the criminal realm. And as is the case with the civil law, citizens agree to be forced to be free in the imposition of punishments associated with criminal acts. Individuals know when consenting to the social contract that they should not harm others. So if they end up doing so, their punishment is nothing more or less than the state forcing them to be free.

The final category here is morals, which Rousseau describes as the "most important of all" (*SC*, 2.12.5, 81 [III: 394]). The French word here is *mœurs*, which can be translated as custom or habit. This fourth type of law is not written anywhere, but rather is found "in the hearts of Citizens" (*SC*, 2.12.5, 81 [III: 394]). *Mœurs* preserve a people more than do the political, civil, and criminal laws combined. He explains that this part of the law is largely unknown to politicians, but is in fact one of the great aims to which "the great Lawgiver attends in secret" (*SC*, 2.12.5, 81 [III: 394]) by virtue of careful legislation reflecting – though not explicitly outlining – the ethos that should dominate the republic.[99] As he explains in 4.7, "A people's opinions arise from its constitution; although law does not regulate morals, legislation does give rise to them" (*SC*, 4.7.3, 141 [III: 458]). He also develops this theme in his *Government of Poland*, where he remarks, "No constitution will ever be good and solid unless the law rules the citizens' hearts. So long as the legislative force does not reach that deep, the laws will invariably be evaded."[100] Over the next several chapters of *Poland* he details how these *mœurs* are to be infused – through education, games, and economic equality. It is only then that love of fellow

---

[99] At least one scholar, Mira Morgenstern, has argued that this reveals Rousseau's "duplicity." She asks, "why is it so necessary for the Legislator to work on the establishment of *mœurs* in secret" unless it is to deceive them about the fact that the constitution lacks the divine origin to which the Lawgiver appeals (Morgenstern 1996, 33–4)?

[100] *Poland*, 179 [III: 955].

citizens can triumph over petty self-interest or private will. Rousseau also calls this "opinion" (*SC*, 2.12.5, 81 [III: 394]).[101] This is opinion in its optimal manifestation. He has already established that opinion can work against the general will insofar as "the opinion that prevails is nothing but a private opinion" (*SC*, 2.3.3, 60 [III: 372]). Public opinion can work either for or against the general will. So long as it embraces the general will, it performs an invaluable function. And if it embraces partial or particular wills, it does the opposite. So everything hinges upon having well-meaning citizens who seek the general will above all.[102] The moment they prioritize the private will at the expense of the general will, all falls apart. They will seek to get around the law any time they perceive it is in their interest to do so.[103] It is worth noting in conclusion that while Rousseau is optimistic here that public opinion can work in the service of the general will, he presents a far less sanguine approach in the *Emile*. Much of what he teaches his young pupil is aimed at freeing him from opinion: "From the bosom of so many diverse passions I see opinion raising an unshakable throne, and stupid mortals, subjected to its empire, basing their own existence on the judgments of others."[104] So Rousseau himself is of diverse opinion on the value of public opinion. Properly conceived, it is a force for great good. But ill-conceived, it is nothing short of a great menace. In either case, however, it is a great force – not to be treated lightly. This is why he will subsequently institute an office of Censor, charged with the task of maintaining public opinion (*SC*, 4.7.2–6).

---

[101] As Jürgen Habermas has noted, the first time Rousseau speaks of public opinion is in his *First Discourse*, where Rousseau speaks of the dangerous literati, who take on public opinion, in the form of religion, fraternity, and patriotism (*First Discourse*, 17–18 [III: 19]). According to Habermas, this is the first reference to public opinion in Western philosophy. See Habermas [1962] 1989, 92–3, 95–8.

[102] Rousseau emphasizes this in a footnote to his *Discourse on Inequality*: "It is up to public esteem to draw the distinction between wicked and good men; the Magistrate is judge only of rigorous right; but the people is the genuine judge of morals; a judge of integrity and enlightenment on this point, sometimes deceived but never corrupted" (*Discourse on Inequality*, 222 [III: 222–3]).

[103] This is, in Montesquieu's terms, the third phase of the Troglodyte society. It is also more or less the fundamental working assumption of most liberal theorists. We must assume the worst about human nature and work with it. Rousseau, by contrast, still holds out some hope that people can be made to see their own interests attached to that of their fellow citizens.

[104] *Emile*, 215 [494]. See also *Emile*, 39 [IV: 39], 68 [IV: 290–1], 83 [IV: 307–8], 152 [IV: 409], 168 [IV: 430], 172 [IV 444], 190 [IV: 462], 244 [IV: 536–7], 253 [549], 254 [550], 255 [551]. Obviously, the threat of opinion is a serious one throughout the *Emile*. This theme is carried over from the Preface to his first major political work, the *Discourse on the Sciences and Arts*: "I do not care whether I please Wits or the Fashionable. There will always be men destined to be subjugated by the opinions of their century, their Country, their Society.... One ought not write for such Readers when one wants to live beyond one's century" (*First Discourse*, 4 [III: 3]).

CHAPTER 3

Book III

OVERVIEW

Book III has two objects. First, Rousseau continues to counsel lawmakers on how to best devise institutions. Second, he provides specific advice on how to maintain the authority of the people in the face of encroaching governmental powers. With regard to institutional design, Rousseau sketches the three fundamental governmental – or executive – forms: democracy, aristocracy, and monarchy. He is very clear throughout Book III and the *Social Contract* generally that there is no unique and universal single best regime type: "Hence the question, which is absolutely the best Government, does not admit to a solution because it is indeterminate.... [There are] as many good solutions as there are possible combinations in the absolute and the relative positions of peoples" (*SC*, 3.9.1, 104–5 [III: 419]). Each has its own particular set of assets and drawbacks. The key is to match the people and their circumstances to the appropriate form of government.

Regardless of which set of institutions a state adopts, it will always be vulnerable to decline and decay. Not even the vaunted constitutions of Sparta and Rome, Rousseau reminds us, were eternal. Most specifically in the latter pages of Book III, he is concerned about the government – however well designed it might have been – and its potential for destroying the state from within. It is an old adage that "power corrupts," and this principle animates Rousseau's concerns here. Specifically, the government or executive branch is a constant threat to the sovereign or legislative branch. And whenever the government succeeds in thwarting the sovereign, it effectively means that a particular will is thwarting the general will. So Rousseau introduces a series of measures to inhibit this kind of encroachment and safeguard the general will against internal threats.

3.1. *Of Government in General*

Book III continues the Book II theme of providing advice to the lawgiver. What kinds of considerations should guide the aspiring lawgiver – or author of constitutions? Of particular interest in Book III, Rousseau lays out the basic principles of the main options for forms of government. He is also concerned here with the various institutional threats to the preservation of just regimes. Chapter One has two important tasks: (1) it must define government generally, and (2) it comprises Rousseau's innovative and central distinction between sovereign and government. These are the central purposes of the chapter – but there are other discussions here worthy of scholarly attention.

All states must minimally possess two powers: (1) legislative, and (2) executive. So it is with all creatures – there must be will and a power to carry out that will, just as the mind tells the body to act and the body carries out that action. Without *both* components, we are impotent, just as are our governments. The legislative power is the will of the government. It can reside *only* in the people, as embodied in the general will. In other words, all sovereignty – which is in effect the legislative power – must reside in the people, as they will what is just. No one else can exercise this power for them, as Hobbes, Burlamaqui, Grotius, Pufendorf, and others suppose.[1] While they share in common the belief that the *sovereign* should make the law, Rousseau is insistent that sovereignty remains with the people all the way through to the point of making the civil laws, whereas the rest view sovereignty as surrendered or transferred to a representative. As becomes clear in *SC*, 3.4, however, this does not necessarily mean that Rousseau is advocating *democracy*.

The other major division is the executive branch. The executive embodies the carrying out of the (general) will. The term "executive" is often synonymous with "government" in Rousseau. This is clear in his first definition of government: "An intermediate body established between the subjects and Sovereign so that they might conform to one another [*correspondence*], and charged with the execution of the laws and the maintenance of freedom, both civil and political" (*SC*, 3.1.5, 83 [III: 396]). The government stands between sovereign and subject. This should sound paradoxical since the sovereign and subject are the same people. Rousseau

---

[1] Hobbes: civil laws can be conveyed by word, writing, "or some other act known to proceed from the sovereign authority" ([1651] 2002, 26.15); Pufendorf: civil laws "are the decrees of the sovereign civil authority" ([1673] 1991], 155 [12.1]).

revels in the paradox, to be sure, but it also has genuine meaning. The executive holds the sovereign people (or, "citizens") to their (general) will. The people need this since they are incapable of doing it on their own, due to temporary weakness or epistemic failures.

Rousseau adds a second definition of government two paragraphs later: it is "the *legitimate* exercise of executive power" (*SC*, 3.1.7, 83 [III: 396]; emphasis added). This emphasis on legitimacy almost certainly means that the executive must work "in accordance with the directives of the general will" (*SC*, 3.1.4, 82 [III: 395]). He adds later in Chapter One, "the Prince's dominant will is or should be nothing by the general will" (*SC*, 3.1.19, 85 [III: 399]). That is, if the people issue laws contrary to the general will, one might imagine the executive is free not to enforce these laws. In fact, a reader might assume that the executive is obligated to ignore those commands. This is because the people are not sovereign in issuing commands serving private wills above the general will. So there is a normative dimension in the executive branch, or an element of judgment. This raises important questions about how an executive might distinguish legitimate from illegitimate laws. Unfortunately, Rousseau does not engage this important question. A related question is how to prevent the executive from abusing this power of judgment. Rousseau has more to say about this in his later political works. He will develop some checks and balances that work this out. This is particularly well-developed in Chapter 8 of his *Government of Poland*, and includes careful Senate oversight of the executive, as well as a strict prohibition against hereditary monarchs, where power might accrue over generations.

There are occasions in his writings when he uses the term "government" more broadly than he does in Book III. In his *Government of Poland*, for example, he employs in the very title the term in its broadest sense of "the state." But for the most part, when he speaks of "government" in apparently technical terms, he is speaking of the executive branch, as he is here and subsequently in the *Emile* and *Letters Written from the Mountain*.[2]

Generally speaking, this distinction between executive and legislative powers, corresponding to differences between government and sovereign, recalls Geneva's own political difficulties. As noted in the Introduction to this volume, Geneva was dominated by two fundamental political institutions: the Small and General Councils. The General Council consisted of all citizens, and it was what Rousseau himself regarded as sovereign. The Small Council, by contrast, consisted of an elite body of wealthy citizens,

---

[2] *Emile*, 463–6 [IV: 844–8]; *Mountain*, 149, 232–3 [III: 770, 808n]; see Gourevitch 1997, l.

which Rousseau regarded most appropriate when maintaining a largely executive function. As he muses in the "Epistle Dedicatory" of his *Second Discourse*, "I should have sought out a Country where the right of legislation was common to all Citizens," but at the same time, "I should ... have fled as necessarily ill-governed a Republic where the People, believing it could do without its Magistrates or leave them no more than a precarious authority, had imprudently retained in its own hands the administration of Civil affairs."[3] The problem in the early eighteenth century was that these distinct roles had been largely ignored in Genevan practice. The General Council met infrequently and with too little authority; the Small Council, or the Government, largely controlled both legislative and executive functions. So these problems were all too real for Rousseau.

There can be no question that Rousseau's distinction here between sovereign and government was read by the Genevan authorities as a critique of their practices. In 1763, Jean-Robert Tronchin, a Genevan magistrate, attacked the *Social Contract*'s distinction between these two powers and defended the authority of the Small Council in a pamphlet entitled *Letters Written from the Country*. Rousseau shortly thereafter defended this distinction in his *Letters Written from the Mountain*, where he reaffirmed his principle of separating powers. Geneva's obvious problem, for Rousseau, was that "the Legislative power and the executive power ... are not distinct." Indeed, one of the primary functions of the sovereign should be to "have inspection over the executive power." But no such thing was happening in practice. While the Genevan constitution was designed to prevent this sort of failure, Rousseau argues, "nothing is more servile than your actual state."[4] The resulting controversy from these allegations, combined with his thoughts on Civil Religion in Book 4, were serious enough that Rousseau would have to flee his native land for England, never to return.

Rousseau's definitions of executive and legislative powers also suggest a separation of powers in Rousseau's system, contrary to what some scholars have suggested. The argument, advanced by Lester Crocker and Jacob Talmon, takes roughly the following syllogistic form:

(1) Rousseau argues that sovereignty is indivisible (*SC*, 57–8 [III: 368–69]).
(2) He also insists that sovereignty is absolute (*SC*, 63 [III: 375]).
(3) The separation of powers constitutes a division of sovereignty.
(4) Therefore, Rousseau must condemn the separation of powers.

---

[3] *Second Discourse*, 136–7 [III: 114].
[4] *Mountain*, 238 [III: 815], 247 [III: 826], and 237 [III: 814].

While the argument itself is valid, it is unsound since one of its premises represents a fundamental misunderstanding of Rousseau's notion of sovereignty. Premise (3) conflates two distinct concepts in the Rousseau lexicon: sovereign and government. The "sovereign" for Rousseau is the united people acting in their public capacity. This definition resembles that suggested in the essays written to advocate the U.S. Constitution's ratification, the Federalist ("the people are the only legitimate fountain of power").[5] Rousseau's critics are right to suggest that this sovereignty cannot be divided. The sovereign, however, must be distinguished from the government. "Government" for Rousseau is "[a]n intermediate body established between subjects and Sovereign so that they might conform to one another, and charged with the execution of the laws and the maintenance of freedom, both civil and political." The fact that he meant for government and sovereign to be distinct is evident in the very definition of this term – that it lies between subjects and sovereign. This distinction is important because it allows Rousseau to separate the powers of the government, not that of the sovereign. This is all that any system of checks and balances does. The Federalists, for example, do not argue for a division of the sovereign people. They argue, rather, for the separation of the branches the sovereign appoints. When Crocker and Talmon make their charges that Rousseau fails to provide the fundamental safeguard against tyranny – checks and balances between separate branches of government – they fail to understand that sovereignty and government are for him two distinct things.

That Rousseau's critics misunderstand his terms is clear in the types of evidence offered for support. Neither Talmon nor Crocker provides any passages from Rousseau that suggest antipathy toward checks and balances. Rather, they seek to associate Rousseau with others who have condemned such measures. Crocker moves from Rousseau's idea of absolute sovereignty to Robespierre's condemnation of the separation of powers within a matter of a few sentences. Likewise, Talmon offers no text of Rousseau's to support his insinuations, but rather relies on an unsubstantiated association with the Physiocrats. After discussing Rousseau's notion of sovereignty, he moves to the Physiocrats, for whom "Parliamentary institutions, the separation and balance of powers, were … impossible as roads to social harmony."[6] He continues afterward to note that they refused to admit to the possibility that the government might abuse its

---

[5] James Madison, Federalist No. 49, 310.
[6] Crocker 1968, 120; Talmon 1955, 45.

power. This may well be true of the Physiocrats; however, it has nothing to do with Rousseau. This is the elementary fallacy of guilt by association. The simple fact is that Rousseau expressly separates the legislative and executive functions: "If the Sovereign [legislature] wants to govern, or the magistrate [executive] wants to give laws ... force and will no longer act in concert, and the dissolved State thus falls into despotism or anarchy" (*SC*, 3.1.9, 83 [III: 397]).

The remaining paragraphs in Chapter One offer specific advice to the lawgiver pertaining to the balance of size of state, on the one hand, and degree of civil liberty, on the other. This is a relevant question in the context of establishing the constitutional authority of the executive or government. His general guidelines governing this matter are especially worth emphasizing: "there is no unique and absolute constitution of Government but ... there may be as many Governments differing in nature as there are States differing in size" (*SC*, 3.1.15, 85 [III: 398]). That is to say, Rousseau rejects the one-size-fits-all solution to government and institutions that some might endorse. One cannot say, for example, that democracy is always the best form of government. Nor can one say the same of aristocracy, monarchy, or any other imaginable form. It depends largely on the context (including, with special emphasis in Chapter One, size).[7]

Some scholars, such as Jonathan Israel, have taken such passages as evidence that Rousseau abandons an "absolute ethics ... the same for all men." According to Israel, Rousseau's "*volonté générale* embodies rather the specific identity of a given body politic that is not, or not so directly, based on any universal ethics." He instead points to what he calls the tradition of "radical enlightenment," embodied in Rousseau's nemeses, such as Baron d'Holbach, as well as eighteenth-century Dutch democrats, who were more committed to a "universal system of rights and egalitarian values."[8]

This reading, however, is insufficiently attentive to the nuances of Rousseau's moral and political ontology. Although Rousseau concedes that different societies demand different sets of laws and institutions, this does not render him a moral or political relativist. To the contrary, he emphatically insists that there is "no more than one good government possible in any one State" (*SC*, 3.1.9, 83 [III: 397]). So there is always a best – and even a singular *right* – answer to the question of what is best

---

[7] See Dent 1988, 213, and Williams 2007a, 114–22.

[8] Israel 2011, 640; Israel 2010, 67. See also Israel 2010, 155–9 for the claim that Rousseau rejects moral and political universals.

in each situation facing a people; but this answer varies according to each set of circumstances. This abstract point of metaphysics applied to politics might be rendered clearer via an analogy. For this purpose, I adapt an example from Stanley Fish.[9] A "good shot" on a basketball court varies according to circumstances. Under "normal" conditions, it is best to shoot from close range without any obstructions. But conditions change all the time. Perhaps the shot clock is about to expire. Perhaps the shooter has been cold all night. Perhaps the game is on the line with two seconds left. Perhaps someone else is open for an even better shot. Perhaps the ball handler is covered – but by someone considerably shorter. Myriad circumstances conspire to dictate whether the shot might be prudent. So although the goal of winning the game always remains the same, there is no precise formula for victory. Circumstances emerge that will change the formula for each game and even each shot. Knowing that one should win the game or make the shot does not tell us precisely *how* to win the game or make the shot. Understanding those conditions and the rules that govern the typical unfolding of those conditions, however, greatly enhances the likelihood of achieving the ultimate aim of winning the game.

Such reflections apply to the practice of institutional choices or regime design, as practiced by Rousseau in the *Social Contract*. As circumstances differ from one culture to another, there can be no single determinate set of principles applying to all. Any set of prescriptions must necessarily take into account the peculiar circumstances of that political moment – such as topography, proximity to other societies, history, religion, economic circumstances, and the character of its people. But nevertheless there are measures by which one can judge institutions better or worse. This standard is inevitably the ideas of justice and the good Rousseau references in *SC*, 2.6 and also in the *Emile*[10] – and the same standards informing the general will.[11]

The particular balancing act Rousseau addresses in Chapter One involves the matters of state size, civil liberty, and authority. The larger a state is, the more authority is required to govern, and the less democratic and civil freedom[12] can be granted. As he says, "the more the State

---

[9] Fish 1989, 123–9.

[10] As the Savoyard Vicar insists in the *Emile*, "Justice is inseparable from goodness.… [F]or the love of order which produces order is called *goodness*; and the love of order which preserves it is called *justice*" (*Emile*, 282 [IV: 588–9]). Since the Lawgiver is charged with establishing order, he is presumably motivated by a love of order, or "goodness." Insofar as he designs these institutions such that order will be maintained suggests "justice."

[11] See the earlier discussion of *SC*, 2.4 in the previous chapter.

[12] Matthew Simpson defines *democratic freedom* in Rousseau as "the collective power of the people to rule themselves" (Simpson 2006a, 2). This is the ability of the citizens to make their own laws.

expands, the more freedom is diminished" (*SC*, 3.1.11, 84 [III: 397]).[13] Political freedom is lost via simple math. Assuming all influence to be equal, which Rousseau elsewhere acknowledges to be a dubious proposition, in a community of a hundred citizens, each citizen has 1 percent influence over the legislative process. In a community of 100,000 citizens, each has 0.001 percent influence. In a community of 100,000,000 citizens, each has 0.000001 percent influence. So as the state grows, each citizen possesses less democratic liberty.

Rousseau also suggests, however, that each citizen also sacrifices civil liberty as the size of the state grows. As its size increases, it requires more "repressive force" (*SC*, 3.1.13, 84 [III: 397]) to govern the subjects.[14] It is easier, for example, to guide people in a small state with suggestions and *mœurs* (*SC*, 2.12.5). But as a state grows, the force of such measures fades. This is one common account for why crime rates are higher in cities – because of the failure of this more moderate form of civil control. So as the state grows, these moderate measures are replaced by laws, which increase in severity with the growth of population. These laws come at the expense of civil liberty. Rousseau warns, however, that there is a genuine limit to how severe these laws might become, since with an increase in state power comes "more temptations and more means to misuse their power" (*SC*, 3.1.14, 84 [III: 398]). So there is some kind of absolute limit on the size of states, where the government's temptation to abuse power becomes irresistible, although he does not provide any numeric threshold for discovering that point. It seems that individuals will have to identify that threshold as it emerges in the course of practice and then adjust accordingly. This adjustment, Rousseau suggests, can be radical. Indeed, if the executive attempts to impose a private will against the general will of the people, "the social union would instantly vanish, and the body politic [would] be dissolved" (*SC*, 3.1.19, 86 [III: 399]). The rule of the strongest would replace the general will.

3.2. *Of the Principle that Constitutes the Various Forms of Government*

In Chapter Two, Rousseau lays out some general principles of government efficiency. The main question concerns the relationship between form of

---

Simpson defines *civil freedom* as "the opportunity for citizens to create lives of their own choosing without coercion by the state or other individuals" (Simpson 2006b, 1). These are the normal liberal freedoms, such as freedom of speech, religion, property, and the like.

[13] Given that securing liberty is one of the great ends of politics for Rousseau (*SC*, 2.11.1), it is clear from these arguments that he prefers smaller states.

[14] Rousseau likely draws this point from Montesquieu's *Spirit of the Laws*, 9.9.

government and executive efficiency. The general answer is: "the more numerous the Magistrates, the weaker the Government" (3.2.4, 87 [III: 400]). In order to understand the logic of efficiency, Rousseau explains that governments frequently operate with as many as three wills. These are the individual will, the corporate will, and the general will.

The individual will pertains only to the single individual person's advantage and not necessarily anyone else. It is not even a faction in the sense that this preference is shared with no one. It is a partial will of one. The corporate will is shared with others with like interests – namely, other magistrates. This is a faction within the government. The final will is the sovereign or general will. Rousseau has addressed this in some detail in earlier passages. Succinctly stated, the general will is the will citizens share in common with all other citizens (*SC*, 3.2.5, 87 [III: 400–1]).

Every magistrate or government official possesses in varying degrees all three of these wills. Yet they pull on magistrates with different degrees of force. The will with the strongest natural force is the *individual will*. Government officials are inevitably tempted to ask how each law and government action affects themselves. The second strongest is the *corporate will*, where magistrates ask how these laws and deeds affect the stability and interests of their institutions. The weakest voice, as Rousseau emphasizes, is the *general will* (*SC*, 3.2.7, 87 [III: 401]). This ordering is precisely the opposite of what would be the case in "perfect legislation" (*SC*, 3.2.7, 87 [III: 401]), where the general will would rule over and dominate the other wills. This is one of the most basic problems of governance – that the inclinations of government are fundamentally opposed to its ends. Rousseau does not answer in Chapter Two how he might solve or at least ameliorate the problem.

He next explores how the size of government influences its activity or relative energy level. Following widely shared conventions of his time, Rousseau posits that small governments are especially adapted to making quick and decisive actions. Indeed, the most active government is "that of a single man" (*SC*, 3.2.8, 88 [III: 401]), or a monarchy. The least active, by contrast, would be a democracy, in which the people enforce their own laws: "it is certain that business gets dispatched less expeditiously in proportion as more people are in charge of it" (*SC*, 3.2.10, 88 [III: 402]).

He concludes this chapter, however, by noting that efficiency is very different from uprightness (*rectitude*) (*SC*, 3.2.13, 89 [III: 402]). And in this case, again, the reality represents precisely the opposite from the morally optimal. Although a single ruler is most efficient, it also embodies the greatest concentration of a private will in its actions. So a single ruler is the most likely to deviate from the general will. The opposite is the case with the sluggish democracy. Although it is slow to move, it is more likely to embody the general will by taking in all of the people.[15]

3.3. *Classification of Governments*

Chapter Three is perhaps the simplest and most straightforward in all of Book III. It is fundamentally a primer for Chapters Four through Seven. His primary task is to outline the basic institutional options for the law-giver. Governments are of three basic varieties: democracy, aristocracy, and monarchy. These distinctions go back as far as Aristotle's *Politics*. Although Rousseau might have most immediately derived these categories from Montesquieu's *Spirit of the Laws*, they were broadly accepted as the alternatives in his milieu. It is worth emphasizing here that Rousseau departs from Montesquieu's addition of a fourth category: Despotism. Montesquieu's careful attention to the operations of a Despotism is particularly frustrating for Rousseau, insofar as Montesquieu was "content to discussion the positive right" of such Governments without sufficient attention to their moral character.[16] In this way, Montesquieu does not differ from Hobbes or Grotius, the targets of Rousseau's critique of amoral politics in *SC*, 1.2.4–5, 1.3, and 1.4.

It is important before pressing forward to recall that "government" has a particular meaning in Rousseau's lexicon. A government is the executive branch.[17] The legislature is not technically part of the government. It stands outside and above the government as sovereign. In this context, Rousseau defines the forms of government. Democracies are those in which the "Sovereign … entrust[s] the charge of government to the whole people or to the majority of the people" (*SC*, 3.3.2, 89 [III: 403]). As will become evident in Chapter 4, this is not precisely what is commonly meant in the twenty-first century as a democracy. Aristocracies "restrict the government into the hands of a small number" (*SC*, 3.3.3, 89 [III: 403]). Finally, monarchies concentrate all the powers of government in a single magistrate. He also calls this "royal Government" (*SC*, 3.3.4, 89 [III: 403]).

Rousseau concedes that these definitions are somewhat indeterminate. A democracy can consist of anywhere from half the citizenry to all. An aristocracy can consist of anywhere from a handful of citizens to half of them. And even a monarchy can range from a single individual to a

---

[15] This does not necessarily guarantee that a democracy would embody the general will. It could exude the will of all instead. See *SC*, 2.3.2, 60 [III: 371].

[16] *Emile*, 458 [IV: 836].

[17] See *SC*, 3.1.5, 83 [III: 396].

handful. He also importantly notes that a government can successfully mix these forms, as was the practice in the Roman Republic.[18]

Finally, it is worth commenting that Rousseau repeats his view from Chapter One that there is no one set form of government valid for all times, places, and contexts.[19] "There has always been much argument about the best form of Government, without considering that each one of them is the best in some cases, and worst in others" (*SC*, 3.3.7, 90 [III: 403]). This reestablishes his view that although there is no one form of government valid for all contexts, there is *always a right and wrong answer* to the question of what is the best in a particular circumstance. So Rousseau is no relativist in the classic sense of saying that political norms are and should be completely relative and free from appeals to a higher norm or standard. There is a "best form of government" in every instance. The answer to the question of what is the best in each case, however, can only be determined by careful investigation of its circumstances. This is why, for example, Rousseau opens his *Government of Poland* by announcing, "Unless one [a Lawgiver] knows the Nation for which one is working thoroughly, one's labor on its behalf, regardless of how excellent it may be in itself, will invariably fall short in application."[20] One can only arrive at the idiosyncratic best solution for each Nation with careful investigation of its culture, economics, climate, geography, topography, history, customs, religion, and other factors. It should never be, to Rousseau's mind, a matter of pure or a priori philosophy.

3.4. *Of Democracy*

Although Rousseau is theoretically open to all forms of government, according to circumstances, he finds each form to have its own peculiar strengths and weaknesses. In this context, his mere page and a half on democracy is dense and fascinating. This is in large part because readers have every reason to believe he will be an enthusiastic supporter of democratic rule. After all, he is as decisive an advocate of popular sovereignty as the world has ever seen. But this turns out not to be the case. In fact, he is strongly opposed to democracy, at least for anything approaching the European states as he knew them. As he has established, sovereignty and government are quite distinct. Sovereignty or the general will is the people

---

[18] See Cicero's *On the Commonwealth*, 1.43–5.
[19] See *SC*, 3.1.15, 85 [III: 398].
[20] *Poland*, 177 [III: 953].

legislating for justice and the common good. Government or the executive carries out those laws. It is worth a careful exploration of the reasons why he thinks democracy is a poor form of government. He offers at least three difficulties associated with democratic governance.[21]

The first problem associated with democracy is the absence of separation of powers (*SC*, 3.4.1, 90 [III: 404]). The legislature and executive are in the same hands.[22] There is no distinction in this case between sovereign and government. As such, there really is no government at all. So there is nothing in place to hold the citizens true to the general will, presumably. It more closely resembles anarchy than governance. It is important to recall, Rousseau does *not* have in mind the representative democracy of the United States, which of course did not exist at the time.

A second danger associated with democracy is letting the legislature enforce the laws insofar as it enhances the opportunities of the private will gaining authority. Private wills go directly from the legislation to action without buffers or checks. As Rousseau emphasizes here, "Nothing is more dangerous than the influence of private interests on public affairs, and the abuse of the laws by the government is a lesser evil than the corruption of the Lawgiver, which is the inevitable consequence of particular considerations" (*SC*, 3.4.1, 90 [III: 404]). The great danger here is that the people could legislate not for the general will, but for the will of all as prejudiced against segments of the community. Without a government to check this possibility, the people have no obstacles against this possibility, which Rousseau takes for an almost inevitable certainty.

A third problem burdening democracy as Rousseau defines it in the *Social Contract* is the practical difficulty of assembling all the people to carry out the administrative work of governance. He adds that, even if they could, they could not establish commissions to carry out the laws without effectively changing the mode of government. So in the strict sense,

---

[21] Following James Miller, I note here that Rousseau employs two conceptions of democracy in his works, pertaining respectively to the executive and legislative functions. The definition operating in the *Social Contract* is the traditional definition of governance by the people. That is, the people are the executives, carrying out the laws. Yet in other works, Rousseau employs "democracy" more loosely and innovatively to suggest what is certainly implicit in the *Social Contract* – namely, popular sovereignty. This occurs, for example, in his *Letters Written from the Mountain*, where he describes a "democracy" as a place "where the People is Sovereign" (*Mountain*, 240 [III: 816]). See Miller (1984, 105–22) for a thorough discussion of this distinction and how it plays out in Rousseau's political works.

[22] To be sure, this fear has already been expressed in Montesquieu. The combination of the various powers of government in one set of hands leads to the fear that "the same monarch or senate that makes tyrannical laws will execute them tyrannically" (*Spirit of the Laws*, 157 [11.6]). This is quoted in Federalist No. 47 by James Madison (Madison [1787–88] 1999, 270).

Rousseau suggests, democracy is simply impossible. Indeed, Rousseau goes so far as to conclude, "If there were a people of Gods, they would govern themselves democratically. So perfect a Government is not suited to men" (*SC*, 3.4.8, 92 [III: 406]).[23]

In spite of the apparently strong conclusion against the possibility of democracy, Rousseau nevertheless spells out the conditions in which a democracy might thrive. First, it would have to be a small state, where the people could easily assemble to carry out the tasks of governance. He adds an important related point here, as well. Its small size would also facilitate conditions where "every citizen can easily know all the rest" (*SC*, 3.4.5, 91 [III: 405]). This is a commonly repeated theme in Rousseau's works. Although all territories have a theoretical best government to suit its circumstances, the best state absolutely would be a small state – largely for the reason he suggests here. Small states facilitate the kind of familiarity between citizens that engenders the general will. Citizens take the interests of others more into account when they actually *know* one another. It is one thing for someone to play loud music at night when he does not know his neighbors. It is quite another – and, I suspect, rarer thing – to do so when he knows them. Knowing them could involve knowing they have young children who go to bed early, they have teenagers with big exams that week, they have jobs for which they have to wake early, they don't like loud music, and so on. And it further means citizens identify with their interests. They genuinely want their neighbors to do well. The smaller the state, the more everyone shares these interests with all citizens. Also, in a small state, all citizens are under the watch of others. As Rousseau writes in his "Letter to d'Alembert," in small cities, citizens are "always in public eye, are born censors of one another and where the police can easily watch everyone."[24] Finally, a small city's lack of cosmopolitanism tends more to the cultivation of virtue, insofar as it is primarily a flaw of large cities and states that citizens are consumed by the need to impress others. This is one of the great themes of his *First Discourse*, also elaborated in his "Letter to d'Alembert." Insofar as citizens are animated by *amour propre*, they are distracted from the needs and interests of their fellow citizens and hence the general will. So small states will for all these reasons almost always be better than large ones – and this goes doubly for democracies.

[23] Despite the apparently blanket statement here that democracy cannot be found anywhere, he subsequently claims in his *Plan for a Constitution for Corsica* that democracy exists in the poorest Swiss cantons (*Corsica*, 127–8 [III: 906]). He also advocates democracy there for Corsica with the caveat that there would be regional assemblies, as opposed to one grand national assembly, which appears to be a concession to practical circumstances.

[24] "Letter to d'Alembert," 61 [V: 54].

A second requirement for democracies is that they retain a "great simplicity of morals to preclude excessive business and thorny discussions" (*SC*, 3.4.5, 91 [III: 405]). This is closely related to the point just made. The larger a state is, the more complex are the perceived interests and needs of the citizens. As the interests and needs grow, so also grows the potential conflict between citizens. Consider, for example, the simple needs of Rousseau's residents of the state of nature, as articulated in Part I of the *Second Discourse*. Their only needs are food, water, shelter, and sex. As long as there are ample resources for everyone, there is no conflict. But as these individuals join civil society, their needs diversify and multiply. In particular, the need for status and superiority becomes especially pressing. But because something like status only exists as a zero-sum commodity (the increased status of one person necessarily implies the lowered status of others), there will be competition and strife. So it is especially important to limit the desires and needs of citizens as much as possible, if one is to approach democratic government earnestly. It should be added, however, that Rousseau repeats this point in *SC*, 4.1.1, 121 [III: 437], hence suggesting this point has broader applications beyond the context of democratic governments. Indeed, all governments benefit from this "simplicity of morals," as Rousseau calls it here.

A third prerequisite for democracy is "equality of ranks and fortunes" (*SC*, 3.4.5, 91 [III: 405]). Vast inequalities in wealth and rank pose big problems, according to Rousseau. Recall his words in the *Second Discourse*: "The rich, for their part, had scarcely become acquainted with the pleasure of dominating than they disdained all other pleasures, and using their old Slaves to subject new ones, they thought only of subjugating and enslaving of their neighbors; like those ravenous wolves which once they have tasted human flesh scorn all other food, and from then on want to devour only men."[25] Obviously, such behavior is inconsistent with democracy and the general will. As Rousseau emphasizes here in Chapter Four, legal equality is a farce without economic equality. And without legal equality, authority becomes despotism. So vast fortunes have no place in a democracy.

The final prerequisite for democracy is the near absence of luxury.[26] For Rousseau, "it corrupts the rich and the poor alike, the one by possession,

---

[25] *Second Discourse*, 171 [III: 175–6]. Rousseau also discusses economic equality at *SC*, 1.9.8.fn, 56 [III: 367]; *SC*, 2.4.8, 63 [III: 374]; *SC*, 2.11.2, 78 [III: 391–2]; *Political Economy*, 19 [III: 258–9].

[26] It is quite possible that Rousseau borrowed this assumption from Montesquieu, who wrote, "The misfortune of a republic is to be without intrigues, and this happens when the people have been corrupted by silver; they become cool, they grow fond of silver, and they are no longer fond of public affairs; without concern for the government or for what is proposed there, they quietly await their payments" (*Spirit of the Laws*, 1.2.2).

the other by covetousness; it sells out the fatherland to laxity, to vanity; it deprives the state of all its citizens by making them slaves to one another, and all of them slaves to opinion" (*SC*, 3.4.5, 91 [III: 405]).[27] This is conceptually a mouthful, as Rousseau here quickly restates his key arguments from his *First Discourse*, where he declares, "luxury is diametrically opposed to good morals."[28] Luxury tends to emerge in larger societies with larger economies. As societies grow in size, they produce more money. More money produces more free time or luxury. And in this free time, citizens turn their thoughts away from goodness and simple virtue and more to trivial or insipid pursuits, such as the arts and sciences. This is not to say that Rousseau condemns the value of art and science altogether. It is appropriate that the most talented pursue these endeavors. But something has gone horribly awry when a virtuous farmer feels he must write beautiful verse in order to be valued as a human being. In fact, these pursuits, possible only with sufficient luxury, distract citizens from virtue. In luxurious societies, virtue is no longer praised; only money and intellectual and artistic accomplishments are. So the rise in luxury eviscerates the virtue democratic societies require. No democracy, on Rousseau's account, can survive it. In this spirit, it is unsurprising that he is quick to tax luxury items in his *Discourse on Political Economy* and in his *Government of Poland*.[29] His discussion in *Poland* is particularly innovative. He argues that it is difficult to eliminate luxury once it arises in society. But one can change the objects of veneration over time with education, replacing meaningless commodities, for example, with strength of character.

3.5. Of Aristocracy

Rousseau once wrote in a letter that the *Social Contract* boils down to two principles: (1) sovereignty belongs in the hands of the people, and (2) aristocracy is the best form of government.[30] The first principle is elucidated in Book II. The second principle is treated here. So we can assume that, although this chapter is brief, it is of high importance. Rousseau's discussion of aristocracy – broadly defined as the rule of the few – first

---

[27] Rousseau variously makes positive (e.g., *SC*, 2.12.5 and 4.7.2–6) and negative (here and also *SC*, 2.3.3) statements pertaining to public opinion. The rule of thumb is that opinion is good insofar as it corresponds to justice and the general will; it is bad insofar as it favors private wills.

[28] *First Discourse*, 18 [III: 19].

[29] *Political Economy*, 35–6 [III: 276–7]; *Government of Poland*, 188–9 [III: 964–6].

[30] Jean-Jacques Rousseau, "Letter to Isaac-Ami Marcet de Mézières, July 23, 1762," cited in Bertram 2004, 97, 159.

addresses its history, its varieties, and the circumstances that contribute to its success.

According to Rousseau, aristocracy can be traced to the very first civilizations. This immediately recalls *SC*, 1.2, "Of the First Societies," in which he traces the earliest modes of political authority to the family. Fathers rule their children and are guided by their natural love for them (*SC*, 1.2.3, 42 [III: 352]). So their intentions are virtually universally upright. He notes here in Chapter Five that authority was based largely on age (hence names like *elders*, *senate*, and *gerontes*), and that citizens respected this authority. Yet, as all things do, this system eventually declined. Rule was no longer determined by age and was now determined by election. The problem is that those elected were largely the rich and powerful. And once they had attained positions of political power, they converted the government into the hereditary aristocracy that had been dominating Europe for centuries leading up to and including Rousseau's own generation. This is his brief speculative political history of the world.

This history also introduces the three varieties of aristocracy: natural, elective, and hereditary. These three forms of aristocracy share some common virtues. Unlike democracies, aristocratic assemblies are relatively easily convened, public business is subjected to more orderly and effective discussion, and they operate more efficiently. He adds that this institutional structure offers a benefit in foreign affairs: its members are received with far greater respect by other states, as compared with an "unknown and despised multitude" (*SC*, 3.5.6, 93 [III: 407]).

Despite these common virtues, there is a vast difference between the varieties of aristocracy in operating principles and prospects for a just society. Rousseau adds very little here to his discussion of natural aristocracy other than that it is really best suited for "simple peoples" (*SC*, 3.5.4, 93 [III: 406]). But as has already been suggested, natural aristocracy is the first mode of government to emerge in civil society, and it is not sustained too terribly long when that society begins to grow. Importantly, however, he describes the Native American communities of his own day as operating along the lines of a natural aristocracy; and he adds that under this institutional structure, "they are very well governed" (*SC*, 3.5.2, 92 [III: 406]). From the pattern of his discussion, however, he is pessimistic that it can be sustained in any larger communities or ones as developed as were to be found in Europe.

Hereditary aristocracies, in which political authority is passed down along family lines, are the "worst of all Governments" (*SC*, 3.5.4, 93 [III: 406]). He does not elaborate here on why this might be the case. But his Genevan predecessor, Jean-Jacques Burlamaqui, found that an heredi-tary aristocracy "inspires the nobility with pride, and entertains, between the grandees and the people, division, contempt, and jealousy, which are productive of considerable evils."[31] This division of people speaks to pre-cisely the kind of factionalization that Rousseau repeatedly identifies as subversive of the general will. Indeed, Rousseau can be found echoing this evaluation in his *Government of Poland*, when he praises the old Polish constitution for its rejection of this hereditary principle. Since power was "not perpetuated in the same families … [the constitution] did not con-centrate absolute force in them; and even when usurped, always returned to its source [the sovereign people]."[32] Readers should note, of course, that this "worst" form of government was also prominent in Rousseau's time. His critique of hereditary aristocracy is certainly a critique of contempo-rary governance.[33]

Finally, Rousseau turns to elective aristocracy, which he deems "the best" (*SC*, 3.5.4, 93 [III: 406]). Calling any mode of government "the best" in apparently absolute terms is a peculiar move for Rousseau in light of his earlier proclamation – just two chapters ago – that "There has always been much argument about the best form of Government, without considering that each one of them is the best in some cases, and the worst in others" (*SC*, 3.3.7, 90 [III: 403]). This could be read as a simple contradiction. Or it could be read as the "best" version of aristocracy. Or it could be the best for the European states Rousseau knew well. Or it could be the best in another absolute sense – that is where all circumstances are optimal.

At any rate, by "elective aristocracy" he clearly envisions a government not where its magistrates are chosen because they are rich and powerful, but where they are selected because of their "probity, enlightenment [*lum-ieres*], [and] experience" (*SC*, 3.5.5, 93 [III: 407]). In the best of all possible elective aristocracies, the people select the wise and virtuous to govern them[34] – contingent on them doing so in the interest of the people [the general will] and not their own personal wills. He concedes, however, that even the best governments eventually decline from such fidelity to the

---

[31] Burlamaqui [1747] 2006, 347 [2.2.40].
[32] *Poland*, 198 [III: 976].
[33] As Helena Rosenblatt observes, in 1750 the old families of Geneva consciously lobbied to establish a hereditary aristocracy in Rousseau's beloved hometown, a fact that undeniably disturbed him. See Rosenblatt 1997, 152–8.
[34] Rousseau's references in Chapter Five to various claims to rule – parentage, age, wisdom, virtue, power, money – recall Plato's "seven titles to rule," as outlined by his Athenian Stranger in the *Laws*, 690a–c. The Stranger concludes that the greatest of these titles is that the wise rule the ignorant. Plato's Stranger concludes that the greatest of the titles to rule is that the wise rule the ignorant (*Laws*, 690b).

general will and slowly and ultimately replace the general will with a corporate or private will.[35]

This decline can be delayed by protecting the circumstances that best
support aristocracy, as Rousseau understands them. Aristocratic governments should be larger than the small states optimal for democracy, but
not so large that the magistrates would exercise independent legislative
judgment, since this fuels their private wills at the expense of the general
will. Further, aristocracies can and should tolerate a bit less equality than
what democracies require. He writes, there should be "moderation among
the rich and contentment among the poor; for it seems that a rigorous
equality would be out of place in aristocracy; it was not even observed
in Sparta" (*SC*, 3.5.9, 94 [III: 407]).[36] So he seems to tolerate inequality
provided the rich maintain a sense of moderation and the poor have what
they need and are satisfied with their allotment.

Rousseau elaborates that this inequality is required to provide magistrates with the time they need to devote to public business. Presumably,
if the magistrates are so poor that they are distracted from public business
in order to support themselves, they will be unable to attend to the public
good. So society must tolerate a degree of inequality in order to facilitate
magistrates tending to the general will.

This immediately raises questions of how Rousseau reconciles this toleration of inequality with his often-repeated condemnations of inequality – both in the *Social Contract* and in his other political works. Namely,
how are these apparent contradictions to be reconciled? It is easy enough
to reconcile Chapter Five's tolerance of inequality with Chapter Four's
intolerance insofar as Rousseau is entertaining two very different forms of
government. But there are many other suggestions throughout the *Social
Contract* and his other works that similarly emphasize the importance of
economic equality.[37]

In this context it is worth considering Rousseau's thoughts on wealth,
on which his conception of elective aristocracy at least partly relies, especially since at least one prominent scholar has argued that Rousseau's entire

---

[35] See *SC*, 3.10–11. As Rousseau writes in his *Reveries of the Solitary Walker*, "Everything is in continual
flux on earth. Nothing on it retains a constant and static form" (*Reveries*, 68 [I: 1046]). This echoes
Plato's similar sentiments in the *Republic* that all forms of government, even the best, are ultimately
doomed to decay (*Republic*, 485b).

[36] This apparently confirms his earlier remark in the "Letter to d'Alembert" that a degree of inequality "can have its advantages" (*d'Alembert*, 115 [V: 105]). He quickly follows this statement, however,
with the qualification that such inequalities ought to have limits since they threaten to corrupt
souls and destabilize states of all kinds.

[37] *SC*, 1.9.8, 56 [III: 367], *SC*, 2.3.4, 60 [III: 372], *SC*, 2.11.2n, 78n [III: 392n].

republic stands on this premise of economic inequality.[38] Rousseau's most extensive treatment of wealth comes in his unpublished fragments "On Wealth and Taste," This essay was at least partly conceived as a reply to someone who has expressed a desire to become wealthy so that he might serve others and promote justice. Rousseau identifies his correspondent as "my dear Chrysophile [*gold lover*]," and explains that any acquisition of wealth can only come at the expense of the impoverishment of others. He might well have recalled in writing this how the Genevan elite of the early eighteenth century had successfully lobbied to eliminate trade restrictions in a way that ultimately reduced the wages of most working Genevans. To acquire wealth only so that one might do good for others, he reasons, is akin to a "charitable man" who "would begin by despoiling all of his neighbors in order to have the pleasure afterward of giving them alms." A person announcing such an ambition must be dismissed either as a "dupe or a hypocrite." If one acquires some money through honest work, it is best to distribute it immediately and then pursue good works with one's hands. He adds, the moments between the acquisition of wealth and its distribution is fraught with dangerous temptations that threaten virtue. For Rousseau, wealth is perhaps the greatest threat to virtue. It is easier, he reasons, to be good when poor. There are relatively few temptations to lead one astray. But wealth provides an abundance of opportunities. Along these lines, wealth simply perverts one's character, according to Rousseau. Although his observations here are based on casual empiricism and broad philosophizing, his arguments have recently been confirmed by studies in contemporary psychology. Greater wealth has indeed been demonstrated to contribute to increased likelihood of dangerous traffic violations, cheating in games, taking valued goods from others (including from children), lying in negotiations, and endorsing unethical behavior in the workplace. Further, argues Rousseau, financial abundance slowly erodes personal happiness: "Cruel anxieties will come to afflict your soul in the bosom of voluptuous pleasures. In your most tumultuous feasts a thousand bitter memories, a thousand fatal pangs of remorse will cry out at the bottom of your heart, louder than all your guests.... What resource will you have left to repulse your attacks?"[39] This, Rousseau confesses, is more than he himself could handle, which is why he has chosen poverty for himself and recommends it to others. So wealth simultaneously threatens justice, the soul, and personal happiness.

---

[38] See McCormick 2007.
[39] "Wealth," 9 [V: 472]; Piff et al. 2012; "Wealth," 13 [V: 477–78].

In this larger context, how is it that Rousseau tolerates wealth here in Chapter Five? Unless he is read as flatly contradicting himself and his principles, it seems likely that the inequality outlined in Chapter Five is fairly modest. Consider that he cites the Spartans as a model of permissible inequality here. Rousseau is surely citing the Sparta established by Lycurgus in the eighth century BCE and not before, since he often cites Lycurgus as a model Lawgiver. Lycurgus' services as a Lawgiver were required in response to a crisis of extreme economic inequality. Wealth had become concentrated in the hands of a few, resulting in arrogance, envy, luxury, and crime.[40] Lycurgus wiped the slate clean, redistributing all wealth and land on a far more egalitarian basis. According to Plutarch, this had the desired effect – crime radically decreased, virtue returned, luxury was largely banished, and Sparta flourished for hundreds of years. Among other measures, although Lycurgus tolerated some inequality of wealth, he struck a blow against the desire for wealth by instituting common meals, whereby rich and poor would eat their meals together, hence eliminating the luxuries and other benefits of wealth. As Plutarch writes, "For the rich, being obliged to go to the same table with the poor, could not make use of or enjoy their abundance, nor so much as please their vanity by looking at or displaying it." Although some wealth differences persisted in this state, "there was now neither avarice nor poverty amongst them, but equality, where every one's wants were supplied."[41]

Finally, it is worth noting that Rousseau opens the chapter with a strange observation that there can be more than one general will operating at the same time. This can be especially confusing, given that some interpreters have read the general will as something like a Platonic idea.[42] How can there be two conflicting ideas of the same thing? The obvious answer is that they cannot be the same thing for Rousseau. It is not quite accurate to call the general will a Platonic idea. The general will, as has been established, draws its substance from the idea of justice, which Rousseau defines as universal, but it is also indeterminate, such that it can take different shapes in different contexts. Among other factors determining the substantive content of the general will are the location and size of the community in which it is found. Consider the following example.[43] A parent

---

[40] See Plutarch, I: 59. Plutach's *Lives* was one of Rousseau's favorite books. As he wrote in his well-known "Letter to Malesherbes," "When I was six years old Plutarch fell into my hands, at eight I knew him by heart" ("Letters to Malesherbes," 574 [I: 1134]).

[41] Plutarch, I: 60–1; Plutarch, I: 74.

[42] E.g., Talmon 1955, 41.

[43] I explore the "indeterminacy" of Rousseau's idea of justice in Williams 2007a, 114–27 and Williams 2010a, 534–8; see also Neuhouser 2008, 211–12.

gets two children to agree that the child with the higher grades on his or her respective report cards will be permitted to sit in the front seat of the car for the following week. The children agree that this is both just and in their interest. In this very limited context, it is fair that the child with the higher grade gets to sit in the front seat. But at the same time, this promise occurs in the context of a greater society with rules of its own. Assume that one morning, the parent must take an elderly and especially tall grandfather to a doctor's appointment. Now there is a greater question of who sits in the front seat – presumably the grandfather, who would be seriously uncomfortable in the back seat. So there are two questions of fairness depending on the sphere of interests being considered. The principle of fairness does not change – but the circle of relevant parties does. In this way, there can be different general wills. A more directly political example would be the multiple general wills that belong to anyone living in a federalist system. There are general wills of the neighborhood, town or city, county, state, and nation. It may be in the provincial interest of New York to send its garbage to New Jersey, for example. But it is probably in the greater interest of the United States as a whole to limit refuse altogether. The abstract idea informing the general will does not change in each instance. That remains the same. But the verdicts rendered by each general will on a particular case may change according to whose interests are affected and how.

3.6. *Of Monarchy*

The final pure form of government is monarchy – and although Rousseau has much to say in this chapter, he has very little good to say about monarchy. Indeed, although it is a possibly legitimate form of government, virtually everything he says about it here suggests the opposite. In fact, Rousseau frequently implies in this chapter that monarchy and republicanism are fundamentally at odds. He defines monarchy as that form of government that is headed by a single individual. As such, it maintains one virtue: it is highly efficient and energetic.[44] In Rousseau's words, "everything responds to the same mover, all of the machine's levers are in the same hand, everything proceeds toward the same goal, no opposing motions cancel one another, and no kind of constitution can be imagined in which less effort would produce greater action" (*SC*, 3.6.3, 94–5 [III: 408]). It gets things done. But this is only a virtue insofar as the

[44] See Montesquieu's *Spirit of the Laws*, 1.5.10.

government aims at the general will. This is all that can be said on behalf of monarchy. As he will argue, most of the time such good intentions are far from the minds of kings.

Three flaws tend to burden monarchies: oppression, incompetence, and instability. The most obvious of these flaws is surely the problem of oppression, which amounts to the suppression of the general will in favor of the king's own private will. Where the government is embodied in one individual, it is least likely to serve the general will. Monarchs tend to desire "absolute" power (*SC*, 3.6.5, 95 [III: 409]). He subsequently elaborates, "The Prince always makes his plans circularly; he wants to command in order to get wealthy and to get wealthy in order to command; he will sacrifice both of them one after the other in order to acquire whichever one he lacks, but it is only so as to succeed in possessing both of the two together in the end that he pursues them separately; for in order to be the master of men and things he must have empire and money at the same time."[45] One of the best ways to consolidate princely power, observes Rousseau, is to win popular affection. But, following Machiavelli, he concedes that this affection is inevitably "precarious and fickle" (*SC*, 3.6.5, 95 [III: 409]).[46] Monarchs will therefore inevitably turn to other means by which they might consolidate their power, including outright "wicked" (*méchans*) behavior, as Machiavelli seems to counsel in the *Prince*.

In this context, Rousseau offers a novel reading of Machiavelli. Niccolò Machiavelli's advice in the *Prince* is notoriously embodied in his advice to inspire fear instead of love, to crush subjects rather than caress, and in his admiration of figures like Cesare Borgia. This has led his readers more commonly than not to conclude that he is either immoral or amoral. Rousseau, however, reads Machiavelli's *Prince* as a "book of republicans" (*SC*, 3.6.5, 95 [III: 409]). That is, Machiavelli pretended to be giving advice to the ruling authorities, when he was in fact revealing their bag of dirty tricks for republican citizens so that they might recognize them and respond accordingly. This interpretation, he argues, is buttressed by Machiavelli's evident republicanism in the *Discourses on Livy* and his *History of Florence*.[47] All this is to suggest that Machiavelli agrees with Rousseau that princes are indeed a great oppressive threat.

---

[45] *Perpetual Peace*, 55–6 [III: 594].

[46] *The Prince*, ch. 17.

[47] Mary G. Dietz has argued that Rousseau's argument is flawed insofar as Machiavelli did not disseminate this text to citizens of Florence, but rather to Francesco Vettori, his contact in the Medici family. See Dietz 1986, 779.

A second weakness of monarchy is its tendency to promote incompetence. Whereas republics foster the ascension of enlightened and capable citizens to positions of power, monarchies promote "petty bungler, petty knaves, [and] petty schemers" (*SC*, 3.6.8, 96 [III: 410]). Rousseau likely was influenced in this reading again by Montesquieu, who wrote, "If one were to doubt the people's natural ability to perceive merit, one would have only to cast an eye over that continuous series of astonishing choices made by the Athenians and the Romans; this will doubtless not be ascribed to chance." Montesquieu goes on to suggest that ambition – far more than virtue – fuels the engine of monarchical governments.[48] This is more than enough for Rousseau to draw the conclusion that ambition is better served in the monarchical context by flattering magistrates than by being virtuous. As such, monarchies are highly unlikely to follow the general will. There is little incentive to do so.

A final flaw of monarchy, according to Rousseau, is the problem of succession, which leads to instability. Whereas in aristocracies, magistrates can be replaced piecemeal with no larger disturbance to the power structure, monarchy offers no similar prospects. Dead kings result in "dangerous intervals" where "intrigue and corruption" are the ruling impulses among citizens (*SC*, 3.6.10, 97 [III: 411]). This problem has been so pervasive that monarchies have typically instituted hereditary succession as the normal means by which to prevent it. Yet for Rousseau, this cure is at least as bad as the disease. In the quest for stability, one receives in exchange the "risk of having children, monsters, [and] imbeciles" as kings (*SC*, 3.6.11, 97 [III: 411]). In fact, the very art of raising children to become rulers almost guarantees the reign of such monsters, according to Rousseau: "Everything conspires to deprive of justice and reason a man brought up to command others. Great pains are taken, so they say, to teach young Princes the art of ruling; it does not appear that this education profits them. It would be better to begin by teaching the art of obeying" (*SC*, 3.6.12, 97 [III: 411]).[49]

This art of obedience, however, should not be celebrated more generally. In fact, the mantra of obedience is particularly dangerous for Rousseau. Echoing his earlier challenge to obedience as a valuable principle in its own right (*SC*, 2.1.3), he laments the proliferation of the principle that

---

[48] *Spirit of the Laws*, 1.2.2, 1.2.7.

[49] It is in this spirit that he subsequently strongly urges Poland to forego the practice of hereditary monarchs. His reasoning there, however, differs slightly from that offered in the *Social Contract*. He argues that a King can always corrupt others "with promises to be redeemed by his successors" (*Poland*, 213 [III: 991]), resulting in a compounding of injustices across generations. As such, both freedom and law, he argues, are surrendered.

subjects should obey even bad kings since they have been sent "as punishments from Heaven" (*SC*, 3.6.16, 99 [III: 413]).[50] He concedes that such obedience might be necessary from time to time, but counseling obedience does not solve the root problem of bad magistrates. A political philosophy whose cornerstone is obedience to authority does not invest enough into the principles of good governance. This is the fundamental problem Rousseau finds burdening the neo-Augustinians.

3.7. *Of Mixed Governments*

After dedicating three consecutive chapters to outlining the three simple forms of government (democracy, aristocracy, and monarchy), Rousseau concedes at the opening of 3.7, "Properly speaking, there is no simple Government" (*SC*, 3.7.1, 99 [III: 413]). A monarch always needs subordinate magistrates to fulfill its tasks, and a democracy always requires some kind of head to coordinate its functions, such as Athens leaned on Pericles. So in some sense, the sharp distinctions between regimes are somewhat academic. Governments, for Rousseau, exist along a continuum from rule by the many to rule by one. They will never occupy either extreme end, but they can certainly incline toward one end or the other – or, for that matter, they can work to strike a balance.

Rousseau asks whether simple or mixed governments are best, and replies that "it should be given the same answer I gave about all forms of Government" (*SC*, 3.7.3, 99 [III: 413]). That is to say, there is no fixed answer for all circumstances. The best constitution for any given state will vary according to its climate, history, economy, geography, topography, religion, and other contingencies.

This being said, simple and complex governments, broadly speaking, have particular characteristics. Simple governments benefit from their simplicity. He does not elaborate, but it is easy to imagine that their simplicity offers a greater likelihood of accountability. That is, when policies fail, citizens will know whom to blame. This is particularly so with aristocracy and monarchy. Even a democracy with a "chief," like Athens' Pericles, offers the possibility of accountability. For this reason, he posits, "In itself

---

[50] Saint Augustine argues that God appoints tyrants as a punishment for various evils (*City of God*, 5.19). Jacques Bénigne Bossuet derives a principle of passive obedience to political authority on the principle that even tyrants have a divine origin and purpose in his *Politics Drawn from the Very Words of Holy Scripture*, ([1709] 1990, 1.6.2). In his notes on the *Social Contract* in the *Pléiade* edition, Robert Derathé also cites Jean Calvin as insisting on obedience as a divine command (Derathé 1964, 1483).

simple Government is best" (*SC*, 3.7.4, 99 [III: 413]). Yet this claim must be tempered by the fact that "in itself" means relatively little to Rousseau in the context of regime types. As he established earlier, even those institutions and laws that are "best in themselves" can be perfectly inappropriate for many or even all societies (*SC*, 2.11.4, 79 [III: 392]).

He concludes Chapter Seven with a consideration of two broad and opposite problems of governance – governments that are too strong and ones that are too weak. His dominant concern is with strong and over-bearing governments that threaten to privilege private wills over the general will. This happens, according to Rousseau, "when the executive Power is not sufficiently dependent on the legislative" (*SC*, 2.11.4 [III 413]). This was frequently a concern he expressed, such as in his *Letters Written from the Mountain*: "Since sovereignty always tends toward relaxation, the government always tends to become stronger. Thus the executive Body ought in the long run to prevail over the legislative body, and when the Law is finally subjected to men, only slaves and masters remain; the State is destroyed."[51] Such governments manifest in the deprivation of civil liberties and can ultimately represent a tyranny. His solution is a separation of powers or division of government, whereby executive authority is distributed among several magistrates. By doing so, he reasons, the private will of the executive is broken up and rendered less capable of resisting the legislative general will. The opposite problem is a government too weak to enforce the general will. The extreme version of this would resemble anarchy or a Hobbesian state of nature. His solution to this trouble is the establishment of tribunals or courts to prosecute particular offenders. In each case, both in governments too strong and too weak, Rousseau finds a solution in the distribution of power and authority.

3.8. *That Not Every Form of Government Is Suited to Every Country*

Chapter Eight is more influenced by Montesquieu than any other in the *Social Contract*. Rousseau acknowledges this in the first paragraph, where he authoritatively cites him in claiming that "liberty is not the fruit of every climate" (187 [III: 414]), a principle he explicitly attributes to Montesquieu. Rousseau will be intimately concerned with the question of context and conditions here more than anywhere else – although he never fully abandons this theme elsewhere. Montesquieu makes this claim in the *Spirit of the Laws*, where he observes, "in warm climates

---

[51] *Mountain*, 263 [III: 808]).

... despotism generally prevails."[52] Montesquieu's arguments stem from a somewhat crude eighteenth-century biology. The principle is roughly this: cold climates contract the extremities, heat relaxes them. The constriction increases strength generally, the relaxation weakens them. Much follows from this, according to Montesquieu. The greater strength of northern Europeans affords them many virtues. It gives them greater confidence, more courage, a better knowledge of their superiority, less desire for vengeance, a higher opinion of their security, more frankness, fewer suspicions, etc. Pretty much the opposite can be said of southern Europeans on Montesquieu's account. They are especially fearful of others. Why? Because of their general weakness and ability to be taken advantage of – "he will fear everything, because he will feel he can do nothing."[53] On this reading, Southerners tend to be lazy. They have "no curiosity, no noble enterprise, no generous sentiment; inclinations will all be passive there; laziness will be their happiness."[54] His arguments ultimately amount to this: because the hot temperatures of some regions relax the morals of their peoples, the governments need to be more severe. So freedom is impossible in certain cultures.

Rousseau, however, constructs a slightly different argument, as he acknowledges in his opening paragraph. His argument is more directly rooted in the fertility of the soil. He first notes that barren and sterile soils should be left uninhabited, or at the most inhabited only by undeveloped peoples. One might then assume that his preference is for the most fertile soils that yield the most food with the least effort. But this is likewise undesirable, albeit for very different reasons. The danger of especially rich soils is their tendency to produce luxury. As Rousseau emphasizes in the *Social Contract* and throughout his writings generally, luxury creates far more problems than it solves. Luxury begets idleness, and idleness leads citizens away from virtue and to obsession with things like the arts and science – which are good for a few citizens, but generally destructive of the masses, as he argues in his *Discourse on the Sciences and Arts*.[55] Additionally, the surplus goods produced by farmers in these lands offer

[52] *Spirit of the Laws*, 5.15 and Book 14 generally.
[53] *Spirit of the Laws*, 14.2.
[54] *Spirit of the Laws*, 14.2.
[55] See also his *Last Reply*, where he responds to the criticism that he questions the value of luxuries. "I am expected to be greatly embarrassed to be asked at what point should limits be placed on luxury. My sentiment is that there should be none at all. Everything beyond the physically necessary is a source of evil. Nature gives us quite enough needs; and it is at the very least exceedingly imprudent to multiply them unnecessarily, and thereby to place one's soul in greater dependence" (*Last Reply*, 84 [III: 95]).

an irresistible temptation to princes who will confiscate them for their own purposes (*SC*, 3.8.7, 101 [III: 416]). Further, since warm countries require fewer laborers to extract food from the land, the population is more dispersed, and the territory is greater. Rousseau worries that this greater territory conspires to keep citizens separated from one another and hence impotent to revolt against despots (*SC*, 3.8.15, 104 [III: 418]). As such, the civil liberty of citizens in fertile lands is under constant threat of a looming despotism.

It is worth raising a final concern Rousseau associates with temperate zones. Warm climates encourage thoughts of luxury and fashion specifically, insofar as the constant temperatures liberate clothing from the utilitarian concerns of variable climates, such as is found in northern territories, and encourage people to dress to impress (*SC*, 3.8.13, 103 [III: 417–18]). In other words, it stimulates the *amour propre* or vanity of citizens, which represents yet one more threat to the fragile general will.

Rousseau's preference is for a middle ground between barren and highly fertile lands. "[P]laces where the excess of produce over labor is moderate suit free peoples" (*SC*, 3.8.7, 101 [III: 416]). Such locations feed the citizens, while keeping them relatively tight together, and do not produce the kinds of luxuries that would corrupt either citizens or princes. They offer the greatest opportunity for the greatest civil liberties and the realization of the general will.

3.9. *Of the Signs of a Good Government*

Chapter Nine opens with Rousseau's reassertion that there is no "absolutely best Government," instead insisting that there are "as many good solutions as there are possible combinations in the absolute and relative positions of peoples" (*SC*, 3.9.1, 104–5 [III: 419]; see also 3.1.15, 85 [III: 398]). This is specifically because his conception of goodness is "indeterminate." This is an important key to understanding the more abstract elements of his political theory, or what might be called his "political ontology." With this term, I refer to the attributes or characteristics of his highest political principles or ideas – those concepts serving as the ultimate source of his moral and political proposals. Such ideas can be either determinate or indeterminate. Determinate ideas might be, for example, the notion that democracy is always the best form of government, as some people believe. John Locke, an important precursor to Rousseau in the social contract tradition, employs determinate ideas in his political theory insofar as he insists that no government has the legitimate authority to inhibit the natural rights of citizens to life, liberty, health, and possessions.[56] These determinate rights are non-negotiable, regardless of circumstances. Indeterminate ideas do not specify any form of government as best – only that there is a best that varies according to situation or circumstance. Nor do they tend to insist on the inviolability of a particular set of rights or privileges. This latter path is Rousseau's. While Rousseau certainly suggests throughout his works that justice and goodness are those highest ideas,[57] he never defines them so determinately that they cannot be realized differently under different conditions.

This raises the tricky question of how a citizen knows the government is doing its job. The most obvious appeal here is the conscience, which if it has been properly developed should inform their judgments about justice and injustice, good and bad. As he writes in his *Emile*, "There is in the depth of souls ... an innate principle of justice and virtue according to which, in spite of our own maxims, we judge our actions and those of others to be good or bad. It is to this principle that I give the name *conscience*."[58]

Yet this conscience, as he illustrates so clearly in the *Emile* and *Second Discourse*, is constantly assaulted by social forces – opinion, *amour propre*, the desire for applause, the lust for power. So the appeal to conscience can in these cases be an appeal to a private will. As such, Chapter Ten offers a shorthand guide for distinguishing good from bad governments: the rate of population growth. "All other things equal, the Government under which the Citizens, without resort to external means, without naturalizations, without colonies, populate and multiply, is without fail the best: that under which a people dwindles and wastes away is the worst" (*SC*, 3.9.4, 105 [III: 420]). It is possible that Rousseau learned this from Machiavelli, who wrote, "Those who desire a city to achieve great empire must endeavor by all possible means to make her populous."[59] This is not precisely Rousseau's point, however, since Machiavelli is concerned here with empire-building, and Rousseau clearly is not. But Rousseau's careful attention to the *Discourses* elsewhere in the *Social Contract* makes this worth considering.

A more immediate influence in this regard, however, is likely to be Montesquieu's *Persian Letters*, which dedicates several pages to outlining concerns about population decline. The character of Usbek expresses

---

[56] John Locke, *Second Treatise*, §6.
[57] *Emile*, 282 [IV: 588–9].
[58] *Emile*, 289 [IV: 598].
[59] *Discourses*, 2.3.

concern about population rates and outlines several possible causes. Most obviously, he observes, the spread of plagues and infectious disease – including sexually transmitted diseases – is a sign of a troubled society. Beyond this, however, Usbek also blames Christianity's prohibition against divorce. To his mind, this only creates more loveless marriages, which yield fewer children. Christianity also produces a class of citizens in monks, priests, and nuns, who are prohibited from reproducing. Beyond Europe, Usbek points to the negative effects of the slave trade in West Africa, the mining industry, settling in lands that ought to be uninhabited (as some colonists of this period attempted), and of economic inequality. Population growth, by contrast, is advanced by benign or good government. Good governments, according to Montesquieu's Usbek, offer the stability necessary to make a decent living, the liberty to make life worth living, and an equality that "brings abundance and life into all parts of the body politic and spreads them everywhere."[60] These latter concerns with liberty, equality, and good governance would certainly have appealed to Rousseau. Some years later, population growth would become a central concern of the Jacobins.

3.10. *Of the Abuse of Government and of Its Tendency to Degenerate*

Rousseau acknowledges in Chapter Ten that all governments are ultimately fated to collapse. He lays out the means by which this might happen in Chapter Ten. The general cause of governmental degeneration is that the government will seek to usurp sovereignty. That is, those in power will seek to take away the legislative power from the people themselves. Or, in other words, they will seek to make the law reflect their private or corporate will, rather than the general will (*SC*, 3.10.1, 106 [III: 421]). So as is generally the case throughout the *Social Contract*, the source of political difficulties can be traced to the failure to secure and vigilantly maintain a robust general will.

Broadly speaking, there are two varieties of degeneration: shrinking and dissolving. A government may shrink in changing from a democracy to an aristocracy, or an aristocracy to a monarchy (*SC*, 3.10.3, 106–7 [III: 421–2]). This is a "natural inclination" or tendency of governments, according to Rousseau. In a footnote, he entertains the argument that Rome is a significant counterexample in starting out with the age of kings and then

---

[60] *Persian Letters*, Letter 72, 206. See Letters 62–72 generally for Montesquieu's treatment of the population question. See also his *Spirit of the Laws*, 23.28, 454.

growing into democracy. He vehemently denies this narrative of Roman political history, however, arguing that the true founding of Rome was with the expulsion of the Tarquins after the rape of Lucretia. Slowly but surely, he laments, this relatively democratic government shrank into the Roman Empire under its respective emperors (*SC*, 3.10.3, 106–7 [III: 421–2]).

The second mode of degeneration is dissolution, and this occupies far more of Rousseau's attention. Dissolution itself can take two forms: (1) princely usurpation of power, or (2) members of the government separately usurping governmental power they should only exercise collectively. Where the prince substitutes his will for the sovereign power, it is not merely the government that degenerates – but in fact the entire state, according to Rousseau.[61] At this point, the prince has become a "master and tyrant" (*SC*, 3.10.6, 108 [III: 422]). The social contract has been entirely dissolved – and the people return to their natural liberty. They have for all intents and purposes been returned to the latter stages of the *Second Discourse*. The government rules by force, not by right. And the people apparently have every right to disobey this so-called government anywhere they can. The government has no moral authority whatsoever.

Rousseau does not elaborate much here on the second form of dissolution – other than to suggest that it is undesirable. But what exactly is it, to have members of the government separately usurping governmental power they should only exercise collectively? He offers a small clue by saying that where this happens, "there are … as many Princes as there are Magistrates" (*SC*, 3.10.7, 108 [III: 423]). This is to say, the government officials are fighting one another for sovereign authority. The government itself is divided among countless private wills, which in turn dissolves the state. The government *ought*, by contrast, to be united in purpose behind the general will.

Following Aristotle, Rousseau identifies the dissolved states as perversions of their original forms.[62] He emphasizes that all of these are variants of anarchy. Democracy becomes ochlocracy or mob rule; aristocracy becomes oligarchy; monarchy becomes tyranny. In his own terms, however, each corruption is characterized by private wills consuming the state at the expense of the general will.

The remainder of Chapter Ten is dedicated to a series of definitions that become more important in subsequent chapters. The definitions hinge

---

[61] This bears obvious resemblance to the last chapter of Locke's *Second Treatise*, esp. §214.
[62] Aristotle, *Politics*, 3.7.

upon distinctions – those being the distinctions between "strict" and "vulgar" definitions or tyranny and then the distinction between tyranny and despotism. Since the general tendency of all governments is to devolve into tyranny, it is especially important to know what it is so one can be vigilant in guarding against its premature emergence.

For Rousseau, there are two ways to define tyranny. The first is the "vulgar" (*vulgaire*) definition. It is important to emphasize that *vulgaire* does not carry precisely the same connotations in eighteenth-century political theory as it does in common parlance today. *Vulgaire* comes from the Latin *vulgaris*, which means what is usual or commonplace, or of the common people. At any rate, this vulgar definition of a tyrant is "a King who governs with violence and without regard for justice and the laws" (*SC*, 3.10.9, 108 [III: 423]). The three important terms here are violence, justice, and law. Rousseau often expresses his distaste for force and violence in politics.[63] But he does not deny the occasional need for it insofar as citizens must be "forced to be free" when circumstances warrant. Violence can be justified for Rousseau only when authorized by positive law. And the law is legitimate for Rousseau only when it is consistent with justice or natural law.[64] So violence can be permissible for a ruler only when it is authorized both by positive and natural law. Any official act of violence in violation of the positive and natural law is therefore the trait of a tyrant. So the commonsense understanding of tyranny importantly includes a violation of both justice and the laws. In this regard, it is worth reconsidering a passage from Book II: "Conventions and laws are therefore necessary to combine rights with duties and to bring justice back to its object" (*SC*, 2.6.2, 66 [III: 378]). For Rousseau, the point of laws is to serve the moral idea of justice. So in this regard, it is fair to read justice and the laws in tandem. That is, if the laws are just, as they must be in order to reflect the general will, then to violate the law is to violate justice.[65]

The second approach to defining tyranny is more technical. Under this definition, "a Tyrant is an individual who arrogates the royal authority to himself without having any right to it" (*SC*, 3.10.9, 108 [III: 423]). This definition permits that a tyrant may be either good or bad. That is, the definition is formal, rather than substantive. It does not require a moral judgment about the ruler's behavior. He notes that this definition was the

---

[63] E.g., *Emile*, 236 [IV: 524].

[64] As he argues in his *Letters Written from the Mountain*, the law must have "nothing contrary to the natural Laws" (231 [III: 807]).

[65] "[O]ne need only be just in order to be sure of following the general will," *Political Economy*, 12 [III: 251].

one most commonly employed by the ancient Greeks. Perhaps the best-known example of this definition was the ancient tyrant, Pisistratus, who seized power by virtue of arriving in Athens with an unusually tall and beautiful woman posing as the goddess Athena.[66] This was neither orthodox nor legal. But nevertheless, Pisistratus was able to consolidate power based on this deception. He then went on, according to Herodotus, to administer "the state according to the established usages, and his arrangements were wise and salutary."[67] So the technical definition of tyranny merely concerns the acquisition of power – not the exercise thereof.

Rousseau employs the "vulgar" definition far more often than the "precise" or technical one. In the *Political Economy*, for example, he refers to the Roman Republic's birth in "the horror of tyranny and the crimes of tyrants." He suggests here the infamous "Rape of Lucretia" in which a nobleman's wife is raped by the son of the king, Tarquin. This incident has everything to do with violence, injustice, and illegality – and nothing to do with the technical seizure of power. Tarquin already had power, according to the positive laws of the existing system. Elsewhere in the *Political Economy*, Rousseau stresses the need for governments to "render justice to all, and above all to protect the poor against the tyranny of the rich."[68] This suggests again a definition of Tyranny as a violation of justice rather than a technical usurpation of power. Rousseau similarly pits Tyranny as against justice in his *Discourse on Heroic Virtue*.[69] This conception of tyranny as opposed to justice is also present in his condemnation of tyrants in Holland and Switzerland (*SC*, 2.8.3, 72 [III: 385]). So it seems that Rousseau is generally comfortable in defining Tyranny in the vulgar sense, although it is generally wise to study context for certainty.[70]

The final distinction of Chapter Ten is that between tyranny and despotism. Rousseau here holds to the precise technical definition of tyranny given previously, identifying the tyrant as "the usurper of the *royal* authority" (*SC*, 3.10.10, 108 [III: 423]; emphasis added). The despot, by contrast, is the "usurper of the *Sovereign* power" (*SC*, 3.10.10, 108 [III: 423]; emphasis added). In other words, the tyrant seizes executive power and then

---

[66] She was actually an ordinary subject named Phya. This story is recounted in Herodotus, *History*, Book I.

[67] Herodotus, *History*, Book I.

[68] *Political Economy*, 22 [III: 262], 19 [III: 258].

[69] *Discourse on Heroic Virtue*, 316, [II: 1274].

[70] In his *History of the Government of Geneva*, Rousseau employs both definitions. He characterizes the early Governments of Geneva as tyrannical while specifically dismissing inquiry into the idea that the Government was founded on usurpation. Then he continues to argue that the rise of the Counts was specifically through usurpation, the technical definition of tyranny (*Government of Geneva*, 105–7 [V: 499–503]). So Rousseau's use of the term is fluid and flexible.

governs according to the general will; the despot sets aside the general will altogether. This is, however, another technical distinction that Rousseau does not seem uniformly to follow. His frequent employment of the vulgar definition of tyranny (as opposed to justice) itself conforms here to his definition of despotism. So in practice Rousseau generally uses the terms tyranny and despotism interchangeably.

3.11. *The Death of the Body Politic*

Repeating a lesson of Chapter Ten, Rousseau opens Chapter Eleven by insisting on the inevitability of political decline. Even the best states, such as Sparta and Rome, are fated to collapse. Here he again apparently draws on the lessons of Plato's Socrates, who observes, "everything that comes-to-be must decay, not even one so constituted [as the ideal regime] will last forever."[71] For Plato, this point is as much metaphysical as it is practical. He distinguishes between the realm of becoming (material substance, which includes political institutions) and being (the immaterial Ideas). Because the Ideas are immaterial, they are not subject to deterioration and exist eternally. Everything in the material realm, however, is created and hence subject to an inevitable decay, including the best political regimes. Something similar appears to underlie Rousseau's observations in Chapters Ten and Eleven. He maintains that citizens should "not dream of making it [the best state] eternal." Such aspirations are patently to "attempt the impossible" (*SC*, 3.11.1, 109 [III: 424]). This can be contrasted with his casual references to "eternal justice" in the *Emile*.[72] So while justice is evidently an immaterial idea existing eternally, regimes are material phenomena subject to decay and decline. The best possible regime is one most closely resembling the idea of justice and aware enough of the signs of decay to slow its inevitability. As Rousseau writes, "it is within the capacity to prolong a State's life as far as possible by giving it the best constitution it can have" (*SC*, 3.11.2, 109 [III: 424]).

To maintain the best states, it is necessary to protect their "heart" – namely, the legislature. For Rousseau, this means specifically the people, but not the people in any such combination. The legislature in his dictionary specifically means the people as they combine to form the general will – in other words, the sovereign. As he declares in Chapter Fifteen,

---

[71] *Republic*, 546a.
[72] *Emile*, 292 [IV: 603], 259 [IV: 556]. In this spirit, it is worth observing that Rousseau describes the general will, itself derived substantively from the idea of justice, as "constant, unalterable, and pure" (*SC*, 4.1.6, 122 [III: 438]).

"law is nothing but the declaration of the general will" (*SC*, 3.15.8, 115 [III: 430]; see also 3.12.1, 110, [III: 425]). So in effect, the best way to preserve a just state is to respect the general will and use it as a guide for all legislation. Anything deviating from justice and the general will only hastens the state's decline: "as soon as the heart has stopped to function, the animal is dead" (*SC*, 3.11.3, 109 [III: 424]). Thus, a state should be vigilant in guarding against the encroachments of *amour propre* he cites in the *First Discourse*, *Second Discourse*, and *Emile*,[73] as well as all manifestations of private wills as opposed to the general will.

In this context of vigilance, it is perhaps surprising to discover what he says next. Rousseau accepts a Lockean tacit consent: "Yesterday's law does not obligate today, but tacit consent is presumed from silence" (*SC*, 3.11.4, 109 [III: 424]).[74] So long as the subjects do not protest the government's actions, the government can assume that they tacitly approve. One potentially troubling implication is that if subjects can be convinced to embrace or tacitly consent to views contradicting the general will, the government's deeds will be assumed legitimate. Rousseau is keenly aware of the dangers invited by this kind of quiescence to unjust regimes. In the *Second Discourse*, he speaks of subjects running to their chains. And in the *Political Economy*, he expresses the concern that the people might be "seduced by private interests which some few skillful men succeed by their reputation and eloquence to substitute for the people's own interest. Then the public deliberation will be one thing, and the general will another thing entirely."[75] Insofar as such manipulations could succeed, it seems that tacit consent in the form of silence may not always serve Rousseau's greater purposes. This presumption of tacit consent reveals a potential soft spot in his political theory. In his defense, Rousseau offers a more robust conception of tacit consent in his *Emile*, published nearly simultaneously with his *Social Contract*. He introduces tacit consent in the context of the near-completion of Emile's education, with only travel and the study of politics remaining on the tutor's syllabus. This process begins with

studying the nature of government in general, the diverse forms of government, and finally the particular government under which he was born, so that he may

---

[73] Frederick Neuhouser stresses that although the *Social Contract* lacks any direct confrontation with *amour-propre*, it "can easily be understood as furnishing the essential elements of the comprehensive response to the problematic consequences of *amour-propre* that Rousseau's thought as a whole aims to offer" (see Neuhouser 2008, 9). See also Cohen 2010, 158.

[74] Rousseau also embraces tacit consent at *SC*, 4.2.6, 123–4 [III: 440]. See Locke's *Second Treatise*, §119–22.

[75] *Political Economy*, 8 [III: 246].

find out whether it suits him to live there. For by right nothing can abrogate, when each man attains his majority and becomes his own master, he also becomes master of renouncing the contract that connects him with the community by leaving the country in which that community is established. It is only by staying there after attaining the age of reason that he is considered to have tacitly confirmed the commitment his ancestors made. He acquires the right of renouncing his fatherland just as he acquires the right of renouncing his father's estate.[76]

This passage suggests that tacit consent is a more active and rational process than implied by the more casual references in the *Social Contract*. Citizens consciously choose to remain in their respective homelands in adulthood, and in the context suggested in *Emile*, after the benefit of education and travel – so that they might compare the merits of their home with other states.

In the spirit of his endorsement of tacit consent, Rousseau accords special respect for "ancient laws" (*SC*, 3.11.5, 109 [III: 425]). If the people have long consented to a law, so the reasoning goes, there can be little question as to its uprightness. There is a good point to be made here. It would seem that the longer laws have endured, the more likely they are to be consistent with the general will. But this again raises a set of concerns about the possibility of long-established tyrannical rules. It is always possible that a set of oppressive rules may very well endure for extended periods. In such cases, respect for "ancient laws" would serve to harm more than promote the general will.

3.12. *How the Sovereign Authority Is Maintained*

The next three chapters represent a natural continuation of the discussion in Chapter Eleven, where Rousseau insists on the importance of protecting the "heart" of the state, namely, the sovereign. He immediately reminds readers in Chapter Twelve that the sovereign's sole task is to legislate – and further, that the only legitimate legislative acts are consistent with the general will. The sovereign only exists for Rousseau *when the people are assembled*[77] and are legislating for the general will. At this point, he concedes the popular opinion of his own day that such assemblies are practically impossible.[78]

[76] *Emile*, 455 [IV: 833].
[77] Richard Fralin notes that the demand for periodic assemblies of the people "was notably absent from the *Dédicace* [of the *Discourse on Inequality*], even though it had been a major goal of Genevan dissidents ever since the days of Pierre Fatio [1662–1707]" (Fralin 1978, 105).
[78] One formulation of this objection comes from David Hume: "all numerous assemblies, however composed, are mere mob, and swayed in their debates by the least motive. This we find confirmed

Rousseau finds this popular opinion, however, to be fundamentally misguided. While popular assemblies are absent among his reading audience, they were once common. The ancient Athenian Assembly is the most striking example. It consisted of all male Athenian citizens and typically met once every month, sometimes more depending on various exigencies that might emerge. Each citizen had the right to speak, provided he could be heard. All citizens also had the right to propose legislation. With a population of approximately 45,000 citizens[79] at the outbreak of the Peloponnesian War, however, many of Rousseau's contemporaries would find Athens too small and quaint to be a useful model. So Rousseau instead turns to the Roman example for more relevant precedent. The Roman Republic[80] had more than 400,000 citizens, who were able to assemble. This example alone, he concludes, "answers all objections: The inference from what is to what is possible seems to me sound" (*SC*, 3.12.5, 110 [III: 426]). It is still unclear that this answers "all objections," since the estimated population in 1760 France was 26 million.[81] So even if one could conceivably assemble 400,000, as Rousseau proposes happened in Rome, it is difficult to imagine how he might have envision this happening in 1760 France. Undoubtedly, however, such an assembly would have been possible in his native city of Geneva. The desire to stress the practical possibility of his own republic is one likely reason that Rousseau dedicates five chapters in Book IV of the *Social Contract* to the institutions of the Roman Republic.[82]

3.13. *How the Sovereign Authority Is Maintained (continued)*

Rousseau continues his discussion of the assemblies in Chapter Thirteen, emphasizing the importance of regular, fixed, periodic meetings of the

---

by daily experience. When an absurdity strikes a member, he conveys it to his neighbour, and so on, till the whole be infected" (Hume [1754] 1994], 228). Some years later, the same view was expressed by James Madison in the *Federalist*: "the more multitudinous a representative assembly may be rendered, the more it will partake of the infirmities incident to collective meetings of the people. Ignorance will be the dupe of cunning, and passion the slave of sophistry and declamation. The people can never err more than in supposing that by multiplying their representatives beyond a certain limit, they strengthen the barrier against the government of a few" (James Madison, Federalist No. 58, 358). These sources and others of this nature are cited in Putterman 2010, 96–7. Putterman offers an extensive defense of Rousseau's preference for large assemblies throughout Chapter Four of his book. He sums up Rousseau's argument thus: "The actualization of 'the most general will' occurs when the greatest number of citizens participate in lawmaking" (Putterman 2010, 110).

[79] This data is from Kitto [1952] 1991, 132, who also includes a useful discussion of the Athenian institutions at 125–35.

[80] Rousseau also cites relevant precedent among the ancient Macedonian and Franconian governments.

[81] Murray 2004, 374.

[82] See Fralin 1978, 112–24.

assembly. Nothing should interfere with these meetings; and if they were to be disturbed or suspended, this would suggest a failure of the state as a whole. There is no fixed formula to establish the frequency with which a people should assemble, but Rousseau offers one guiding principle. The stronger the government, the more often its assembly should meet. This effectively functions as an executive check in Rousseau's balance of governmental powers,[83] a check necessitated by the very tendency of this power to encroach upon the legislature, substituting a private will for the general will, as detailed in *SC*, 3.6. In his *Letters Written from the Mountain*, he similarly calls on the legislature to exercise "inspection over the executive power," insisting that there is no state in which the sovereign lacks such an obviously required function.[84]

Rousseau acknowledges the objection that the assembly of citizens in a city like Rome or Athens, however, is quite different from the modern state of France, for example, characterized by a large territory, millions of citizens, and multiple cities. He entertains two popular solutions to this problem. First, sovereignty might be shared across the various cities of a larger state. Second, there should be one dominant sovereign city governing the inferior ones.

He finds the first proposed solution unacceptable on the principle that sovereignty cannot be divided (*SC*, 2.2). Earlier, Rousseau deduces two conclusions from this principle: (1) that legislation must be derived from *all* of the citizens, and not merely a part; and (2) that sovereignty cannot be divided between branches of government – that there must be a supreme sovereign branch, namely, the legislature. It is not entirely clear here why this forecloses the possibility of legislation being drawn from many people across different cities, unless Rousseau is especially concerned that they assemble *together in one place*. In this case, his objection is more practical than it is principled. Further, the notion that sovereignty cannot be divided among powers is of no immediate relevance to the question of whether it can be shared among cities.

One possible solution is to have one major (capital) city reigning as sovereign over subordinate others. But Rousseau expressly rejects this proposal on the principle that "the essence of the political body consists in

---

[83] Some scholars, such as Arthur M. Melzer, postulate that Rousseau "does not create real checks and balances" (Melzer 1990, 209). Melzer maintains, technically speaking, all governmental powers are subordinate to the sovereign power of the legislature. For all practical purposes, however, Rousseau's system here conforms to what most understand to be a functioning system of checks and balances, even where sovereignty is not shared across branches. While it may not be a balancing of *sovereign* power, it is a balance of *institutional* power.

[84] *Mountain*, 247 [III: 826].

the concurrence of obedience and freedom, and that the words *subject* and *sovereign* are identical correlatives whose idea is combined in the single word *Citizen*" (*SC*, 3.13.5, III [III: 427]).[85] His point is reasonably simple: a people ought not be subject to laws that they have no part in shaping. This is a foundational principle of democratic legitimacy. Indeed, this was no small problem in Rousseau's day. One may argue this was precisely the problem of colonial governance in the eighteenth century – a sovereign imposing laws over subordinate subjects lacking any role in their creation. In the parlance of the American colonists, "no taxation without representation."

Rousseau also expresses a general distaste for the creation of large states here, which inevitably have their "natural inconveniences" (*SC*, 3.13.6, III [III: 427]). He does not spell out these "inconveniences" here – but they are perfectly evident throughout his other works, especially the "Letter to d'Alembert." The dominant virtue of smaller states, according to Rousseau, is that citizens are always present to one another. That is, they cannot hide. This provides a considerable obstacle for those who might otherwise be tempted to privilege their private wills over the general will. For example, someone who cheats in business can continue for a long time to deceive new customers in a large state. But in a smaller state, the deceiving merchant will be revealed, scorned, and punished with a lack of customers much sooner as the merchant's behavior quickly spreads by word of mouth spreads to all citizens. Additionally, Rousseau insists that smaller states tend to excite the passions less, which keeps *amour propre* – one of the greatest fuels for the private will – from overcoming citizens. That is, the larger the society, the more temptations there are to stand out among the crowd – and the less one considers the common good. Finally, Rousseau adds that citizens of smaller states are generally more talented and inventive, since the pressures to conform to fashions and the like is greater in larger states. He adds in his *Political Economy* more specifically economic and political problems. This includes the fact that larger states are more expensive to maintain, and further that often the resources of one territory are used to devour another one within the same state, which "upsets the balance between production and consumption." Finally, in his *Government of Poland*, he writes that large states are "the first and principal source of the miseries of humankind, and above

---

[85] This definition of *citizen* differs from the definition he offers earlier that a *citizen* is a participant in the sovereign authority (*SC*, 1.6.10, 51 [III: 362]). Here he seems to add the additional condition that a *citizen* is also someone who is a subject. While this is technically true for all citizens when they are not legislating, it is not a condition imposed on the earlier definition.

all of the countless calamities that sap and destroy politically organized peoples."[86] Specifically, he celebrates the fact that all citizens in small states know one another and the fact that evils threatening the general will cannot easily go undetected.

This being said, Rousseau is sensitive to the problem that small states, for all their virtues, might be militarily vulnerable to the larger ones: "how are small States to be given enough force to resist the large ones?" (*SC*, 3.13.6, III [III: 427]). His answer is to appeal to history: "in the same way that formerly the Greek cities resisted the great King, and more recently Holland and Switzerland resisted the House of Austria" (*SC*, 3.13.6, III [III: 427]).

All this being stated, Rousseau is not unaware of the growing European trend in favor of larger states. The France in which he wrote the *Social Contract* was one such example.[87] So he offers some suggestions for how to build a larger state at least moderately consistent with his general political principles, even if inherently inferior to the small states he prefers. Specifically, he recommends that no one city function as a permanent capital. The capital should rotate among the established cities. Further. he emphasizes that no matter where citizens might live, they should all be accorded the same set of rights. Finally, each corner of the state should be developed as equally as possible so that no one city or region might come to dominate another.

3.14. *How the Sovereign Authority Is Maintained (continued)*

Chapter Fourteen represents the third consecutive chapter dedicated to maintaining the sovereign authority of the legislature, which is a strong indication of just how central this institution is to his political program. In Chapter Twelve, he draws attention to the importance of there being a physical assembly of the legislature; in Chapter Thirteen, he insists that those assemblies must be regular; in Chapter Fourteen, he now places special emphasis on its vulnerabilities to the encroachments of the executive or government itself on the legislature.

---

[86] "Letter to d'Alembert," 59–60 [V: 54–5]; *Political Economy*, 28 [III: 268]; *Government of Poland*, 192 [III: 970]. In fact, the chapter title addressing this problem in Poland is called "The Radical Vice."

[87] Another example was Poland, which Rousseau was subsequently to advise on constitutional matters. He here offers two lines of advice consistent with the *Social Contract*. First, investigate all possible routes by which to shrink the size of the state, hence experiencing the full benefits of small states. Second, failing that, he urges a federalist system, in which the virtues of the small state might be imitated, if imperfectly. See *Poland*, 193–4 [III: 970–1].

Rousseau has already intimated the dangers of the executive branch. Its role is to stand between sovereign and subject (*SC*, 3.1), i.e., lawmaker and law-abider. This essential role is fraught with the numerous temptations of power. The most common mode of government in the eighteenth century, of course, was some version of monarchy, which amplified these temptations to the point of irresistibility, where monarchs sought to make their power "absolute" (*SC*, 3.6.5, 95 [III: 409]). While this tendency is not for Rousseau technically "natural," since the natural condition of humanity is goodness, it is nevertheless virtually inevitable in civil society, where the *amour propre* of all individuals, government officials especially, fosters a preference for the private over the general will. This tendency is compounded where the government has no official legislative role, insofar as an executive "has to recognize an actual superior" (*SC*, 3.14.2, 112 [III: 428]). Its jealousy of the legislative power should rightfully alert the sovereign to the precariousness of its own position.

As such, the legislature in any republic must be especially vigilant against this brooding threat. While the obvious modern answer here would require more checks and balances (which Rousseau implements elsewhere), his solution here is more consistent with an earlier tradition: increased virtue. The best way to protect against executive encroachments against the legislature is to cultivate the development of virtuous citizens. It is worth emphasizing that the virtue Rousseau wants to cultivate is more important for citizens than it is for the rulers. "When citizens are greedy, cowardly, pusillanimous, more enamored of repose than of freedom, they do not long hold out against the redoubled efforts of the Government" (*SC*, 3.14.2, 112 [III: 428]).[88] Insofar as citizens are prone to these vices, they facilitate the executive's encroachments. Their greed may foster the effective employment of bribes; their pusillanimity makes them increasingly vulnerable to threats; their preference of repose over freedom fosters easy bargains and sacrifices of their freedoms with long-ranging consequences. The evidence for the importance of this point in Rousseau's political thought can be extrapolated from the basic framework of his *Emile*, published the same year as the *Social Contract*. The *Emile* consists of five books – the first four and a half of which are dedicated to the cultivation of a virtuous pupil. The final half chapter is dedicated to situating this pupil in political society. Likewise, in his *Government of Poland*, he

---

[88] In this spirit, Rousseau writes in his *Political Economy* of the importance of having "illustrious warriors ... preach courage" and "upright magistrates ... teach justice" so as to perpetuate the civic virtues once they are established" (*Political Economy*, 22 [III: 261]).

stresses the importance of an education for virtue and civic love before he moves on to address Poland's institutions. Finally, in his *Discourse on Political Economy*, he insists that in order to facilitate an effective political system, one must first "make virtue reign."[89] In all these cases, virtue is in essence substantively synonymous with the general will.[90] For Rousseau, it would make little sense to embark on a political project like a state and its attendant laws without having first made some considerable efforts in securing the virtue of its citizens. Indeed, failing to do so means "the Sovereign authority finally vanishes, and most Cities fall and perish before their time" (*SC*, 3.14.2, 113 [III: 428]).

3.15. *Of Deputies or Representatives*

Chapter Fifteen is close to the longest chapter in Book III and one of its more controversial, at least to contemporary political minds. Rousseau sternly cautions against representative government – the backbone of governments that would follow in his wake. Readers should keep a few things in mind before moving forward, however. First, representation was relatively uncommon in the centuries leading up to Rousseau. It existed in England – at least insofar as the wealthy or nobles could be said to represent the people more broadly. It was more or less absent in Continental Europe. Second, Rousseau had a mixed relationship with representation throughout his career as a political thinker. He seems to accept it in the *Political Economy*, he rejects it here, and he accepts it again in the *Government of Poland*. Third, political representation was thought to originate in feudalism – in which case, representation was nothing more than an elaborate form of class oppression.[91] So it is possible to have at least a small sense now – heading into Rousseau's remarks – of why it is that he might have been so staunchly opposed to a doctrine that strikes most today as so sensible.

He offers three broad arguments against representation: (1) it facilitates the influence of money on politics, (2) it fosters political apathy, and (3) it threatens realization of the general will. It would seem that the most intuitively resonant argument would be the first – that representation facilitates the improper influence of money on the political process. The

---

[89] *Emile*, 455–71 [IV: 833–55]; *Poland*, 189–93 [III: 966–70]; *Political Economy*, 13 [III: 252].

[90] "[V]irtue is nothing but … conformity of the particular will to the general will" (*Political Economy*, 13 [III: 252]).

[91] See Fralin 1978, 15–16, 22–6. According to Fralin, the first to connect representation and feudalism was none other than Baron d'Holbach, who did so in his *Encyclopedia* entry on *Répresentation*.

long and continuing history of corruption in representative politics provides constant reminders of this danger. Yet Rousseau's argument is not
quite so obvious. Instead of speaking to the capacity of money to corrupt
a representative, he instead focuses on how money corrupts the citizens
themselves. He conceives of political representation as a form of paying
someone to take on a task that one is too lazy or incompetent to take
on oneself. But the consequences in the task of political representation
are far graver, according to Rousseau. In paying someone to legislate on
my behalf, I have surrendered my own civic duty. I have transferred or
alienated my own sovereignty. He insists at the very outset of Chapter
Fifteen, "public service … [is] the Citizens' principal business" (*SC*, 3.15.1,
113 [III: 428]).

He develops this point in the next paragraph. Citizens must be cau-
tioned generally against the tendency to pay for services that they could
perform themselves: "it is the softness and love of comforts that change
personal services into money. One gives up a portion of one's profit in
order to increase it in leisure…. In a truly free State the citizens do everything with their hands and nothing with money" (*SC*, 3.15.2, 113 [III:
429]).[92] Rousseau speaks of a hyper-self-reliance in this regard. The more
citizens pay others to take on their duties for them, the more they find
themselves at others' whims. It is ultimately tantamount to a kind of slavery for Rousseau: "Give money, and soon you will have chains. The word
finance is a slave's word" (*SC*, 3.15.2, 113 [III: 429]).

A second and related argument against representation is that it fosters
political apathy. In paying others to represent them, citizens inevitably
find themselves caring less about the policy decisions shaping their lives.
Rousseau assumes – not unreasonably – that the less personally involved one
is, the less one cares about its operations. He has in mind again the assemblies of ancient Athens[93] and Rome, which required citizen involvement

---

[92] On this point, see Rousseau's *Plan for a Constitution for Corsica*, in which he suggests that it would
be best to come as close as possible to eliminating money from the state altogether: "If Corsica
needed foreigners it would need money, but being able to be self-sufficient, it does not need it;
and since it is useful only as a sign of inequality, the less of it that circulates in the Island the more
real abundance will reign there" (*Corsica*, 140 [III: 921]). See also his *Separate Fragments* written in
preparation for *Corsica*, 157 [III: 941] and 161 [III: 946].

[93] The Greeks did not have representatives – but Rousseau's contemporaries argued this was only
possible because they had slaves to do all their work for them at home, thus freeing them up for
the business of politics. Now that slavery is a thing of the past, the people simply do not have the
time to participate in politics. They must therefore resort to representation as the "next-best-thing."
Rousseau finds this argument unacceptable – even as he acknowledges some truth in the basic
facts. Citizens simply have to buckle up, so to speak, and find the time to participate. The alternative is slavery for the citizens themselves (*SC*, 3.15.9–12, 115–16 [III: 430–1]).

in legislation. The Greeks did not have representatives – but Rousseau's contemporaries argued this was only possible because slave labor afforded citizens the luxury of spare time for the business of politics. With the elimination of pervasive slavery, so the argument goes, eighteenth-century Europeans simply lacked the time for this level of civic engagement. They must therefore resort to representation as the "next-best-thing." Rousseau finds this argument unacceptable – even as he acknowledges some truth in the basic facts. Citizens simply have to find the time to participate. The alternative is slavery for the citizens themselves (*SC*, 3.15.9–12, 115–16 [III: 430–1]). Insofar as citizens maintained active participation in the assemblies, they were likely to see to it that their laws were just. But in handing the reins over to representatives, Rousseau reasons, citizens will focus their interests elsewhere – most likely to the "hustle and bustle of commerce and the arts" (*SC*, 3.15.2, 113 [III: 429]).[94] These distractions from civic duty amount to nothing less than the near-certain death of the republic: "As soon as someone says about the affairs of the State, *What do I care?* the State has to be considered lost" (*SC*, 3.15.3, 113–14 [III: 429]).

The third and main reason why Rousseau opposes representation, however, is the threat it poses to the general will. This is, in fact, the underlying premise of the first two arguments. The point of legislation is to realize the general will.[95] As Rousseau often insists, "the law is nothing but the declaration of the general will" (3.15.8, 115 [III: 430]). So any degree to which representation threatens this principle renders it illegitimate. The problem appears to be that this is precisely what representation does. Rousseau's discussion of the feudal tradition of representation here is illuminating – since the feudal "representatives" were scarcely what James Madison would desire for the institution: "As it is essential to liberty that the government in general should have a common interest with the people, so it is particularly essential that the branch of it under consideration should have an immediate dependence on, and an intimate sympathy with, the people."[96] The feudal representatives were, by contrast, aristocrats who had virtually nothing in common with their serfs. They represented "corporate interests," in Rousseau's terminology – scarcely the general will toward which legislation should be aimed. It is on these grounds that he remarks, "Sovereignty cannot be represented for the same reason it cannot

---

[94] This suggests the connection between the *First Discourse* and the *Social Contract*. Citizens distracted by the excitement of the arts and sciences do so at the cost of their civic engagement, which in turn results in the downfall of the republic itself.

[95] See *Government of Poland*, 206 [III: 984].

[96] Madison, Federalist No. 52, 324.

be alienated; it consists essentially in the general will, and does not admit of being represented; either it is the same or it is different; there is no middle ground" (*SC*, 3.15.5, 114 [III: 429]). The general will *must* be ratified by the people if it is to be called the general will. Anything short of this is a corporate or private will. Under the best of circumstances, an enlightened and benevolent representative legislature might pass just laws – but it cannot create the general will; this can only be done by the people themselves.

3.16. *That the Institution of the Government Is Not a Contract*

This is one chapter title that neatly sums up its essential thesis: the establishment of a government or executive is *not* a contract. Rousseau has at least two important reasons for building an argument to support this conclusion. The first is that other philosophers are arguing that government is established through contract. The Genevan political theorist, Jean-Jacques Burlamaqui, outlined a theory of government in which it was established in a contract between it and the people. He specifies three different social contracts. The first is the social contract in which all prepolitical individuals agree to form a society. The second is a contract agreeing to a particular constitution. The final is "another covenant" investing power in "one or more persons." It specifically calls for a "submission of the strength and will of each individual to the will of the heart of the society." So by Burlamaqui's account of the institution of government, each citizen necessarily surrenders his or her will. Samuel Pufendorf outlines a similar argument. For him, "After the decree concerning the form of government, a new pact will be needed to constitute the person or persons on whom the government of the group is conferred."[97] It is on this basis, for Pufendorf, that "subjection" to the government is established. But this language – Pufendorf's "subjection" and Burlamaqui's "submission" of the will – is entirely at cross-purposes with Rousseau's conception of the social contract.

Rousseau's principled rejection of institution of government via contract is that there is no contract with the magistrates. In his words, "It is absurd and contradictory for the Sovereign to give itself to a superior;

---

[97] Burlamaqui [1747] 2006, 293 [2.1.4.15.3]; Pufendorf, *Of the Law of Nature and of Nations*, 1.7.2.8. Notably, Hobbes differs from Burlamaqui and Pufendorf on this point, insisting that there is no contract with the government, largely since government and sovereign are the same in his system (see Hobbes [1651] 2002, 18.4, 18.6). Hobbes and Rousseau agree that the only contract is the one the people make among themselves to form a society.

to obligate oneself to obey a master is to return one's full freedom" (*SC*, 3.16.4, 116 [III: 432]). For Rousseau, the sovereign people cannot surrender their authority in a contract, which amounts to surrendering their democratic freedom. Contracts imply obligations and duties. These obligations and duties cannot be generated in a contract with an unequal partner in the magistrates, whom Rousseau designates as "servants," not sovereigns.[98] Contracts can only be made with equals, not subordinates. To imply that a sovereign can contract with a government is tantamount to saying that a government is of equal status as the sovereign – that is, it is sovereignty itself, and as such can impose its will on the people. For Rousseau, this is one more possible route to despotism, where the government could use the pretense of a contract to buttress its efforts to consolidate power.

3.17. *Of the Institution of Government*

Whereas Chapter Sixteen was dedicated to explaining what the institution of government is *not*, Chapter Seventeen is dedicated to explaining what it *is*. Government is *not instituted* by virtue of a contract between sovereign and magistrates. Government *is, rather, appointed* by the sovereign. This process, however, is "complex" (*SC*, 3.17.1, 117 [III: 433]) and requires several steps of reasoning.

The first step in appointing a government, according to Rousseau, is to choose a form of government (namely, a constitution of institutional arrangements, such as democracy, aristocracy, or monarchy). The people do this as a sovereign act of legislation. It presumably satisfies the criteria for legislation insofar as it is a general rather than particular act informed by the general will. But this immediately raises a question. Rousseau had earlier suggested that work of constructing and instituting a constitution falls not directly to the sovereign but rather to the lawgiver (*SC*, 2.7.1–4, 68–70 [III: 381–2]). He invests great effort there in sketching an individual of superhuman intelligence, who establishes a constitution while not being

---

[98] Specifically, he insists that Magistrates merely obey their Sovereign, not the other way around (*SC*, 3.18.1, 118 [III: 434]). Rousseau's conception of rulers as servants can be traced back as far as Plato: "I have now applied the term 'servants of the laws' to the men usually said to be rulers, not for the sake of an innovation but because I hold that it is this above all that determines whether the city survives or undergoes the opposite. Where the law is itself ruled over and lack of sovereign authority, I see destruction at hand for such a place. But where it is despot over the rulers and the rulers are slaves of the law, there I foresee safety and all good things which the gods have given to cities" (*Laws*, 715d). This can be effectively contrasted with Edmund Burke's insistence that "it is not true that they [kings] are, in any ordinary sense (by our constitution, at least) anything like servants; the essence of whose situation is to obey the commands of some other and to be removable at pleasure" (Burke [1790] 1987, 26).

in a position to benefit from any of its laws. There is no reference to this figure, however, and precisely the moment when the Lawgiver is required. One scholar, N. J. H. Dent, argues that this is because the Lawgiver is not in fact required by any argument in the *Social Contract* outside of 2.7.[99] Dent's argument is provocative, but the text at least in 3.17 here is consistent either with the people choosing a constitutional form themselves or with a lawgiver assuming this task for them. This being said, it is peculiar that Rousseau does not evoke the lawgiver at precisely the moment when it seems required by his earlier argument.

Regardless of how the constitution is chosen by the people, the choice of magistrates is a second and distinct step in the process of instituting a government. Rousseau emphasizes that while the formulation of a constitution is a general act and hence a "law," the choice of magistrates or a government is not general and hence not a law, but rather a "particular act" (*SC*, 3.17.3, 117 [III: 433]). This seems troublesome for Rousseau insofar as he specified earlier that the sovereign lacks the authority to make particular determinations (*SC*, 2.4.5, 62 [III: 373]). He solves this problem by suggesting the people have the right to make this particular determination because they are for a brief moment the government themselves. That is, they are a momentary democracy. This, of course, raises questions pertaining to Rousseau's own doubts about the success of democratic governments, culminating in the conclusion, "If there were a people of Gods, they would govern themselves democratically. So perfect a Government is not suited to men" (*SC*, 3.4.8, 92 [III: 406]). Why, then, does Rousseau insist that all states must be democratic at their origins? It is presumably because of the very transient nature of this political moment. To corrupt a people with luxury, for example, is an extended process of cultivating *amour propre*. Presumably, Rousseau's reliance on democracy here assumes that there will be insufficient time for democratic vices to corrupt the state before it carries out its singular duty of appointing magistrates. As a government, then, citizens are then entitled to conduct particular acts – most immediately, choose particular magistrates. Rousseau insists there is nothing peculiar in this: "It takes place every day in the Parliament of England where the lower House on certain occasions turns itself into a Committee of the whole, the better to discuss business, and thus becomes a simple commission rather than the Sovereign Court" (*SC*, 3.17.6, 118 [III: 434]).

---

[99] Dent 2005, 140–2.

3.18. *Means of Preventing the Usurpations by the Government*

In Chapters Sixteen and Seventeen, Rousseau argues that the government is appointed rather than established by a contract. He explores one of the most important consequences of this mode of instituting magistrates in Chapter Eighteen – namely, that because there is no contract between citizens and government, the people or sovereign may dissolve the government at its pleasure. This is yet another check built into Rousseau's institutional system. The government is nothing more than a "provisional form ... until such time as it [the Sovereign] pleases to order it differently" (3.18.2, 119 [III: 435]).[100] It is important to draw attention here to the fact that Rousseau characterizes the nature of governments as quite subordinate to the sovereign people. As there is no contract between the people and the government; there is only the issue of government's obedience to the people. As soon as it deviates from their will, which is specifically the general will, the people can go about the business of removing and replacing it.

The question of governmental change, however, is a tricky one. Deviations from the general will or common good are bad in themselves; but they cannot be treated simply in themselves. The fact is that changing the law or government on every such minor or momentary deviation is itself disruptive to the common good. As Aristotle cautions, "something and in certain cases law should be changed; but when we look into the matter from another point of view, great caution would seem to be required. For the habit of lightly changing the laws is an evil, and when the advantage is small, some errors both of lawgivers and rulers had better be left; the citizen will not gain so much by making the change as he will lose by the habit of disobedience."[101]

Rousseau is sympathetic to Aristotle's argument. He acknowledges, "changes are always dangerous, and ... one should never touch an established Government unless it becomes incompatible with the public good" (*SC*, 3.18.3, 119 [III: 435]). So he is far from counseling revolution at a modest or momentary deviation from the general will. Such disruptions promise to do more harm than good. At the same time, however, this is more a matter of prudence than right. Strictly speaking, the people reserve

---

[100] As Ethan Putterman remarks, the crucial point is that the government "can never be dismissive of the popular will without fear of political retribution" (Putterman 2010, 155).

[101] Aristotle's *Politics*, 2.8, 1269b12–19. In a similar manner, this moderately skeptical attitude toward change was articulated in the twentieth century by Michael Oakeshott, who writes, "the disruption [of change] entailed has always to be set against the benefit anticipated" (Oakeshott 1991, 411).

the right to change governments at whim, the same way, he says, they are free to change their military generals. It is important, however, to bear in mind that Rousseau is not necessarily thinking of something so radical as the American or French revolutions. A change in government can be as orderly as the change of power in parliamentary democracies, when the people determine that one party is more likely to pursue the general will than another. But it is clear from the nature of Rousseau's remarks here that such changes *can include* very disruptive ones, which is why he thinks it the better part of prudence to embark upon them only when "an established Government ... becomes incompatible with the public good."

Along these lines, Rousseau cautions the reader to be observant of important distinctions, including legitimate legislation from "seditious tumults" and the will of the people from the "clamors of faction." Most emphatically, he again warns that the "Prince can very easily expand them [his constitutional authorities] and, on the pretext of public calm, prevent assemblies intended to restore good order" (*SC*, 3.18.4, 119 [III: 435]). In making his point, he cites the Roman Decemvirs. The Decemvirs was assembled by the Romans in 452 BCE with the purpose of drawing up a legal code in one year's time. All other governmental agencies were suspended, and all of their decisions were to be final and without appeal. They completed their Law of the Twelve Tables in 450, but then refused to relinquish power at that time. Machiavelli notes in his *Discourses on Livy*, "These Ten conducted themselves very civilly" at first, attempting to build a basis of public trust for their future usurpations and tyranny.[102] Rousseau himself emphasizes the Decemvirs' unwillingness to relinquish power and preventing the legislative body from assembling. This is how all powers, he laments, "sooner or later usurp the Sovereign authority" (*SC*, 3.18.4, 119 [III: 435]).[103]

In order to forestall such eventualities, Rousseau proposes that each Legislative session open with two questions:

(1) *"[W]hether it please the Sovereign to retain the present form of Government.*

(2) *"[W]hether it please the People to leave its administration to those who are currently charged with it.* (*SC*, 3.18.7–8, 120 [III: 436])

---

[102] Machiavelli, *Discourses on Livy*, 86 [1.40]. See Livy 2002, 233–59 [3.33–54]. Of particular emphasis in Livy (and possibly of great interest to Rousseau) is his emphasis that "For the *decemvirs*, personal favor was equated with justice" (Livy 2002, 237 [3.36]).

[103] It is worth recalling that for Rousseau, to usurp the Sovereign authority is precisely the definition of a despot (*SC*, 3.10.10, 108 [III: 423]).

The first question offers the people the opportunity of transforming, for example, from a monarchic government to an aristocratic one. The second offers the possibility of removing one set of magistrates in favor of another. The point of both questions, however, is to refresh the spirit of the social contract and the general will more broadly.

He closes Book III with a radical conclusion: "there is no fundamental law which could not be revoked, not even the social pact; for if all the citizens were to assemble to break this pact by a common accord, there can be no doubt that it would be most legitimately broken" (*SC*, 3.18.9, 120 [III: 436]). This speaks to the strength and absolute sovereignty of the people when assembled. There is no externally binding reason why a state should exist against the will of the people, provided they make this decision for the right reasons. No state is eternal. He has already argued that governments are fated to decay. It is not difficult to deduce that entire societies likewise face the same fate. It is possible for Rousseau, under such circumstances, that this people might effectively re-institute itself at least once (*SC*, 2.8.5, 73 [III: 386]).[104] He is not optimistic, however, that this resurrection can be repeated beyond this. It seems thereafter a people is either destined to dissolve into anarchy, break up into new different civilizations, or suffer under tyranny.

---

[104] It is possible here that Rousseau has in mind the birth of the Roman Republic in the wake of Tarquin's abuses.

CHAPTER 4

Book IV

The final nine chapters of the *Social Contract* have two broad and related purposes: legislating and then maintaining the general will. Chapters One through Three speak to the practical issue of how a people might perform their duties as legislators. In Rousseau's vocabulary, they outline how the sovereign effectively legislates the general will. It is one thing to say that the people must agree on the general will for them to legislate. It is quite another to make it happen in the real world, since as Rousseau's great admirer, Immanuel Kant, once lamented, "Nothing straight can be constructed from such warped wood as that of which man is made."[1] Despite this, Rousseau is persuaded that measures can be taken to improve the likelihood of the people legislating the general will, including virtue (*SC*, 4.1.1) and supermajoritarianism (*SC*, 4.2.11).

The final substantive chapters of the *Social Contract* are dedicated to a discussion of the Roman Republic, often cited by Rousseau as an inspiration and model for his political theory. Here he discusses and adapts several of its institutions to his own purposes – primarily to maintaining the integrity of the general will. The Comitia and Tribunate combine as institutional bodies that might represent the *general* nature of the general will, insofar as the Comitia and Tribunes combine to represent the two classes of citizens that have historically combined to destroy all polities – namely, rich and poor. Rousseau suggests in these pages that representing both in a reasonable way might help maintain the general will. His chapter on the dictatorship speaks of the need to preserve the general will through times of crisis. His chapter on censorship addresses institutional measures by which public virtue might be maintained. And finally, his discussion of the civil religion in Chapter Eight offers spiritual reasons to inspire

---

[1] Kant [1795] 1996. 46.

citizens to civic duty, while also keeping the ominous threat of external religious authorities at bay, since they pose their own threats to the general will. He concludes in Chapter Nine by suggesting that the general will would ultimately also have to be protected in the context of external threats in the international sphere.

4.1. *That the General Will Is Indestructible*

Book IV notably opens with a return to the central and dominant concept of Rousseau's political philosophy: the general will. This represents thematic continuity with the opening chapters of both Books II and III. Book II opened with a discussion of sovereignty, which Rousseau defines as virtually synonymous with the general will. He specifically stresses there that "the general will alone can direct the forces of the State" (*SC*, 2.1.1, 57 [III: 368]). Book III opens with a discussion of government, which is to take its directives only from the general will (*SC*, 3.1.4, 82 [III: 396]). Yet at the same time, he acknowledges the difficulty in achieving this lofty though necessary ambition. Powerful princes tend to privilege their private or selfish wills over the general will or common good (*SC*, 3.1.19, 85–6 [III: 399]). So it is only appropriate that Rousseau would open his final book with another return to his central theme: how can one foster the development of a general will, protect it from nefarious particularizing forces, and empower it to govern? These are the central questions of the *Social Contract*, and they figure large in Book IV, Chapter One.

In returning to the general will in the first paragraph, Rousseau also returns to the first two *Discourses*. In other words, the solution to the problem of the general will lies in understanding its connection to these two essential preliminary works. As he wrote in his *Dialogues*, in order to understand his works of political philosophy it is necessary to "follow the chain of their contents." To facilitate the general will, he writes in the *Social Contract*, citizens should be "upright and simple" since those individuals "are difficult to deceive" (*SC*, 4.1.1, 121 [437]). "Simple" citizens – individuals largely unaffected by the negative manifestations of *amour propre* – are precisely those found to be lacking in the *First Discourse*. They do not pursue poetry or philosophy to impress their neighbors with their erudition. They do not study natural science to parade their intellectual might. They likely have neither erudition nor intellectual might, since these faculties are largely developed for the purpose of demonstrating their relative superiority over others. As Rousseau writes in his *Second Discourse*, already in early society, "Everyone began to look at everyone else and wished to be looked at himself.... The one who sang or danced best; the handsomest, the strongest, the most skillful, the most eloquent came to be the most highly regarded, and this was the first step at once toward inequality and vice." This effect is multiplied by the relative sophistication of any given society. The more developed it is, the more arts and letters it possesses, the more advanced its sciences, the more opportunities there are for others to engage in this unceasing contest for recognition and praise. This is precisely the problem Rousseau describes in the *First Discourse*, where otherwise simple and upright citizens feel compelled to demonstrate their worthiness to others in specifically these arenas. In doing so, they set aside what is truly valuable, however: their uprightness. The worst offenders of Rousseau's milieu are the *Philosophes*, an exceptionally learned group of Enlightenment thinkers, many of whom were deeply involved with the assembly of the *Encyclopédie*. He describes them in his *Reveries* as "not even concerned" about whether their arguments "were true or false."[2] What instead mattered to them was how clever others perceived them to be. This is precisely the worst disposition one could find in a citizen – since a commitment to the truth is tantamount to a commitment to justice.[3] In other words, to sacrifice truth in favor of vanity is the same as disregarding justice and the general will. It is inherently selfish and anti-social. For all these reasons, Rousseau prefers that his citizens be simple. The less sophisticated they are, the fewer temptations they have to sacrifice others to the altar of their own egos.

Further, as Rousseau also notes in the opening paragraph of Book IV, the more sophisticated subjects are, the more vulnerable they are to being duped. This seems counterintuitive, yet he has a compelling implicit argument underlying this assertion. A truly simple person is difficult to manipulate through flattery, bribes, or other machinations. Someone without ambitions of being the brightest person in the room does not respond to flattery of his intelligence. Someone without expensive taste in furnishings is more difficult to bribe with generous or extreme cash offers. So for this reason, too, Rousseau is concerned to keep citizens as simple as possible. It is noteworthy in this regard that the student reared in his pedagogical treatise, the *Emile*, is no boy genius. He is a child with no special or technical interests in philosophy, poetry, or the higher natural sciences. Simple persons have no use for wealth, opulence, or praise.

---

[2] *Dialogues*, 211 [*OC*, I: 933]; *Second Discourse*, 166 [III:169]; *Reveries*, 29 [I: 1013].
[3] "Justice and truth are two synonymous words" (*Reveries*, 51 [I: 1032]). Though, to be sure, Rousseau's thoughts on this matter are nuanced and somewhat ambiguous. See Grant 1997, Gourevitch 1994, and Kateb 1980.

They only know what is good and seek to do it. This is what makes for an ideal Rousseauean citizen.

It should go without saying, however, that simplicity is not synonymous with stupidity. Rousseau's citizens retain a kind of moral intelligence in the absence of their social sophistication – one perfectly adequate for the kind of political reasoning required of them. He envisions them "attending to affairs of State under an oak tree and always acting wisely" (*SC*, 4.1.1, 121 [III: 437]). This is the kind of intelligence he initially describes in the concluding paragraph of his *First Discourse*: "Are not your principles engraved in your hearts, and is it not enough in order to learn your Laws to return into oneself and to listen to the voice of one's conscience in the silence of the passions?"[4] In other words, he speaks of a native moral intelligence or conscience that exists prior to and independent of one's socially constructed ideas. The safeguarding and careful development of this faculty is the fundamental theme of Rousseau's *Emile*. As should be evident here, it is absolutely central to his democratic politics. Insofar as this conscience flourishes among the citizens, the general will and hence the state will flourish. Insofar as it is neglected in favor of vanity, wealth, and the desire for approval, the general will withers on the vine and despotism takes seed.

Beyond describing the types of citizens most favorable to cultivating and maintaining the general will, Rousseau also provides more clues about the content of the general will itself in 4.1. The general will is here characterized by "Peace, union, [and] equality" (*SC*, 4.1.1. 121 [III: 437]). This is not the first time he has described the tight relationship between the general will and equality. Earlier, Rousseau emphasizes the importance of equality for the general will (*SC*, 2.1.3, 57 [III: 368]), insofar as it takes the interests of all citizens equally into account, instead of sacrificing the legitimate interests of some in favor of the illegitimate interests of others. Equality in this context is contrasted with partiality, the opposing force threatening the general will. One of the most important ways to promote this kind of equality is to promote a degree of economic equality, as he stresses in 1.9.8n, since radical wealth stratification results in divergent interests and the ascendancy of privates wills at the expense of the general will.

Here in 4.1, Rousseau stresses the connection of equality to peace and union. The more equal citizens are (presumably both in rights and wealth), the less conflict and the more unity. This points to his deep commitment to fraternity. Social, economic, and political equality all foster

[4] *First Discourse*, 28 [III: 31].

more broadly shared affections for fellow citizens. One's interests do not stop at the front door. They extend down the block, throughout the community, and eventually to the national border.[5] This fraternal love – fostered in large part by equality – helps facilitate the general will. Wherever this equality is abandoned, this fraternal love disappears, and "the social knot begins to loosen and the State … weaken[s]; when particular interests begin to make themselves felt, and small societies influence the larger society, the common interest diminishes and meets with opposition, votes are no longer unanimous, and the general will is no longer the will of all, contradictions and disagreements arise, and the best opinion no longer carries the day unchallenged" (*SC*, 4.1.4, 121–2 [III: 438]).

Fraternal love facilitates what he earlier posited in Book II – that the general will is an "admirable accord between interest and justice" (*SC*, 2.4.7, 62 [III: 374]). By fostering love of fellow citizens, Rousseau hopes to make individuals love what is just. This is almost necessarily the case since instances of injustice are characterized by unfairly favoring one person or group over another person or group. If all citizens are equally valued and cherished, then there is no cause for such partiality. Perhaps the most (in-) famous example of such impartiality is Plato's city of Kallipolis, described by Socrates in the *Republic*, where the rulers are prohibited from having their own families or property. Socrates suggests that through such proscriptions, governments have no self-interest to defend, and will incline to the common good. Rousseau first pursues this end in his *Political Economy* by promoting patriotism. "Certain it is that the greatest marvels of virtue have been produced by love of fatherland: this gentle and lively sentiment which combines the force of *amour propre* with all the beauty of virtue, endows it with an energy which, without disfiguring it, makes it into the most heroic of all passions." It is insufficient to assume that most citizens simply reason it is best to serve the common good. They are most effective and most just when they are infused with a passionate love of homeland and fellow citizens. One must, so to speak, merge the energy and vigor of the private will with the justice of the general will. After elaborating in the *Political Economy* with the examples of Socrates and Cato, Rousseau insists that this passionate love of country and fellow citizens is only possible in the context of political

---

[5] Rousseau favors patriotism over cosmopolitanism. As Jason Neidleman argues, this is not so much because Rousseau is philosophically opposed to a universal fraternity, but simply because he thinks its abstractness is ultimately beyond the reasonable capacity of most. As Rousseau writes, "Patriotism and humanity … are two virtues incompatible in their energy, and especially among an entire people. The Legislator who wants them both will get neither one nor the other. This compatibility has never been seen and never will be, because it is contrary to nature, and because one cannot give the same passion two aims" (*Mountain*, 149 [III: 706]).

and economic equality. It is impossible to foster fraternal love where justice is ignored and the laws fail to protect the poor from the usurpations of the rich. "It is, therefore, one of the most important tasks of government to prevent extreme inequality of fortunes." Without this equality, there is little to protect "good morals, respect for the laws, love of fatherland, and the vigor of the general will."[6] This is the argument underlying Rousseau's value of fraternity and commitment to equality in 4.1.

Subsequently, he elaborates in his *Government of Poland* that a citizen can arrive at this fraternal love through an education that will make him "patriotic by inclination, passion, necessity." Ideally, "this love makes up his whole existence; he sees only his fatherland, he lives only for it; when he is alone, he is nothing: when he no longer has a fatherland, he no longer is, and if he is not dead, he is worse than dead." This is cultivated through games that stress equality and fraternal love, as well as the need to win the right kind of public approbation.[7] Along these lines, Rousseau also stresses in his "Letter to d'Alembert" the value of public festivals and balls, which have the effect of making everyone feel as though part of one large family where everyone's interests count.[8] All these rituals and festivals promote the same value of fraternal love. And for Rousseau, where citizens genuinely love one another, the general will stands its best chance of becoming and remaining sovereign. Without this, the best one can hope for is the liberal option of all of these interests colliding and cancelling one another out.

If a state succeeds in cultivating this fraternal love on the broad scale, Rousseau observes, there is little reason to multiply the number of laws and regulations (*SC*, 4.1.2, 121 [III: 437]).[9] If people genuinely care about one another and have a strong sense of justice, they will not need anyone to *force* them to do anything. They will do the right thing on their own accord. Compare this with Thomas Hobbes, who makes law a central element of his politics. He needs many laws because human nature itself is never transformed.[10] Hobbes either never considers fostering this kind

---

[6] *Political Economy*, 16 [III: 255], 19 [III: 258], 20 [III: 259].

[7] *Poland*, 189 [III: 966], *Poland*, 191 [III: 968]. Striving for public approbation seems to run at cross-purposes with other elements of Rousseau's philosophy, insofar as it is mixed with the volatile *amour propre*. It seems in this context, assuming Rousseau is not contradicting this general concern in his works, that he means it appropriate for citizens to win public approval so long as that judgment is based on the general will itself.

[8] "Letter to d'Alembert," 131 [V: 119].

[9] This echoes the same point made earlier in his *Political Economy*, 14 [III: 253].

[10] This reading of Hobbes has been challenged by Richard Tuck, who describes a more "utopian" and even "Rousseauean" Hobbes than others in this regard. For him, the institution of Hobbes's commonwealth parallels Rousseau's, insofar as it transforms human nature. It purges individuals of the

of love, or he tacitly thinks it quixotic and foolish. His citizens therefore remain just as selfish as they ever were. The only way to keep them in line is to threaten them with punishment for anti-social behavior and back it up with violence when required. In Rousseau's state, by contrast, citizens are largely self-regulating.[11] There is a great advantage in Rousseau's approach, as he is well aware. In a Hobbesian state, where subjects are kept in check by fear, they have little incentive to obey the law when the sovereign's attention is turned elsewhere. A state animated by fraternal love provides no incentives for evading the law and social obligations: "They will obey the laws and not elude them because they will suit them and will have the inward assent of their wills. Loving their fatherland, they will serve it out of zeal and with all their heart." For Rousseau, the law may supplement this civic virtue, but it cannot replace it: "nothing can replace morals in sustaining government."[12]

If a state fails to cultivate this kind of fraternal love, Rousseau asks, "Does it follow that the general will is annihilated or corrupted?" His answer is firm: "No, it remains constant, unalterable, and pure" (*SC*, 4.1.6, 122 [III: 438]). Citizens always retain a sense of the general will. The problem is that it can be subordinated to private or corporate wills. When someone consciously follows his self-interest to the common good, "he does not extinguish the general will within himself, he evades it" (*SC*,

---

passions that burden them in the state of nature and replaces them with others more conducive to peace. See Tuck 2004, 132–8. To be sure, Tuck is correct in his description of the behavior of Hobbes's subjects. Yet it is less clear that their internal motivations are transformed. As Hobbes insists, even in the commonwealth they are fundamentally motivated by fear. The fear of one another is exchanged for the fear of the Leviathan. And they also remain, I think, egoistic. It is simply a more complex egoism, whereby one's interest is now served by behaving in accordance with the laws of nature by virtue of the laws and sanctions imposed by the Leviathan.

[11] Of course, Rousseau's approach here also differs from Madison in Federalist No. 51. For Madison, "It may be a reflection on human nature that such devices [as checks and balances] should be necessary to control the abuses of government. But what is government itself but the greatest of all reflection on human nature? If men were angels, no government would be necessary" (Madison [1787–88] 1999, 290). To be sure, Rousseau does not entirely disagree with Madison. If he did, he would have neither provisions for a government nor a need to force people to be free. So he knows that some laws will, of course, be necessary. But the point is to motivate the people to be as good as possible at first, so that the resulting government is as small and unobtrusive as possible.

[12] *Poland*, 184 [IV: 961]; *Political Economy*, 13 [III: 252]. It is worth comparing Rousseau again with James Madison on the question of virtue. Madison writes in Federalist No. 10 that "we know that neither moral nor religious motives can be relied on as an adequate control [on factions]" (Madison [1787–88] 1999, 75). This being said, Madison writes in Federalist No. 56 that although there are obvious failings in human nature, "there are other qualities in human nature which justify a certain portion of esteem and confidence. Republican government presupposes the existence of these qualities in a higher degree than any other form" (343). So while there are times when Rousseau and Madison seem to be proposing fundamentally different kinds of programs, on other occasions the differences seem to reside in the relative degree to which each relies on the morality of their citizens.

4.1.6, 122 [III: 438]). This is the sense of conscience that he describes in the *Emile* and elsewhere. It is "engraved in all hearts." It is "an innate principle of justice."[13] The problem is that it is subject to much diversion and obfuscation. But as it is *innate*, it can never be eliminated.

4.2. *Of Suffrage*

Rousseau's chapter on voting is particularly important insofar as it explains how the general will is realized in legislation. This is precisely his goal – to convert the general will into public law. And it is a goal that is no doubt broadly shared in principle. Of course, ideally he desires that everyone agrees on the general will in complete harmony or concord. There is nothing better than having everyone unanimously agree to craft perfectly just legislation. This is presumably most likely to occur under the conditions described in the previous chapter, where equality and fraternity reign. By contrast, states characterized by "long debates, dissensions, disturbances, signal the ascendancy of particular interests and the decline of the State" (*SC*, 4.2.1, 123 [III: 439]). While unanimity seems perhaps an impossible standard, Rousseau certainly makes a reasonable point. When legislators largely or especially unanimously agree, the general will is almost certainly well-guarded. Where legislators clash, it is almost certainly the case from a Rousseauean perspective that at least one side has privileged its own interests at the expense of the general will. By this measure, of course, it seems that few Western democracies today measure up to Rousseau's ideal state.

Of course, there is a dangerous flip side of faux harmony against which Rousseau sternly cautions. Citizens might also unanimously agree when they have "fallen into servitude, [and] no longer have freedom or will. Then fear and flattery turn voting into acclimations" (*SC*, 4.2.3, 123 [III: 439]). This is most obviously the state he depicts in Part Two of his *Discourse on Inequality*, where citizens have been driven either by fear, flattery, or outright deception into servitude. They are even drawn in by the promise of being preserved in "everlasting concord."[14] Their consent is unanimous, but dubious, since they have been lured into a despotic trap, where their wills are sacrificed to the particular wills of the moneyed and powerful. Rousseau associates this explicitly with the politics of the Roman Empire, where unanimity was more the outcome of fear than of fraternity and the general will.

---

[13] *First Discourse*, 28 [III: 30]; *Emile*, 289 [IV: 598].
[14] *Second Discourse*, 173 [III: 177]. See also *Poland*, 217 [III: 996].

Of course, even under the best of circumstances, unanimity is virtually impossible. Furthermore, there is a specific sense in which it is undesirable for Rousseau. There was one political system in the seventeenth and eighteenth centuries notorious for its legislative unanimity requirement: Poland. Rousseau addresses this mechanism, called the *liberum veto*, specifically in his *Government of Poland*, which he describes as a "fatal abuse" and an "instrument of oppression." The problem with a requirement for legislative unanimity is how easily it facilitates the power of factions and private interests. An enterprising wealthy party need only buy the vote of one legislator to kill off measures otherwise destined to serve the common good. So while Rousseau is enthusiastic about a populace that organically arrives at unanimity, he steadfastly rejects it as a required standard for legislation, so much so that he insists, "This barbarous right must be abolished and the death penalty imposed on anyone who might be tempted to exercise it."[15]

Nevertheless, he retains this standard for the social contract itself.[16] This is not to say that everyone present in a state of nature must agree to live together as one civic union in order for that union to exist. Rather, it means that no one can be coerced into joining that civic union in the first place. All members must give their free consent: "for the civil association is the most voluntary act in the world; every man being born free and master of himself, no one may on any pretext whatever subject him without his consent" (*SC*, 4.2.5, 123 [III: 440]). Those refusing to join the association are considered to be "foreigners among the Citizens" (*SC*, 4.2.6, 123 [III: 440]). They presumably receive fewer of the protections and carry fewer responsibilities than do citizens, although Rousseau does not here specify how limited this might be. In his *Political Economy*, he insists that the state's general will does not apply to foreign visitors. For them, the state's general will is merely another particular will. This makes sense to a point, insofar as a state has its own interest independent of aliens. At the same time, however, his treatment raises questions. Do visitors lack basic rights of life and liberty when passing through another land? It is difficult to imagine Rousseau denying that foreigners lack any protections or considerations of justice when visiting or even residing in another land. Yet he does not provide any principled ground to support such protections.

---

[15] *Poland*, 216 [III: 995], 218 [III: 996].

[16] Rousseau first asserted the necessity of unanimity in *SC*, 1.5.3. He reaffirms this even amidst his denunciation of the *liberum veto* (*Poland*, 217 [III: 996]).

Settlers, however, are a different matter from visitors. Anyone taking up residence in the state implicitly or tacitly consents to obey the sovereign: "to dwell in the territory is to submit to sovereignty" (*SC*, 4.2.6, 123 [III: 440]; see also 3.11.4, 109 [III: 424]). This principle of tacit consent was articulated in John Locke's *Second Treatise on Government*, where he argues, "every man, that hath any possessions, or enjoyment, of any part of the dominions of any government, doth thereby give his *tacit consent*, and is as far forth obliged to obedience to the laws of that government."[17] This may seem an alarming doctrine, especially where a government holds someone captive either by force or deprivation of the resources to escape. Anticipating this objection, Rousseau does add an important caveat. If someone is *forced* to be there against his will, he cannot be thought of as tacitly consenting. And his notion of being forced there is generously broad – including being deprived of shelter and food, in addition to being the object of threats and violence. This would suggest a kind of response to Hume's objection to tacit consent, as proposed by Locke. Hume objects that individuals cannot be obligated to consent to laws when lacking the resources to escape.[18]

For those remaining according to their own explicit or tacit consent, all other decisions will be handled by a majority of citizens (*SC*, 4.2.7, 124 [III: 440]). Rousseau acknowledges, however, that this immediately raises an uncomfortable question: "how can a man be both free and forced to conform to wills which are not his own?" (*SC*, 4.2.7, 124 [III: 440]). In other words, why should someone voting against the majority accept the majority's decisions? This is a way of revisiting the "forced to be free" paradox Rousseau introduced in Book I (*SC*, 1.8.8, 53 [III: 364]). What right does a state have to compel subjects with force to obey its laws, especially when they explicitly reject those laws when acting in their capacity as sovereigns?

Rousseau's answer to this question is simple on the surface, but potentially troubling: "when the opinion contrary to my own prevails, it proves nothing more than that I made a mistake and that what I took to be the general will was not" (*SC*, 4.2.8, 124 [III: 441]). This seems to imply that the majority is, in effect, tantamount to the general will itself – in other

---

[17] *Second Treatise on Government*, §119.
[18] "Can we seriously say, that a poor peasant or artisan has a free choice to leave his country, when he knows no foreign language or manners, and lives from day to day, by the small wages which he acquires? We may as well assert, that a man, by remaining on a vessel, freely consents to the dominion of the master; though he was carried on board while asleep, and must leap into the ocean, and perish, the moment he leaves her" (Hume [1748] 1994, 193).

words, that it is impossible for the majority to err. That is, the will of all would be the general will. If this were true, it would violate much of what Rousseau maintained earlier about the distinction of the general will from the will of all (*SC*, 2.3.2, 60 [III: 371]), about the faulty deliberations of the people (*SC*, 2.3.1, 59 [III: 371]), and the moral uprightness of the general will itself.[19] So to understand the ontological status of majoritarianism in this particular sense of it being infallible would be to read against the entire spirit of Rousseau's political thought. Indeed, the very next paragraph of Chapter Two clarifies this point with an essential caveat: "This [the fact that the minority voter is misguided] presupposes, it is true, that all characteristics of the general will are still in the majority: once they no longer are, then regardless of which side one takes there is no longer any freedom" (*SC*, 2.3.9, 124 [III: 441]). Stated otherwise, these remarks only apply insofar as the will of all coincides with the general will. And presumably, insofar as the majority will deviates from the general will, one is relieved from the burdens of obeying those laws.[20]

To appreciate the point Rousseau means to emphasize here, consider the following example. When an industrialist is a member of a political community, he has both an individual and a general will. His general will demands that harmful pollutants be kept out of rivers and lakes. Yet his private or individual will worries that environmental regulations could be personally costly. So when the opportunity to vote on environmental regulations presents itself, he votes against them. It is in this spirit that Rousseau suggests that he has erred on the general will. The community has a better conception of the general will than any one individual. A single individual or even a small group of people might find it advantageous to pollute the local waters. But it is highly improbable that an entire community would do the same. Or at least this is true so long as Rousseau's prescriptions concerning economic equality are in place. In the absence of this equality, it is more feasible that particularly wealthy citizens might influence others through a greater share of public discourse or even veiled threats about killing local jobs.

The remaining question, however, is: how are subjects obligated to obey laws to which they might have objected? Returning to the polluting industrialist example, what if he opposes environmental regulations, insisting that he has an individual right to operate his factory according

---

[19] *Political Economy*, 12 [III: 251].

[20] A different account of how Rousseau might justify the imposition of majority rule on dissenters can be found in Cohen 2010, 74–82.

to his own lights? How, then, can Rousseau say he is being forced to be free when he is doing what he thinks right? He has a simple answer, if not one that might satisfy all readers. We *do agree* to put ourselves under the direction of the general will, as he notes at *SC*, 1.6.9 and 4.2.8. Insofar as the environmental regulations conform to the general will, the industrialist in a genuine sense agreed to obey that law or be forced to do so. He has agreed to do what is right – even where his myopic view of what is right deviates from genuine right in specific instances. If he did not want to find himself in the position of being forced to do what is right, he should not belong to a society governed by the general will.

In Chapter Two Rousseau also provides specific advice on how to vote in order to help maintain the republic: "When a law is proposed in the People's Assembly, what they are being asked is not exactly whether they approve or reject it, but whether it does or does not conform to the general will" (*SC*, 4.2.8, 124 [III: 440–1]). Citizens are not to vote in accordance with their private wills; they must vote for the general will. Insofar as they vote in any other fashion or with any other considerations, they thereby vote for a partial interest and hence vote illegitimately.

Both paragraphs eight and nine insist on a strict fidelity to the general will. Yet it is unclear to this point what mechanisms are in place to enforce this outcome. Specifically, how can citizens be assured that their votes are consistent with the general will? Rousseau has already provided guidance to increase this likelihood by virtue of his recommendations to promote equality and fraternity. Yet despite these measures, it is clearly possible that a majority may violate the general will.

In this context, Rousseau offers yet one more measure to improve the odds of bringing the will of all in agreement with the general will. On particularly important matters, supermajoritarian rules should be applied. That is, majorities in excess of 50 percent plus one should be required on the most important legislative matters – what he calls "Laws" (*loix*), as compared with matters of business (*affaires*) (*SC*, 4.2.11, 125 [III: 441]). He is more explicit on this matter in his *Government of Poland*, where he specifies (as an example though, not as a fixed or eternal rule) that "when it comes to legislation [*legislation*], one might require at least a three-quarters majority, two-thirds in matters of state [*les matieres d'Etat*], no more than a bare majority for … business of routine and immediate interest [*affaires courantes et momentanees*]."[21] The fundamental point is straightforward. The more important or momentous the decision, the greater the majority that is required to enact the people's will. In simple matters, such as setting the date when taxes are due, for example, a simple majority is sufficient.[22] By contrast, if part of the constitution requires amending, something closer to a three-quarters vote would be advisable. As Melissa Schwartzberg has argued, Rousseau's implicit logic here is compelling.[23] The greater majority that is required, the less one can simply vote on the basis of one's private will. It may be possible, for example, to find a bare majority of citizens willing to sacrifice others to promote their selfish interests. For example, it might be possible to find a majority of citizens willing to support a measure that would cut education for the poor. But when a supermajority requires that those same oppressed individuals be included in the voting bloc to enact that bill, its chances of legislative success diminish greatly. That is, supermajorities require that nearly everyone's interests be taken into consideration as a matter of procedure. So supermajorities are especially helpful in bringing about the general will, as they almost by definition frustrate private wills (provided the people are well-informed and uninfluenced by flattery and opinion). Supermajorities are still not the same as the general will – they are real-world approximations.[24] But their construction offers great strides in that direction.

While Rousseau's arguments for supermajoritarianism are compelling, it is worth pausing to consider some difficulties associated with this solution. First, any vote beyond a normal majority is likely to slow down the legislative process. This may not always be worrisome insofar as it can slow down impassioned majorities otherwise bent on wholly irrational paths. But on other occasions, where it delays necessary and timely legislation, this can be a burden on the common good. Second, and likely more troublesome for Rousseau, is the fact that supermajority requirements make it possible for a relatively small group of partial or factious interests to kill off legislation aimed at promoting the general will. This kind of concern animated the decisions of the American Founders, who opted in most instances for a simple legislative majority rule (excepting constitutional amendments, treaty ratification, and the overriding of presidential vetoes). Alexander

---

[22] This raises unanswered questions for Rousseau concerning what constitutes a matter of business requiring majority vote and what can be determined by the government itself. He does not engage this question.

[23] Schwartzberg 2008, esp. 414–19. This account differs from that offered by David Estlund, who argues, "Rousseau conceived voters as giving their opinion on an independent matter of fact – the content of the general will – and held that the answer receiving the majority of votes under certain conditions was guaranteed to be correct" (Estlund 1989, 1318). See also Brian Barry ([1965] 1990, 292–93), where he compares Rousseau with Condorcet's jury theorem.

[24] Consider where a supermajority might oppress a very small minority, or consider how a supermajority might be constructed on the basis of demagoguery and flattery.

Hamilton lamented that such procedures resulted in "contemptible com-promises of the public good," and James Madison likewise perceived that supermajoritarianism would enable "an interested minority ... [to] take advantage of it to screen themselves from equitable sacrifices to the gen-eral weal."[25] Defenders of Rousseau have at least one conceivable reply to such objections. Whereas Madison and Hamilton largely assume human nature to be irretrievably corrupt, Rousseau works to cultivate virtuous citizens, largely immune to the lure of partial interests. This would func-tion to limit the eventualities feared by Madison and Hamilton. No one could deny that some would resist the bonds of fraternal love. It is clear enough throughout Rousseau's political writings that many would. But Rousseau presumes that at least a supermajority of them would embrace their fellow citizens' interests as equally valid as their own. So here, as in many moments in the *Social Contract*, he relies on civic virtue as a means to maintain the republic.

4.3. *Of Elections*

Although Rousseau does not advocate a democratic form of government (*SC*, 3.4), his commitment to popular sovereignty makes him a kind of democrat. One of the most important functions of the people in their capacity as citizens is to appoint magistrates to handle the affairs of government.[26] These are the members of the executive branch, as is known in contemporary parlance, ranging from modest bureaucrats to a ruler. As he suggested earlier, magistrates – especially princes, if they are to exist at all – must be animated by the general will.[27] So the main issue for Chapter Three is how magistrates might be selected such that they most likely act in accordance with the general will.

There are two primary modes by which magistrates may be appointed: lot and election. In aristocracies, Rousseau observes, voting is appropriate.[28] Appointment by lot is most appropriate for democracies, Rousseau

---

[25] Alexander Hamilton, Federalist No. 22, 144; James Madison, Federalist No. 58, 359.

[26] Notably, Rousseau insists that the appointment of magistrates is a moment – though a fleeting one – of pure democracy. That is, when the people select magistrates, they temporarily act as the government themselves. After this moment, the government takes its more permanent form, depending on the constitution (*SC*, 3.17.5, 117–18 [III: 433–4]).

[27] *SC*, 3.1.19, 85 [III: 399].

[28] He does not attempt to explain why this is the case. One might deduce this, however, from his description of aristocracies at *SC*, 3.5. Aristocracies ideally involve the selection of magistrates defined by their "probity, enlightenment, [and] experience" (*SC*, 3.5.5, 93 [III: 407]), which is unequally distributed through the population. Voting for magistrates according to the general will would presumably involve choosing those most exemplifying these traits.

reasons, because in a democracy "magistracy is not an advantage but a burdensome charge" (*SC*, 4.3.3, 125 [III: 442]).[29] Bearing in mind Rousseau's conception is of a place defined by its uniquely high level of civic virtue and is without luxury or wealth disparity, it is easy to see that no citizens would be eager to rule insofar as they lacked the motives and incentives to use the office to enrich themselves or promote their selfish interests. Ruling is not an opportunity to be exploited; it is a burden that must be fulfilled. So to avoid imposing this burden by active choice, which can be an unjust imposition to people with better things to do, lot imposes government service by making the choice mechanical: "Only the law can impose this charge on the one to whom the lot falls. For then, since the condition is equal for all and the choice does not depend on human will, no particular application can distort the universality of the law" (*SC*, 4.3.4, 125 [III: 442]). Yet Rousseau reminds his readers that there is no "genuine Democracy" on earth. While one can expect people to enlarge their wills and take the interests of others into account much of the time, it is impossible to expect that everyone will shed their individual wills at all times.

Since most governments, however, will be mixed,[30] it is generally prudent to employ both modes of appointment. Rousseau finds this in the selection of magistrates in the Venetian Doge, a set of magistrates appointed in an impossibly baroque combination of lot and election.[31] In such circumstances, it is best to divide these modes of selection according to the talents demanded by the particular office. For offices requiring specific skills, such as military posts, Rousseau prefers appointment by election.[32] For those offices requiring only "good sense, justice, [and] integrity," such as judicial appointments, it is best to appoint citizens by lot. He naturally assumes here that citizens in a republic would possess precisely these traits, as these attributes merely describe the virtuous citizen fostered in *SC*, 4.1 and elaborated in *Emile*, the *Discourse on Political Economy*, and the *Government of Poland*. From a certain point of view, of course, Rousseau places enormous faith in ordinary citizens – the kind of faith not commonly found in most countries today calling themselves

---

[29] He specifically notes that this association of democracy and selection by lot differs from the reasons provided by Montesquieu that "*it leaves every Citizen with a reasonable hope of serving the fatherland*" (*SC*, 4.3.2, 125 [III: 442]). See Montesquieu's *Spirit of the Laws*, 1.3.17 ([1748] 1999).

[30] Rousseau posits, "Properly speaking, there is no simple Government" (*SC*, 3.7.1, 99 [III: 413]), and subsequently repeats, "there is no genuine Democracy" (*SC*, 4.3.7, 126 [III: 443]).

[31] Mowbray and Gollmann 2007. Rousseau had some familiarity with the Doge from his time spent in Venice. See his *Confessions*, 261 [I: 310].

[32] He confirms this in his *Government of Poland*, where he insists, "it is important, in the selection of officers, not to take into account of birth, position, and wealth but only of experience and talent" (*Poland*, 236 [III: 1016]). A lottery system is obviously incapable of making these distinctions.

"democracies." Few would seriously consider appointing citizens by lot to serve most bureaucratic posts. But from another point of view, this is precisely the faith modern democracies place in their citizens when selecting them for jury duty – and the lottery method remains the same.

4.4. *Of the Roman Comitia*

Chapter Four begins a sequence of five consecutive chapters dedicated to analyzing key elements of the Roman Republic. It has long been known that Rousseau was fond of the ancients, with a particular affection for the Roman Republic. This affinity is evident in his many appeals to civic virtue which underlie much of the *Social Contract*. But it is also readily apparent in his embracing of specific Roman institutions, which includes here the comitia, the tribunate, the censor, the dictator, and finally the practice of a civil religion. Each of these institutions is dedicated less to establishing the general will than maintaining it. The dominant approach of most scholars to understanding these chapters (with the exception of Chapter 8) is simply to ignore them. C. E. Vaughan remarks in his otherwise comprehensive treatment of Rousseau's political philosophy, "It must be confessed ... that these four chapters [*SC*, 4.4–7] are barely relevant to the subject, and quite unworthy of the setting in which they stand." Robert Derathé is equally dismissive, remarking, "It is clear, in effect, that the essay in four chapters on Roman political institutions have only a distant relationship with the *Principles of Political Right*."[33] Yet Rousseau himself cautions against this reading: "the historical sketch of Roman administration ... will explain more concretely all the maxims which I might establish" (*SC*, 4.3.10, 126–7 [III: 443]). Readers should take these words to heart before succumbing to the temptation of skipping over these chapters, as they speak to the crucial matter of preserving the general will through institutional measures.

Before considering Rousseau's account of the Comitia and its specific virtues, it is helpful to have a sense of this institution as it existed in Rome. The Roman Republic of the fourth century enacted the bulk of its important laws in its assemblies.[34] These were not representative, as is largely found in contemporary republics, but quite immediately sovereign in Rousseau's sense. All citizens were free to attend the gatherings as

---

[33] Vaughan [1915] 1962, II: 109n1; Derathé 1964, 1495n1. Both this passage and Vaughan's are cited approvingly in Masters 1968, 305–6.

[34] See Boatwright, Gargola, and Talbert 2004, 67–71.

they saw fit. Attendance generally increased with the gravity of the issues at hand. The assemblies were called to order by particular office holders, such as consuls, praetors, and tribunates, who also controlled the meeting agendas. The assembled citizens had the task of voting their proposals up or down. The Comitias were three such assemblies. The *Comitia Tributa* was an assembly of the thirty-five Roman tribes, relatively egalitarian across class in composition. Each tribe, regardless of wealth or class, possessed exactly one vote. Since the rural regions had more total tribes, the *Comitia Tributa* tended to favor the interests of simple farmers over urban concerns (although the distance required to reach the assemblies was sometimes prohibitive for the farmers, which tended toward equalizing urban and rural influence). The *Comitia Centuriata*, by contrast, was divided into many centuriates, each possessing one vote. These certainly favored the more urban and wealthy interests since the rich held a large number of sparsely populated centuriates. Indeed, voting in the *Comitia Centuriata* was ordered de facto according to wealth. Often, matters were decided before the poorer centuriates (*proletarii*) even had an opportunity to cast a vote. An additional Comitia existed in the earlier days of the Roman Republic as well, the *Comitia Curiae*, which passed certain laws, confirmed governmental appointees, and also approved adoptions.

Rousseau opens Chapter Four with a caveat: early and especially founding history consists largely in speculation and fable rather than in reliable records (*SC*, 4.4.1, 127 [III: 444]). While historians can know the relatively recent past with much greater certainty, the founding times of Rome, for example, are simply beyond their grasp. This is not especially problematic for Rousseau in this chapter, since he does not need to know the origins so much as the principles of the subject under consideration. But it is worth drawing attention to the use of "conjectures" and "fables" because of his employment of them elsewhere in his work. He cites his reflections on early society in his *Second Discourse*, for example, as nothing but "conjecture." And he subsequently defines "fables" in his *Reveries of the Solitary Walker* as fictions "which have a moral purpose" to "wrap useful truths in easily perceived and pleasing forms."[35]

---

[35] *Second Discourse*, 125 [III: 123]; *Reveries*, 48 [I: 1029]. When he recommends the judicious use of fables in the *Emile*, the Tutor does not attempt to pass off these tales as actual historical facts (*Emile*, 247–9 [IV: 540–3]). He references a series of fables involving talking crows, cicadas, frogs, and mules, and emphasizes that these are to be taught to "men" (*Emile*, 249 [IV: 542]), not young children, who are too young to separate allegory from truth (*Emile*, 112–16 [IV: 351–7]). There is no reason to believe that he intends to pass these tales off as factual and historical accounts of real events.

The first twenty paragraphs of Chapter Four are largely dedicated to sketching the complicated class structure underlying the Roman Comitia. The precise means of deriving the classes are less important to Rousseau than the composition and tendencies of those classes in the context of their respective comitias. In spelling out the origins of the comitia, he emphasizes early Rome's special love of rural life. Even the most distinguished Roman citizens preferred the "simple and hardworking life" to the "idle and loose life of the Roman Bourgeois" (*SC*, 4.4.9, 129 [III: 446]). This Roman bias is entirely consistent with Rousseau's preference for the simple virtue of rural citizens, described in the *First Discourse*, the *Discourse on Political Economy*, the "Letter to d'Alembert," the *Government of Poland*, and elsewhere in the *Social Contract* (e.g., *SC*, 4.1.1, 121 [III: 437]). And insofar as the Comitia succeeded, he avers, "it could only be made to work because of the first Romans' simple morals, their disinterestedness, their taste for agriculture, their contempt for commerce and the ardor for gain" (*SC*, 4.4.19, 131 [III: 448]).

Rousseau discusses three comitias in the central portion of Chapter Four: the Curiae, the Centuriate, and the Tribal. According to Rousseau, Romulus founded the Curiate in order to establish mutual checks between the Senate and the people – while maintaining his own power over both. It functioned well enough throughout the age of the Roman kings and into the early years of the Republic, balancing the competing interests of both rich and poor. But its great vice was its emphasis on urban Rome at the expense of rural Rome, hence making it favorable to "tyranny and evil designs" (*SC*, 4.4.34, 135 [III: 452]). By Rousseau's established standards, it failed insofar as it did not represent and include citizens from all classes, since according to Book I, "For a will to be general, it is not always necessary that it be unanimous, but it is necessary that all votes be counted; any formal exclusion destroys generality" (*SC*, 2.2.1n, 58n [III: 369n]). The exclusion of rural populations presumably constitutes a "formal exclusion" in precisely this sense. The Roman institution eventually fell into disuse, its functions being usurped by the Lictors.

The second comitia was the Centuriate, which at first clearly favored Patrician or aristocratic interests. As Rousseau concedes, although the Centuriate represented all Roman classes, "the first Class [the wealthiest] comprised ninety-eight [of one hundred ninety-three centuries in the Centuriate]," resulting in the fact that "this first Class by itself alone prevailed over all the others by the number of its votes" (*SC*, 4.4.28, 133 [III: 450]). This had the effect of its decisions being "settled more often by majorities of cash than of votes" (*SC*, 4.4.28, 133 [III: 451]). So it would seem that the Centuriate was the least suited to Rousseau's political philosophy. But Rousseau continues his analysis of the Centuriate by observing its moderating features. First, the wealthy included not only the Patricians (historically wealthy and exclusive families), but also several Plebeians with historically different and opposing interests – specifically ones who presumably defended their friends and family among the poor. Second, the Centuriate adopted a unique voting procedure that moderated its class bias. Instead of voting in order of wealth, which would set a biased precedent in the first Century for the Centuries to follow, they instead chose a Century by lot (which by definition could have been from any class). This Century was known as the *praerogativa*.[36] It would then cast its vote alone the first day. The other Centuries had a day thereafter to ponder the choice of the randomly selected Century and generally followed its model, regardless of class. Rousseau concludes, "In this way the authority of example was withdrawn from rank and given to lot in conformity with the principle of democracy" (*SC*, 4.4.31, 134 [III: 451]). He adds that this extra day itself was helpful for the other Centuries to cast their votes on the basis of knowledge rather than impulse.

Whereas the Tribal Comitia seems at least partly sympathetic to Rousseau's repeated condemnations of wealth and privilege, it possesses a fatal flaw. The Tribal Comitia, while having extensive Plebeian representation, formally excluded Patricians.[37] As such, it possessed precisely the same vice as that which burdened the Curiae, in Rousseau's theory: the formal exclusion of any group from political participation constitutes a violation of the general will. Excluding any class of citizens from its deliberations, the Tribal Comitia could only offer "simple particulars" (*SC*, 4.4.32, 134 [III: 451]) rather than laws and elected officials chosen for their accord with the general will.

Rousseau concludes on the basis of this review that only the Centuriate offers even the pretense of legislating according to the general will: "Certain it is that the whole majesty of the Roman People resided only in the Comitia by Centuries, which alone were complete; for the Comitia by Curiae lacked the rural tribes, and the Comitia by Tribes lack the Senate and the Patricians" (*SC*, 4.4.34, 135 [III: 452]). He quickly adds an essential caveat to this conclusion, however. The Centuriate functioned best when the people were virtuous. Much of this virtue among the Romans, according to Rousseau, can be attributed to their practice of open balloting. He

---

[36] See Nicolet 1980, 258–67.

[37] Rousseau refers to them here as members of the "Senate" (*SC*, 4.4.32, 134 [III: 451–52]). See Nicolet 1980, 228.

reasons that a citizen was "ashamed to cast his vote publicly for an unjust opinion or an unworthy candidate" insofar as each was known and held publicly accountable for his vote in the Comitia.[38] Given the prevalence of secret ballots today, this position seems somewhat counterintuitive. But Rousseau has an argument. He suggests that after open ballots were replaced by secret ballots between 139 and 107 BCE, people could vote according to their particular wills without fear of civic scorn. Rousseau undervalues the positive value in secret ballots – that no one is subject to unjust pressures and retributions for voting their conscience. Reading Rousseau's passionate defense of the open ballot, however, reminds us today that this can sometimes come at the cost of facilitating particular over general wills.

Despite this flaw associated with secret ballots, Rousseau disagrees with Cicero[39] that they contributed to the downfall of the Roman Republic. Here he abandons the more utopian elements of his republican philosophy to espouse practical reality. The laws for a virtuous people do not suit a corrupt one. It was a great pity for Rome to lose virtuous citizens; it was a tragedy that the laws were not adjusted accordingly. He finds a more successful example of such adaptation in Venice: "Nothing proves these maxims better than the long life of the Republic of Venice, which still retains a simulacrum of existence, solely because its laws are suited only to wicked men" (*SC*, 4.4.36, 135 [III: 453]).[40] This has two important implications for Rousseau's political thought generally. First, it reaffirms the doctrine found throughout the *Social Contract* that context matters (eg., *SC*, 2.11.4, 79 [III: 392]; *SC*, 3.1.15, 85 [III: 398]; *SC*, 3.3.7, 90 [III: 403]). While he suggests that his ultimate principles are eternal or fixed, applying them in particular circumstances requires contextual sensitivity and flexibility. Second, although Rousseau generally prefers a polity build on civic virtue and fraternal love, he understands the realities of politics sufficiently to suggest an alternative based on more selfish or even wicked citizens. This gives rise to more liberal readings of Rousseau – "liberal"

---

[38] Rousseau seems to be borrowing his argument here from Montesquieu [1748] 1989 14 [1.2.2].

[39] Cicero writes, "Who does not realize that the entire authority of the optimates was stolen by the [secret] ballot law? When the people were free they never wanted it, but they demanded it when they were beaten down by the oppressive power of leading citizens. And in fact, there are records of harsher verdicts against very powerful men given by voice than by ballot. For that reason the power should have been deprived of their excessive desire for balloting bad causes rather than giving the people a hiding place in which the written ballot could conceal a flawed vote while the respectable citizens were ignorant of each person's sentiments. Therefore no respectable citizen has ever been found to propose or support such a measure" (*On the Laws*, [3.35]).

[40] It is quite possible that Rousseau derived this point from Machiavelli's *Discourses*, 1.18.

specifically in the traditional sense of downplaying the role of civic virtue among citizens. This is not the only occasion in the *Social Contract* on which Rousseau makes this specific concession to reality (e.g., *SC*, 2.3.4, 60 [III: 372]). Any system that includes checks and balances by definition assumes flawed individuals inhabiting it.

Of course, Rousseau in effect seamlessly combines these two elements of his political philosophy here. There can be little question that he retains something of an ideal republic in his mind based on the most fundamental ideas of his political philosophy. This ideal republic is built upon a foundation of civic virtue and fraternal love, where citizens actively pursue the common good with as much vigor as we might expect normally to find others pursue their own private goods. This is the republican Rousseau that dominates the *Social Contract* and offers the most memorable passages. But he never allows readers to forget that "each people has to be assigned a particular system of institutions which is the best, not perhaps, in itself, but for the State for which it is intended" (*SC*, 2.11.4, 79 [III: 392]). Since most peoples lack the virtue required for the best solution, it is necessary to give them a different set of laws. Insofar as Rome failed to take the declining virtue of its citizens into account, the state itself failed. One cannot govern a wicked people with laws constructed for virtuous ones.

4.5. *Of the Tribunate*

The second institution of the Roman Republic to receive Rousseau's extended attention in Book IV is the Tribunate. Given the relative tendency of the Comitia Centuriate to represent the wealthy classes, the Tribunate offers something of a balance, insofar as its historical origins are grounded in protecting the poorer segments of Roman society.[41] As is the case with all institutions Rousseau endorses, he holds a well-functioning Tribunate to be a useful mechanism in preserving the general will: "A wisely tempered Tribunate is the firmest bulwark of a good constitution" (*SC*, 4.5.4, 137 [III: 454]). Its function is a largely negative one, however. It serves the general will by frustrating private wills.

Rousseau assumes more familiarity with the Tribunate here than he does with the Comitia, so it is especially important to consider here the

---

[41] Given the prevalence of Machiavelli's influence in these chapters, it is quite possible that Rousseau might have had in mind his *Discourses* here, including 1.2–3, which emphasizes the Roman Republic's checking and balancing of wealthy and poor interests. He subsequently celebrates the Tribunate in particular for its function as "a check on the ambition of the nobility" (*Discourses*, [3.11]).

historical origins and functions of this institution. The Tribunate emerged in the early Roman Republic out of "The Conflict of the Orders," itself a struggle between the poor Plebeians and wealthy Patricians. In the earliest days of the Republic, Rome was dominated by the Patricians, who controlled most of the political and religious institutions. Being largely shut out of these institutions, the Plebs let it be known that they wished to end the Patrician monopoly on political and religious offices, and additionally sought to redress a number of economic grievances, including debt, hunger, and land distribution, that had long favored the Patricians.[42] To achieve their goals, the Plebs withdrew from their civic duties on three occasions (494, 450, and 287 BCE), which amounted to a massive general strike against the Patricians. The first of these resulted in the election of two Plebeian magistrates of the Republic, known as Tribunes. This number sometimes changed, ranging from two to ten. At the outset, the Plebs characterized the Tribunes as special. They were declared "sacrosanct," which amounted to their being absolutely untouchable. Any harm done to a Tribune was out of the question, and this was backed up by the threat of popular riots. The Tribunes had the right to convene the Plebeian Counsel and act as its leader, which also gave them the right to propose legislation. Tiberius Gracchi employed this legislative power for his program of land reform in an effort to reduce radical wealth inequalities in Rome. Beyond this – and more important for Rousseau's purposes – the Tribunes also acquired powers in the Patrician Senate. Most notably, this included a *veto power* over bills deemed to be unfriendly to the Plebs. The authority of the Tribunes was eventually co-opted by the Emperors, especially Caesar Augustus, who found the "sacrosanct" status useful in consolidating his powers.

Rousseau describes the Tribunate's function as largely negative. Neither legislative nor executive, it is defined most fundamentally by its veto power: "while it can do nothing, it can prevent everything" (*SC*, 4.5.3, 137 [III: 454]). He is fond of the Tribunes, as they are carrying out their mission in a virtuous republic and the office is well-balanced in the context of the greater Constitution. In this context, he posits, the Tribunate is nothing less than a "preserver of the laws [*loix*] and of the legislative power" (*SC*, 4.5.2, 136 [III: 454]).[43] Since Rousseau earlier defines the laws as the legislative will of the people conforming to the general will (*SC*,

---

[42] See MacKay 2004, 33–5.

[43] It is perhaps in this spirit that Rousseau is comfortable with the sacrosanct nature of the Tribunes – insofar as their task is to protect the sovereign general will, which itself is for Rousseau "sacred, and inviolable" (*SC*, 2.4.9 63 [III: 375]).

2.6.5, 67 [III: 379]), it is safe here to draw the inference that the primary function of the tribunate is to protect the general will. This makes sense given the historical association of the tribunate with the vast majority of lower-class citizens in Rome.[44] No will can be general without considering the poor citizens' interests. Without this, all wills are merely particular or partial. He affirms this reading by emphasizing that "proud Patricians, who always despised the entire people, were forced to yield before a plain officer of the people wielding neither patronage nor jurisdiction" (*SC*, 4.5.3, 137 [III: 454]).

Rousseau adds an unexpected twist. Although readers are unlikely to be surprised that the tribunates must protect the sovereign people against the schemes of the government, he adds that it is sometimes appropriate that the tribunates "uphold the Government against the People" (*SC*, 4.5.2, 136 [III: 454]). He cites Venice's "Council of Ten" as a model in this regard.[45] Members of this council were appointed by the Great Council for one-year terms exclusively, so as not to consolidate power; and no family could have more than one representative. It functioned largely as an internal police force, protecting against armed rebellion and "any noble acting as if above the law, and any attempt to organize a faction or party even if merely by soliciting and swapping votes."[46] Insofar as they kept citizens bound by the law and prevented the formation of factions, it is easy to see how the Council of Ten would have appealed to Rousseau – and how it would protect the government from ill-intentioned segments of the people. He had earlier condemned factions as "small associations [operating] at the expense of the large association" (*SC*, 2.3.3, 60 [III: 371]). There he attempts to stifle their formation by limiting communication among citizens while deliberating about legislation. But with the office of Tribunes in Book IV he offers an institution charged with the task of dismantling them. This is a modest admission on Rousseau's part that while the ideal republic has no factions, it is better to be safe than sorry. Expect that citizens will inevitably be drawn to factions, Rousseau advises, and establish methods to cope with them.

---

[44] This raises questions, however, about why the Tribunes would be consistent with the general will, while he quickly dismisses the Tribal Comitia in *SC*, 4.4.32 for its failure to consider the interests of *all* citizens rather than simply the poor class. It would seem that the Tribunes and Tribal Comitia are representing the same class of citizens.

[45] The "Council of Ten" was established in 1310 to address significant problems of unrest and possible insurrection. While it thrived at times, by the eighteenth century it had often become secretive and a source of liberal suspicion (see Norwich 1989, 597).

[46] Lane 1973, 116.

Of course, so long as the Tribunates are virtuous themselves, Rousseau's plan is defensible. The problem, however, is that the tribunates themselves are as subject to vice and factionalization as the citizens.[47] He acknowledges that the Roman Tribunes were ultimately corrupted when merged with the office of Emperor, starting with Caesar Augustus, who along with his successors used his sacrosanct status to destroy freedom. Corruption also eventually overtook the Venetian Council of Ten, which had become by his own day a "Tribunal of blood, equally abhorrent to the Patricians and the People" (*SC*, 4.5.5, 137 [III: 455]). While the precise source of Rousseau's anger here is unclear, there is no doubt that he had witnessed at least some of the Venetian government's foibles first-hand, while working there as a young man. In his *Confessions*, he writes, "I had opportunities to notice the defects of that much-vaunted government."[48] More specifically, the Tribunate is most dangerous, according to Rousseau, when it usurps the executive power (*SC*, 4.5.5, 137 [III: 454]).

Rousseau makes his point with a brief discussion of the decline of the Spartan Ephors (*SC*, 4.5.3), resulting in the murder of the just King Agis. They had been originally conceived as overseeing the king and ensuring his fidelity to the law. In the third century BCE, Agis took office only to inherit a significant moral and economic crisis. The story of Agis has been told by one of Rousseau's favorite authors, the Roman historian, Plutarch. Plutarch records that Agis assumed the kingship just as "the love of gold and silver had once gained admittance into the Lacedaemonian commonwealth, it was quickly followed by avarice and baseness of spirit in the pursuit of it, and by luxury, effeminacy, and prodigality in the use. Then Sparta fell from almost all her former virtue and repute."[49] This love of money and its associated vices Plutarch attributes directly to the influx of wealth after Spartan victory in the Peloponnesian War. One of its most direct consequences was the concentration of wealth in a few hands, while the large number of the poor suffered in misery. Agis saw that the best hope for Sparta's resurrection was to equalize wealth among citizens, which

---

[47] Rousseau here is following Montesquieu, who attacks the Tribunes for "usurp[ing] the executive power of which it is but the moderator" (*Considerations on the Causes of the Greatness of the Romans and Their Decline*, 84).

[48] At least some of these defects were already present by the seventeenth century, when, according to Lane, "The ten had come to symbolize the concentration of power in a narrow oligarchy" (Lane 1973, 403). Rousseau continues to suggest that his Venetian experience was formative in his political thought: "I had seen that everything depends radically on politics, and that, from whatever aspect one considers it, no people ever would be anything other than what it was made into by the nature of its Government" (*Confessions*, 342 [I: 407]).

[49] "Agis" in *Plutarch's Lives*, II: 317.

would end greed and restore virtue. The Ephors, by this time the great beneficiaries of this wealth, were deeply offended and threatened. They conspired and executed King Agis so that they might keep their wealth and privilege, hastening the end of Sparta's glory years. This is the pattern Rousseau finds followed in Rome and Venice.

To avoid this fate by institutional means, Rousseau insists that the Tribunate should not be a permanent body. There should be periods during which it is suspended entirely. These gaps with no Tribunate should be long enough to prevent the Tribunes from consolidating factious power, but short enough to thwart other factions from gaining traction. This seems a relatively modest measure by which to limit a power with such a mixed historical record. But perhaps it would be best to read this in the context of other non-institutional measures, and here again the story of Agis is apt. The Ephors grew factious because of their concentrated wealth.[50] One must recall the special importance for Rousseau of preventing just these radical inequalities. "Do you, then, want to give the State stability? bring the extremes as close together as possible; tolerate neither very rich nor beggars. These two states, which are naturally inseparable, are equally fatal to the common good; from one come the abettors of tyranny, and from the other tyrant; it is always between these two that there is trafficking in public freedom; one buys it, the other sells it" (*SC*, 2.11.2n, 78n [III: 392n]). So the institutional mechanism of periodically suspending the Tribunate is in fact a secondary measure to the primary one of keeping wealth relatively equal. This primary measure for Rousseau fosters the virtue that limits or even obviates the need for coping with the worst tendencies of the Tribunates, and places them in a position to carry out their important chores consistent with the general will.

4.6. *Of the Dictator*

Rousseau's penultimate chapter on Roman institutions is on the office of dictatorship. The term "dictator" has understandably taken on pejorative meanings in the wake of the twentieth century. Yet such associations are very far from the institution's origins and Rousseau's understandings. He outlines the theoretical necessity of the dictatorship as stemming from the rigidity of the laws: "The inflexibility of the laws, which keeps them

---

[50] Rousseau's anger in recounting this tale is consistent with his many pronouncements throughout his writings that wealth should be kept relatively equal. This counters the argument of John McCormick, for example, who finds Rousseau to be a defender of wealth and privilege in these chapters on the Roman Republic. See McCormick 2007.

from bending to events, can in some cases render them pernicious, and through them cause the ruin of a State in crisis" (*SC*, 4.6.1, 138 [III: 455]).[51] This problem has been long acknowledged in the history of political thought. Thomas Aquinas, for example, wrote, "Now, it happens often that the observance of some point of law conduces to the common weal in the majority of instances, and yet in some cases is very hurtful. Since, then, the lawgiver cannot have in view every single case, he shapes the law according to what happens most frequently, by directing his attention to the common good. Wherefore, if a case arise wherein the observance of that law would be hurtful to the general welfare, it should not be observed."[52] Such issues were more recently raised when Abraham Lincoln blockaded Confederate ports, suspended habeas corpus, and even issued the Emancipation Proclamation. It is difficult to argue that he had constitutional authority for any of these actions. Lincoln himself admitted as much in asking with regard to the suspension of Habeas Corpus, "are all the laws, but one, to go unexecuted, and the government itself go to pieces, lest that one be violated?"[53] Lincoln implicitly invoked something like the dictatorial powers Rousseau outlines here in Chapter Six.

The historical origins of the office can be traced back to the Roman Republic. The dictator was a constitutional office, established for certain special conditions. Specifically, the Consuls appointed a dictator during times of military crisis or emergency. The office was to last six months or until the end of the crisis, whichever was shortest. Their power was extensive – their acts were not subjected to any veto power. With the exception of Sulla and Caesar, most all terms ended before six months had expired.

Machiavelli was among the most adamant supporters of the dictatorial powers in early Modernity. In his *Discourses on Livy*, he makes a careful case for their constitutional place. When faced with a crisis requiring extraordinary measures to ensure survival, he reasons, a republic has three choices. First, it may do nothing and perish. This is hardly an option. Second, it may grant extraordinary powers to some person or persons without any institutional foundation or limits. This amounts to little more than handing over the republic – in which case, tyranny follows. The third

---

[51] See also Montesquieu's *Spirit of the Laws*, 16 [1.2.3]. Montesquieu understands this institution in specifically anti-democratic terms as being aimed at mitigating the passions of an inflamed public, rather than in defending the state against external enemies.

[52] This is St. Thomas's "City Gate" example, where he authorizes the violation of a city ordinance mandating the shutting of a city gate at a fixed time, in order to admit back to the city the city's defenders. See Aquinas 2003, 69.

[53] Lincoln, quoted in Brest, Levinson, Balkin, and Amar 2000, 225. See the discussion of the constitutionality of Lincoln's acts generally, 219–31.

option is to have institutional foundations for and limits on those extraordinary powers – namely, to have an office of dictatorship. For Machiavelli, this is the only responsible way to address such crises that pose existential threats. He emphasizes that dictators have strict term limits of six months, which obviates tyrannical ambitions. And while the dictator has exceptional powers, "he could not do anything that might diminish the state, as taking away authority from the Senate or from the people." So no dictator could change the constitution, which is fixed. Under these circumstances, Machiavelli reasons, "it was impossible for him to escape his limits and to hurt the city." In the absence of this office, one could imagine a well-intentioned extraordinary tyrant doing great good for the republic. But the very fact of going outside the law to do so sets a bad precedent: "for if one sets up a habit of breaking the orders [laws] for the sake of good, then later, under that coloring, they are broken for ill."[54]

Rousseau's arguments in Book IV, Chapter Six are largely faithful to Machiavelli's. The only possible justification for establishing a dictator is the "greatest dangers" when "the salvation of the fatherland is at stake" (*SC*, 4.6.3, 138 [III: 456]). Such occasions call for a dictator, whom Rousseau also calls the "worthiest person" [*au plus digne*] (*SC*, 4.6.3, 138 [III: 456]). He does not offer great detail on what constitutes this worthiness, but he does suggest that dictators would view this charge more as a burden than as a privilege or an opportunity. Given his fondness for Machiavelli's treatment of the subject, it is possible that he had in mind someone like Cincinnatus. As Machiavelli reports, he "was plowing his small villa, which did not surpass a limit of four *jugera*, when the legates of the Senate came from Rome to convey to him the election to his dictatorship." Cincinnatus proved to be an effective dictator in the minds of his contemporaries and subsequent commentators. And when he was done, he returned to the poverty of his own farm, perfectly content, since "four *jugera* of earth was enough to nourish him."[55]

Once in office, this worthy individual then does the most extraordinary thing – he suspends the sovereign authority. This is a singular moment in

---

[54] *Discourses on Livy*, 1.34. Precisely this kind of reasoning was employed in U.S. Supreme Court Justice Jackson's concurrence in the *Steel Seizure* case. In response to Harry Truman's seizure and forcible re-opening of the steel mills to support the steel production for the war, Jackson wrote, "I am not alarmed that it would plunge us straightaway into dictatorship, but it is at least a step in that wrong direction."

[55] *Discourses on Livy*, 3.25. Near the conclusion of Rousseau's *Emile*, the tutor comments that "the Romans went from the plow to the consulate. If the prince or the state calls you to the service of the fatherland, leave everything to go fulfill the honorable function of citizen in the post assigned to you" (*Emile*, 474 [IV: 860]). This seems to be a reference to the model of Cincinnatus.

the *Social Contract*, as the sovereign people have a unique and generally inviolable character. Rousseau thus parses his words very carefully here. Although the sovereign authority has been suspended, the general will has not – a stunning revelation, given that the general will and sovereign have been synonymous throughout the *Social Contract* to this point. He had announced early in Book Two that "sovereignty … is nothing but the exercise of the general will" (*SC*, 2.1.2, 57 [III: 368]).[56] The general will is what the people want, as that will corresponds to justice. Sovereignty, as he suggests in Book II, is the *exercise* of that will. So here in Book IV, the sovereign authority has been suspended insofar as the people are not actively implementing the general will. This has been temporarily delegated to the dictator. The fundamental question here is how a dictator – or *anyone* for that matter – can act on the general will in place of the people. This is because Rousseau makes an important presupposition about the general will here. In cases where the republic's very existence is in question, "the general will is not in doubt, it is obvious that the people's foremost intention is that the State not perish" (*SC*, 4.6.4, 138 [III: 456]).[57] That is, the dictator need not consult the people. He knows for a fact – insofar as he is as "worthy" as Rousseau supposes – the content of the general will. He must do what is necessary to save the republic. In broadly virtuous states, such as the early Roman Republic, he reasons, it was not difficult to find such worthy individuals to assume the dictatorship. Citizens were trusting, and officers were responsible. But as the Republic aged, virtue declined. This meant that the citizens grew more circumspect about the possibility of finding qualified "worthy" dictators. So they hesitated to evoke the office. Perhaps surprisingly, Rousseau chides Rome for being too untrusting and not seeking a dictator when they most needed one.

To illustrate the need for a dictator, Rousseau spends three paragraphs summarizing and evaluating Cicero's behavior during the Roman "Catiline Affair," in 63 BCE. Catiline was an associate and alleged "henchman" of Sulla, the notorious one-time Roman General, Consul, and even dictator. Sulla's notoriety stemmed from using his forces to march on Rome itself.[58] After Sulla's retirement, Catiline forged a political career of his own, twice running for consul and losing in 64 and 63 BCE. Unable to accept his

---

[56] See also the *Emile*: "the essence of sovereignty consists in the general will" (*Emile*, 462 [IV: 842]).

[57] Rousseau expressly states this "obvious" doctrine in his *Political Economy*: "this general will … always tends to the preservation and the well being of the whole and of each part" (*Political Economy*, 6 [III: 245]).

[58] Plutarch records that Catiline's infamy also stemmed from "deflowering his virgin daughter, and killing his own brother" (Plutarch's *Lives*, II: 415).

losses, he began assembling his own forces in Etruria. The Senate responded by passing its "Final Decree" – a measure authorizing the consul, Cicero, to act as a de facto dictator.[59] It is this ad hoc measure circumventing the constitutional office of dictator that Rousseau finds most disturbing.

At any rate, Cicero employed his new powers to put down the rebellion, driving Catiline into exile. Within a matter of weeks, however, Catiline was at it again – only this time to be quickly struck down. This did not, however, put an end to Catiline's cause. In December of 63 BCE, the rebels resumed conspiring to effect a Roman civil war. Yet word quickly reached Cicero once again, who this time had the conspirators arrested. Without the benefit of a trial, he dramatically ordered and carried out their immediate execution on the basis of the "Final Decree" passed some months earlier to address the first rebellion.

Rousseau acknowledges that Cicero's measures were effective in ending the rebellion. But he also laments the fashion in which Cicero handled this affair. In applying the "Final Decree," after the decree had already expired, to a different (albeit related) crime that inspired said decree, Cicero overstepped his authority and ordered illegal executions (*SC*, 4.6.10, 140 [III: 457]). Rousseau notes that such authority would be within the rights of a legitimately appointed and constrained dictator. The subtle, yet essential, difference between Cicero's actions under the "Final Decree" and the same actions that might have been conducted by a dictator is in their legality. Had a dictator pursued and executed the conspirators, this would have been perfectly legal. And when the crisis subsided, or six months had passed, the dictator would step down and return to private life. But Cicero violates the law in conducting the same acts. And in doing so, he establishes a dangerous precedent for his successors – in privileging efficiency over legality.

Rousseau acknowledges that many fear the office of dictator. Indeed, the associations of dictatorship and tyranny precede the ugliest twentieth-century manifestations of this pairing. It was Julius Caesar who declared himself "Dictator for Life" [*Dictator perpetuo*] to consolidate the powers of the Roman Emperor and hastened the end of the Republic. To assuage this fear, Rousseau places careful limits on this office so that it may not result in a Caesar. First, he insists that although the dictator acts on behalf of the sovereign people, he may not legislate as a sovereign

---

[59] In Plutarch's account: "the senate made a decree to place all in the hands of the consuls, who should undertake the conduct of everything, and do their best to save the state. This was not a common thing, but only done by the senate in case of imminent danger" (Plutarch's *Lives*, II: 418).

(*SC*, 4.6.4, 139 [III: 456]). Only the sovereign people may enact laws. The sovereign may neither pass laws nor alter the constitution. Insofar as this constraint is effective, no dictator has the right to declare himself or anyone else "Dictator for Life." Second, along these lines and consistent with the Roman Republic, the dictator's office is to be strictly limited to six months. He is emphatic that this power "can never be extended" beyond that term (*SC*, 4.6.11, 140 [III: 458]).[60] This being said, it is difficult to know how effective these constitutional provisions might be in the face of a dictator determined to become a tyrant or emperor. There was no provision in the Roman Republic to facilitate Caesar's extension of his legitimate powers to dictator for life. Yet it happened. Rousseau himself subsequently concedes that the dictatorship in Rome ended up destroying the laws.[61] Presumably here as elsewhere in Rousseau's system, much hinges on the degree of virtue possessed by the citizens and its magistrates. Insofar as the dictator is "worthy" as he demands, the threat of tyranny would be minimized.[62] And where the citizens are virtuous, they would presumably ignore instructions from any would-be tyrant neglecting the general will and terminate his reign before the six months expired. As Karl Loewenstein observed, there was "not a single instance of the ninety-odd dictatorships of the [Roman] republican period" in which an abuse of power took place.[63]

But Rousseau himself acknowledges elsewhere the dangers inherent in relying on the people. As he argued in his *Discourse on Political Economy*, corruption is always possible where "the people is seduced by private interests which some skillful men succeed by their reputation and eloquence to substitute for the people's own interest." Here, too, Rousseau's primary

---

[60] He notes that the Roman Decemvirs indeed took the prerogative of violating this type of constraint with disastrous consequences. Rousseau undoubtedly draws this point, once again, from Machiavelli's *Discourses*. The Decemvirate was assembled by the Romans in 452 BCE with the purpose of writing a code of law in the span of one year. All other government agencies were suspended during this period, and all their decisions were to be final and without appeal. The Decemvirate was led by Appius Claudius Crassus and Titus Genucius Augurinus. In 450, they completed the Law of the Twelve Tables, which was to be their major achievement. But when their term was up, they refused to leave office. Appius made things worse by attempting to make a young woman his personal sex slave, prompting her father's mercy killing and outrage from the Roman people. The Decemvirate eventually stepped down in 449. For Machiavelli, this unfortunate turn was primarily because the Decemvirate got *all power*, whereas the Dictators still operated simultaneously with the Senate, consuls, and tribunes. "So the Senate, the consuls, the tribunes, remaining in their authority, came to be like a guard on him [the Dictator] to make him not depart from the right way." Without this check on their power, "they were able to become insolent" (*Discourses on Livy*, 1.35; see also 1.40).

[61] *Poland*, 219 [III: 998].

[62] See Putterman 2010, 166–7.

[63] Loewenstein 1973, 79.

resource in the face of seductive appeals to private interests is public virtue. "Do you wish the general will to be carried out? See to it that all
particular wills take their bearings by it; and since virtue is nothing by this
conformity of the particular will to the general will, to say the same thing
in a word, make virtue reign." It is in this spirit that he offers his final
criticism of Cicero, who, "though a Roman, loved his glory more than his
fatherland" (*SC*, 4.6.10, 140 [III: 457]). Rome narrowly escaped from the
Catiline affair on the fumes of its ancient commitment to virtue. But it
would not survive much longer, as this virtue faded, only to be replaced
by the rise of personal glory and oratory. It is for this reason that he writes
in his *First Discourse* that as soon as "Rome filled up with Philosophers
and Orators," virtue began its steady, inevitable, and disastrous decline.[64]
In the end, for Rousseau, institutional checks can only guarantee so much.
Beyond this point, a state is only as successful as it is virtuous.

4.7. *Of Censorship*

If Chapter Six speaks to the need for a virtuous citizenry, Chapter Seven
provides some means for maintaining that requisite virtue required of both
citizens and rulers. Rousseau outlines the relationship of virtue to the general will in his *Political Economy*, where he explains, "virtue is nothing but
[the] conformity of the particular will to the general will."[65] So maintaining the general will depends on a virtuous citizenry. It is the task of the
censors to keep a virtuous populace virtuous.[66] As he does with the dictator, the tribunate, and the comitia, he derives this institution from the
peak of the Roman Republic. It was originally established in the middle
of the fifth century BCE for the simple task of taking a census, or count-
ing citizens for representation purposes (so that each class was represented
accurately) and assessing property for tax purposes. Two censors were
elected to office by the *Comitia Centuriata* for five-year terms, but eventually these terms were cut to eighteen months because the long terms were
associated with tyrannical tendencies. Although not a prerequisite, most
censors were former consuls.

The most striking function of the censors was one that exceeds any
function typically associated with contemporary census bureaus: moral

---

[64] *Political Economy*, 13 [III: 252]; *Discourse on the Sciences and Arts*, 13 [III: 14]; see also 10 [III: 10].
[65] *Political Economy*, 13 [III: 252].
[66] Montesquieu had addressed the role of the Roman censors before Rousseau, noting that this "very
wise institution" was able to correct "the abuses that the law had not foreseen, or that the ordinary
magistrate could not punish" (Montesquieu [1734] 1999, 86).

censure. This was a central – and Rousseau argues, crucial – element of the Roman institution. In assessing individuals for the census, censors also assessed citizens morally. This began with the question of whether or not they cultivated their land adequately, but grew to include evaluations pertaining to military cowardice, dereliction of civil duties, various forms of corruption, and debt. The censors publicly condemned citizens failing in any of these regards. Completion of this evaluation and condemnation culminated in a ritual of purification called the *lustrum*. Although the censors lacked the power to sanction citizens in the fashion of the courts, as Anthony Lintott has observed, "the loss of status involved in *infamia* of any kind was a serious matter in a society where ambition was focused on glory and a good name."[67] It was precisely this aura of infamy that the censors imposed on citizens, which would follow and plague them for years thereafter.

Rousseau's adaptation of the Roman censors is exclusively focused on their capacity as moral judges. Specifically, he charges his censors with declaring and upholding "public opinion" (*l'opinion publique*). In assigning this peculiar task to the censors, he draws on a conception introduced earlier in the *Social Contract*. In Book II, Chapter Twelve, Rousseau outlines the four types of laws operating in a republic. The first three are common legal concepts: political, civil, and criminal law. The final category, however, is less typically explored in political and legal philosophy: morals (*mœurs*), customs (*coutumes*), and "above all … opinion [*l'opinion*]" (*SC*, 2.12.5, 81 [III: 394]). These laws are crucially different from all others insofar as they are not precisely codified in legislation – although legislation may well take its cues from public opinion. Instead, these laws are to be found "in the hearts of the Citizens" (*SC*, 2.12.5, 81 [III: 394]). In Book II, the lawgiver attends to the task of establishing opinion at the outset of the republic itself – by virtue of "particular regulations which are but the ribs of the arch of which morals, slower to arise, in the end form the immoveable Keystone" (*SC*, 2.12.5, 81 [III: 394]). Since Rousseau singles out Solon, Numa, and Servius for their attention to promoting equality in their early laws, this had the effect of assuring that the general will would thereafter be "enlightened" (*SC*, 2.3.4, 60 [III: 372]). It is quite possible that this is the kind of law he has in mind here. That is, by shaping laws that advance equality, the general will ultimately takes root in the citizens' hearts.

Rousseau now emphasizes the importance of public opinion to a thriving republic before suggesting how the censors offer an institutional

[67] Lintott 1999, 119.

mechanism for maintaining the opinion established by the lawgiver. He acknowledges, "Among all peoples of the world, not nature but opinion determines the choice of their pleasures" (*SC*, 4.7.3, 141 [III: 458]). This is an important reemphasizing of a fact declared earlier that the social contract involves "changing human nature" (*SC*, 2.7.3, 69 [III: 381]). The natural pre-societal sentiment of compassion described in the *Second Discourse* is replaced in the social world by public opinion.[68] Provided those opinions are consistent with what is truly virtuous, the state is well-positioned to thrive. The problem is in assuring that the people indeed love the right things. Although they always want to love what is fine (*beau*), they are sometimes confused about the true value of things (see also *SC*, 2.3.1, 59 [III: 371]). This can be true even if a republic has a highly skilled and virtuous lawgiver, who establishes an ideal public opinion. It therefore falls to the censors to maintain public opinion, which is the republic's backbone.

The censors thus must be established early in a republic, before public opinion has an opportunity to decline. Rousseau is well aware of this problem of decayed morals. It is an obsession in his pedagogical novel, *Emile*, to protect the young pupil from the forces of public opinion. Raising young Emile in a corrupted society, the mentor aspires to shape a man "who depends as little as possible on the authority and opinion of others."[69] The *Emile*, however, represents a very different scenario from that presented in the *Social Contract* in a central respect. Public opinion has already been corrupted in the *Emile*. To follow it would be to push that society further off its cliff. In the *Social Contract*, by contrast, Rousseau is working to shape and maintain a society in which public opinion is pure and good. In this world, it is right for citizens to look to public opinion for their social cues – as is their tendency, regardless.

Insofar as the censors have a strong public opinion to maintain, and protect it well, the republic is in a particularly advantageous position. They overstep their bounds, however, if they seek to depart from public opinion. To the extent that they do so, their decisions "are vain and without effect" (*SC*, 4.7.1, 141 [III: 458]).

Rousseau indicates in a footnote that he has already addressed these themes in his "Letter to d'Alembert." Although the "Letter" is largely dedicated to arguing against the presence of a theater in the city of Geneva, it is ultimately concerned with protecting that city's morals or its public

---

[68] See the *Second Discourse*, 154 [III: 156–7].
[69] *Emile*, 254 [IV 550].

opinion. To illustrate how a government might work to maintain or ever so slightly manage and manipulate public opinion, he dedicates a long digression to the tribunal of the marshals of France, established by Louis XIV with the intention of putting an end to the practice of dueling. It failed in this endeavor – but for reasons Rousseau finds compelling. He endorses the idea of such a tribunal insofar as he finds the practice of dueling to be morally wrong, and further because the outright legal banishing of such a practice would be effectual in itself. He acknowledges that it is tempting to abolish undesirable practices with simple acts of legislation – but opinion is largely impervious to legal solutions. To effect desired changes, one must change opinion itself.

Louis XIV conceives the tribunal to make this kind of change: "It was established to change public opinion about duels, the redress of offenses and the occasions when a brave man is obliged, under penalty of disgrace, to get satisfaction for an affront with sword in hand."[70] He acknowledges the failure of the institution to achieve its aim – but offers several respects in which its measures might have been more effective. First, it should have had a different name – the *Court of Honor*. This name removes all suggestions of violence, which is important insofar as violence is never effective as a device to change people's opinions. The title also suggests the two key elements of public opinion – honor and shame.[71] Rousseau presumes that everyone desires honor and shuns shame. The Court of Honor would thus dispense honor and shame rather than corporal punishment, prison terms, and monetary fines. Failing to appear before the Court itself would be a striking sign of shame – whereas appearing before the Court would signify honor. So drawing on the same sense of honor that inspires people to duel, the Court can compel disputants without violence.

Second, Rousseau insists that the members of the Court must be especially distinguished. The judges must themselves be received by public opinion as honorable. Without this status, their pronouncements would be of little consequence. He admits that standards of honor might vary according to the opinion of a particular land. But insofar as a state has a warrior culture, it is prudent to select celebrated and decorated war veterans. This provides some assurance that their decisions will resonate with public opinion. Ultimately, he hopes to cultivate a revered and

---

[70] "Letter to d'Alembert," 67 [V: 62].
[71] "Letter to d'Alembert," 68 [V: 62]. It is possible that Rousseau here follows Pierre Bayle and Bernard Mandeville. See Bayle [1681] 2000), §172; Mandeville, *Fable of the Bees,* Remark C.

unchallenged institution where "the princes ought to tremble at the very name *Court of Honor*."[72]

Third, the court must be careful not to depart sharply from existing public opinion. If it intends to change opinion, it must do so slowly and deliberately. The people will fiercely resist any sudden challenge to public opinion. By slowly and "artfully manipulating" existing opinions, slightly more enlightened views can be "gradually substituted" for "ferocious prejudice[s]." Following this principle, Rousseau cautions that the court should not begin by outright banning duels. Such a measure would only result in secret duels and contempt for authority. Instead, the court should intervene only modestly at first – permitting many requested duels among disputants. As the court's moral authority continues to grow, it can then become "more severe [in prohibiting duels] until the legitimate occasions had been reduced to nothingness, the point of honor had changed principles, and duels were entirely abolished."[73]

Toward the end of his discussion of the Court of Honor, Rousseau leaves little doubt about the importance of this diversion: public opinion is "queen of the world ... not subject to the power of kings; they themselves are her first slaves." Yet he notes in the *Social Contract* that opinion has been entirely neglected by modern states. They have left the people to shape opinion, however the wind may blow. This is one presumable cause of the duels he found so distasteful. But it is also the source of the esteem his contemporaries have for the sciences and the arts, which he laments in the *First Discourse*. And it has also resulted in the love of commerce and gain at the expense of civic duties.[74] It is the unique and essential task of the censors to steer the people from these false idols and to keep them as faithful as possible to the original and true virtues present at the republic's founding.

Of course, it is not difficult to conceive potential problems with this office. One of Rousseau's most vocal critics in the early nineteenth century, Benjamin Constant, described the censorship as wielding an inherently "discretionary" or "arbitrary" power. The actions of the censor would be anchored only in the judgment of the censor. Therefore, the presence of even one factious or selfish office-holder threatens to undermine the purposes toward which Rousseau is striving. Naturally, Rousseau presumes here a highly virtuous censor – but it is indeed a high standard to presuppose that *all* censors would be as virtuous as the office demands.

---

[72] "Letter to d'Alembert," 72 [V: 66].
[73] "Letter to d'Alembert," 69 [V: 63], 70–1 [V: 65].
[74] "Letter to d'Alembert," 73–74 [V: 67], 67 [V: 61].

Constant offers a second objection, as well. He doubts that any populace would take its moral direction from a magistrate: "It would rebel against any positive authority which wanted to give it greater precision. If the government of a modern people wanted, like the censors of Rome, to censure a citizen arbitrarily, the entire nation would protest against this arrest by refusing to ratify the decisions of the authority."[75] To be sure, Constant imagines a different sort of citizenry from Rousseau – one more distinctively modern and independent in nature. In some sense, Rousseau's own temperament shared much of this modern nature. But he expected that individuals in a proper republic would feel their identity most fundamentally as citizens participating in the general will – not in resisting it. So for Rousseau – here as elsewhere in these chapters – the success of his prescriptions relies crucially on the virtue of both the citizens and magistrates.

4.8. *Of Civil Religion*

The final substantive chapter of the *Social Contract* is dedicated to what Rousseau calls the "civil religion" (*la religion civile*). As scholars have noted, this chapter was a late addition. Rousseau had written several drafts of his *Institutions politiques*, from which the *Social Contract* was drawn, without any suggestions of this chapter. It was only added late to the *Geneva Manuscript* before making its way into the *Social Contract*. Some scholars have even observed that while the rest of the *Geneva Manuscript* has been written in "Rousseau's fairest hand," the chapter on civil religion was "scribbled, in a hand often most indecipherable," suggesting it was a first draft written in great haste.[76] But, despite its late addition to the text, of all the chapters in the *Social Contract* this was almost certainly the most controversial in his own epoch. It was his remarks here, combined with related ones in the *Emile*, that got him banished from France and fueled book burnings in Geneva. It was these passages that forced him to flee to England. And it was ultimately these pages that forced him to live out his last decade in relative anonymity, under an assumed name. One of Rousseau's contemporaries and interlocutors, Christophe de Beaumont, the Archbishop of Paris, described Rousseau's doctrines here as "erroneous, impious, blasphemous, and heretical … suited to overturning natural Law

---

[75] Constant [1819] 1988, 322.
[76] See Vaughan [1915] 1962, I: 434–5; Kelly and Masters 1994, 240n41; Derathé 1964, lxxxii–lxxxiii; and Ball 1995, 118–19.

and to destroying the foundations of the Christian religion." Rousseau was accused of fomenting atheism and threatening to break all social bonds in civil society. Readers can understand why an Archbishop might have so vigorously opposed Rousseau's words – it was the power of such figures and institutions that was most threatened by his doctrines.[77]

While orthodox Catholics and Calvinists took Rousseau for a radical on the basis of Book IV, Chapter Eight, the *Philosophes* took these pages to be reactionary against progress and the Enlightenment itself. Beginning with La Mettrie, it became fashionable within certain intellectual corners of Paris to question God's existence. Two of the fiercest atheists happened to be Rousseau's occasionally dear friends: Baron d'Holbach and Denis Diderot. They argued that not only was God's existence opposed to a rational understanding of the physical universe – it was also opposed to a rational understanding of the *moral* universe. Holbach argued passionately, "Religion has ever filled the mind of man with darkness, and kept him in ignorance of his real duties and true interests. It is only by dispelling the clouds and phantoms of Religion, that we shall discover Truth, Reason, and Morality."[78] Holbach thought this equally true of Enlightenment Deism as he did of Christianity. Rousseau's remarks here in Chapter Eight must be understood at least partly in the context of a response to what he regards as this growing menace. This is clear from one of his later works, the autobiographical *Dialogues*:

But this infatuation with Atheism is an ephemeral fanaticism, a product of fashion that will be destroyed by it too; and the enthusiasm with which the people surrender to it shows it is nothing but a mutiny against its conscience, whose murmur it feels with resentment. This convenient philosophy of the happy and rich who build their paradise in this world cannot long serve as the philosophy of the multitude who are the victims of their passions, and who – for lack of happiness in this life – need to find in it at least the hope and consolations of which that barbarous doctrine deprives them. Men nurtured from childhood by an intolerant impiety pushed to fanaticism, by fearless and shameless libertinage; youth without discipline, women without morals, peoples without faith, Kings without law, without a Superior whom they fear and free of any kind of limit, all the duties of conscience destroyed, patriotism and attachment to the Prince extinguished in all hearts, and finally no social bond other than strength: it seems to me one can easily foresee what must soon come of all that. Europe prey to masters taught by their own teachers to have no guide than their interest nor any God besides their passions, at times secretly starved, at times openly devastated,

[77] Quoted by Kelly and Grace 2001, xvi. Rousseau would subsequently respond to all such charges in his public letter to Beaumont and his *Letters Written from the Mountain*.

[78] Holbach [1772] 2006, III.

inundated everywhere with soldiers, Actors, prostitutes, corrupting books and destructive vices, seeing races unworthy to live be born and perish in its bosom, will sooner or later feel that these calamities are the fruit of the new teachings, and judging them by their deadly effects, will view with the same horror their professors, the disciples, and all those cruel doctrines which, conferring absolute empire over man to his senses and limiting everything to the enjoyment of this brief life, make the century in which they reign as despicable as it is unhappy.[79]

The threats of atheism, according to Rousseau, are many – and they strike the core missions of the *Social Contract*. Atheism attacks the conscience, which is the repository of citizens' idea of justice – itself the substantive core of the general will. It promotes egoism and libertinism, which undermines virtue and civic duty. It destroys patriotism, which helps preserve the general will. And it frees kings from their obligations to the law and hence the general will – namely, it destroys the rule of law. In short, Rousseau makes it very clear here just how crucial some form of religious belief is to his political project. And the very heart is found in Chapter Seven. Without *some kind of God*, the political project is almost doomed to spectacular failure. At the same time, however, it is not clear that existing modes of religion are adequate to what politics requires of religion. It must be a certain kind of religion.

Yet these pages are not intended merely to address the threats of dogmatic religiosity on the one side and a dogmatic atheism on the other. In many ways they draw the reader's attention back to the fundamental themes of the *Social Contract* – the general will, fraternity, republicanism, and fidelity to the law. Whereas it was the task of Book II to establish a republic governed by the general will, it is the task of Book IV to maintain that general will. The quasi-Roman institutions of Chapters Four through Seven represent one approach to this maintenance via the magistrates. But his civil religion – while also Roman in spirit – is an approach to general will-maintenance through a system of beliefs appealing to the citizens directly. This chapter can be divided into roughly three sections: (1) a brief history of religion and politics, (2) a discussion of the types of religion and their relation to politics, and (3) his positive recommendations for a civil religion.

Rousseau's history of religion and politics opens with the striking observation that the earliest governments were all theocracies. He reasons that this makes good sense. It takes a long time for people to accept the rule of their fellows.[80] That is, they can accept the superiority of gods much

---

[79] *Dialogues*, 242, [I: 970–2]. See also Damrosch 2005, 219–20.
[80] To be sure, Rousseau counsels religious sentiment at the founding of republics, as well. See *SC*, 2.7. Consider also Kant's remark that the law must be thought of as having "arisen not from human

more easily than they can of other humans. So every early society has gods at the head. And because every society had its own god, there were as many gods in early times as there were states. These early societies fought often because of this religious plurality. Different states recognized different masters. Many think that there were no "wars of religion" in early societies, but Rousseau rejects this conclusion on the grounds that all political wars were in fact wars of religion. This is because politics and religion were so closely intertwined. Yet in this epoch, the Romans were especially clever. When they conquered enemies they did not destroy their gods. These "conquered Gods" were incorporated into the state religion – Paganism. This provided religious and political unity.

All of this, however, was sternly challenged by Christianity, which is distinguished by its separation of theology and politics. The Christians embrace and prioritize the "new idea of a Kingdom of the other world" (*SC*, 4.8.8, 144 [III: 462]). The Pagans did not trust the motives of the Christians, suspecting that their professed humility was in fact a clever guise to usurp Rome's political authority. Rousseau argues that the Romans were right to harbor such suspicions, since the "humble Christians" ultimately "changed their language" and established in the Roman Catholic Church, "the most violent despotism in this world" (*SC*, 4.8.9, 145 [III: 462]).[81] Yet as the Pope was not strictly speaking a political ruler, this left Europe with two masters: the political ruler of any given state and the Pope. This division of loyalties has consistently frustrated attempts at effective politics, as Rousseau explains later in the chapter. Since this time, the bifurcation of political and religious authority has dominated and troubled the West.[82]

The Europeans are burdened by this failure to coordinate religion and politics. Both England and Russia have historically intended to unite the two, but fail in practice. Rousseau surprisingly gives credit to Thomas Hobbes for correctly understanding the problem. As Hobbes argues, where "these two powers [civil and religious] oppose one another, the commonwealth cannot but be in great danger of civil war and dissolution."[83] Rousseau approves of Hobbes's solution in blending the two powers into one. But Hobbes makes a great mistake, in supposing that this

---

beings but from some highest, flawless lawgiver; and that is what the saying 'All authority comes from God' means" ([1797] 1996, 462).

[81] Rousseau's attitude toward Catholicism is outlined in Grimsley 1968, 77–8.

[82] The modest exception to this rule was Islam for a brief period of time, which Muhammad established as a theocracy, uniting political and religious authority (*SC*, 4.8.11, 145 [III: 463]).

[83] Hobbes [1651] 2002, 29.15.

can be done with Christianity. The nature of this religion makes this combination impossible – because "the interest of the priest would always be stronger than that of the State" (4.8.13, 146 [III: 463]).[84]

Rousseau concludes his history of religion and politics in Europe with a discussion of Pierre Bayle and Warburton.[85] Pierre Bayle argues that religion was unnecessary for politics.[86] For him, a society of atheists functions just as well as a society of believers – since all citizens are ultimately motivated by honor and shame rather than religious ideas. Warburton, by contrast, argues that only Christians are suitable for a republican society (see also *SC*, 2.7.12, 72 [III: 384]). Rousseau rejects both claims. Against Bayle and his *Philosophe* disciples, Rousseau believes citizens require *some* religious foundation. Against Warburton and Catholic France, Rousseau holds that Christianity is the wrong religion for building a strong community guided by the general will.

After sketching out the history of religion and politics in the Western world, Rousseau describes the three modes of religion with relation to politics, as thus far practiced. He finds flaws with all of them, leaving his own alternative for the final few paragraphs. The first – and least viable – solution to the problem of the relationship of religion to politics is what he calls "the religion of the Priest" (*SC*, 4.8.16, 147 [III: 464]). This includes Lamaism[87] and the Roman Catholic Church. The problem with both is that they establish hierarchies of authority independent from the

---

[84] Rousseau's criticism of Hobbes is, in a way, formulated by Machiavelli long before Hobbes was born. He condemns the Catholic Church for its division of political power in Italy between itself and various political powers. "[T]he church has kept and keeps this province divided. And truly no province has ever been united or happy unless it has all come under obedience to one republic or to one prince, as happened to France and to Spain" (*Discourses*, 1.12). The fundamental problem, from Machiavelli's perspective, is that it is neither too strong to seize all political power, nor sufficiently weak to avoid dividing the citizens' loyalties. So it occupies the undesirable middle, in which citizens find themselves pulled unproductively in different directions.

[85] While Rousseau cites Warburton, it is also true that one of Rousseau's early heroes, Bernard Lamy (see *Confessions*, 194 [I: 232]), also advocates a Christian republic. Rousseau deeply admired Lamy's Platonism, but could not follow Lamy's departure from Plato on the matter of a Christian republic. Lamy wrote, "the republic of Jesus Christ is more holy by far, as well as richer in goodness, than that of Plato" (quoted in Hendel 1934, II: 229).

[86] Bayle says, "We can say without indulging in false oratory that human justice is the cause of the virtue of most people, for as soon as it fails to punish the sinner, few people keep themselves from the sin," which is really to say that it is threat of punishment, not religious faith, that keeps subjects in order (Bayle, *Various Thoughts on the Comet of 1680*, §161). Both believers and nonbelievers act precisely the same way in this respect.

[87] The term "Lamaism" refers to what is now called "Tibetan Buddhism." This term was largely a Protestant epithet employed by historians of religion, philologists, and imperialists to impugn Tibetan Buddhists as corrupted in a fashion resembling the Roman Catholic Church. For them, and likely for Rousseau here, followers worshipped the Pope and the Lama, not the teachings of Christ or Buddha. My thanks to Cameron Warren for clarification on this matter.

political system. This becomes problematic as soon as the inevitable happens – that the religious authority demands different principles from the state and vice-versa. Citizens are forced to choose their master – either the church *or* the state – since they cannot serve both with equal fidelity. The moment this occurs, the state itself is threatened and potentially undermined. One can see this phenomenon of a forced choice in modern-day Tibet. In January 2006, the Dalai Lama prohibited the wearing of furs, in response to a growing trend of Tibetan Buddhists donning fur skins. The Chinese government responded by specifically requiring that citizens wear these garments, in direct defiance of the Lama. They must either defy their political ruler or defy their spiritual ruler. Setting aside important questions of Tibetan sovereignty (on which Rousseau would surely have much to say), the Chinese Tibetan Buddhists have precisely the divided loyalties Rousseau thinks fatal to any healthy regime. So long as one has two independent masters, to his mind, one is doomed to be a poor citizen. As he concludes his treatment of the religion of the Priest, "Everything which destroys social unity is worthless: All institutions which put man in contradiction with himself are worthless" (*SC*, 4.8.17, 147 [III: 464].

The second mode of religion is the "religion of the Citizen." This is a variant of the theocracies that emerged with the earliest political communities, where there is "no other pontiff than the Prince, nor other priests than the magistrates" (*SC*, 4.8.18, 147 [III: 465]). Unlike the religion of the Priest, this at least has advantages, according to Rousseau. By uniting religion and the state so tightly, it links the laws with the divinity. Insofar as citizens obey the law, in other words, they are also pious. Crime is impious. This religion, however, possesses deep and pernicious flaws. The complete union of church and state fosters a kind of nationalistic fanaticism: "it makes a people bloodthirsty and intolerant; so that it breathes only murder and massacre, and believes it performs a holy deed in killing whoever does not accept its Gods" (*SC*, 4.8.19, 147 [III: 465]). This mode of religious faith is based on a "divine civil or positive right" (*SC*, 4.8.15, 146 [III: 464]), such that all of the state's commands are accepted as true and divine. This is a formula for tyranny internally and imperialism externally. It is tyrannical insofar as it allows for no reasonable toleration of diverse views within the state. Either one accepts the full slate of state beliefs or one is impious and hence a threat to that state. It is imperialistic insofar as everyone outside of the state is by definition impious and hence a threat both to their gods and their state. So, despite the virtues Rousseau first attributes to the religion of the citizen, it is largely pernicious.

The final option is the "Religion of man." This is Christianity as it may have once and ideally existed, not as he finds it in eighteenth-century Europe. It is specifically the Christianity of the Gospels. Rousseau elaborates little on its content here, other than to identify it as a "saintly, sublime, genuine Religion, men, as children of the same God, [where] all recognize one another as brothers" (*SC*, 4.8.20, 147 [III: 465]). He notes elsewhere that although the "Gospel is full of unbelievable things, of things repugnant to reason," at the same time the core messages of this Scripture are true.[88] Rousseau often repeated that he was a Christian – "not as a disciple of the Priests, but as a disciple of Jesus Christ."[89] Christ's teachings, on his reading, emphasize universal fraternity and charity. These elements represent the very best in Christianity, and likely are the reason he is comfortable – by this definition of the religion – in calling himself a Christian.[90]

Beyond the moral appeal of Christianity, Rousseau also reports some of its social and political virtues. First, as has already been mentioned, Christianity promotes a broad sense of fraternity among citizens. This element of the Christian religion was already well-known among and advocated by some of the most prominent early Enlightenment philosophers. Among them was Gottfried Wilhelm Leibniz, who argued that Christianity rightly demands a "charity regulated by wisdom" where the wise make "the felicity of others" their own.[91] Additionally, Christianity encourages citizens to fulfill their civic duties,[92] it fosters virtuous magistrates and rulers, its followers would scorn luxury and vanity, and its soldiers would be fearless in battle, convinced that this life is relatively

---

[88] *Emile*, 308 [IV: 627].

[89] "Letter to Beaumont," 47 [III: 960].

[90] *Mountain*, 147 [III: 704]. At the same time, he acknowledges that insofar as Christianity becomes the Religion of the Citizen, Christian charity is "little troubled … by injustice and cruelty" (*Emile*, 304 [III: 621]). Along these lines, he announces in his *Letter to Beaumont*, "I am a Christian, and sincerely a Christian, according to the doctrine of the Gospel" (47 [IV: 960]). It is likely, however, that this embrace of Christian morality has far more to do with charity or neighborly love than with the Golden Rule, which he notes is "subject to a thousand exceptions" (*Geneva Manuscript*, 2.4.16, 161 [IV: 329]). Rousseau goes on in the next paragraph to cite "*love thy neighbor as thyself*" as a noble deduction from the "universal Law of the greatest good of all." One finds the inverse of the conception of Christianity in Part II of the *Second Discourse*, where the wealthy are animated not by a love of their neighbors, but rather "the pleasure of domination" and desire to be "subjugating and enslaving their neighbors" (*Second Discourse*, 171 [III: 175]). This in part might explain how the spirit of the Gospels permeates his works more broadly.

[91] Leibniz, quoted in Riley 1996, 141. Rousseau was an admirer of Leibniz, having commented, Leibniz "died laden with goods and honors, and … even deserved more" (*Last Reply*, 82 [III: 92]).

[92] Perhaps a reference to Matthew 22:21: "They say unto him, Caesar's. Then saith he unto them, Render therefore unto Caesar the things which are Caesar's; and unto God the things that are God's."

meaningless. Obviously, most of these elements of the religion are consistent with Rousseau's political project.

But the virtue associated with its soldiers simultaneously suggests for
Rousseau the religion's fatal flaw for republican politics. Christianity's
emphasis on the next life diminishes the importance of *this* life – the
life in which Rousseau means to enact his republic. As he does so often
throughout Book IV, he is again drawing on Machiavelli, who writes in
his *Discourses*:

Our religion has glorified humble and contemplative more than active men. It
has then placed the highest good in humility, abjectness, and contempt of things
human; the other [ancient] placed it in greatness of spirit, strength of body, and
all other things capable of making it very strong. And if our religion asks that you
have strength in yourself, it wishes you to be capable more of suffering than of
doing something strong. This mode of life thus seems to have rendered the world
weak and given it in prey to criminal men, who can manage it securely, seeing
that the collectivity of men, so as to go to paradise, think more of enduring their
beatings than of avenging them.[93]

Rousseau is likewise concerned that Christian indifference to earthly existence would facilitate the abuse of power. Its exclusive "concern with the
things of Heaven" would render citizens largely unconcerned with the
machinations of potential tyrants (*SC*, 4.8.25, 148 [III: 466]).[94] To focus
too much on the problems of this world would be to distract individuals from their main tasks of faith and eternal salvation. Further, the very
act of driving out a tyrant would require acts fundamentally opposed to
the true Christian: violence and bloodshed. Finally, tyrants are further
emboldened by the fact that Christians care little whether they are free or
serfs in this world. A slave has just as much chance to gain salvation as a
master, if not more. So Rousseau's Christian has no incentive to fight off
tyranny. They accept their chains with a large degree of indifference. Such
complacence is utterly incompatible with what Rousseau requires of his
citizens, who must always be on guard against the encroachments of its
government and its usurpers.

Beyond this, Christians make poor soldiers. While they have the one
distinct virtue of being fearless of men, they lack the passion required of
great and effective troops. They will fulfill their duties, Rousseau acknowledges, but dispassionately: "they know better how to die than to win" (*SC*,

---

[93] *Discourses*, 2.2.
[94] Indeed, for Saint Augustine, for example, the presence of tyrants could be read as a sign of the
justice of God, who is punishing citizens for their sins. See *City of God*, 5.19; Proverbs 8:15; and Job
34:30.

4.8.27, 149 [III: 466]). Confronted by troops with any kind of commitment to the present world, they will be destroyed easily. So in the end, for Rousseau, "Christianity preaches nothing but servitude and dependence. Its spirit is too favorable to tyranny for tyranny not always to profit from it. True Christians are made to be slaves; they know it and are hardly moved by it; this brief life has too little value in their eyes" (*SC*, 4.8.28, 149 [III: 467]).

Rousseau's rejection of a Christian republic is followed by a final option: a civil religion. This is the third and final section of Chapter Eight. He clarifies the purpose of his civil religion in his *Letters Written from the Mountain*:

> The enterprise was bold, but it was not rash, and without circumstances that it was hard to foresee, it ought naturally to succeed. I was not alone in this sentiment; very enlightened people, even illustrious Magistrates thought as I did. Consider the religious condition of Europe at the moment I published my book [*The Social Contract*], and you will see that it was more than probable that it would be welcomed everywhere. Religion, discredited everywhere by philosophy, had lost its ascendency even over the people. The Clergy, obstinate about propping it up on its weak side, had let all the rest be undermined, and, being out of plumb, the entire edifice was ready to collapse. Controversies had stopped among the different parties, because none care about his own anymore. In order to remove the bad branches they cut down the tree; in order to replant it, it was necessary to leave nothing but the trunk.

He continues that the true purpose of his civil religion was to establish a "universal peace" and emphasize that in pushing aside the many disputes that characterize public life, "at bottom all were in agreement" that "everywhere one ought to serve God, love one's neighbor, [and] obey the laws."[95] Rousseau understood himself as a moderate in a world of extremists – dogmatic Christians and dogmatic atheists. He genuinely believed, however, there was a firm middle ground of shared beliefs that could bring the extremes together, offer civil peace, and ultimately promote the general will. This is his ambition in the remaining pages of Chapter Eight.

He stresses at the outset of his discussion the *civil* element of civil religion, noting that its tenets are not so much "dogmas of Religion" but rather "sentiments of sociability" (*SC*, 4.8.32, 150 [III: 468]). Insofar as they constitute "dogmas of Religion," they are those that engender the love of civic duties (*SC*, 4.8.31, 150 [III: 468]). This being said, his civil religion includes some substantively religious dimensions. Positively speaking, the

---

[95] *Mountain*, 227 [III: 802].

civil religion requires five doctrines. First, one must believe in a "powerful [*puissante*], intelligent, beneficent, prescient [*prévoyuante*], and provident [*pourvoyante*] Divinity" (*SC*, 4.8.33, 150 [III: 468]). These divine attributes, Rousseau believes, are broadly shared across any number of reasonable people of faith. They are also largely consistent with the conception of God his Savoyard Vicar outlines in the *Emile*.[96] The Vicar argues for the existence of a God largely on the basis of the striking order and beauty of the natural world, in the same spirit that Isaac Newton was persuaded that his discovery of the laws of nature only confirmed the existence of a higher intelligence. The fact that the universe is so well ordered is sufficient for the Vicar to arrive at God's existence, power, intelligence, and prescience. The Vicar quickly concludes that God must be benevolent since no creature of such immense power would have any need for wickedness, which itself is merely a means for compensating for various weaknesses.[97] Rousseau provides a separate account of God's providence in his *Letter to Voltaire*, which defends Leibniz's doctrine that God has legislated the best of all possible worlds. This emerges from the same tradition that produces Rousseau's general will in the *Social Contract*, albeit this version is largely theological. By "provident," Rousseau means that God has created general rules that govern the universe – both physical *and* moral.[98]

The next three tenets of the civil religion come as a logically linked set of doctrines: (2) that there is an afterlife, (3) that the just are happy, and (4) that the wicked are punished.[99] All of these propositions are again defended by Rousseau's Vicar in the *Emile*.[100] His argument takes the following form:

1. God is good and just.
2. Yet the wicked prosper and the good suffer on earth.
3. A good god prohibits the prolonged profiting by the wicked and suffering of the just.

---

[96] That the God of the *Social Contract* substantively resembles the God of Rousseau's Savoyard Vicar has been argued in Cladis 2006, 194.

[97] *Emile*, 275–7 [IV: 579–81].

[98] Rousseau explicitly states that God creates the moral laws earlier in the *Social Contract* (*SC*, 2.6.2, 66 [III: 378]). Rousseau's Savoyard Vicar endorses God's creation of the laws of the physical universe in the *Emile* (275–6 [IV: 579]). See also the *Letter to Voltaire* (242 [IV: 1070]).

[99] A description of Rousseau's conception of "paradise" can be found in Grimsley 1968, 87–107; a description of Rousseau's conception of hell can be found in Grimsley 1968, 123–9.

[100] *Emile*, 282–3 [IV: 589–90]. Rousseau also addresses these points in his earlier *Letter to Voltaire*, where he is a bit more circumspect: "I do not know whether this just Being will not some day punish every tyranny exercised in his name; I am quite sure, at least, that he will have no share in them" (244 [IV: 1072]).

4. Therefore, the soul must be immortal so that God can punish the wicked and reward the just.

The Vicar immediately adds the caveat that while the wicked are likely to be punished in the hereafter, eternal punishment is inconsistent with the premise of a good God.[101]

The fifth and final positive doctrine of Rousseau's civil religion is the "sanctity of the social Contract and the Laws" (*SC*, 4.8.33, 151 [III: 468]). In this doctrine, he is again likely finding inspiration in Machiavelli's *Discourses*. Machiavelli stresses Numa's appeal to religion as the source of Rome's laws, such that citizens associated infractions against the state with infractions against God.[102]

The civil religion also includes one negative tenet: that intolerance is unacceptable. He had earlier defined intolerance in his *Letter to Voltaire*: "I call intolerant on principle any man who imagines that one cannot be a good man without believing everything he believes, and mercilessly damns all those who do not think as he does."[103] In the *Social Contract*, Rousseau means specifically theological intolerance. Individual citizens and presumably organized religions within the state *must* tolerate all religious views consistent with the positive dogmas of the civil religion. But he adds that civil intolerance follows on the heels of religious intolerance: "It is impossible to live in peace with people one believes to be damned: to love them would be to hate God who punishes them; one must absolutely bring them back [to the fold] or torment them" (*SC*, 4.8.34, 151 [III: 469]).

While intolerance is often and rightly associated with some modes of religious belief, Rousseau is quick to add in his *Letter to Voltaire* that it is a vice of some atheists as well: "if there were intolerant nonbelievers who wanted to force the people to believe nothing, I would banish them no less sternly than those who want to force the people to believe whatever they please."[104] To be sure, he has in mind his former *Philosophe* friends, like Baron d'Holbach, although surely not all of them.[105] As with the religiously devout, there are tolerant as well as intolerant nonbelievers.

---

[101] See also the "Letter to d'Alembert," 12 [V: 12].

[102] See Machiavelli's *Discourses*, 1.11. To be sure, this is close in spirit to the "religion of the citizen" which Rousseau earlier rejected (*SC*, 4.8.18, 147 [III: 465]). He does not spell out here how he differs from the rejected option.

[103] *Letter to Voltaire*, 245 [IV: 1073].

[104] *Letter to Voltaire*, 245 [IV: 1073].

[105] One of the noblest characters in *Julie*, Wolmar, was an atheist for a significant time. Rousseau explains how Wolmar was disillusioned about religion from an early age by witnessing the various abuses of the Church. By the time he is able to overcome his indignity and examine the Gospels soberly, "his faith had already closed itself to truth, his reason was no longer accessible

Oddly, however, the same Rousseau who insists on a far-reaching tolerance adds that "If anyone, after having publicly acknowledged these … dogmas, behaves as if he did not believe them, let him be punished with death; he has committed the greatest of crimes, he has lied before the laws" (*SC*, 4.8.32, 150 [III: 468]). Why does he insist on such a severe penalty for a seemingly simple hypocrisy? To answer this, readers have to appreciate what would constitute a sign of hypocrisy. The sign of hypocrisy is almost certainly anti-social behavior. This can be deduced from the dogmas themselves. Nonbelievers may exist, but how is one to tell? Likewise, how might the state determine whether a citizen believes in the hereafter? Evidence can only be found in actions or deeds rather than in internal beliefs. And the relevant deeds would seem to be criminal acts, violating the "sanctity of the social Contract and the Laws." So one might very well read the impious here as "criminals." This mitigates some of the extreme nature of Rousseau's remarks.

It does not mitigate it entirely, however. There are at least two troublesome elements even on this charitable reading. First, one might reasonably wonder, if a law-abiding citizen simply confessed to his own atheism, whether Rousseau would still demand the death penalty. That this is an open question in the *Social Contract* is enough to be deeply troubling. In Rousseau's defense, he inserts a relevant footnote in his discussion of the virtuous atheist in his novel, *Julie*: "no true believer can possibly practice intolerance or persecution. If I were a judge, and the law prescribed the death penalty against atheists, I would begin by having burned for atheism anyone who came to turn in someone else."[106] This suggests that Rousseau would not actively seek out atheists for persecution.

A second concern is that he does not distinguish here between petty and serious crimes. Would a jaywalker not also deserve the death penalty by violating the sanctity of the laws? Surely, it is difficult to imagine Rousseau demanding such severity – but he does not suggest how to distinguish the jaywalker from mass murderers or those guilty of treason against just governments. He only identifies one broad category of those who behave as if they do not believe in the dogmas of the civil religion.

A final concern, of course, is the possibility that a civil religion might be commandeered by enterprising and manipulative individuals for purposes

to certitude." By the end, he straddles the line between faith and atheism as an agnostic. It is perfectly obvious throughout the novel that Wolmar is upright, virtuous, and a model citizen. To be sure, however, Wolmar is also depicted as an individual of rare moral fiber. See *Julie*, 482–3 [II: 590].

[106] *Julie*, 482 [II: 590].

other than those intended by Rousseau. Undoubtedly, the most infamous such historical episode was Robespierre's Cult of the Supreme Being, which was intended, according to Carol Blum, as a "literal enactment of Rousseau's prescription."[107]

These flaws being acknowledged, Rousseau's purpose for the civil religion is important – and deeply attached to his larger ambitions for a just republic. The desired effect of all the dogmas is, Rousseau reminds readers, to provide extra incentive for citizens to be moral and fulfill their civic duties (*SC*, 4.8.31, 150 [IV: 468]). This is another way of suggesting that the civil religion is aimed at supporting and buttressing the general will. As it is the subject of the last substantive chapter of the *Social Contract*, it may in a sense be read as the last line of defense against threats to the general will. By this juncture, Rousseau has introduced countless measures to improve the likelihood that citizens will behave sociably in concert with the general will. These measures have included reason, various institutional mechanisms, public opinion, and the bonds of civic fraternity. But it is presumably possible that some individuals might escape the effects of these various measures. There is no question that he thought this was the normal circumstance in his own times, where "the wicked man prospers, and the just man remains oppressed."[108] Insofar as his citizens believe in God, divine rewards and sanctions, and the divine quality of the laws themselves, Rousseau is persuaded that they have one more reason to behave sociably. Acting criminally in the pursuit of a private will subversive of the general will merits divine sanctions. Acting virtuously in service of the republic brings divine rewards. In this way, Rousseau follows a long tradition, stemming back to Plato's Myth of Er and Cicero's Dream of Scipio.[109] Both of the ancient precedents conclude their descriptions of a republic with an account of the afterlife, where civic virtue is richly rewarded in the hereafter. One can never know with certainty whether this turns out to be true, Rousseau would concede. But that is not his immediate concern. The important consideration is that citizens act as if it were true. As Ronald Grimsley has suggested, "In Rousseau's view, considerations of public order far outweigh any questions of the truth or falsity of particular religious dogmas. The effectiveness of a national religion is to be determined by its ability to strengthen the unity and stability of the State rather than by its spiritual value."[110] Its status as subservient to politics,

[107] Blum 1986, 249.
[108] *Emile*, 282 [IV: 589].
[109] *Republic*, 614b–21c; *On the Commonwealth*, Book 6, §8–29.
[110] Grimsley 1968, 82.

however, does not render it insignificant. To the contrary, Rousseau was persuaded that his religious views were not only crucial to the success of the *Social Contract*, but could one day "bring about a revolution among men, if good sense and faith are ever reborn among them."[III]

4.9. *Conclusion (On International Relations)*

The reader has every right to expect a grand summary of the themes of the *Social Contract* in its conclusion, but it instead reads like an apology for an abrupt ending. It is clear enough from Rousseau's own words here and in the "Notice" (*SC*, 40 [III: 349]) that he had clearly run out of time and energy to produce as much as he thought his topic deserved. Nevertheless, he provides at least hints in the Conclusion of how he might have brought the *Social Contract* to a more glorious close. Specifically, it would turn to international relations, including "the right of nations, commerce, the right of war and conquests, public right, leagues, negotiations, treaties, etc." (*SC*, 4.9.1, 152 [III: 470]). And although he says nothing here about the substance of his views on these matters, he has left enough clues elsewhere in his writings to construct a reasonable accounting. This notably includes his short essays, *The State of War* and the *Judgment of the Plan for Perpetual Peace*, both of which were written some years before publication of the *Social Contract*. It is likely that had Rousseau the energy, he would have developed the reflections outlined in these works in Chapter Nine. Fortunately, however, Rousseau's thoughts in these earlier works are developed sufficiently to constitute a significant contribution in their own right. Perhaps the most influential theorist of international relations in the latter half of the twentieth century, Kenneth N. Waltz, suggests that Rousseau invented an entirely original manner of conceiving relations between states.[112] Of Rousseau's two most relevant works, broadly speaking, *The State of War* offers his understanding of war largely as an empirical phenomenon. The *Judgment of the Plan for Perpetual Peace* represents his evaluation of a sincere attempt to put an end to wars.

[III] *Reveries*, 34 [I: 1018].
[112] Waltz attributes what he calls the "Third Image" of international relations to Rousseau. The "First Image" understands human nature to be the cause of war (as in Hobbes). The "Second Image" understands the structure of individual states to be the cause of war (e.g., that liberal or republican states, for example, might be less prone to war, or that capitalist states might be more inclined to war). The "Third Image" views the causes of war to be sewn into the very nature of the international system. This is explored later. See Waltz 1959, 165–86.

The State of War is a fragmentary and incomplete work.[113] Yet these frag-ments suggest a highly original understanding of the nature of war. His departure points are, as they were in Book I of the *Social Contract*, the philosophies of Thomas Hobbes and Hugo Grotius.[114] Hobbes argues that the natural condition of humanity is nothing less than a state of war. This rests on the underlying assumption of a deep, pervasive, and some-what myopic egoism animating all human behavior in the state of nature. Everyone is selfish and knows everyone likewise to be the same. So given the lack of external constraints on behavior in the state of nature, indi-viduals are constantly engaged in offensive or defensive campaigns – or at least preparing for them. Hobbes goes on to suggest that while this condi-tion has a domestic solution in the contract that established the sovereign Leviathan, it remains more or less permanently true of international rela-tions, where all countries exist in a state of war with one another.

Rousseau's problem with Hobbes's account of human nature and the natural condition of war is that he and his disciples "confuse natu-ral man with the men they have before their eyes." In observing those with "unbounded and uncontrollable greed" surrounding him, Hobbes has erred in assuming this is humankind's natural condition. Rousseau does not expend much effort in explaining why Hobbes is wrong, hav-ing sketched these arguments extensively in his *Second Discourse*. The con-densed version in the *State of War* emphasizes that natural human beings desire very little. "Man is naturally peaceable and timorous."[115] It is only socialized individuals who exhibit acquisitive and socially destructive traits. It is only by stirring *amour propre* and fueling it by rewarding those very destructive behaviors that brings about what Hobbes calls "natural." Hobbes is right to identify Parisians and Londoners, for example, as egois-tic to the highest degree. The big mistake is to assume that this is natural.

Hobbes's mistake in understanding human nature is compounded by another error in applying this logic to the state of war. Rousseau paints Hobbes's natural men as desiring to destroy all the rest of humanity.[116] But Rousseau argues that no one – not even those motivated by "unbounded

---

[113] The issues surrendering its nature in this regard are outlined in Roosevelt 1987.

[114] In framing Rousseau's *State of War* as a response to Hobbes and Grotius, I follow Roosevelt 1990, chapters 1 and 2. Roosevelt's treatment of Rousseau's international relations theory is likely the definitive one in English. See also Hoffmann and Fidler 1991; Pangle 1999, 185–91.

[115] *State of War*, 164 [III: 611]; *State of War*, 165 [III: 601]; *Second Discourse*, especially 151–4 [III: 153–7]; *State of War*, 166 [III: 601].

[116] It should be said, it is unclear that this reading of Hobbes can be sustained by Hobbes's actual words.

and uncontrollable greed" – can really be said to desire such a thing. This is because pure acquisition is not anyone's ultimate goal. The real goal – whether it be for Hobbes's natural man or Rousseau's socialized one – is to lord those acquisitions and that power over others: "before whose eyes will he display his power?" Rousseau asks. As such, the inclination of socialized and *amour-propre*-inflamed individuals is not a war of all against all. Those at the top do not seek to kill their neighbors. As described in Part II of the *Second Discourse*, they rather seek to make them their slaves. This is the condition of despotism, where those lacking power are "all in chains" – presumably, the very same chains Rousseau finds individuals wearing at the outset of the *Social Contract*. For Rousseau, this despotism is technically not a state of war, which he defines as "the manifest will to destroy one another."[117]

The reason he does not call this "war" has to do in part with his response to Grotius. Grotius had defined two major categories of war in his *Rights of War and Peace*: private and public.[118] On his account, a private war takes place "between private Persons, without public Authority."[119] A public war, by contrast, takes place between public entities with public authority. Rousseau denies, however, that conflicts between individuals can properly be called war: "the state of war can … not obtain among individuals."[120] These conflicts might be more properly called quarrels – since they tend to be of very short duration and lack the greater permanence attached to war. Such is the nature of tension and violence between individuals. The only conflict deserving of the name "war" is a public one between states.

The origin of the conflict between states represents perhaps Rousseau's most original contribution to international relations theory. Understanding why states conflict with one another hinges on a difference between natural human beings and states. Natural human beings have a limit to their satiation, since a stomach, for example, can only hold so much food. While it might make sense in the state of nature for one person to knock another over the head to steal his freshly killed rabbit, there is no point in taking more than one can eat. So there are natural limits on the amount individuals might desire to acquire by violence from others.[121] By contrast,

---

[117] *State of War*, 165 [III: 601]; *State of War*, 165 [III: 601]; *State of War*, 173 [III: 1903].

[118] See *The Rights of War and Peace*, Book I, Chapter 3. There is for Grotius an additional third category of "mixed" wars, partly public, partly private.

[119] *Grotius*, 240 [1.3.1].

[120] *State of War*, 167 [III: 602].

[121] Though, to be sure, if one considers socialized individuals animated by *amour propre*, the limits on satiation expand dramatically. This is because *amour propre* is artificial. The desire for honor and praise has no natural limits. So if individuals think they can gain in the public eye by harming

there is no end to what a state might acquire and enjoy as booty from conquering another state. This is exacerbated by the fact that states are necessarily subject to the forces of *amour propre*: "since the size of a body politic is purely relative, it is forced constantly to compare itself in order to know itself."[122] A state can increase its sense of value only in relation to others. It is "better" than other states in that it is larger, wealthier, more powerful, and the like. The most obvious way it can attain this status is by conquering its neighbors. So in the international sphere, there will always be incentives for war. This is built into the international system.

Now Grotius's definition of war is relatively straightforward: it is "the State or Situation of those ... who dispute by Force of Arms."[123] This is a largely traditional conception of war, drawing on its most obviously vicious elements. So the apparent means of war by this standard definition all involve force. Yet Rousseau's analysis of war draws on the nature of the state itself. Since the heart of every state, according to Rousseau, is its "social pact" – itself "inscribed in the general will"[124] – there are numerous points of vulnerability in warfare. This leads to another strikingly original element of Rousseau's theory of war. The social pact is embedded in its government, laws, morals, goods, possessions, and citizens. So a war often does include violent assaults against citizens. But on Rousseau's understanding, a successful campaign can also target the government, laws, and morals of its enemy's citizens. As Grace G. Roosevelt has observed, Rousseau's theory of war extends beyond violent assaults to "espionage, economic exploitation, and cultural subversion."[125] One can grasp in reading this why Rousseau's reaction against the construction of a theater in Geneva was so profound. Corrupting a state's morals can be more effective than muskets and cannons in conquering another land.

Whatever means a state employs, however, the ends are the same. The purpose and very definition of a war, according to Rousseau, is to "destroy one's enemy." He insists that in order for a conflict to meet the standard of "war," this purpose must be "steady, considered, and manifest." An impassioned, but ephemeral, lashing out typical of individual relations would fail to qualify as a war. War requires "reason," which itself generates "lasting resolve."[126]

others, they could presumably do so without end. In a well-constructed republic, however, the incentives are probably minimized.

[122] *State of War*, 169 [III: 605].
[123] Grotius, 134 [1.1.2.1].
[124] *State of War*, 171 [III: 1900].
[125] Roosevelt 1990, 56.   •
[126] *State of War*, 173 [III: 1903].

The inconveniences of war are obvious enough. The real question, for Rousseau, is whether anything can be done to stem them. On this matter, there is some debate among scholars. Stanley Hoffmann, for example, is persuaded that for Rousseau "in the world as it is," most otherwise seemingly plausible solutions to the problem of war are largely "impossible." By contrast, Grace G. Roosevelt is more optimistic that Rousseau offers reasonable alternatives to the pessimistic conclusion that war is a permanent fixture of international relations.[127]

Generally speaking, Rousseau offers two means by which war might be escaped. The two solutions are vastly different in nature. The first is largely isolationist. The second is a radical opposite: a confederation of nations that might establish a collective security.[128]

The first solution hinges upon the spread of Rousseau's ideal republics. He initially defines a republic in Book I of the *Social Contract* as the union of all citizens under the guidance of the general will (*SC*, 1.6.9–10 [III: 361]). He subsequently adds a second definition: "any State ruled by laws, whatever may be the form of administration" (*SC*, 2.6.9, 67 [III: 379]). Since Rousseau defines legitimate laws as conforming to the general will (*SC*, 2.6.5, 67 [III: 379]), it is evident that his conception of a republic presupposes all the benefits of living according to the general will. Among other consequences for Rousseau, this means the minimization of international trade.

Throughout the eighteenth century, it was common among intellectuals to argue that international commerce would ease tensions between states. This doctrine is known as *doux commerce*. Its most vocal supporters included Bernard de Mandeville, Jean-François Melon, and David Hume,[129] all of whom argued that trade tended to relax tensions and improve morals. Among Rousseau's contemporaries, Montesquieu wrote, "The natural effect of commerce is to lead to peace. Two nations that trade with each other become reciprocally dependent."[130] Rousseau acknowledges the argument on the very first page of his *First Discourse* that "commerce" has the alleged advantage of "rendering men more sociable by inspiring them to please one another." Yet in Part II of the same essay he describes a system overtaken by "commerce and money" at the expense of morals and virtue. An obsession with trade and money leads necessarily to wealth, which results in the burdens of luxury. He expands his critique

---

[127] Hoffmann 1983, 326; Roosevelt 1990, 6.
[128] In laying out these two options, I am largely following Roosevelt 1990, chapters 3 and 4.
[129] See Rosenblatt 1997, 53–60.
[130] *Spirit of the Laws*, 338 [4.20.2].

of *doux commerce* in his subsequent exchanges in defense of the *First Discourse*. In his *Last Reply*, he writes that the views of Melon represent "odious maxims which only tend to destroy and debase virtue." And in the *Preface to 'Narcissus'*, he finds it "horrifying to see how far the maxims of our ratiocinating century have carried contempt for the duties of man and citizen."[131] The more that individual citizens engage in commerce, the more they celebrate themselves over the community as a whole. This has the effect of eroding the general will, which requires for its very existence the prioritization of the community over the individual.

The core of Rousseau's argument against *doux commerce* appears to be that it draws on *amour propre*. One seeks profits not in order to benefit others mutually, but rather "to raise his own advantage above theirs and at their expense."[132] This does not improve relations, as Mandeville and others argue – it instead makes civic relations more hostile and manipulative. For Rousseau, both esteem and profits operate as a zero-sum game. This suggests why trade represents a great danger to international peace. Commerce necessarily implies winners and losers.[133] The acquisition of wealth for one nation requires impoverishing another. So to the extent that an entire state can be animated by *amour propre*,[134] it will seek to enrich itself by menacing its neighbors.

The solution to this problem is to minimize commerce and consequently return to embrace the principles of the general will – each state on its own. A small virtuous republic can supply all of its own needs, according to Rousseau.[135] Citizens do not assess their own value according to their wealth; they assess themselves according to their degree of virtue. It would stand to reason, hence, that with fewer incentives to acquire wealth, citizens would cease threatening one another.

Relatedly, Rousseau also observes that self-sufficiency places one state less at the mercy of another – which can also reduce the need for warfare. As he comments in his *Corsica*, "Even if you have all the wealth in the world, if you do not have anything with which to nourish yourself you are dependent on others. Your neighbors can give your money whatever value they please because they can wait; but the bread that we need has an indisputable value for us and in every sort of commerce it is always the least

---

[131] *First Discourse*, 6 [III: 6]; *First Discourse*, 18 [III: 19]; *Last Reply*, 84 [III: 95]; *Narcissus*, 98 [III: 966]. I am guided here by Rosenblatt 1997.

[132] *Narcissus*, 100 [III: 969].

[133] Though among Rousseau's contemporaries, economists such as David Hume would argue the opposite – namely, that international trade can be win-win (Hume [1752b] 1994).

[134] *State of War*, 169 [III: 605].

[135] *Corsica*, 140 [III: 921].

hurried person who gives the law to the other."[136] Although Rousseau does not develop this point as it affects international relations, it is not difficult to imagine its implications. A dependent state is always at the mercy of others. It can only seek to overcome its dependency either by becoming self-sufficient or by conquering the territories on which it depends. In many respects, this latter option explains much of the colonial spirit of the sixteenth century to the present. It is perhaps not a coincidence that this conflict emerged along with commercial culture.

The appeal to small republics is certainly an ideal Rousseauean solution. There is a second possibility, however, that relies on virtue in a different way: to construct a confederation of states structured for the mutual security and advantage of all. Rousseau evaluated just such a proposal in his summary of the Abbé de Saint-Pierre's *Plan for Perpetual Peace* and his subsequent *Judgment* of that piece. The Abbé de Saint-Pierre suggested a confederative government uniting the various European states under one uniform international law. His plan was the archetype of a certain species of Enlightenment thinking that placed supreme faith in reason. Princes would understand themselves to exist in a state of war and then reason their way to a felicitous peace through confederation. It would ultimately bring complete security of the state, of the prince and his family, greater freedom and commerce, reduced expenditures on military, and greater glory.

Rousseau acknowledges the Abbé's aim of perpetual peace to be "by its object the one [plan] most worthy of occupying a good man." Its advantages are for him "immense, clear, undeniable."[137] Yet at the same time, he is insistent that it is utterly impossible under the present conditions. The root of the problem, as is so commonly Rousseau's diagnoses of social problems, is excess and poorly directed *amour propre*. In this instance, this has everything to do with the princes themselves, who are incapable of distinguishing their real from their apparent interests. He argued in the *Social Contract* that the dominant institution of hereditary monarchy had been nothing short of disastrous.[138] Rousseau finds confirmation of this disposition in their approach to war. As found throughout Europe, princes want war for myopically selfish reasons. They are falsely persuaded that war serves their

---

[136] *Corsica*, 127 [III: 905].

[137] *Judgment*, 53 [III: 591].

[138] "Everything conspires to deprive of justice and reason a man brought up to command others. Great pains are taken, so they say, to teach young Princes the art of ruling; it does not appear that this education profits them. It would be better to begin by teaching the art of obeying" (*SC*, 3.6.12, 97 [III: 411]).

own private interests. Specifically, they are optimistic that war "provides a pretext for extortions," which ultimately will enhance their wealth and power. This drive to war for myopically selfish reasons is also shared by a prince's ministers, who "need war to make themselves necessary."[139]

So long as princes and magistrates motivated by passion, *amour propre*, and a narrow sense of self-interest populate Europe, the confederations that might bring an end to war are utterly naïve. Rousseau does not mince words here. Although the Abbé de Saint-Pierre's plan was "very wise, the means for executing it make one feel the author's simplicity.... Let us agree that ... he judged the means for establishing them [his plans for a confederation] like a child."[140] He was simply too sanguine that princes would have the wisdom to understand that perpetual peace was in everyone's interest and then the courage to pursue that course of action. For this reason, scholars such as Stanley Hoffman have concluded that for Rousseau, "in the world, such as it is, such a universal state is impossible."[141]

What would it take, then, to implement the Abbé's noble, if utopian, plan? Uncharacteristically, Rousseau explicitly considers violence as a means to peace: "what is useful to the public hardly finds its way in except by force, considering that private interests are almost always opposed to it." For all of Rousseau's reputation as a muse to revolutionaries, this is the one instance in his works in which he expressly considers violence as a means to achieve noble political ends. Yet as soon as he offers it for consideration, he retreats from the thought, noting that such efforts could likely "cause more harm all at once than it would prevent for centuries."[142]

For all of this pessimism about establishing a lasting peace among states, Rousseau surely retains some hope. A few years after recording his thoughts about the Abbé's plan, he briefly returns to consider the plague of war in his *Emile*. Near his conclusion, he again points to the menace of war – but this time appealing more hopefully to the

kind of remedies ... provided by leagues and confederations, which leave each state its own master within but arm it against every unjust aggressor from without. We shall investigate how a good federative association can be established, what can make it durable, and how far the right of confederation can be extended without jeopardizing that of sovereignty.[143]

---

[139] *Judgment*, 54 [III: 593]; *Judgment*, 56 [II: 595].
[140] *Judgment*, 56–7 [III: 595].
[141] Hoffmann 1963, 326.
[142] *Judgment*, 60 [III: 599]. More typical of Rousseau: "violent means do not suit the just cause" (*Mountain*, 269 [III: 852]).
[143] *Emile*, 466 [IV: 848].

It is unfortunate, however, that while Emile's tutor points to the importance of these lessons, he never articulates them. We are merely left with the tantalizing prospect that Rousseau had somehow resolved in his mind the impasse with which he concludes his judgment of the Abbé's proposal.

Grace Roosevelt is nevertheless persuaded that Rousseau has in essence sketched the outlines of such a plan in the very nature of Emile's education.[144] Since the problem he identified earlier is the lack of virtue and wisdom among the princes, the solution is to make them both wiser and more virtuous. In this spirit Roosevelt emphasizes those passages in the *Emile* that speak to the importance of building on *amour propre* in a healthy way. A good education acknowledges an inclination toward selfishness, but then extends it more broadly. One begins by loving oneself, and it is natural enough for this to be extended to family and friends. The great challenge is to extend that same love to "the abstract idea of humanity." This is crucial in inculcating the pupil's love of justice, which is nothing less than a "love of mankind." This love of mankind, in turn, engenders a love of peace, since no one who loves humanity would seek to harm it. Armed with this love of humanity, "If he sees discord reigning among his comrades, he seeks to reconcile them; ... if he sees two men who hate each other, he wants to know the cause of their enmity."[145] The remaining pages of the pedagogical novel, on Roosevelt's reading, are (among other purposes) dedicated to building up sufficient force of will to overcome the temporary passions and apparent interests that might divert someone from justice and true interests. The lack of this will and judgment is precisely what burdens the princes Rousseau condemns in his *Judgment of the Plan for Perpetual Peace*. So it stands to reason that the education of Emile provides in it the solution to the otherwise apparently intractable problem of war. It is not, however, a likely solution. Rousseau conceded that the *Emile* was impracticable for mass implementation. But it might also be possible that for Rousseau's world, it could have been proven a useful training for individuals destined to assume power.[146]

As in the individual state, for Rousseau, the prospects for success hinge largely upon the degree to which the citizens and its government embrace virtue. He announced the centrality of virtue in his first constructive work

---

[144] See Roosevelt 1990, esp. 163–73.

[145] *Emile*, 233 [IV: 520]; *Emile*, 252 [IV: 547]; *Emile*, 251 [IV: 545].

[146] Though it is important to bear in mind that being raised to assume power is deeply problematic for Rousseau. As he laments in the *Social Contract*, "Everything conspires to deprive of justice and reason a man brought up to command others" (*SC*, 3.6.12, 97 [III: 411]). See also the *Poland*, 213–14 [III: 991–2].

on politics, the *Discourse on Political Economy*, where he admits that the temptations of political power are indeed great, and that the institutional measures for combating them are ultimately limited. In the end, "the only effective instrument is virtue, and the magistrate's integrity is the only curb capable of restraining his greed."[147] Create a state conducive to the cultivation of virtue, and peace is more within reach.

This raises the final matter of whether or not there can be a general will across state lines. There are two respects in which this question might be posed. First, is it logically possible in Rousseau's scheme to imagine such a general will? Second, is it practically possible? There are good grounds to believe that the answer to the first question is "yes." The general will has, broadly speaking, two demands: (1) that its content conforms to justice and the common good, and (2) that the people themselves will it. He makes both components clear in his *Political Economy*, where he describes the body politic as "a moral being that has a will." This moral being with a will is nothing less than the "general will, which always tends toward the preservation of well-being of the whole and of each part." He continues in the next paragraph, however, to observe that this "rule of justice" [the general will], dependable with respect to all citizens, can be false with respect to strangers."[148] This might suggest that the general will is of necessity limited to states – and not to an international community. But this is not necessarily implied. Recall that in the *Social Contract*, Rousseau suggests that there can be more than one general will operating in the same society at the same time (*SC*, 3.5.1, 92 [III: 406]).[149] It is easy enough to imagine how this might operate in a territory characterized by federalism. There can at one time and place be general wills of a city, a state or province, and a nation. Insofar as the general will of the city is concerned, the interests of people from other cities are largely irrelevant. Insofar as the general will of the state or province is concerned, the interests of residents of others states are largely irrelevant. And insofar as the general will of a nation-state is concerned, the interests of people outside of that nation-state are largely

[147] *Political Economy*, 26 [III: 265]. In the same spirit Rousseau insists in his "Fragments on the *Polysynody*" that "Of all the qualities of a political thinker, the most necessary is a true desire to procure the public good, if genius makes one find the means to do it, it is virtue that makes one seek them; thus something other than talents is needed to govern well and as soon as it is a question of someone else's interest, the head always goes badly as long as a beautify soul does not lead it" ("Fragments on the *Polysynody*," 105 [III: 652]).

[148] *Political Economy*, 6 [III: 245]; *Political Economy*, 7 [III: 245].

[149] As James Miller observes, "There are as many general wills as there are genuine communities" (Miller 1984, 62). See also Tracy B. Strong, who argues that for Rousseau, "I can have several general will in myself, depending on in how many social forms I find myself ([1994] 2002, 83).

irrelevant. So while it might be in the service of the one state or province's general will to dump all of its nuclear waste in another state or province, this may not necessarily conform to the broader national general will.

By this reasoning, there may be a general will for a continent or even the entire globe. While a general will of a nation-state would consider the interests of people within its borders, an international general will would consider the interest of everyone regardless of borders. Presumably, it was something like this that motivated the Abbé de St. Pierre, whose ambition Rousseau endorses as a "moral truth."[150] He goes on to describe a "common good" for the "European Republic" – which, although not a fully global union, transcends traditional national borders. So if the people of the world could agree to an international general will, it would exist. In a scenario where one is subject to multiple general wills simultaneously, it is fair to ask which general will takes precedence. Rousseau does not address this question directly, but it is not too much of a stretch to suggest that the larger the scope of the general will, the more weight it might have. In his *Emile*, he posits that "the more one generalizes this interest [*amour propre*], the more it becomes equitable, and the love of mankind is nothing other than the love of justice." This suggests that the more generalized the will, the more just it is. So if one is at least measuring obligations by the standard of justice, the most general will would trump less generalized wills.[151]

This raises the second main concern about an international general will: is it feasible or practicable? To be sure, it encounters many obstacles, several of which Rousseau identifies. One of these obstacles is the simple fact that there is no impulse to form a "general society of mankind" in the state of nature. In response to Denis Diderot's claim that there is a natural impulse toward cosmopolitanism in the state of nature,[152] Rousseau is skeptical in his *Geneva Manuscript* that natural human beings have the capacity to extend their conception of the good beyond their immediate self-interest. Indeed, he observes that the idea of a "common brotherhood [*fraternité*] of all men spread rather late" in human history, emerging as an aspiration only with the spread of Christianity.[153]

Of course, much the same could be said of the love of fellow citizens in a city-state. While natural human beings feel compassion for others, they do not *love* them or see the interests of others as equally valid as their own.

[150] *Judgment*, 53 [III: 591].
[151] (*Emile*, 252 [IV: 547]).
[152] Diderot 1992, 17–21. See Roosevelt 1990, ch. 3.
[153] *Geneva Manuscript*, 158 [III: 287].

and more popular literature. It may be useful, however, to conclude this book by lingering a bit amidst some judicially selected evidence of his centrality and uniqueness; to do so can only sharpen our understanding of the problems he has left us to grapple with. I would like to approach this matter of his uniqueness and centrality by considering not only how he follows and then deviates from the paths that existed when he wrote his *Social Contract*, but also how subsequent political philosophers have built on his foundation and deviated where they thought necessary. In selecting a small group of interlocutors for Rousseau here, I apply three criteria. First, Rousseau's predecessors must have had some discernible effect on his own development. Second, his successors must acknowledge Rousseau's influence on them to at least some degree. Third, I choose philosophers engaged largely in constructive political philosophy, in the tradition of the *Social Contract*, rather than in the more critical tradition of his *Discourses*.

5.1 PLATO

There is good reason to begin a comparative inquiry about Rousseau with Plato. Rousseau reports spending his formative years with "Socrates and the divine Plato."[2] He personally owned a copy of Plato's complete dialogues, which he read and thoughtfully marked.[3] In the *Emile* he praises Plato for "purif[ying] the heart of man" and for writing the *Republic*, which he describes as "the most beautiful educational treatise ever written."[4] Rousseau even once wrote a dialogue, "On Theatrical Imitation," in the voice of Plato, systematically repeating Plato's arguments from Book X of the *Republic*, arguments clearly paralleling Rousseau's own thoughts as spelled out in the *First Discourse* and *Letter to d'Alembert*. Charles Hendel characterized Rousseau's interest in Plato as an "obsession," and contemporary commentators continue to find Rousseau's relationship to Plato a fruitful avenue for gaining further insight into his political thought.[5]

Plato's Socrates rests the *Republic's* city of Kallipolis on a tight set of related premises. Its primary assumption is the well-rehearsed theory of forms or ideas. Although he acknowledges the existence of material

---

[2] "The Banterer," 4 [II: 1124].
[3] This can be found and examined today at the British Library in London, document #G.16721-5. An historical account of Rousseau's personal copy of Plato's dialogues can be found in Silverthorne 1973.
[4] *Emile*, 40 [IV: 250].
[5] Hendel, I: 29; See, for example, Hall 1982; Trachtenberg 2001; Gouhier 2005, Maloy 2005; Williams 2007a; Cooper 2008; and Cusher 2010.

substance, the most valuable and important realm is that of immaterial ideas, universal and eternal – "always the same in all respects." Sitting atop his doctrine of ideas is the idea of the good, and Plato makes knowledge of the realm of universal ideas, and especially of the good, the single greatest requirement of all rulers. Rulers must master the form of the good, which is the ultimate source of truth: "what gives truth to things known and the power to know to the knower is the form of the good."[6] And since only few possess the requisite talents to know the good, the ruling class is necessarily a small elite that wields its immense power wisely, according to its knowledge of philosophical ideas.

On the surface, it is difficult to imagine what Rousseau's political thought might have in common with Plato's. Most notably, Rousseau specifically disdains the "jargon of metaphysics" and places ultimate political authority not with an elite few, but with the entire body of citizens. Further, Rousseau himself specifically distances the *Social Contract* from "the *Republic of Plato* ... [and] the land of the chimeras."[7] This is all true, but Rousseau's Platonic faith is not so easily disavowed.

While Rousseau disdains the "jargon" of metaphysics, his dispute is not with metaphysics as such but with professional philosophers who use metaphysics as a means of impressing others and rising up the social hierarchy. Philosophers carried a social weight in the eighteenth century that is difficult to imagine in the twenty-first. Just as Newton became famous for his physics, Descartes became famous for his metaphysics. And with potential social rewards comes a host of intellectually inferior or dishonest characters, eager to philosophize in order to ascend the social ranks. First come the great geniuses – then come the lesser imitators. This is the spirit of his argument against philosophers in the *First Discourse*. This is perfectly clear on a close read of the *First Discourse*, where he remarks, for example, "How sweet it would be to live among us if the outward countenance were always the image of the heart's dispositions; if decency were virtue; if our maxims were rules; if genuine Philosophy were inseparable from the title of Philosopher!"[8]

This raises the obvious question of what constitutes "genuine Philosophy" in Rousseau's lexicon. He provides a straightforward answer to this question in his conclusion: "Are not your principles engraved in all hearts, and is it not enough in order to learn your Laws to return into

[6] *Republic*, 484b; *Republic*, 476cd, 484c; *Republic*, 505a; *Republic*, 508e.
[7] *Emile*, 274 [IV: 577]; *Mountain*, 234 [III: 810].
[8] *First Discourse*, 7 [III: 8].

oneself and listen to the voice of one's conscience in the silence of the passions? That is genuine Philosophy, and let us know how to rest content with it." Genuine Philosophy, in simple terms, is nothing other than the moral principles residing in the conscience. Rousseau explains further in the *Emile* that the conscience itself consists in "an innate principle of justice," which, like Plato's ideas, is eternal.[9]

Further, although Rousseau specifically eschews metaphysics as practiced by his contemporaries, he develops a metaphysics of his own, most substantially in the voice of the Savoyard Vicar in the *Emile*.[10] Included in his metaphysics is his substance dualism – the doctrine that there are two kinds of substance, material and immaterial. Material substance includes all the matter present in the physical world. It necessarily comes into and goes out of existence – like any tree, rock, house, or animal. Immaterial substance includes things like eternal ideas (such as beauty, justice, or goodness) and the soul. It is by its nature eternal. For Rousseau, human beings are composites of these two kinds of substance; their bodies are material and fleeting, their souls immaterial and immortal. Rousseau embraces this philosophical dualism – which dates back to Plato's dialogues – against the materialism of the *Philosophes*, who insist that everything (including each human being) is made exclusively of matter.

Rousseau shares much in common with Plato in all these regards. He employs Plato's doctrine of dualism; he considers genuine Philosophy to be of special importance; and he identifies justice as being one of the immaterial substances and necessarily eternal.

Yet Rousseau is sincere when he suggests that the *Social Contract* is far removed from Plato's *Republic*. The differences largely emanate from the matter of the extent of epistemic access to the eternal ideas. Whereas Plato's ideas are accessible only to the few, Rousseau's notion of the conscience is theoretically present in everyone. For him, even the most ordinary minds are capable of knowing the "true principles of the just, the true models of the beautiful, all the moral relations of beings" since they are "all imprinted on his understanding."[11] This is not the same as saying that they can grasp the fine points of Leibnizian metaphysics or Berkeley's epistemology. But these matters are entirely beside the point for Rousseau.

---

[9] *First Discourse*, 28 [III: 30]; *Emile*, 289 [IV: 598]; *Emile*, 259 [IV: 556], 292 [IV: 603].
[10] Some have suggested that the Vicar is not voicing Rousseau's own views (e.g., Melzer 1990, 30). I do not follow this suggestion, largely because Rousseau frequently embraces the Vicar's views throughout his writings in his own voice. See Williams 2007a, 62–4.
[11] *Emile*, 253 [IV: 548].

It is ordinary people's capacity to understand justice that facilitates Rousseau's democratic politics – and this separates him from Plato's *Republic*, which openly condemns popular government. Since for Plato's Socrates the masses can never practice philosophy and therefore will never understand justice and goodness, it stands to reason that they should be largely excluded from legislation and ruling. By contrast, for Rousseau, the people should legislate because they know what is most relevant – justice itself, which is the source of the general will.[12] This key assumption underlies Rousseau's commitment to the doctrine of popular sovereignty.

There is another, closely related, respect in which Rousseau's *Social Contract* deviates from Plato's *Republic*. Rousseau's republic requires the actual consent of its people. This is the principle of legitimacy, which animates both the general will and the social contract itself. Rousseau's political society can only come into existence by individuals consenting to live together under the guidance of the general will. In order for the contract not to be "an empty formula," it must be understood as an agreement to "obey the general will" (*SC*, 1.7.8, 53 [III: 364]); and one of its most important elements is the very act of willing. As Patrick Riley properly emphasizes, the general will is for Rousseau "'the most voluntary act in the world,' and … 'to deprive your will of all freedom is to deprive your actions of all morality.'"[13] The very category of legitimacy grounded on free consent was unknown in the ancient world. So in an important sense, Rousseau combines important features of both ancient and modern political philosophy. From the ancients, he borrows Plato's commitment to an "eternal" conception of justice. But in order for this conception of justice to be active and legitimate, it must be validated through the modern device of popular consent.

5.2 *Machiavelli*

In the most obvious sense, it seems foolish to suggest that Rousseau has much, if anything, in common with Niccolò Machiavelli. Machiavelli's infamous pronouncements that it is often better to be feared than loved, better to be cruel than compassionate, and his general counsel on how to secure ill-gained territories, suggests a worldview entirely foreign to Rousseau. Yet Rousseau's own words suggest a surprising sympathy for the Florentine diplomat. He cites Machiavelli authoritatively throughout

---

[12] See Appendix A, A.4.1.
[13] Riley, 2001b, 127, quoting *The Social Contract*, 4.2.5, 123 [III: 440] and 1.4.6, 45 [III: 356].

the *Social Contract*, describing him as an "honest man and a good citizen" (*SC*, 3.6.5n, 95n [III: 409n]). Given Machiavelli's generally notorious reputation in respectable circles throughout early modern Europe (and even today), it would be surprising if his own mother rendered such a sympathetic verdict on his character. Yet it is precisely on the basis of Rousseau's reading of Machiavelli's infamous *Prince* that he arrived at this assessment.

In his *Prince*, Machiavelli offers advice to would-be kings on how to acquire and maintain power. As Quentin Skinner has persuasively outlined, he reverses the time-honored advice of the ancients, specifically Cicero.[14] Cicero's moral philosophy, for the present purposes, is relatively simple: it is always prudent to do what is moral. Does one sell a house infested with termites without informing the prospective buyer? Absolutely not. Why not? First, because it is morally wrong, and second, because one's reputation would suffer, resulting in infamy and isolation. By contrast, Machiavelli suggests that prudence should be separated from morality – and, often, preferred to it. Among the most important tasks of a Machiavellian ruler is to set aside moral questions when necessary;[15] getting hung up on morality will only bring certain and rapid demise to one's reign. So Machiavelli counsels deception, violence, and cultivating a generally fearsome reputation among the population to maintain power and order.

This outline of Machiavelli's *Prince*, again, offers little to suggest any reason why Rousseau might have found the work so appealing. Yet Rousseau, indeed, has a very unorthodox reading of the text, outlined briefly in a footnote at *SC*, 3.6.5:

Machiavelli was an honest man and a good citizen: but being attached to the house of the Medici, he was forced during the oppression of his fatherland to disguise his love of freedom. The very choice of his execrable Hero suffices to exhibit his secret intention, and the contradiction between the maxims of his Book on the Prince and those of his discourses on Titus Livy and of his history of Florence proves that this profound politician has so far had only superficial or corrupt Readers.

Rousseau argues that due to a reasonable expectation of persecution for his real republican views, Machiavelli had to conceal these views in favor of an outward show of love of tyranny. In short, Machiavelli's *Prince* is a clever satire[16] about a tyrant ruling not only immorally, but presumably

---

[14] See Skinner [1981] 2000, 46–53.
[15] *Prince*, ch. 8.
[16] Rousseau speaks of Machiavelli as a satirist in his *Political Economy*, 9 [III: 247].

also ephemerally.[17] Any princes actually ruling on the principles expressly avowed in the *Prince* are likely to find themselves quickly unemployed.

The main evidence for Rousseau's interpretation is Machiavelli's *Discourses on Livy,* which Rousseau cites enthusiastically and authoritatively in the *Social Contract.* Unlike the *Prince,* the *Discourses* speak to governing a republic. As such, the *Discourses* outwardly embrace a set of values almost entirely opposed to those found in the *Prince.* Most fundamentally, the *Discourses* make it clear that it is not the interest of an individual ruler that should animate a republic, but rather the general good: "it is not the particular good but the common good that makes cities great."[18] In prioritizing the common good, Machiavelli speaks in language resembling Rousseau's general will, insofar as it also distinguishes a *general* good from a *particular* good. It is this privileging of the common good over the private good of any class of citizens that animates the republican tradition, in which Machiavelli plays a large role.

The ability to place the common good over personal good is also, in fact, the defining feature of individual virtue, as understood by the republican Machiavelli of the *Discourses.* As J. G. A. Pocock has observed, in Machiavelli's republicanism "[t]he republic or polity was … a structure of virtue: it was a structure in which every" citizen would place "the common good before his own."[19] So whereas in the *Prince* he seems to celebrate "heroes" like Cesare Borgia, in the *Discourses,* he chooses to celebrate figures like Cincinnatus, who readily abandoned his private life on a moment's notice to serve his fellow citizens. This relationship of an ethic of the common good to virtue can also be found in Rousseau, who

---

[17] Rousseau's interpretation is largely in accord with Spinoza's approval of Machiavelli's most democratic sentiments in the *Political Treatise*: "But what means a prince, whose sole motive is lust of mastery, should use to establish and maintain his dominion, the most ingenious Machiavelli has set forth at large, but with what design one can hardly be sure. If, however, he had some good design, as one should believe of a learned man, it seems to have been to show, with how little foresight many attempt to remove a tyrant, though thereby the causes that make the prince a tyrant can in no wise be removed, but, on the contrary, are so much the more established, as the prince is given more cause to fear, which happens when the multitude has made an example of its prince, and glories in the parricide as in a thing well done. Moreover, he perhaps wished to show how cautious a free multitude should be of entrusting its welfare absolutely to one man, who, unless in his vanity he thinks he can please everybody, must be in daily fear of plots, and so is forced to look chiefly after his own interest, and, as for the multitude, rather to plot against it than consult its good. And I am the more led to this opinion concerning that most far-seeing man, because it is known that he was favorable to liberty, for the maintenance of which he has besides given the most wholesome advice" (*Political Treatise,* [5.7]). A more recent endorsement of this reading can be found in Benner 2009.

[18] Machiavelli, *Discourses,* 130 [2.2]; see also 179 [2.22], 267 [3.22].

[19] Pocock 1975, 184.

expressly defines "virtue" in his *Political Economy* as "nothing but this conformity of the particular will to the general will."[20]

Further, the *Discourses* offer a conception of liberty that would certainly appeal to Rousseau. As Quentin Skinner has outlined, "republican liberty" is distinct from "modern liberty" insofar as where the latter seeks merely to remove impediments to action, the former strives to be free from the arbitrary will of others.[21] This suggests that republican liberty can only be broadly satisfied in the context of self-rule – where the subjects are in some meaningful sense their own masters. And in this respect, the *Discourses* reveal Machiavelli to be a great advocate for republican liberty. Early in Book 1, he insists that "every city ought to have its modes with which the people can vent its ambitions…. The desires of free peoples are rarely pernicious to freedom because they arise either from being oppressed or from suspicion that they may be oppressed." He continues in Book 2 to observe that a love of liberty was in fact the greatest guardian against invasion and collapse. The love Rome's neighbors had for their civic liberty was the greatest obstacle to Roman expansion. Machiavelli notes, however, that whereas this love of liberty was widespread in ancient times, it is almost completely absent in his own.[22] This conception of liberty informs Rousseau's conception of democratic liberty that places a central importance in the citizens acting as their own legislative body. By virtue of self-rule, they almost necessarily free themselves from external and internal modes of tyrannical power, "since no will can consent to anything contrary to the good of the being that wills" (*SC*, 2.1.3, 57 [III: 368]).

Given these elements of Machiavelli's *Discourses*, it is no wonder that Rousseau was drawn to his peculiar reading of the *Prince* as satire. By approaching Machiavelli in this fashion, he is able quickly to dismiss the most disturbing elements of the *Prince* and to keep all that he admires in the *Discourses*. As such, in all the above respects, Rousseau is extending the republican tradition as found in Machiavelli. But he departs in significant respects – both in more ancient and more modern directions.

One important respect in which he deviates from Machiavelli in the ancient direction is in foundational matters. While both Machiavelli and Rousseau profess fealty to the common good, they clearly mean different things by the phrase. When Machiavelli speaks of the common good, this is frequently in the context of a republic's capacity for expansion. He

---

[20] *Political Economy*, 13 [III: 252]; see also 15 [III: 254].
[21] See, for example, Skinner 2008, ix.
[22] *Discourses*, 17 [1.4]; *Discourses*, 129–33 [2.2].

casually cites, for example, the fact that as soon as Rome was freed from the tyranny of King Tarquin and embraced republican liberty, it rapidly expanded in "dominion" and in "riches." Even more explicitly, he later confirms that "Rome had as its end empire and glory."[23]

Rousseau never suggests in the *Social Contract* that a successful republic can be measured either by its wealth or its military successes. As he observes in the *First Discourse*, a virtuous republic will be effective in repelling external threats. But he never confuses an expansionist military policy with the end of republican politics. In fact, he states quite the opposite, noting in his *Judgment of the Plan for Perpetual Peace* that the lamentable fact about European princes is their consuming desire for "extending their domination abroad and rendering it more absolute at home." He continues further to observe that some would cynically present such domination as necessary to, or even constitutive of, the "*public good*," when it is precisely the opposite.[24]

In this respect, Rousseau's affection for justice as the common good distinguishes him from Machiavelli. Justice is desirable for its own sake, not because it fosters an ability to plunder or dominate others. Rousseau wants to anchor the common good in a fixed, eternal idea. This is an artifact of his Platonism, not to be found in Machiavelli's republicanism.

A second element in which Rousseau resists Machiavelli's modernism is in their respective attitudes toward dissension in a republic. Machiavelli expressly observes that there are two possible kinds of republics: those that eschew dissension and those that embrace it. Machiavelli is strikingly comfortable with dissension. Unlike Rousseau, he casually adopts a dismal view of human nature ("it is necessary to whoever disposes a republic and orders laws in it to presuppose that all men are bad"). This nature cannot be changed. It can only be channeled into directions conducive to the common good. As Quentin Skinner summarizes, "the law can be used to coerce and direct us in just such a way that, even if we continue to act solely out of a corrupt desire to further our own individual or factional advantage, our motivations may be capable of being harnessed to serve the common good." Machiavelli's direction is distinctly modern, insofar as he turns these selfish forces against one another to push citizens in the direction of their common interests. Each class of citizens should have its respective governmental presence, resulting in a checking and

---

[23] *Discourses*, 129 [2.2]; *Discourses*, 146 [2.9]. As Cary J. Nederman observes, "conquest and imperial expansion … [are] the ultimate goals of politics" in Machiavelli's writings. Nederman 2009, xi.

[24] *Judgment*, 54 [III: 592].

balancing familiar to most contemporary students of politics. So in the end, a successful large republic, like Rome, will "make a place for tumults and universal dissensions," especially where its ambition is to "arrive at … greatness."[25] Given Machiavelli's inclination toward expansion, the acceptance of disharmony is a necessary component of republican success.

By contrast, Rousseau speaks emphatically and repeatedly against this solution (e.g., *SC*, 2.3.3, 60 [III: 371], 3.18.4, 119 [III: 435]). Of course, in the first instance, he denies Machiavelli's assumption that human beings are naturally wicked. They may well have been corrupted in most instances by society, but there is at bottom a pure, decent core in all people. Encouraging conflict and dissension is only likely to exacerbate the negative effects of *amour propre*.

As such, the general will is importantly different from Machiavelli's common good in another respect. He wants his citizens not to arrive at the common good by accident, happenstance, or even merely by virtue of the institutions of a wise lawgiver. He deeply wants his citizens to *will* the common good. The general will after all is a general *will*. There is an obvious appeal in this approach. If all citizens truly want what is good for everyone, society ceases to be a place where one must constantly be on guard against the machinations of one's selfish neighbors and becomes instead a setting in which one can enjoy a life free from these consuming worries and move forward to enjoy other pleasures. Of course, on the more troublesome side of the equation, it is fair to ask whether or not it is possible for a community to attain a unified will.[26]

This concept of will also employs a modern element absent in Machiavelli. As was the case in the Plato comparison given earlier, Machiavelli lacks a conception of legitimacy crucial for Rousseau. It is not merely enough that there be a ruling conception of the common good. The people must choose it for themselves in order for the state to have its legitimacy. In modernity, this conception of legitimacy is tightly connected with the familiar conception of consent found in Hobbes, Locke, and the American Declaration of Independence. In taking seriously the principle of legitimacy, Rousseau pays tribute to the distinctly modern notion that the individual will matters. It is inadequate to say simply that

---

[25] *Discourses*, 15 [1.3]); Skinner 2002, 177–8; *Discourses*, 22, 23 [1.6].

[26] In these respects, one might argue, as I suggested earlier, that Rousseau has placed certain "back-up" measures in the *Social Contract* to address such failures, including checks and balances and even the possible use of more Machiavellian opposed interests. This can be found, for example, in the earlier treatment of *SC*, 2.3.4. It seems clear enough from Rousseau's arguments, however, that these are generally second-best alternatives.

justice and the common good are in fact good. Individual citizens must in fact give their assent to their goodness and to the institutions and laws that purport to work toward these ends. So at one and the same time, Rousseau is more ancient than Machiavelli in some respects and more modern in others.

5.3 *Hobbes*

Rousseau has a complex relationship with Thomas Hobbes. Most obviously, Rousseau dedicated a substantial portion of his *Second Discourse* to critiquing the Hobbesian assumption that humanity is naturally vainglorious and violent. Throughout the essay, he repeatedly speaks of Hobbes's tendency to read humanity's artificial or social traits as natural. Typical of these attacks, he insists, "let us not conclude with Hobbes that because he has no idea of goodness [natural] man is naturally wicked, that he is vicious because he does not know virtue, that he always refuses to those of his kind services which he does not believe he owes them."[27] Yet Rousseau's critique of Hobbes hardly stops at the front door. It is a thorough critique of nearly the whole structure – from his metaphysics to his politics. For this reason, Rousseau lashes out against Hobbes with more apparent abhorrence than he directs to any other canonical philosopher. He variously identifies Hobbes as a muse of "dangerous reveries," a "sophist," "blasphemer," the author of a "horrible system," and an advocate of "principles ... destructive of every republican Government."[28]

Yet at the same time, many commentators perceive great similarities in the constructive politics of Hobbes and Rousseau. Leo Strauss, for example, holds that Rousseau "agrees with Hobbes in finding the principle of natural law in the right of self-preservation." Roger D. Masters finds that Rousseau is drawn in his first draft of the *Social Contract* to employ the exact same proofs as Hobbes and to embrace "the Hobbesian critique of traditional natural right." Arthur M. Melzer has pushed this relationship perhaps the furthest:

The purpose of the official doctrine Rousseau elaborates in the *Social Contract* is essentially the same [as Hobbes's in the *Leviathan*] ... Hobbes and Rousseau in fact share an identical view of the central political task (albeit with a different understanding of the ultimate goal): both are obsessed with closing off every

---

[27] *Second Discourse*, 153 [III: 153]. See also 132 [III: 132]; 135 [III: 136].
[28] *First Discourse*, 27 [III: 28]; *Emile*, 458 [IV: 836]; "Legal Profession," 379; *State of War*, 163 [III: 610]; *Mountain*, 235 [III: 811].

possible challenge to the law, both seek an airtight state with an "infallible" sovereign.

According to Melzer, Rousseau, with Hobbes, abandons any real thought of establishing a "moral" regime in favor of a Hobbesian sovereign, "who creates the standard he enforces."[29] And, to be sure, there is something in these associations. Rousseau himself acknowledges in his *Second Discourse*, "Hobbes very clearly saw the defect of all modern definitions of Natural right."[30] With regard to civil religion, Rousseau praises "the philosopher Hobbes … [as] the only one who clearly saw the evil and the remedy, who dared to propose reuniting the two heads of the eagle, and to return everything to political unity, without which no State or Government will ever be well constituted" (*SC*, 4.8.15, 146 [III: 464]). And he does not hesitate in his *State of War* to identify Hobbes as "one of the finest geniuses that ever lived."[31] So indeed, Rousseau's relationship with Hobbes is undoubtedly the most complex of his many relationships with the great philosophers.

Hobbes's political philosophy is importantly grounded in his theory of nature. He is a materialist, meaning that everything existing must necessarily be composed of matter. To speak of *immaterial substance*, for example, is for Hobbes nothing short of absurdity. Further, because everything in Hobbes's world is made of matter, this means that everything is likewise necessarily subject to the laws of physics. This is the doctrine of determinism. Most controversially and dramatically, this includes the actions of human beings, whose actions are every bit as determined by these laws as the motions of alligators or stones. So the very notion of *free will* is, like immaterial substance, also an absurdity. A "will," as Hobbes understands it, is nothing more or less than "the last appetite, or aversion, immediately adhering to the action or to the omission thereof." In the broad sense, the last appetite or "will" of all individual is that which promotes what they call "good" or pleasurable, or helps in averting "evil" or the unpleasant. Since the greatest evil in this understanding of the word is the fear of a violent death,[32] this looms large in the will.

Hobbes builds his political philosophy from these simple assumptions in the context of what he calls the state of nature – a theoretical historical condition prior to the existence of government, laws, or organized society

---

[29] Strauss [1953] 1965, 266 – Strauss continues shortly thereafter to speak strongly to this affinity by stressing Rousseau's "loyalty to the spirit of Hobbes" in these matters (Strauss [1953] 1965, 267; Masters 1968, 267; Masters 1968, 351; Melzer 1990, 125; Melzer 1990, 143).

[30] *Second Discourse*, 151 [III: 153].

[31] *State of War*, 164 [III: 611].

[32] Hobbes [1651] 2002, 5.5; 5.5; 6.53; 6.7; 6.11, 13.9.

of any kind. In the absence of any overpowering authoritative constraints, individuals are entirely free to pursue their pleasures as far as they see fit. But since the pleasure of one is often the pain of another (such as in the possession of a tidbit of food or even in the choice of mates), conflict is inevitable – to the point where Hobbes asserts that the state of nature is nothing other than a state of war. Since this state of war is "solitary, poor, nasty, brutish, and short,"[33] individuals soon realize that their survival is best assured by agreeing to a contract with one another to exit the state of nature, abandon their natural rights to harm one another at their pleasure, and rest all authority in a sovereign Hobbes calls a "Leviathan."

Since the Leviathan is not party to the contract, but rather a beneficiary of a contract between everyone else, it is free from the obligations imposed on everyone else: Hobbes's Leviathan possesses absolute authority over all subjects. There is no appeal above the Leviathan, whom Hobbes calls a "mortal god."[34] Nor are there any limits on what it might command.[35] The law is whatever the sovereign commands – regardless of content. This is the doctrine of legal positivism, where there are no moral standards to which the laws must conform in order to be considered "laws." Further, the Leviathan rules by virtue of its capacity to maintain a healthy fear of punishment among subjects – such that the consequences of being anti-social are more fearsome than the perceived benefits of being anti-social. The Leviathan will remain in power so long as its power and force are sufficient to keep the populace in sufficient fear. Finally, while Hobbes is open in theory to different regime types, he is explicitly partial to monarchy, which he thinks most likely to offer the stability necessary for effective rule.[36]

Rousseau shares significant elements of Hobbes's political philosophy. He agrees that political society must come about by consent in order to assure its legitimacy.

But what is the foundation of this obligation? That is what Authors are divided upon. According to some, it is force, according to others, paternal authority; according to others, the will of God. Each establishes his principle and attacks that of the others: I have not done otherwise myself, and following the soundest

---

[33] Hobbes [1651] 2002, 13.8, 13.9.

[34] Hobbes [1651] 2002, 18.4, 20.8; Hobbes [1651] 2002, 17.13.

[35] Though, to be sure, Hobbes thinks it prudent for the Leviathan to conform to the laws of nature, which promise not only to serve the public good, but also to extend the duration of the Leviathan's rule.

[36] Hobbes [1651] 2002, 19.4–9. For an elaboration on Hobbes's arguments for monarchy, see Kapust 2011, esp. 688–9.

portion of those who have discussed these matters, I posited as a foundation of the body politic [in the *Social Contract*] the convention of its members.[37]

This is precisely what Rousseau does in *SC*, 1.2–6, where he attacks all the perceived alternatives to forming a political community, such as those found in Grotius, Filmer, and Aristotle. This sets him apart from both Plato and Machiavelli, where consideration of consent and legitimacy are largely absent.[38] Further, he agrees with Hobbes that this contract should result in a sovereign, who maintains final political authority, although they disagree substantially on where sovereignty should be located. Finally, he agrees with Hobbes that laws will play a crucial role in serving the goals sought in the social contract.

Rousseau's disagreements with Hobbes, however, are deep, and they begin with the metaphysics. Whereas Hobbes presupposes materialism and determinism, Rousseau posits dualism and free will. These doctrines are implicit in the *Social Contract*, but they underlie its most basic principles. He engaged them extensively elsewhere because they informed the intellectual milieu in which he existed. The mid-eighteenth-century Parisian *Philosophes* were dominated by the materialism and determinism of thinkers like Baron d'Holbach and Denis Diderot. Rousseau attacked these doctrines head-on in his *Profession of Faith of the Savoyard Vicar*, which constitutes dozens of pages of his *Emile*. He posits there that human beings are composed of two substances – a material body and an immaterial soul. Each component of humanity has different animating principles: "Conscience is the voice of the soul; the passions are the voice of the body." Insofar as human beings are animated by the passions, their actions are determined, as Hobbes had suggested. But insofar as they are animated by their conscience, which he also calls "an innate principle of justice," they act freely.[39]

Rousseau's commitment to the doctrine of free will underlies his doctrine of the general will. The general will, that is, must be a free will. There is no "general will" where citizens are not genuinely free. This is clear in his *Second Discourse*, where individuals agree to social contract, but only as part of a grander manipulative scheme. And this animates the further operations of the general will legislating in society. The general will is only legitimate insofar as the people arrive at their legislative decisions freely. If

---

[37] *Mountain*, 231 [III: 806].

[38] Cary J. Nederman has, in fact, observed, "Machiavelli's political theory … represents a concerted effort to exclude issues of authority and legitimacy from consideration" (Nederman [2005] 2009).

[39] *Emile*, 283 [IV: 589–90]; *Emile*, 286 [IV: 595]; *Emile*, 289 [IV: 598].

they have been manipulated, coerced, or misled, such that they are not led by their conscience or sense of justice, then there is no general will. This is easily contrasted with Hobbes, who concedes that it does not matter for his purposes whether people are coerced by fear into their consent.[40] A "will" for his purposes is merely the last disposition or appetite in deliberations. But for Rousseau, the will must be free, if the general will can be said to exist at all.

Further, Rousseau's metaphysics also presupposes justice to have the same ontological status as free will – namely, it is immaterial. As such, it is "eternal"[41] and "universal" (*SC*, 2.6.2, 66 [III: 378]). By contrast, for Hobbes, justice is simply the performance of contract. So whereas for Hobbes there is no idea of justice to which the sovereign is accountable, for Rousseau there is always an idea of justice that serves as a higher standard to which laws must conform. This is why Rousseau insists that the social contract contain "nothing contrary to the natural Laws."[42] It is also why he maintains that "Conventions and laws are ... necessary to combine rights with duties and to bring justice back to its object" (*SC*, 2.6.2, 66 [III: 378]).[43] Further, it is why "the first and greatest public interest is always justice."[44] And because there is a standard above the positive laws themselves, this affords Rousseau a definition of "tyranny," largely absent in Hobbes, whose sovereign's commands can be simply arbitrary. For Hobbes, a tyranny is simply a "misliked" monarchy.[45] By contrast, Rousseau permits himself to employ the "vulgar" or common notion of monarchy, whereby a king "governs with violence and without regard for justice and the laws" (*SC*, 3.10.9, 108 [III: 423]). For Hobbes, violence is part of the skill of ruling, and the Leviathan is always above the laws. Rousseau's commitment to an eternal principle of justice is precisely a solution to the arbitrariness of Hobbes's sovereign commands.

Finally, it must also be said that Hobbes and Rousseau presuppose very different psychologies. For Hobbes, fear is the primary motive for civic or legal behavior. Fear is what drives individuals to the social contract, and fear is what keeps them in line thereafter: "Of all passions, that which inclineth men least to break the laws is fear."[46] This is because the punishment

[40] Hobbes [1651] 2002, 14.27.
[41] *Emile*, 259 [IV: 556], 292 [IV: 603], 473 [IV: 857].
[42] *Mountain*, 231 [III: 807].
[43] I elaborate on this point substantially in Appendix A, A.4.1.
[44] *Mountain*, 301 [III: 891].
[45] Hobbes [1651] 2002, 19.3.
[46] Hobbes [1651] 2002, 27.19. It should be mentioned that in one instance Hobbes urges the sovereign to teach subjects the "commandment" of "mutual charity," namely that "*Thou shalt love thy*

will presumably make the prospect of being punished far more unpleasant than the potential rewards of violating the law. Rousseau likewise thinks laws and punishment a necessary component of political society. But the sword is in an important sense less integral to him than it is in Hobbes. This is because of his reliance on fraternal love.

The tradition of fraternal love has a long and important role in the history of political thought. Most immediately for Rousseau, it could be found in the work of François de Fénelon, whom Rousseau singles out as one of the most admirable French writers of his age. Fénelon's *Telemachus* is, in fact, the first book that Rousseau has Emile read when preparing for citizenship as an adult.[47] Understanding the reasons for this choice is fruitful for understanding the comparison here with Hobbes and for gaining a genuine foothold into the moral psychology of the Rousseauean citizen. Fénelon stresses "pure love" of God, which must be expressed in a love of God's law of charity, or love of others. As he writes in his "On Pure Love," "Nothing is so odious as this idea of a heart always occupied with itself: nothing delights us so much as certain generous actions which persuade the world (and us) that we have done good for the love of good, without seeking ourselves therein."[48] This view obviously made a large impression on Rousseau, who remarks in his autobiographical works that Fénelon opened hearts to "genuine charity"[49] and was one of the rare authors who had done "honor to modern times."[50]

This tradition of charity can also be found in Fénelon's contemporary, G. W. Leibniz, who had sparred with Hobbes in insisting that the successful polity requires charity, which he describes as "the habit of rejoicing in the happiness of another.... [Of] converting the happiness of another into one's own," independent of "hope, fear, and ... regard for any question of utility."[51] Both Fénelon and Leibniz are part of an early modern Christian Platonic tradition that fuses Platonic ideas with Christian charity – both of which are absent in Hobbes. Of course, the very notion of fraternal love central to Christian doctrine can be found earlier in Plato, whose

---

neighbor as thy self (Hobbes [1651] 2002, 30.13). This being said, the doctrine of charity is scarcely discussed throughout *Leviathan* as an animating principle of his state.

[47] *Emile*, 467 [IV: 762].

[48] François de Fénelon, "On Pure Love," quoted in Riley 1994, xxi.

[49] *Confessions*, 519 [I: 620].

[50] *Dialogues*, 158 [I: 863]. Fénelon's influence on Rousseau has been traced in Patrick Riley 1994. See also Williams 2007a, 36–40. For a sustained treatment of Fénelon's doctrine of charity, see Hanley 2011.

[51] Leibniz [1693] 1972, 171.

Socrates and Athenian Stranger in the *Republic* and *Laws* labor tirelessly to prevent dissension and to promote filial bonds among citizens.[52]

Rousseau is utterly confident that no society can be held together merely by fear or calculations of pure self-interest. A successful republic must necessarily cultivate the kind of love found in Plato, Leibniz, and Fénelon. He wants to cultivate this love, for example, by the salutary force of living in a small city and also with civic festivals that bring citizens together in joyous moments. But he also wants to promote this love with a love of the community itself, the likes of which are to be found nowhere in Hobbes. This is perhaps most evident in a passage from the *Government of Poland*: "They will obey the laws and not elude them because they will suit them and will have the inward assent of their wills. Loving their fatherland, they will serve it out of zeal and with all their heart."[53] This can easily be contrasted with Hobbes, who suggests that subjects obey the laws because they fear the consequences of disobedience. This also implies that where those consequences are less likely (such as when the attention of the state is turned elsewhere), one is more or less free to act selfishly with impunity. Rousseau wants to eliminate the prospect of such calculi by creating subjects who have no desire to injure their fellows or the republic at large. Rather, insofar as it is possible, he seeks to replace Hobbesian egoism with a fraternal love among citizens. This is the considerable appeal of his approach over Hobbes's.

5.4. *Immanuel Kant*

As many philosophers may have influenced Rousseau's political thinking, there are at least as many he would go on to influence himself. Perhaps the most notable of these was his contemporary, Immanuel Kant. In some autobiographical reflections, Kant confesses Rousseau's influence:

I am by inclination an investigator. I feel a complete thirst for knowledge and an eager unrest to go further in it as well as satisfaction at every acquisition. There was a time when I believed that this alone could constitute the honor of mankind, and I had contempt for the rabble who know nothing. *Rousseau* brought me around. This blinding superiority disappeared, I learned to honor human beings, and I would find myself far more useless than the common laborer if I did not believe that this consideration could impart to all others a value in establishing the rights of humanity.[54]

---

[52] See Seung 1996, 99–106, 253–5.
[53] *Poland*, 184 [IV: 961].
[54] Kant [1764–65] 2005, 7.

This is not mere idle praise. Kant describes a profound and heartfelt reaction to Rousseau that really did amount to a permanent change in his valuation of his fellows. This reaction to Rousseau has fueled numerous legends about Kant, including the well-documented fact that the only object hanging in Kant's home was a portrait of Rousseau, directly above his writing desk,[55] and the possibly apocryphal (but perfectly plausible) tale that Kant only interrupted his ritualistic daily walk on one occasion – to complete reading Rousseau's *Emile*.[56]

The imprints of Rousseau's thought on Kant's practical philosophy can be found throughout his works. Rousseau's conception of virtue as a struggle of the will against inclination, for example, would shape Kant's notion of the "good will" central to his ethics. Yet Rousseau's influence over Kant's political philosophy is equally pervasive, if less well known. Only four years after the publication of the *Social Contract*, Kant began to appropriate the general will in his own, still developing, political theory. In *Dreams of a Spirit-Seer*, he describes a conflict between two forces – self-interest and charity – that correspond well to the private will and general will. In the spirit of Rousseau, Kant interprets self-interest largely as an "alien will," contrary to a more compelling "secret power [that] requires us to adjust our intentions to the welfare of others." As he makes clear, this "secret power" is nothing other than the general will:

Thus we see that, in most secret motives, we are dependent upon *the rule of the General Will* [*des allgemeinen Willens*], and from it springs in the world of all thinking natures a *moral unity* and systematic constitution according to purely spiritual laws. If one wishes to call this compulsion we feel in us to harmonize our will with the General Will "*moral feeling*," then one speaks of it only as an appearance of what actually takes place in us, without considering its cause. Thus *Newton* called the certain law governing the tendencies inherent in all particles of matter to draw closer to each other their *gravitation*.... Should it not be possible to represent the phenomenon of the moral impulses in thinking natures, who are reciprocally related to each other, likewise as the effect of a genuinely active force through which spiritual natures flow into one another such that the moral feeling would be this felt dependency and an effect of the natural and universal reciprocal interaction through which the immaterial world attains its moral unity by forming itself into a system of spiritual perfection in accordance with the laws governing its own cohesion?[57]

---

[55] Kuehn 2001, 272.
[56] Cassirer [1945] 1963, 1.
[57] Kant [1766] 2002, 20; Kant [1766] 2002, 21.

Consistent with the general will tradition developed in Malebranche and secularized by Rousseau, Kant's early formulation of the general will suggests the dangers of partiality and the moral superiority of the general. Furthermore, Kant also follows Rousseau in suggesting (without necessarily demonstrating) that the general will emanates from an innate conscience.

His early thoughts on the general will are inchoate, however, and he does not begin to seriously incorporate it into a political philosophy until the 1790s. In 1793, he explicitly implements the general will at the first stages of his theory by positing that the public law must be derived from "no other will than that of the entire people (since all decide about all, hence each for himself); for it is only to oneself that one can never do wrong." By contrast, "no particular will can be legislative for a commonwealth." So the basic law, he concludes, "can arise only from the general (united) will of the people."[58] At this stage of his argument this "basic law" is synonymous with the "*original contract*." He goes on, however, to incorporate it at most every level of his theory. The general will not only informs the social contract, but also informs the legislative authority, informs the executive authority, and functionally serves as sovereign.[59]

In most all of these respects, Kant's conception of the general will parallels Rousseau's. Furthermore, Kant also follows Rousseau in understanding the general will as related to eternal or transcendent ideas, insofar as it is itself a Platonic idea. He expressly makes this claim in his *Contest of the Faculties*:

All forms of state are based on the idea of a constitution which is compatible with the natural rights of man, so that those who obey the law should also act as a unified body of legislators. And if we accordingly think of the commonwealth in terms of the concepts of pure reason, it may be called a Platonic *ideal (republica noumenon)*, which is not an empty figment of the imagination, but the eternal norm for all civil constitutions whatsoever, and a means of ending all wars.[60]

This was not an isolated statement of his Platonism. Kant had also argued in his *Critique of Pure Reason* that the ideal constitution, which allows "*the greatest possible human freedom* in accordance with laws by which *the freedom of each is made to be consistent with that of all others*," was emphatically a Platonic idea calling for "respect and imitation."[61] As Riley has observed,

[58] Kant [1793] 1996, 295.
[59] Kant, *Metaphysics of Morals*, 457, 470, 479.
[60] Kant [1798] 1991, 187.
[61] Kant [1781/87] 1965, 312–13.

Kant was especially attracted to Plato's insistence that moral and political ideas must be abstracted from empirical forces.[62] In other words, the general will is itself an idea. This makes it even more abstract than Rousseau's account, since for Rousseau the general will must be in fact willed in order to exist. For Kant, the general will itself is an idea, capable of being known "a priori."[63]

In transforming Rousseau's general will from a fusion of ancient idealism and modern voluntarism into a pure idea, Kant has in effect removed the empirical will from the general will. The "will" of Kant's general will is instead an idealized, reasoned will, as he makes clear in *Theory and Practice*: the general will is "*only an idea* of reason, which, however, has its undoubted practical reality, namely to bind every legislator to give his laws in such a way that they *could* have arisen from the general will of a whole people and to regard each subject, insofar as he wants to be a citizen, as if he has joined in voting for such a will.... In other words, if a public law is so constituted that a whole people *could not possibly* give its consent to it ..., it is unjust; but if it is *only possible* that a people could agree to it, it is a duty to consider the law just."[64] So whereas for Rousseau the will must be real, for Kant that will is hypothetical. A whole people would only consent to laws that conform to the general will, so any legislation satisfying this test is just and valid, regardless of the empirical origin of that law.

5.5 HEGEL

Kant might have been the last philosopher to speak of Immanuel Kant with unbridled enthusiasm. But he is obviously not the last to have been substantially shaped by Rousseau's influence. Kant's great successor, G. W. F. Hegel, fits this characterization well. As a student, Hegel followed Kant's model, being easily seduced by the power of Rousseau's ideas and the lure of his prose. He was known as a pupil to neglect his required readings in seminary in order to consume Rousseau's works; and his classmates remembered him writing "*Vive Jean-Jacques*" in their yearbooks.[65] Yet Rousseau does not loom so large as Kant as an explicit interlocutor in Hegel's mature scholarship. And Hegel's mature assessment of Rousseau is more measured than the attitudes expressed in his youth. He is critical of

---

[62] Riley 1993, 14–19.
[63] Kant [1795] 1996, 345.
[64] Kant [1795] 1996, 296–7.
[65] See Pinkard 2001, 27.

Rousseau's formulation of the general will, and works to develop what he considers to be a superior alternative. Nevertheless, Rousseau's footprints can be found in Hegel's most important works.

Hegel embraces Rousseau's ambition that the general will be "the principle of the state." Yet he is troubled by what he takes to be Rousseau's understanding of that principle. Specifically, he is concerned that the "union of individuals [*der Einzelnen*] within the state ... becomes a *contract*, which is accordingly based on their arbitrary will and opinions."[66] In other words, Hegel views Rousseau as a theorist of popular positivist political morality. Or, to put this in Rousseau's own terminology, Rousseau conflates the general will with the will of all (*SC*, 2.3.2, 60 [III: 371]). Whatever the citizens agree to must necessarily be law, on Hegel's reading of Rousseau.[67] This amounts to equating Rousseau with the positivist Hobbes: there are no substantive moral constraints on the sovereign's edicts. To make this point perfectly clear, Hegel attributes the "most terrible and drastic" events of the French Revolution to Rousseau's allegedly arbitrary general will.

At the same time, however, Hegel is persuaded that Rousseau's general will is salvageable. Following Rousseau's themes, if not always his precise vocabulary, Hegel cites the existence of two wills: an objective and a subjective, corresponding roughly to Rousseau's general and particular wills. The objective will for Hegel is the Spirit or *Geist*, which he identifies in the *Introduction to the Philosophy of History* as "general and abstract." Elsewhere, he labels this objective will the "general will" [*allgemeine Wille*], which he characterizes as "the will of all *individuals* as such." He distinguishes this general will, as do his historical predecessors, from particular wills, "factions," or "atomic point[s] of consciousness."[68] Being abstract, however, this general and somewhat remote will fails to inspire individuals to action on its behalf.

Instead, individuals are naturally motivated by the subjective or private will that derives from "human need, drive, inclination, and passion." At a base level, this subjective will is fundamentally selfish or egoistic. It seeks to satisfy its own demands on its own terms. The aim of politics is to harness its energy, since as Hegel observes, "*nothing great* has been

---

[66] *Philosophy of Right*, 277 [§258].

[67] The most detailed accounts and defenses of Hegel's reading of Rousseau can be found in Ripstein 1994 and Nuzzo 2011. A different approach, but again a defense of Hegel as an improvement over Rousseau in important respects, can be found in Church 2010.

[68] E.g., Hegel, *Phenomenology of Spirit*, 357; see also 363. See also Hegel's *On the Scientific Ways of Treating Natural Law*, 132–5.

accomplished in this world *without passion.*" Yet it is virtually impossible to expect these subjective wills of citizens driven by passions and private inclinations of various citizens to coincide: "the particular will *for itself* is *different* from the universal, [and] its attitude and volition are characterized by arbitrariness and contingency." As he notes later, a purely "natural will," unshaped by politics and history, is "*in itself* a force directed against the Idea of freedom," insofar as it is subject to precisely a *natural* force. In this way, the raw particular or subjective will is unfree or determined, since "The uncivilized [*ungebildete*] human being lets everything be dictated to him by brute forces and by natural conditions."[69] To bring subjective and objective wills together requires not natural forces, but cultural and conventional ones.

The goal of the state then is to channel this passion of the subjective will into the cause of the objective or general will. As Hegel writes in the *Introduction*, "a state is well constituted and internally strong if the private interest of the citizens is united with the universal goal of the state, so that each finds its fulfillment and realization in the other." This is why for Hegel "freedom" only exists for those who have merged these two wills. Duties imposed by the general will are the only "*limitation[s]* ... to the drives of the natural will." By contrast, "The individual," for Hegel, "finds his *liberation* in duty."[70] This is very much in the spirit of Rousseau, who insists that in political society, citizens are only free insofar as they conform their behavior to the general will. Insofar as they deviate from the general will, they are subject to forces external to their consciences and wills – such as inclinations, opinion, threats of violence, and the manipulations of enterprising sophists.

Whereas Rousseau brings about the union of individual wills with the general will through fraternity and a shared commitment to the terms of the social contract, Hegel offers a different route. While the goal of bringing about a union of subjective and objective wills is in some sense the goal of all states at all stages of history, *history itself* is the ultimate force pushing these two wills together. This is true even though throughout history its agents are unaware of this incremental merger: "in world history the outcome of human actions is something other than what the agents [motivated by their subjective, private wills] aim at and actually achieve, something other than what they immediately know and will. They fulfill

---

[69] *Introduction to the Philosophy of History*, 25; *Introduction to the Philosophy of History*, 26; *Elements of the Philosophy of Right*, 113 [§81]; *Philosophy of Right*, 120 [§93]; *Philosophy of Right*, 136 [§107] – see also 169 [§139] and *Phenomenology of Spirit*, 370.
[70] *Introduction*, 27; *Philosophy of Right*, 192 [§149].

their own interests, but something further is thereby brought into being."[71]
This "something further" is the general or universal will found at the end
of history, as Hegel conceives it. It is at this stage that their consciousness
takes full shape and they will the general will *as the general will.* Freedom,
for Hegel, is realized by individuals who freely choose to will the general
will. This historically driven merger of the particular with the general will
is thus different in method from Rousseau, who, if anything, views history as pushing these two wills apart (e.g., *SC*, 3.11.1, 109 [III: 424]).

5.6. RAWLS

The nineteenth and twentieth centuries operate in Rousseau's considerable
wake. Yet much of this relatively pessimistic period takes its cue from his
more critical works, rather than his constructive *Social Contract.* While
it embraces the deconstructive lessons of the *Second Discourse*, it has
eschewed the largely constructive ones of the *Social Contract.* This dichot-
omous relationship to Rousseau's critical and constructive philosophy is
well illustrated in Friedrich Engels's *Anti-Dühring*, which condemns the
Social Contract for promoting "nothing more than the idealized kingdom
of the bourgeoisie," yet simultaneously celebrates the *Second Discourse*,
which lays out "not only a sequence of ideas which corresponds exactly
with the sequence developed in Marx's *Capital*," but also "a whole series
of the same dialectical developments as Marx used."[72] Rousseau's influence
over critical political philosophy lingers in this spirit throughout the twentieth century, insofar as he offers an early account of class conflict, ideol-
ogy, and the assorted tools the bourgeois employed to maintain power.

So although Rousseau's critical philosophy continued a vibrant life into
the twentieth century, his constructive political philosophy declined as a
model for political reform. Where the far left, as exemplified previously
by Engels, viewed the *Social Contract* as a means to maintain bourgeois
power, more traditional liberals viewed Rousseau's politics to be a means
by which tyrants might consolidate power under the ruse of a "general
will." As Bertrand Russell mused during World War II, "At the present
time, Hitler is the outcome of Rousseau; Roosevelt and Churchill, of
Locke."[73] Partly on this narrative, Anglo political philosophy superseded
Rousseau's influence in much of the Western world. Some of this was
Locke's doctrine of natural rights, as cited by Russell. Some of it was the

---

[71] Hegel, *Introduction*, 30.
[72] Friedrich Engels [1878] 1939), 24, 153–4.
[73] Russell [1945] 1972, 623.

utilitarian philosophy of Jeremy Bentham and John Stuart Mill, which made the greatest aggregate happiness the aim of politics. There was considerable debate over the meaning of "happiness" among nineteenth- and twentieth-century philosophers, but this debate itself was far more pressing over this period than issues more directly relevant to Rousseau's *Social Contract*.

Much of this changed in 1971 with the publication of John Rawls's *A Theory of Justice*, likely the most influential work of constructive political philosophy in the past century. Rawls takes the shortcomings of utilitarianism as a departure point for his own approach, which he traces back to seventeenth- and eighteenth-century social contract theory, explicitly including Rousseau's *Social Contract*, which he considers "definitive of the contract tradition." Rousseau's appeal to Rawls is also evident in Rawls's lecture notes, where he posits, "Rousseau's ideas are deep and consistent … hang[ing] together in one unified view." More informally and provocatively, a former student reports Rawls once casually remarking that his "two principles of justice could be understood as an effort to spell out the content of [Rousseau's] general will."[74] So it can be argued that as Rawls reinvigorated an interest in constructive non-utilitarian political philosophy, he simultaneously brought more attention to problems central to Rousseau's *Social Contract* and general will.

Rawls's approach to the social contract is in certain obvious ways unique. He presents the social contract as a kind of thought experiment,[75] the "original position," into which anyone can enter at any time in order to generate principles of justice. All one needs to do is abstract from one's present circumstances and consider what set of political rights and institutions might be most desirable. But he adds a crucial constraint in the original position: the "veil of ignorance." The veil of ignorance, among other conditions, demands that no one in the original position "knows his place in society, his class position or social status; nor does he know his fortune in the distribution of natural assets and abilities, his intelligence and strength, and the like."[76] The effect of these constraints in choosing a political community suggests what Rawls might have meant when he claimed that his theory aimed to articulate the general will.

---

[74] Rawls 1971, 11n4; Rawls 2007, 192; Cohen 2010, 2. This echoes what Rawls himself suggests about Rousseau's influence on Kant: "Kant sought to give a philosophical foundation to Rousseau's idea of the general will" (Rawls 1971, 264).

[75] He emphasizes this is a "purely hypothetical situation" (Rawls 1971, 12).

[76] Rawls 1971, 137.

Rousseau's general will similarly asks citizens not to promote their self-interest as particular individuals. By replacing the particular will with the general will, citizens are required to consider the greater good of the entire community. Along these lines, Rawls insists that any principles emanating from the original position under the veil of ignorance "should be general." Without the ability to know anything about oneself, Rawls suggests, generality is the only way to proceed. It is irrational to design a society that would privilege particular interests, even for the most base and selfish individuals, who would not hesitate to sacrifice all of humanity to their own desires, if one has no idea where one ranks on the social hierarchy. So it only makes sense to establish "principles ... universal in application."[77]

Rawls generates two general principles of justice in his original position. The first principle establishes that "Each person is to have an equal right to the most extensive total system of equal basic liberties compatible with a similar system of liberty for all."[78] This includes civil liberties such as the freedom of conscience, freedom of speech, freedom of assembly, freedom of action where that action does not harm others, and freedom of political participation. Although in many respects these liberties are drawn from the Anglo tradition independent of Rousseau, Rousseau similarly makes efforts to protect certain civil and political liberties in the *Social Contract*.[79] Rousseau is perhaps most passionate in defending religious liberty, taking the stance that "one must tolerate all those which tolerate the others insofar as their dogmas contain nothing contrary to the duties of the Citizen" (*SC*, 4.8.35, 151 [II: 469]).[80]

Rawls's second principle of justice requires that "All social primary goods – liberty and opportunity, income and wealth, and the bases of self-respect – are to be distributed equally unless an unequal distribution of any or all of these goods is to the advantage of the least favored."[81] This second principle seeks to promote the kind of economic equality Rawls thinks anyone in the original position would consider fair. Animating this choice is the assumption that most advantages people exploit in the social world

---

[77] Rawls 1971, 131, 132; see also 235–43. For Rousseau's presentation of the same principle, see Appendix A, A.3. For a comparison of Rousseau and Rawls's veil of ignorance see Dagger 1981, 360–61.

[78] Rawls 1971, 250, 302.

[79] See Simpson 2006b, ch. 3.

[80] Rawls offers more precision on the same point: "[J]ust citizens should strive to preserve the constitution with all its equal liberties as long as liberty itself and their own freedom are not in danger. They can properly force the intolerant to respect the liberty of others, since a person can be required to respect the rights established by principles that he would acknowledge in the original position" (Rawls 1971, 219).

[81] Rawls 1971, 303.

are arbitrary from a moral point of view. No one, for example, deserves to be born a billionaire, as some are, simply by virtue of the identity of their parents. Pushing this logic further, neither does anyone deserve to be born with special natural gifts for financial analysis, throwing a ball, or for that matter, dancing. Such wealth and talents are merely the outcome of the social and genetic lotteries. In making this claim, Rawls seems implicitly to be operating with the same concerns that worry Rousseau in the transition from the state of nature to civil society. In the state of nature, there are surely very different natural aptitudes, but they only lead to social inequalities in civil societies where those talents are identified and valued. A fundamental problem with the social contract of the *Second Discourse* is precisely that those orchestrating the agreement know precisely who they are and how they might guarantee their holdings and the privileging of their talents indefinitely. The basic dignity of the individual – that which most inspired Kant about Rousseau – seems almost beside the point. And it seems that this concern underlies Rawls's second principle of justice, which seeks to ameliorate those social inequalities that are arbitrary from a moral point of view.

Since Rawls wants people in the original position to *choose* a society governed by these two principles of justice, this gives his theory of justice the dimension of will that stems from the general will tradition of Rousseau. As he specifies, "a society satisfying the principles of justice as fairness comes as close as a society can to being a voluntary scheme, for it meets the principles which free and equal persons would assent to under circumstances that are fair."[82] In this way, Rawls carries on the general will tradition in the Kantian spirit, where there may be not an actual moment of consent, so much as principles that would meet with consent were the people afforded the opportunity to evaluate those principles.

Much like Rousseau and Kant, then, Rawls with his two principles of justice celebrates and prioritizes the ideas of liberty and equality.[83] As such, his two principles of justice have a kind of status as ideas. Kant had specified that his idea of a constitution was a Platonic idea, eternal and not contingent on agreement for its substantive content. So while human beings can assent to be governed by those principles, they cannot simply make justice whatever they might like it to be – especially where it might favor the interests of some over others. This is largely consistent

---

[82] Rawls 1971, 13.
[83] "If one inquires into precisely what the greatest good of all consists in, which ought to be the end of every system of legislation, one will find that it comes down to these two principle objects, *freedom* and *equality* (*SC*, 2.11.1, 78 [III: 391])."

with Rousseau's notion of justice as universal and eternal. It is precisely on this point that Rawls departs most dramatically from his early modern predecessors. Although there are indications in his early formulations of his theory that he is inclined to draw on metaphysical ideas as a source of his political principles,[84] the general trajectory of his theory pushes him away from such foundations. This is embodied in his maxim that his conception of justice is "political, not metaphysical." As he explains, "Political liberalism … aims for a political conception of justice as a freestanding view. It offers no specific metaphysical or epistemological doctrine beyond what is implied by the political conception itself." Instead of locating his ideas in the murky realm of metaphysics, he instead locates them in his political culture. As such, Rawls finds "a tradition of democratic thought" as his "fund of implicitly shared ideas or principles."[85] The ideas of liberty and equality are desirable and worthy of promoting because they already exist in the relevant political communities. So the community itself is the source of Rawls's political ideas.

Rawls's "political, not metaphysical" approach offers a specific advantage over the tradition found in Rousseau and Kant. Namely, he avoids appeals to metaphysically ambiguous or controversial concepts. Like Habermas, who defines the twentieth century as a "postmetaphysical age," Rawls is keen to avoid relying on ideas that cannot be empirically understood, quantified, and measured. In the eighteenth century, Rousseau and Kant had relied on a kind of intuitionism or "inner sentiment" that in the contemporary age lacks scientific and, in many circles, intellectual legitimacy. By contrast, in appealing to the political culture of a specific community, Rawls has offered a source of ideas that can be empirically grasped and measured. Social scientists can presumably identify and measure the values of that community, such that their content can be easily understood.

At the same time, however, Rawls abandons the intial appeal of those metaphysical conceptions. As suggested earlier (§5.3), one of the driving forces behind Rousseau's turn to an eternal idea of justice was the desire to avoid the arbitrariness of Hobbesian sovereign commands. Like Rawls, Hobbes eschews abstract metaphysics in favor of the tangible and material. In his case, the Leviathan's commands offer a palpable source of norms valid for its political community. Rawls likewise avoids the metaphysical realm. But instead of locating his values in the commands of a particular sovereign, he derives them from political culture. The impetus

---

[84] Seung 1993, 40–5, 63–70.
[85] Rawls, [1985] 1999, 388–414; Rawls [1993] 2005, 10; Rawls [1993] 2005, 14.

to escape metaphysical controversy is similar in Hobbes and Rawls, nevertheless, and the result is potentially the same – namely, arbitrariness. This is because the political culture of any particular community is as theoretically arbitrary as the commands of a Leviathan. To be sure, Rawls very much has in mind the norms of robust democratic cultures. But if the political culture is the ultimate source of values, then a society with objectionable principles, for example, would then presumably validate and even privilege objectionable laws. There is no external standard by which to invalidate or even judge those laws in a meaningful way. Rousseau, in fact, read Montesquieu as doing the same as Rawls, by simply describing a society's values rather than prescribing them where necessary. In his *Emile*, he clarifies the difference between his project and Montesquieu's and expresses his disappointment with this otherwise very impressive thinker: "he was careful not to discuss the principles of political right. He was content to discuss the positive right of established governments, and nothing in the world is more different than these two studies."[86] He continues to emphasize that one must know what *should be* before assessing what *is*. Political philosophy, in other words, must necessarily be a normative project. The great appeal of Rousseau in this regard is the depth of his conviction in the objective value of liberty and equality. As Rousseau argues, the principles of liberty and equality are not merely important for preexisting democratic cultures, but rather "ought to be the end of *every* system of legislation" (*SC*, 2.11.1, 78 [III: 391]; emphasis added). It is this positive, normative vision that fuels his bitter attack against society as described in the first two discourses; and it is the same set of normative values that provides the substantive vision of the *Social Contract*. This unabashed normative vision distinguishes Rousseau from most serious attempts to articulate these values in recent decades[87] – and it is simultaneously a source of concern for some and his appeal to others.

---

[86] *Emile*, 458 [IV: 836].

[87] One noteworthy exception in this regard is Ronald Dworkin, who has expressly committed himself to a transcendent conception of justice. See Dworkin 2011, 7–9; Dworkin 1986, 424–25; and Dworkin 1985, 219.

On the General Will

Among the many potential frustrations confronting readers of the *Social Contract* is the simple fact that Rousseau never commits to spelling out the meaning of his most important concept, the general will, in anything approaching a straightforward or analytic fashion. As Bertrand Russell remarked, regarding the all-important details of the general will, "Rousseau leaves us in the dark." He introduces the general will several pages into the text (*SC*, 1.6.9, 50 [IV: 361]), and does so without so much as a hint of definition. As he progresses, the general will becomes increasingly and obviously central to his program – so much so that Judith Shklar commented, "the general will is Rousseau's most successful metaphor. It conveys everything he most wanted to say."[1] But he never offers the kind of systematic account that such concepts typically demand. It is difficult to say precisely why Rousseau fails to do so. It is presumably *not* because he was averse to straightforward definitions. In his *Second Discourse*, he is remarkably and admirably direct in defining his central terms of equality, *amour propre*, *amour de soi*, and *pitié*. He also offers precise definitions of terms like "citizen," "subject," "state," "republic," "tyranny," and "despotism" throughout the *Social Contract*. One possible reason he never offers a systemic account of the general will is simply that the term was already known to most of the book's target audience of erudite political thinkers.

A.I. A BRIEF HISTORY OF THE GENERAL WILL

As Patrick Riley has outlined with admirable clarity, Rousseau did not invent the general will. He rather developed a concept that had emerged decades earlier in early modern French philosophy of religion. Early modern theologians were deeply concerned with the problem of how to

---

[1] Russell [1945] 1972, 698; Shklar 1969, 184.

reconcile God's will that everyone be saved[2] with the widely held belief that only some would be. Nicolas Malebranche would employ the general will to address questions of both natural science and salvation. With regard to nature, he compares ignorant and enlightened agents as they navigate their ways through the world. A relatively ignorant man "undertakes new plans at every moment," constantly grasping and flailing at every step. By comparison, the enlightened agent "compares and weighs all things," developing plans only on the basis of carefully considered evidence. Rather than grasping and flailing, moving from one plan to another, the enlightened agent devises a single plan taking everything into consideration. Of course, for Malebranche, the wisest of all beings is God, who as an efficient planner necessarily "acts through general wills," hence "establish[ing] a constant and lawful order." He later clarifies the operations of God's general will in natural science with an example: "If … one drops a rock on the head of passers-by, the rock will always fall at an equal speed, without discerning the piety, or the condition, or the good or bad dispositions of those who pass by." This is because God has ordained a general law of gravity that determines the speed and trajectory at which objects fall. God's law, again, is general, not particular.

God likewise legislates the laws of grace. Grace is not decided in a series of idiosyncratic and particular cases. Rather, God ordains "laws which are very simple and very general" – indeed, the most simple, fruitful laws "worthy of his wisdom," such that he can save "as many persons as he can save, acting according to the adorable laws which his wisdom prescribes to him."[3]

While Malebranche is particularly engaged with theological matters, Riley draws attention to his political overtones. He regularly speaks of God "legislating" his laws of nature and grace, of their "wisdom" and "justice," and of their admirable morality. Many of these themes can be found in his treatment of the particular will. Individuals dissatisfied with God's general will, such as when life does not go their way, demand miracles of God. That is to say, they reject generality in favor of particularity – they want God to disrupt his legislation so that he might perform special favors on their behalf. Malebranche scarcely masks his contempt for such requests, which would put particular individuals at the center of the moral universe. This desire "flatters the self-love [*amour propre*] which relates everything to itself."[4] It also betrays an ignorance that fails to comprehend that the general laws are in fact the best.

---

[2] 1 Timothy 2: 4.
[3] Malebranche [1680] 1992, 126–7, 137, 130–1; See also Nadler 2010, 118–24.
[4] Riley 1986, 30–1; Malebranche [1680] 1992, 137.

One other important element of Malebranche's theory of the general will is his thoroughgoing Platonism. God's laws are not valid simply because they come from God. In contemporary political theory terms, he rejects a kind of divine command theory of legal positivism, where God's laws' contents are perfectly arbitrary, subject to divine whim. Such in Malebranche's view is the "bizarre" theory of Thomas Hobbes, which, he charges, posits precisely this kind of particularity and arbitrariness. A sovereign unconstrained by fixed standards is capable of anything – even the most bizarre and morally offensive. By contrast, for Malebranche, God chooses his laws because he is "wise, just and good … such that his wills are not at all purely arbitrary – that is to say that they are not wise and just simply because he is all-powerful … but because they are regulated by the eternal law … a law which can consist only in the necessary immutable relations which are among the attributes and perfections which God encloses in his essence."[5] For Malebranche, there is an eternal and explicitly Platonic conception of justice and order to which even God himself must conform.

Metaphysical issues aside, however, the theological matter of how to reconcile God's will that everyone be saved with the belief that only some are was deeply vexing for early modern Christians. Malebranche's appeal to God's general will offers a kind of ingenious solution. He argues, in effect, that if we do not appeal to God's general will, we say that God wills damnation upon particular individuals. To be sure, such a theology is available. But it was distinctly unpleasant and unappealing for those who wanted to emphasize God's straightforward goodness. Malebranche's solution salvages God's wisdom, goodness, and justice.

On Malebranche's model, the responsibility for anyone being damned does not fall on God. It falls on individual free will or liberty. When individuals use their wills to follow their God-implanted inclinations to be good and follow God's laws, salvation follows. When they employ their wills for their own particular pleasures, contrary to God's laws, each of these wills is "unjust, it is ungrateful, it is blind."[6] Put simply, following God's general will results in salvation while following one's own particular will results in damnation. Malebranche goes so far as to suggest that God has in fact implanted a knowledge of his general will in each individual, just as Rousseau refers to "the sentiment of the just and the unjust innate in the heart of man."[7] It is not difficult to see in Malebranche's theological

---

[5] Quoted in Riley 1986, 56.
[6] Malebranche [1680] 1992, 171.
[7] *Emile*, 66 [IV: 286]; see Malebranche [1680] 1992, 172.

formulation a foundation for Rousseau's secularized discourse, with the question of salvation replaced by the common good.

A.2. THE *WILL* OF THE GENERAL WILL

On the preceding narrative, it was largely left to Rousseau to secularize and politicize the general will. For Riley, the theological tradition of the general will was more or less "ready-made for his purposes" insofar as both terms – will and generality – figure centrally in his political theory.[8] But it is in the articulation of this secularized general will that Rousseau is notoriously sketchy. In the account that follows, I spell out the various elements of the general will as clearly as possible. Along the way, I make some interpretive choices about how best to make sense of various ambiguities in Rousseau's texts, acknowledging here that strong cases are available for alternative readings. Readers are encouraged to examine Rousseau's words carefully for themselves to judge the merits and demerits of my and other available interpretations of the general will.

Rousseau stresses the importance of the will repeatedly throughout his works, including the *Social Contract*. To be sure, the will for him is expressly a *free will*.[9] He identifies it early in his *Second Discourse* as one of the defining features of humanity. Whereas an animal is "nothing but an ingenious machine ... man contributes to his operations in his capacity as a free agent."[10] It is for Rousseau this unique ability to shun inclination and impulses that separates him from all other species. Furthermore, it is this freedom of the will that imparts to humanity its distinctly moral nature, since virtue itself requires "not only ... being just, but ... being so by triumphing over one's passions."[11]

This freedom takes center stage early in his *Social Contract*. In Book I he emphasizes that the "transition from the state of nature to the civil state produces a most remarkable change in man by substituting justice for instinct in his conduct, and endowing his actions with the morality they previously lacked." By bringing about laws and a general sense of order, human beings are afforded the ability to cultivate their freedom and

---

[8] Riley 1986, 181–2.

[9] To be sure, there are some who have disputed the role of free will in Rousseau's political philosophy, including Masters 1968 (69–71), Melzer 1990 (30), and Strauss [1953] 1965 (271n).

[10] *Second Discourse*, 140 [III: 141]; see also *Emile*, 359 [IV: 695].

[11] "Letter to Franquières," 281 [IV: 1143]. In his *Reveries*, he similarly observes, there is no virtue "in following our inclinations and in giving ourselves the pleasure of doing good when they lead us to do so.... [but only] in overcoming them when duty commands in order to do what duty prescribes" (*Reveries*, 77 [I: 1052–3]).

act as moral beings. They are finally *free from* "physical impulsion" and "inclinations" and are now *free to* act in accordance with their duties. As such, Rousseau writes of the citizen, "his ideas are enlarged, his sentiments ennobled, [and] his soul is elevated" (*SC*, 1.8.1, 53 [III: 364]).

The institution of free wills among citizens, however, is not merely an end in itself, as important as that is. A free will is also necessary for Rousseau in order to maintain and implement legislation, which must itself conform to the general will. People lacking free will are incapable of performing their central task as citizens. This is why he so vigilantly works to protect their freedom. The painful absence of free will is perfectly evident in Part II of the *Second Discourse*, where individuals hoping that they might be "securing their freedom" in fact secure only despotism. Rousseau makes it perfectly clear that they lack free will under this regime: "there would … no longer be any question of morals and virtue."[12] They have surrendered the freedom necessary to exercise their moral capacities. This is one reason why there is no mention of the general will in the *Second Discourse* – its fundamental prerequisite is entirely absent.

While Rousseau's conception of the free will is crucial, it is also very fragile. Myriad obstacles threaten it from all imaginable angles. Many originate in *amour propre*, which prompts individuals to seek external approval. In the *First Discourse*, he describes how the arts prompt citizens to seek public applause rather than attend to their civic duties. They are thus no longer their own masters, lacking freedom insofar as the whims of the audience's taste guide their every move. In the *Second Discourse*, he describes how *amour propre* compels a kind of endless quest for power, where even the most powerful become "slaves" as they "come to hold Domination dearer than independence." And even though such despots may appear free to the casual observer, they are not. They are entirely beholden to those who would tremble below them. They must constantly be responsive to the whims of the people in order to maintain their positions of power. In the *Political Economy*, he warns against the corrupting forces of money, where the quest for wealth finds citizens selling their freedom and virtue for cash.[13] He sums up many of these concerns when expressing his ambitions for Emile:

Nurtured in the most absolute liberty, he conceives of no ill greater than servitude. He pities these miserable Kings, slaves of all that obey them. He pities these false wise men, chained to their vain reputations. He pities these rich fools,

---

[12] *Second Discourse*, 173 [III: 178]; *Second Discourse*, 185 [III: 191].
[13] *Second Discourse*, 183 [III: 188]; *Political Economy*, 19 [III: 258–59].

martyrs to their display. He pities these conspicuous voluptuaries, who devote their entire lives to boredom in order to appear to have pleasure. He would pity even the enemy who would do him harm, for he would see his misery in his wickedness. He would say to himself, "In giving himself the need to hurt me, this man has made his fate dependent on mine."[14]

In conspiring to undermine the free will, all of these factors also threaten to undermine the general will central to the *Social Contract*. Rousseau expressly warns against the temptations of power (*SC*, 3.6), the corrupting effects of money (*SC*, 1.9.8n, 2.11.2n), and excess sophistication (*SC*, 4.1). The capacity of these menaces to rob citizens of the free exercise of their own will represents a constant threat hovering over Rousseau's republic and the governance of the general will. So the general will rests on the existence and careful maintenance of the will itself.

A.3. FORMAL ELEMENTS OF THE GENERAL WILL

A general will must not merely issue from a free will – it must also be general. As Patrick Riley has observed, "Even if 'will' is a central moral, political, and theological notion in Rousseau, this does not mean that he was willing to settle for just any will."[15] Virtually all Rousseau scholars agree on this much. But debate begins precisely on the dimensions and nature of that will. Specifically, there is considerable debate on whether or not the general will is largely a formal or procedural concept on the one hand, or a substantive one on the other. These two terms deserve careful definitions. Substantive political ideas promote specific political principles. They are not value-neutral. They have content and can be inherently controversial because in choosing to privilege some ideas, other ideas are rejected or at least accorded lower priority.

To avoid these problems associated with substantive political ideas, some philosophers appeal to formal or procedural norms. To call something "formal" or "procedural" is to say that its content is determined by a procedure. The laws of a democracy, for example, are often determined by the formal procedure of majority vote. In the philosophical realm, the procedure of subjecting a maxim to Kant's test of the categorical imperative or R. M. Hare's prescriptivism generates the content of permissible moral actions. The great appeal of formal or procedural accounts in moral and political theory is their apparent impartiality. In the abstract, at least,

---

[14] *Emile*, 244 [III: 536].
[15] Riley 1986, 243.

procedures take no sides. The drawback of employing strictly formal procedures is their lack of content.

Rousseau scholars disagree on whether his constructive political theory is fundamentally formal or substantive. Some are persuaded that his political philosophy consists largely in procedures that generate outcomes but have no content before those procedures are implemented in any given circumstance. Roger D. Masters, for example, argues that "[a]lthough the just and legitimate end of civil society is defined in terms of the general will, the general will itself is not that just end properly speaking; rather it is a formal requirement which must be fulfilled by the laws which constitute any legitimate regime." John T. Scott is persuaded that "Rousseau abandons all *substantive* standards of justice and law, whether they be from God or nature. He does speak of all justice coming from God, but he means this first in a purely *formal* sense pertaining to order and generality, and, second, he reverses the priority of justice and law." Steven Smith describes Leo Strauss's Rousseau as employing a "purely formal mechanism of 'generalization,'" where substance is so absent that even "cannibalism is as just as its opposite."[16] Perhaps the most elaborate reading of Rousseau as a strict formalist comes from Gopal Sreenivasan, who argues that the general will results whenever four conditions have been met in deliberation:

(1) the subject matter of the deliberation is perfectly general, and
(2) the conclusions of the deliberation apply equally to all the members of the community, and
(3) all the members of the community participate in the deliberation, and
(4) all parties to the deliberation think for themselves.[17]

All of these formalist readings capture an element of truth in the general will. Rousseau was clear that the formation of a general will must satisfy formal criteria. Most notable among these are two distinct formal dimensions of generality, corresponding with Sreenivasan's conditions (1) and (2): *generality in derivation* and *generality in application*. A general will must "issue from all in order to apply to all" (*SC*, 2.4.5, 62 [III: 373]). Of the former, Rousseau is quite explicit: "For a will to be general, it is not always necessary that it be unanimous, but it is necessary that all votes be counted; any formal exclusion destroys generality" (*SC*, 2.2.3n, 58n [III: 370n]). This is one of the most democratic elements in Rousseau's political

---

[16] Masters 1968, 327–8; Scott 1994, 490–1; Smith 2011.
[17] Sreenivasan 2000, 574. See also Bertram 2012, 405.

philosophy. This general derivation is necessary in two respects. First, it is a bedrock principle of his republicanism that all citizens possess a dignity and a kind of right to participate in the politics that regulate their own affairs. Second, deriving the general will from all those affected by it makes that will more likely to reflect the substantive values Rousseau associates with the general will. As Charles Hendel observed, "the general will is more likely to emerge if there is the broadest possible basis of suffrage and an absolutely free exercise of their own personal judgment by every individual in the State."[18] The need for a general derivation of the general will becomes apparent in considering its opposite: factious particular wills. It is the nature of a faction that it is *not* derived from the whole of the people. It almost necessarily, then, aims not to serve the whole people, but rather merely a subset thereof. The insistence on the general derivation of the general will is, therefore, a crucially democratic element of Rousseau's politics – so crucial, as he says, that any formal exclusion of participation in the derivation of the general will "destroys [its] generality" and hence its sovereignty.

The general will must also be general in its application. It cannot apply merely to a segment of the citizens. It must apply to all. To legislate such that laws only apply to some segment of the population and not others amounts to placing some above the laws. In the most obvious respect, those passing and enforcing the laws cannot set themselves above the law. This is the rule of law.[19] In this spirit, Rousseau in his *Second Discourse* approvingly cites an Edict from Louis XIV:

Let it … not be said that the Sovereign is not subject to the Laws of his State, since the contrary proposition is a truth of the Right of Nations, which flattery has sometimes challenged, but which good Princes have always defended as a tutelary divinity of their States. How much more legitimate it is to say with the Wise Plato that the perfect felicity of a Kingdom is that a Prince be obeyed by his Subjects, that the Prince obey the Law, and that the Law be right and always directed at the public good.[20]

What Rousseau admires in Louis XIV's words is his complete submission to the rule of law. His reference to Plato certainly resonated with Rousseau, who knew Plato's dialogues intimately. Plato had insisted in his *Laws* that rulers must be "servants" to the law.[21] Elsewhere in the *Second*

---

[18] Hendel 1934, II: 192. See also Neuhouser 1993, 390.

[19] For a discussion of the rule of law in Rousseau's conception of democracy, see Cohen 2010, 135–6. See also Miller 1984, 35–6 and Mason 1995, 121–38.

[20] Louis XIV, quoted in the *Second Discourse*, 178 [III: 183]; italics in original.

[21] "I have now applied the term 'servants of the laws' to the men usually said to be rulers, not for the sake of an innovation in names but because I hold that it is this above all that determines whether

Discourse, Rousseau elaborates that if he had the opportunity to choose the place of his birth, he would have chosen the one in which "no one inside the State could have declared himself to be above the law.... For, regardless of how a government is constituted, if there is a single person in it who is not subject to the law, all the others are necessarily at his discretion."[22] Rousseau continues in his *Social Contract* to describe those who would place themselves above the laws as the very definition of despots (*SC*, 3.10.10, 108 [III: 423]).[23] One of the central goals of any serious political proposal, then, is to "*find a form of Government that might place the law above man*."[24] To establish the rule of law in this fashion is necessarily to establish the generality of application.

There is another related formal dimension of the generality of application: all laws must be directed to the *common good*. While "good" itself is a substantive term, "common" in this context is a formal one. In the opening sentence of Book II, he insists: "The first and the most important consequence of the principles established thus far is that the general will alone can direct the forces of the State according to the end of its institution, which is the common good" (*SC*, 2.1.1, 57 [III: 368]).[25] It is in this context that he introduces an essential distinction between particular and general wills. A particular will aims only at the good of some subset of the population. A general will serves the good of the entire community. In a transparent example, a corporation might lobby for relaxing environmental standards so that it can freely pollute a river in order to augment its profits. Yet the citizens rely on that very river for fresh drinking water. This would clearly violate the spirit of the common good Rousseau has in mind. At the very least, even to see such a policy entertained in a legitimate political process, the corporation would have to argue that the jobs and wealth generated for the community represent a greater contribution

the city survives or undergoes the opposite. Where the law is itself ruled over and lacks sovereign authority, I see destruction at hand for such a place. But where it is despot over the rulers and the rulers are slaves of the law, there I foresee safety and all good things which the gods have given to cities" (*Laws*, 715d). Plato re-states this principle many pages later: "it's necessary for human beings to establish laws for themselves and live according to laws, or they differ in no way from the beasts that are the most savage in every way" (*Laws*, 874e–75a). Rousseau's interest in Plato's *Laws* is well-documented in Silverthorne 1973. Silverthorne examines Rousseau's personal copy of Plato's *Laws*, which includes many suggestive marks and comments. He notes that just as Plato had called magistrates "servants of the laws," Rousseau likewise calls them "minstres des lois" (Silverthorne 1973, 245; Plato's *Laws*, 715d; *Political Economy*, 10 [III: 249]).

[22] *Second Discourse*, 115 [III: 112].

[23] See also *SC*, 4.6.5n, 139n [III: 456n]; *SC*, 2.6.7, 67 [III: 379]. See also *Mountain*, 230 [III: 805]; 237 [III: 814]; 261 [III: 842]; 269 [III: 852]. See also "Letter to d'Alembert," 115 [V: 105].

[24] "Letter to Mirabeau," 270.

[25] Or as he posits in the *Political Economy*, "the general will is always for the common good" (8 [III: 246]). See also *Geneva Manuscript*, 1.5 [III: 305].

to the common good than does clean drinking water. To ask for such specific favors in policy is very much akin to Malebranche's example of the individual asking God for a personal miracle. It is born of a selfish inclination where individual factions value themselves above the community at large. Such inclinations ultimately violate the general will as Rousseau understands it. As he clarifies in his *Letters Written from the Mountain*, a Law "is a public and solemn declaration of the general will, on an object of common interest. I say, on an object of common interest; because the Law would lose its force and would cease to be legitimate if the object did not matter to all. By its nature Law cannot have a particular and individual object."[26] So any attempt to pass off individual interests as the general will is, in Rousseau's words, illegitimate.

A.4. SUBSTANTIVE ELEMENTS OF THE GENERAL WILL

While the formal criteria of the general will are necessary conditions for generating a general will, Rousseau also associates that will with specific substantive ideas. As Frederick Neuhouser has insisted in his influential reading, "the general will ... is more than a set of purely formal criteria for the legitimacy of legislation; the general will, as Rousseau conceives it, also has a content." Along these lines, Joshua Cohen has recently called the procedural or formal reading of the general will "perverse." Cohen argues that the procedural reading demands that each vote under the formal constraints constitutes a "prediction about what the result of the collective vote will be" – an absurdity as voting is not a prediction but an attempt to promote the common good.[27]

But perhaps the most obvious shortcoming of the formal or procedural reading of the general will is that it neglects to ask why Rousseau chooses the particular formal constraints he does. Namely, why does he insist that laws must be derived from everyone, must apply to everyone, and serve objects of common interest? There is no satisfactory way to answer these questions by appealing to more formal procedures. Gopal Sreenivasan, for example, never suggests *why* Rousseau chooses his set of formal constraints as opposed to another. Why not choose another set of procedures? Why not choose simple majoritarianism, for example? Or why not choose only to consider the interests of those in the top 10 percent of income? Or, conversely, why not choose only to consider the interests of those at

---

[26] *Mountain*, 232 [III: 807–8].
[27] Neuhouser 1993, 388; Cohen 2010, 77–8.

the bottom 10 percent of income? This is the spirit of Hegel's critique of Kant's formal test of the categorical imperative. A formal procedure or test "does not get very far.... [O]ne content is just as acceptable to it as its opposite."[28] The most logical reason anyone chooses to implement a set of formal rules is because those rules tend to promote certain substantive values. Requiring unanimity by juries represents a procedural rule. But that rule is chosen because of the underlying substantive value it means to promote – arriving at true verdicts. Factual truth, in this instance, is the desired substantive outcome (not that it is the inevitable outcome). The formal rule in baseball that a ball hit over the fence in fair territory constitutes a home run (rather than a foul or an out) is meant to promote that substantive value that a well-struck ball should be rewarded. Rousseau likewise has substantive values in mind in choosing his formal constraints for legislative deliberation. Specifically, I argue, he identifies three tightly related values: justice, goodness, and equality. And in doing so, I respond to some of the arguments by those who read Rousseau as more strictly formal than substantive.

A.4.1. *Justice*

There is little disputing Rousseau's love of justice. In his *Letters Written from the Mountain*, he declares that "justice and the public good" are the first rules of governance. In his "Letter to d'Alembert," he identifies "Justice and truth" as "man's first duties." In his *Reveries*, he declares, "My moral being would have to be annihilated for justice to become unimportant to me."[29] The question for some scholars is whether or not this love of justice has anything to do with the general will. Roger D. Masters, for example, never denies Rousseau's love of justice, but suggests that it is separate from his political theory. Arthur M. Melzer is even more direct: "If Rousseau favors the general will, then, it is most certainly *not* as the *embodiment* of justice but rather as a hardhearted and practical *replacement* for it." And most recently, Jonathan Israel has posited that Rousseau's general will does not "need to conform to justice."[30]

---

[28] *Phenomenology*, 257.
[29] *Mountain*, 249 [III: 828]; "Letter to d'Alembert," 3 [V: 3]; *Reveries*, 81 [I: 1057].
[30] See Masters 1968, 323–34 and 73–89; Melzer 1990, 157; Israel 2011, 640. See also Melzer 1990, 135; Simpson 2006b, 29, 42; and Scott 1994, esp. 490–2. Melzer's case is fully developed in chapters 8 and 9 of his *Natural Goodness of Man*. I address Melzer's argument in more detail in Williams 2007a, 108–14.

In arguing that the general will is independent from justice, Melzer, Matthew Simpson, John T. Scott, and others, cite text from the *Geneva Manuscript* in which Rousseau claims that "law precedes justice, not justice the law."[31] They draw on this passage to claim that the general will (the source of law in Rousseau) is entirely distinct from justice. Yet this is somewhat misleading in two respects. First, in one sense Rousseau is speaking not of metaphysical principles, but of psychology. Prior to the social contract being agreed, the idea of justice exists, but it does not animate individuals, who are instead guided by pity, *amour propre*, and *amour de soi-même*.[32] They are insufficiently socialized to have developed the faculty of reason necessary for understanding justice rationally. They only develop this faculty after the introduction of the laws (*SC*, 1.8.1, 53 [III: 364]). Second, although the *idea* of justice is itself "eternal," its *application* is conditional. It only applies when everyone agrees to be governed by it. So in this way, the law must be instituted first for justice to be realized. As John B. Noone, Jr. observes, "There is a natural law [in Rousseau], but in order for it to be operative certain conditions must be fulfilled; in the absence of these conditions it is not obligatory." He continues, "Thus, the real thrust of Rousseau's argument ... is not to deny that there is an objective standard of justice but to question whether or not the state of nature embodied conditions under which there would be an interest in being just."[33]

Despite the claims of the formalist readers, there are firm textual bases for believing precisely what they would deny – that an objective or even transcendent conception of justice is part of the core meaning of the general will. In his *Political Economy*, Rousseau writes, "the most general will is also the most just." He later adds in the same essay, "one need only be just in order to be sure of following the general will."[34] In the *Social Contract*, he concedes that although accessing the eternal idea of justice can be difficult, it is the very task of conventions and laws "to bring justice back to its object" (*SC*, 2.6.1, 66 [III: 378]). Elsewhere, Rousseau associates justice and the general will in such a way as to suggest that they depend on or

---

[31] *Geneva Manuscript*, 2.4, 160 [III: 328]; Melzer 1990, 135; Scott 1994, 490; see also Simpson 2006b, 29, 42.

[32] See, for example, *Second Discourse*, 154 [III: 157].

[33] Noone 1972, esp. 30, 32. See also Grimsley 1972, 68–9.

[34] *Political Economy*, 8 [III: 246]; *Political Economy*, 12 [III: 251]. Rousseau around the same time also employs the terms "justice" and the "general will" synonymously in his *Geneva Manuscript*, 157 [III: 286]. As Charles W. Hendel later summarizes, Citizens "are to have recourse to the general will or the spirit of the law, or what is declared to be the very same thing, 'the idea of justice'" (Hendel 1934, I: 118).

explain each other. For example, he frequently cites the general will as the guiding force of the law,[35] and at the same time, he insists that the laws of the state must also be just. He expressly declares in his *Letters Written from the Mountain*, "The first and greatest public interest [and hence the object of law and the general will] is always justice."[36]

Justice in Rousseau can be understood in its metaphysical, epistemic, and substantive attributes. Metaphysically, he describes justice as "universal" (*SC*, 2.6.2, 66 [III: 378]) and "eternal."[37] To claim that justice is universal is to posit that it is the same everywhere. He makes this clear in the words of *Emile*'s Savoyard Vicar: "Cast your eyes on all the nations of the world, go through all the histories. Among so many inhuman and bizarre cults, among this prodigious diversity of morals and character, you will find everywhere the same ideas of justice and decency, everywhere the same notions of good and bad." Scratching beneath the surface of various cultural differences, according to Rousseau, one quickly discovers that moral principles, including justice, are the same. In responding to his early modern predecessors, such as Locke and Montaigne, who would claim the opposite, Rousseau asks "whether there is a country on earth where it is a crime to keep one's faith, to be clement, beneficent, and generous, where the good man is contemptible and the perfidious one honored?"[38]

The likely reason why justice is universal for Rousseau is because it is eternal. For a value to be eternal means it never changes. It always has been and always will be the same. It is neither created nor destroyed; it is a fixed condition of the universe. And of great significance to Rousseau, human beings cannot define eternal ideas any way they wish. As he posits in the *Social Contract*, "What is good and comfortable to order is so by the nature of things and independently of human conventions" (*SC*, 2.6.2, 66 [III: 378]). The existence and substantive content of justice transcends anything that might happen in this world. Whether or not it applies to human circumstances, however, depends on the willingness of communities to adopt it as their legal foundation and enforce it. While the idea of justice is eternal, it is unreasonable to expect everyone to obey it when there are no sanctions attached to its violation. This is why he insists that

---

[35] E.g., *SC*, 2.1.1, 57 [III: 368], 2.6.7, 67 [III: 379], 3.15.8, 115 [III: 430]; *Political Economy*, 9 [III: 247]; *Mountain*, 232 [III: 808].

[36] *Mountain*, 301 [III: 891]; see also 231 [III: 807], 249 [III: 828].

[37] See also "Letter to d'Alembert," 66 [V: 61]; *Emile*, 259 [IV: 556], 292 [IV: 603], 473 [IV: 857]. Rousseau cites this passage concerning "eternal justice" in his *Letter to Beaumont*, 39 [IV: 950]; see also *Julie*, 69 [II: 84]; "Letter to M. l'Abbé de Carondelet," 273.

[38] *Emile*, 288 [IV: 597–98]; *Emile*, 289 [IV: 599].

"Conventions and laws are therefore necessary to combine rights with duties and to bring justice back to its object" (*SC*, 2.6.2, 66 [III: 378]).[39]

Epistemically, this idea of justice is generally accessible to humankind via the conscience, which his Savoyard Vicar defines as an "innate principle of justice."[40] The conscience lurks throughout his political works. In his *First Discourse*, he concludes his screed against the arts and sciences by pleading for humanity to appeal to its conscience: "Are not your principles engraved in all hearts, and is it not enough in order to learn your Laws to return into yourself and to listen to the voice of one's conscience in the silence of the passions?" In his "Last Reply," he counsels, "the best guides which honest men can have are reason and conscience." In his *Second Discourse*, he similarly implores his readers "to return to the depths of your Heart and consult the secret voice of your conscience."[41]

He develops his most extensive thoughts on the conscience in the *Emile*, where he suggests that one of the central aims of education is to foster and protect the conscience against all forces that threaten to obscure it. The foundations of the conscience are "innate" and "graven in our hearts by the Author of all justice." As he writes in Book IV of the same treatise, "The true principles of the just … are imprinted on his [Emile's] understanding." Yet this sentiment for children is indeterminate and undeveloped. Through the careful and incremental introduction of reason, a child can eventually develop this innate sense (such as the sense of injustice experienced in being the victim of theft) to be the "infallible judge of good and bad which makes man like unto God." Ultimately, for Rousseau, "[t]he more one generalizes this interest, the more it becomes equitable, and the love of mankind is nothing other than the love of justice." Rousseau stresses that this is all possible despite the fact that Emile possesses a modest or "ordinary" intellect.[42] Distinguishing himself from Plato's theory of philosopher-rulers in the *Republic*, he holds that it takes

---

[39] Christopher Bertram explores Rousseau's eternal or transcendent conception of the general will and its relationship to its democratic dimensions (Bertram 2012).

[40] *Emile*, 289 [IV: 598]. Earlier in his own voice, he writes that "the sentiment of the just and the unjust [are] innate in the heart of man" (*Emile*, 66 [IV: 286]). See also his *Moral Letters*, 195 [IV: 1108]).

[41] *First Discourse*, 28 [III: 30]; "Last Reply," 82 [III: 93]; *Second Discourse*, 119 [III: 116]. Rousseau also offers an extended example of a juror guilty of the very crime he is judging to press the case that there is a conscience – or innate principle of justice – that stands independently of all self-interest and can motivate even the most vile among us ("Letter to d'Offerville," 263–4).

[42] *Emile*, 100n [IV: 334n]; *Emile*, 253 [IV: 548]; *Emile*, 98–9 [IV: 331]; *Emile*, 290 [IV: 601]; *Emile*, 252 [IV: 547]; *Emile*, 245, 393 [IV: 537, 746]. Laurence D. Cooper stresses Emile's ordinariness and its relationship to philosophic wisdom (Cooper 2008, 176). An extended account of this cultivation of the conscience can be found in Hanley 2012. See also Cooper 1999 and Marks 2006.

no special intellectual tools to access the conscience and understand justice. One need only be human and be generally protected from the various assaults on our innate understanding. This broadly accessible understanding of justice is importantly linked to Rousseau's democratic sympathies.[43]

In the *Social Contract*, Rousseau makes relatively few explicit references to the conscience. In Book I, he notes that the conscience rejects the doctrine that might makes right (*SC*, 1.3.3, 44 [III: 355]), suggesting that the conscience of *Emile* and his early political works is very much in play as a measure of justice and injustice in the *Social Contract*. More broadly, however, Rousseau insists in Book IV that his citizens be "upright and simple" (*SC*, 4.1.1, 121 [III: 437]). Along these lines, he attributes the success of the Roman Republic in part to the "simple morals" of its citizens (*SC*, 4.4.19, 131 [III: 448]). These words also well describe Emile's role in the political world, where "great [intellectual] talents are less necessary than a sincere love of justice." Rousseau would subsequently describe himself as such a simple man in his autobiographic works, noting, by contrast, "The reflective man is the man of opinion; it is he who is dangerous."[44] This simplicity is precisely the disposition that best facilitates the cultivation of a "single will, which is concerned with their common preservation, and the general welfare" (*SC*, 4.1.1, 121 [III: 437]). The derivation of the general will from the principle of justice rooted in the conscience is apparent later in the same chapter when he notes, "Even in selling his vote for money he does not extinguish the general will within himself, he evades it" (*SC*, 4.1.6, 122 [III: 438]). That is to say, the corrupt citizen cannot eliminate the innate conscience, but rather endeavors to ignore it. The conscience is the lifeblood of the general will in a flourishing republic – and even when ignored it serves as a haunting reminder of the state's failures.

A.4.2. *Goodness*

To claim that the notion of justice informing Rousseau's general will is substantive is not simply a matter of metaphysical or epistemological correctness. Most fundamentally, Rousseau asserts in the *Emile*, "Justice is inseparable from goodness." He clarifies this relationship a few sentences later: "the love of order which produces order is called *goodness*; and the love of order which preserves order is called *justice*." Since for Rousseau God is the creator or Author, God's most fundamental virtue is

---

[43] See Williams 2012, 114–22.
[44] *Emile*, 458 [IV: 837]; *Dialogues*, 114 [I: 808].

this goodness, as we are reminded in the very opening sentence of *Emile*: "Everything is good as it leaves the hands of the Author of things; everything degenerates in the hands of man." As he describes in painstaking detail throughout the *Discourses*, human beings in their present state almost seem single-mindedly determined to disrupt that order. Human goodness, what Rousseau calls "love of [one's] fellows," is what enables people to restore that order (insofar as anything does). This establishment of order as goodness is embodied in the task of the lawgiver. Fraternal love as goodness informs Rousseau's descriptions of his favorite historical lawgivers: Moses, Lycurgus, and Numa. Moses labored tirelessly to establish "all the bonds of fraternity"; Lycurgus worked to cultivate an "ardent love of fatherland"; and Numa sought to unite brigands "into an indissoluble body ... by attach[ing] them one to another." In all three cases, the effect was the same for Rousseau: each "sought bonds that might attach the citizens to the fatherland and to one another."[45]

Insofar as they succeed in restoring this order, it is essential that citizens preserve some of that love – this preservation is the virtue of justice. So justice clearly involves the love of one's fellow citizens, which helps clarify why Rousseau, who is far from an orthodox Christian by the standards of his times or those of the present, claims to be "Christian, and sincerely Christian" – insofar as one understands the "essential truths of Christianity" to be embodied in the Gospels' doctrine of charity or fraternal love.[46]

A.4.3. *Equality*

Embodied in the doctrine of charity or fraternal love, and also central to Rousseau's conceptions of justice and the general will, is equality. This is one of the most readily identifiable elements of justice and hence the general will. It is the social and economic inequality of subjects described in Part II of his *Second Discourse* that renders it so wicked. In the *Emile*, he indicates that the general will "always tends to equality." In the *Government*

---

[45] *Emile*, 282 [IV: 588–9]; *Emile*, 37 [IV: 245]; *Emile*, 285 [IV: 593]; *Poland*, 180–1 [III: 957–58].

[46] "Letter to Beaumont," 47 [IV: 960]; Rousseau specifically cites Galatians 5:14 in this context ("For all the law is fulfilled in one word, even in this; Thou shalt love thy neighbour as thyself"). To be sure, there are also important doctrines associated with Christianity which Rousseau finds inconsistent with his political program, too (e.g., *SC*, 4.8.21–30, 147–9 [III: 465–7]; see also his "Letter to Usteri"). Finally, it is worth observing in this context that Jean Calvin, whom Rousseau praises earlier in the *SC* (2.7.9n, 70n [III: 383n]) for his lawgiving achievements in Geneva, argues that the proper foundation of legislation is the moral law, which he defines as "love [of] our fellow man with unfeigned love" (Calvin [1536] 1991, 67).

of Poland he describes equality as "the principle of the constitution." And in the *Social Contract*, he contrasts the particular will, which "tends, by its nature, to partiality," with the general will, which tends "to equality" (*SC*, 2.1.3, 57 [III: 368]). But it is in his *Letters Written from the Mountain* that he speaks most clearly to the relationship of equality to justice: "The first and greatest public interest is always justice. All wish the conditions to be equal for all, and justice is nothing but this equality."[47] In an important sense this conception of equality is embodied in his commitment to the rule of law, which insists that all subjects are *equal* under the law – there are no exceptions among citizens, regardless of class, position, or origin.

The equality of citizens under the law, however, is extremely fragile without a commitment to economic equality.[48] Rousseau speaks repeatedly to this concern. In the presence of extreme wealth inequality, he remarks in his *Political Economy*, citizens can be sure that the wealthy will employ the "pretext of the public good" to assault the poor and confiscate their remaining resources. A just government, therefore, evidences a "strict integrity to render justice to all, and above all [seeks] to protect the poor against the tyranny of the rich." It accomplishes this primarily by "prevent[ing] extreme inequality of fortunes."[49] Although he first explores this doctrine in his *Political Economy*, it clearly animates the *Social Contract* (*SC*, 1.9.8n, 56n [III: 367n]; 2.10.5, 77n [III: 390n]; 2.11.2, 78 [III: 391–2]; 3.4.5, 91 [III: 405]; 3.5.9, 94 [III: 407]). This connection is perhaps clearest in Book II:

Do you, then, want to give the State stability? bring the extremes as close together as possible; tolerate neither very rich nor beggars. These two states, which are naturally inseparable, are equally fatal to the common good; from one come the abettors of tyranny, and from the other tyrant; it is always between these two that there is trafficking in public freedom; one buys it, the other sells it. (*SC*, 2.11.2n, 78n [III: 392n])

Given his definition of justice as the "love of order which preserves order," it is easy to grasp why the equality of fortunes is a matter of justice for Rousseau. This equality helps to preserve civil order or "stability." Inequality of riches means that the wealthy will inevitably exploit the poor, resulting in class warfare and its accompanying instability.

---

[47] *Emile*, 463 [III: 842]; *Poland*, 215 [III: 994]; *Mountain*, 301 [III: 891].

[48] Joshua Cohen and Frederick Neuhouser speak to the importance of wealth equality in Rousseau (Cohen 2010, 53, 117, 140, and 164; Neuhouser 2008, 165–6). Perhaps the most extensive accounts, however, can be found in Vaughan 2008, 65–81 and Scholz 2013.

[49] *Political Economy*, 19 [III: 258].

Beyond this, however, wealth inequality tends to corrupt both rich and poor citizens. In a society where some wield considerable surpluses, and others are destitute, both are driven to make regrettable choices subverting the general will. The recent college placement test scandal in New York[50] is an apt illustration of how wealth inequalities fuel these problems. Those with enormous financial resources have employed their wealth to hire others to take their college placement exams. This frees the rich from the burden of working to maintain their relative privilege. Further, those taking the exams in their place are, presumably, driven by their relative poverty to risk prison sentences and significant fines. A just society, along Rousseau's lines, would reduce wealth at the top to reduce the temptation to hire professional test-takers; it would simultaneously reduce poverty at the bottom to reduce the likelihood that the poor would be tempted to risk prison sentences for cash.

It is no surprise, then, that in his most practical political works, he aggressively employs models of taxation that work to promote this equality.[51] In the *Government of Poland*, he implements a property tax. In the *Political Economy*, he recommends "heavy taxes" on all luxury items, and is further willing to entertain the possibility of taxing the rich citizen "up to the full amount that exceeds his necessities." It is only in the most utopian of his practical works, the *Plan for a Constitution for Corsica*, that his taxation is financially modest, inasmuch as citizens are encouraged to pay their taxes in produce and public service. But this presupposes an initial absence of significant inequalities that would require rectification through the tax code. He stresses to the Corsicans, "The fundamental law of your foundation ought to be equality. Everything ought to be related to it." In order to achieve this, he seeks to locate most property in the hands of the state. But even here, Rousseau is concerned about drifts toward inequality – so he speculates on the necessity of inheritance taxes that "tend to bring things back to equality so that each might have something and no one have anything in excess."[52]

Without this wealth equality undergirding equality under the rule of law, the rule of law and "justice" itself are suspect. It is great wealth itself

---

[50] See http://www.nytimes.com/2011/12/02/education/on-long-island-sat-cheating-was-hardly-a-secret .html?hp. Accessed December 2, 2011. Not only does the article note how the rich and fiscally needy are pressed into dubious moral choices, it also observes that some of the needy are driven to take the exams to improve their social standing among their peers.

[51] For a balanced reading of Rousseau on wealth that weighs his obvious aversion to inequality with other elements of his political philosophy, see Simpson 2006a, 81–5.

[52] *Poland*, 232 [III: 1011]; *Political Economy*, 36 [III: 276], 31 [III: 271]; *Corsica*, 151 [III: 935], 149 [III: 932]; *Corsica*, 130 [III: 909–10]; "Separate Fragments" from *Corsica*, 160 [III: 945].

that emboldens individuals to pervert the essential meanings of these core Rousseauean values. This is perfectly apparent in the narrative of the *Second Discourse*, where the wealthy "institute rules of Justice and peace to which all are obliged to conform." It is those very laws and principles that conspire forever to fix "the Law of property and inequality" in favor of the privileged class.[53] For this reason, Rousseau cautions elsewhere against "[t]hose specious names, justice and order, [which] will always serve as instruments of violence and as arms of inequity."[54] Eliminate the inequality of wealth, and the state has gone some distance to protect the equality and justice residing at the heart of the general will.

A.5. SOVEREIGNTY, JUSTICE, AND THE GENERAL WILL

The general will is closely related to two other concepts: justice and sovereignty. I have already suggested that justice is the substantive core of the general will. But it is not synonymous with the general will. Similarly, Rousseau associates the general will with sovereignty: "sovereignty ... is nothing but the exercise of the general will" (*SC*, 2.1.2, 57 [III: 368]). And in the *Emile* he writes, "the essence of sovereignty consists in the general will."[55] Yet sovereignty is not identical to the general will. Understanding how the general will is related to, yet distinct from, justice and sovereignty clarifies all three terms.

Jacob Talmon once wrote, "Ultimately, the general will is to Rousseau something like a mathematical truth or Platonic idea. It has an objective existence of its own, whether it is perceived or not." Talmon's assessment is incorrect, but for reasons that sharpen the meaning of the general will and its relationship to justice. The general will is not, precisely speaking, an eternal mathematical truth or a Platonic idea. It is *not* eternal in that it is contingent upon being willed for its very existence. The general will is emphatically a will. As Patrick Riley argues, Rousseau needs the general will to be a *will* and not merely an idea because that will is required for *legitimacy* and *obligation*. These are uniquely modern notions, absent in the ancient thought of Rousseau's heroes, such as Plato, Numa, or Lycurgus. As Riley writes, the general will is ultimately a "fusion of the generality (unity, commonality) of antiquity with the will (consent, contract) of modernity."[56] It does not stand alone merely as an idea of

---

[53] *Second Discourse*, 173 [III: 178].
[54] *Emile*, 236 [IV: 524]. See also *State of War*, 162 [III: 609].
[55] *Emile*, 462 [IV: 842].
[56] Talmon 1955, 41; Riley 1982, 108, 109.

generality, justice, or the common good. The general will represents the citizens' consent to those notions. And it does not, strictly speaking, exist without that consent. Therefore, it is not a Platonic idea in the sense suggested by Talmon.

This being stated, the general will must conform to an eternal idea of justice. Its content cannot be arbitrary. This is evident in his rejection of the exploitative laws established in the *Second Discourse*. It is also apparent in his distinction between the general will and the will of all (*SC*, 2.3.2, 60 [III: 371]). Consent to unjust principles cannot result in a general will. It results perhaps in a victorious particular will and a will of all. But it cannot be a general will. This is the unique marriage of ancient and modern political theory suggested by Riley. The substantive content of the general will, as a commitment to justice and the common good, is derived from ancient political theory; citizens' obligation to conform to justice and the common good is generated by their consenting to those very principles. This consent is the modern device of obligation, as established in the social contract tradition.[57] By willing justice, the citizens impose upon themselves an internal reason[58] to hold themselves up to the highest standards. They also simultaneously pledge themselves accountable to official sanctions, should they fail to do so. Without this crucial element of willing, Rousseau would be simply espousing a preexisting tradition of celebrating or promoting justice and the common good. It is this explicit consent to or willing of those principles – and its accompanying accountability – that separates him from the ancient tradition. It is his substantive commitment to those ancient principles that separates him from his contemporaries. So while the general will is not an eternal or Platonic idea itself, it is necessarily derived from such notions.

The fact that the general will must conform to the idea of justice clarifies some of the most perplexing passages on the general will. For example, when Rousseau posits that "the general will is always upright," this is not a call to affirm the doctrine that the people are always right, and certainly not that the government is always right, as is sometimes suggested. It is simple deduction drawn from definitions. If the general will must be just, in order to be a general will, then it necessarily follows that it

---

[57] This tradition largely extends from Thomas Hobbes, who writes, "it is DUTY, not to make void that voluntary act of his own" ([1651] 2002, 14.7). Rousseau, however, importantly differs from Hobbes insofar as Hobbes conflates this obligation to uphold "voluntary act[s]" with the very meaning of justice.

[58] Samuel Pufendorf describes "creating an obligation" as the "imposi[tion of] an internal necessity" (Pufendorf [1673] 1991, 29 [1.2.7].

is "always upright." As Rousseau continues, "it does not follow … that the people's deliberations are always equally upright" (*SC*, 2.3.1, 59 [III: 371]). This is because the people may deviate in their deliberations from the idea of justice. If the people's will so deviates, then it is merely a "will of all" and not a general will. This is not to say that this renders Rousseau's theory impervious to thoughtful criticism on such matters. After all, a state may use the pretext of the general will always being upright to enforce unjust policies – insofar as it convinces the populace that the general will is something other than what Rousseau takes it to be. Rousseau's defenders have available responses to such challenges, but they are certainly serious objections.

Another concept closely linked to the general will is *sovereignty*.[59] As discussed previously, Rousseau often speaks of the two terms as synonymous, and throughout this book I have largely treated them as such. But there is a modest, yet significant, difference. The general will is the citizens' willing of justice and the common good. Sovereignty is the *exercise* of that will by the people in their capacity as legislators. As he states in Book II, "sovereignty … is nothing but the exercise of the general will" (*SC*, 2.1.2, 57 [III: 368]). An act of legislation derived from the general will is, thus, an act of sovereignty. This connection is clarified in Book III: "The Sovereign, having no other force than the legislative power, acts only by means of the law, and the laws [are] nothing but authentic acts of the general will" (*SC*, 3.12.1, 110 [III: 425]). Any act of legislation deviating from the general will is hence invalid law. This is a rejection of the doctrine of legal positivism that insists that law can be completely divorced from moral principles.[60]

To be sure, the general will is a broader concept than sovereignty. Sovereignty is merely an application of the general will. For this reason, it is possible to speak of the general will outside of specific acts of legislation. For example, Rousseau specifies in the *Social Contract* that the executive does not legislate. It cannot, therefore, issue acts of sovereignty. Nevertheless, "the Prince's dominant will is or should be nothing but the

---

[59] As Timothy O'Hagan notes, "Sovereignty and the general will are tied conceptually to one another. When a people exercises its sovereignty it is expressing its general will" (O'Hagan 1999, 78).

[60] As Maurizio Viroli has observed, "Rousseau holds that there is an authority which transcends that of kings themselves and this authority is none other than the natural law" (Viroli 1988, 133; Viroli here cites Rousseau's *Government of Poland*, 196 [III: 973]). For an elaborate reading of Rousseau as a natural law theorist opposed to positivism, see Derathé 1970; see also Cohen 2010, 66, 162. For a contrary reading, see C. E. Vaughan [1915] 1962, I: 16–19; see also I: 424. This doctrine of positivism is traditionally associated with Thomas Hobbes (e.g., [1651] 2002, 26.2, 30.20). As A. P. Martinich has observed, however, Hobbes himself occasionally deviated from this doctrine (e.g., [1651] 2002, 26.40). See Martinich 1992, 112–34.

general will" (*SC*, 3.1.19, 85 [III: 399]). So the executive must always be aware of the people's will, in accordance with the idea of justice. And if the prince finds himself unable to locate the general will, insofar as the people have not publicly deliberated on a matter of particular executive interest, then the executive must go back to the substantive root of the general will itself, justice, since he reminds his readers that "for chiefs to know well enough that the general will is always on the side most favorable to the public interest, that is to say, the most equitable; so that one need only be just in order to be sure of following the general will." This is most evident in his institution of the dictator in Book IV, only possible in moments of peril in which the general will has not been declared in legislation. Despite this legislative silence, Rousseau is comfortable in insisting that "the general will is not in doubt, [since] it is obvious that the people's foremost intention is that the State not perish" (*SC*, 4.6.4, 138 [III: 456]). This is precisely what Rousseau's conception of justice as defined in the *Emile*, "love of order which preserves order," would suggest.[61] So justice and the general will exist where sovereignty is absent. This clarifies the intimate and necessary relationship of sovereignty to the general will and of the general will to justice.

A.6. IMPLEMENTING AND MAINTAINING THE GENERAL WILL

It is one thing to insist that laws must conform to the general will, itself derived from an eternal idea of justice. It is quite another to make this happen in the real world. Of course, at some level Rousseau is perfectly aware that such ambitions are quixotic. He once described schemes like Plato's Kallipolis in the *Republic* as belonging to the "land of the chimeras."[62] He is also clearly aware that however well-established a state might be, it is inevitably subject to the laws of decline and decay. While ideas of a republic may be perfect in theory, they are necessarily imperfect in empirical reality. The impossibility of a perfect eternal regime is no excuse, however, for shirking the responsibility of making a good faith effort to come as close as is practically possible to instituting and maintaining such a regime.[63] The measure of success in a republic amounts, as

---

[61] *Political Economy*, 12 [III: 251]; *Emile*, 282 [IV: 588–9].

[62] *Mountain*, 234 [III: 810].

[63] This is precisely the position adopted by the authors of the U.S. Constitution, some twenty-seven years after the publication of the *Social Contract*: "Concessions on the part of the friends of the plan, that it has not a claim to absolute perfection, have afforded matter of no small triumph to its enemies. 'Why,' say they, 'should we adopt an imperfect thing? Why not amend it and make it perfect before it is irrevocably established?' This may be plausible enough, but it is only plausible.

Zev Trachtenberg has remarked, to a "society's *first formulating* and then *enforcing* its general will."[64]

A.6.1. Enacting the General Will

To enact the general will is, most simply, to legislate. Rousseau describes the core essence of this process in Book IV:

The constant will of all the members of the State is the general will.... When a law is proposed in the People's assembly, what they are being asked is not exactly whether or not they approve the proposal or reject it, but whether it does or does not conform to the general will, which is theirs; everyone states his opinion about this by casting his ballot, and the tally of the votes yields the declaration of the general will (*SC*, 4.2.8, 124 [III: 440–1]).

Implementing the general will, in other words, requires that citizens vote in favor of the public good, rather than private interests. To facilitate this outcome Rousseau introduces institutional and extra-institutional measures. Institutionally, he promotes supermajoritarianism, whereby the more important the matter, the larger majority is required for acting upon it (*SC*, 4.2.11, 125 [III: 441]). As Melissa Schwartzberg has argued, the more citizens required to agree on substantive matters of policy, the less likely the outcome is to be partial or unjust.[65]

Most measures for ensuring the people legislate a general will, however, are largely extra-institutional. Most immediately, Rousseau insists that, before casting their ballots, citizens must be "adequately informed" and have "no communication among themselves" (*SC*, 2.3.3, 60 [III: 371]). Voting on the basis of ignorance does not bode well for arriving at the general will. Those without a handle on the relevant facts are vulnerable to the manipulations of artful private interests. Further, communication among citizens only multiplies opportunities for self-interested parties to form coalitions. While it is unclear that Rousseau desires the complete

---

In the first place I remark, that the extent of these concessions has been greatly exaggerated. They have been stated as amounting to an admission that the plan is radically defective, and that without material alterations the rights and the interests of the community cannot be safely confided to it. This, as far as I have understood the meaning of those who make the concessions, is an entire perversion of their sense. No advocate of the measure can be found, who will not declare as his sentiment, that the system, though it may not be perfect in every part, is, upon the whole, a good one; is the best that the present views and circumstances of the country will permit; and is such an one as promises every species of security which a reasonable people can desire" (Alexander Hamilton, Federalist No. 85, 522–3).

[64] Trachtenberg 1993, 7.
[65] Schwartzberg 2008.

elimination of all conversations among citizens, which is frankly unthinkable, he certainly does worry that extensive communication only fosters well-organized factious interests, who would use such opportunities to collude and spread misinformation in order to promote private wills.

More fundamentally, however, legislating the general will requires that the citizen be "upright and simple" (*SC*, 4.1.1, 121 [437]). By this Rousseau really means that the citizens must be virtuous. Base and selfish people rarely if ever prefer the general will to their own. In fact, they only choose the general will on those rare occasions when it appears aligned to their own myopic private wills (*SC*, 2.1.3). Given the unlikelihood of this concurrence among base people, it is a high priority for Rousseau to cultivate citizens virtuous enough to enact the general will. In fact, so tightly related are virtue and the general will for Rousseau that he defines a "virtuous" man in the *Political Economy* as he who "conforms" his particular will "in all things to the general will."[66]

This is one reason why the *Emile* plays an important role in Rousseau's political philosophy. The pedagogical novel declares early in Book I that "one must choose between making a man or a citizen, for one cannot make both at the same time."[67] This has led some scholars to the conclusion that Rousseau radically separates the *Emile* from his *Social Contract* as two very different solutions to the problems endemic to modernity. Yet as Frederick Neuhouser has persuasively argued, although Rousseau is very much interested in making Emile a virtuous "man" in Books I–IV of the *Emile*, the novel itself culminates in introducing Emile to a political society governed by the general will – that is, it makes him a citizen.[68] As is evident in the *Social Contract* itself, a political society governed by the general will demands virtuous citizens. So Rousseau's politics draws specifically on the attributes exemplified in individuals like Emile.

Furthermore, Rousseau's conception of virtue specifically relies on the freedom of the will. "This word virtue means *force*. There is no virtue without struggle, there is none without victory. Virtue consists not only in being just, but in being so by triumphing over one's passions, by ruling over one's heart."[69] The strength of will necessary to overcome the passions and inclinations can only originate in a free will. This is why the *Social Contract* requires that freedom be safeguarded as a top priority:

---

[66] *Political Economy*, 15 [III: 254]; see also 13 [III: 252].
[67] *Emile*, 39 [IV: 248].
[68] Neuhouser 2008, 21, 172–3. See also Strong [1994] 2002, 137–8.
[69] "Letter to Franquières," 281 [IV: 1143].

If one inquires into precisely what the greatest good of all consists in, which ought to be the end of every system of legislation, one will find that it comes down to two principle objects, *freedom* and *equality*. Freedom, because any individual dependence is that much force taken away from the State; equality, because freedom cannot subsist without it. (*SC*, 2.11.1, 78 [III: 391])

As Rousseau suggests here, freedom is the lifeblood of the state. When individuals lose their freedom – whether to the wiles of skilled rhetoricians, to the burdens of poverty, to the temptations of fantastic wealth, to threats of blunt violence, or even to the whims of their own passions – the general will is itself threatened. The general will, as established, must come from all citizens. If a significant portion of those citizens are not legislating from the perspective of a perfectly free will, the general will ceases effectively to come from all. And when it merely comes from *some*, it will likely only benefit some. This is why Rousseau connects equality so closely with freedom in this passage. A certain amount of material equality is required for citizens to legislate freely. Those with too little are too desperate to maintain a free will – they will sell their will too easily to the first comers to promise a bill of goods, as occurs in Part II of the *Second Discourse*. Those with too much develop a mania only for more and more, hence becoming slaves to their own passions. So economic equality not only preserves the rule of law; it also preserves the free will necessary to legislate the general will.

A.6.2. *Maintaining the General Will*

Maintaining the general will largely depends on maintaining those resources required for enabling it in the first place. Central among these, again, is virtue. Just as citizens require virtue to establish the general will, they need to remain virtuous in order to preserve it throughout the life of a republic. One of the ways Rousseau commonly recommends maintaining this virtue is to keep the state as small as is possible. In the *Social Contract*, he specifically cites small size as a virtue of democracies, since "every citizen can easily know all the rest" (*SC*, 3.4.5, 91 [III: 405]). But it is clear from reading Rousseau more broadly that small republics are not only good for democracies, strictly speaking; smallness is an asset for any republic aspiring to virtue. In his "Letter to d'Alembert," he notes that in small cities, citizens are "always in public eye, are born censors of one another and ... the police can easily watch everyone."[70] Further, a small

---

[70] "Letter to d'Alembert," 61 [V: 54]. See also *Poland*, 193 [III: 970].

city's lack of cosmopolitanism tends to the cultivation of virtue, insofar as it is primarily a flaw of large cities and states that citizens are consumed by the need to impress others. This theme dominates the *First Discourse*. Insofar as citizens are animated by *amour propre*, they are distracted from the needs and interests of others and hence the general will.

Beyond this, 4.7–8 of the *Social Contract* is dedicated to institutional measures to help maintain the general will. The censor, for example, is expressly assigned the task of "maintain[ing] morals by preventing opinion from becoming corrupt" (*SC*, 4.7.6 [III: 459]).[71] Likewise, his civil religion is intended as a device that inclines citizens "to love of one's neighbor, to justice, to peace, to the happiness of men, to the Laws of society, to all the virtues."[72] In short, the civil religion is yet another support for maintaining the relative purity of the general will in the face of all those obstacles that conspire to fragment and defeat it.

To be sure, however, the greatest support for maintaining the general will through Rousseau's political writings is fraternity. This love of fellow citizens is alluded to in the *Social Contract* and developed more substantially in other political writings. His most commonly deployed device to advance the spirit of fraternity is patriotism. In the *Political Economy*, he praises this love of fatherland as a "gentle and lively sentiment which combines the force of *amour propre* with all the beauty of virtue." Patriotism builds on the energy inherent in self-love and generalizes it to all citizens. In his *Government of Poland*, he develops the love of country as the animating principle of all public education, in which a student will learn to see "only his fatherland; he lives only for it; when he is alone, he is nothing."[73] The more citizens embrace the interests of their fellows as equally weighty to their own, the more vigor the general will acquires. Rousseau explores the consequences of failing to establish these bonds in Book IV of the *Social Contract*:

when the social knot [*le lien social*] begins to loosen and the State ... weaken[s]; when particular interests begin to make themselves felt, and small societies to influence the larger society, the common interest diminishes and meets with opposition, votes are no longer unanimous, and the general will is no longer the will of all, contradictions and disagreements arise, and the best opinion no longer carries the day unchallenged (*SC*, 4.1.4, 121–2 [III: 438]).

---

[71] As he claims two paragraphs earlier, the censor "can be useful in preserving morals, never in restoring them" (*SC*, 4.7.4 [III: 459]).

[72] *Mountain*, 140 [III: 695].

[73] *Political Economy*, 16 [III: 255]; *Government of Poland*, 189 [III: 966].

The "social knot" of which he speaks here is the fraternal love among citizens. It is clear in this passage that this fraternity is crucial to maintaining the general will. It expands the sense of "I" to "we." Citizens imbued with this love pursue the public good with the same vigor that base individuals can be expected to pursue their myopic self-interest. As such, the spirit of fraternity is a powerful tool – and probably a necessary one – for maintaining the general will.

A.7. CONCLUSION

At the outset of this appendix, I cited Judith Shklar. It is worth repeating her words again: "the general will is Rousseau's most successful metaphor. It conveys everything he most wanted to say." Understanding the general will requires a thorough tour of Rousseau's constructive political thought more broadly. In this respect, readers can appreciate why he does not simply define the general will in the *Social Contract*, which would otherwise seem to be a great service to his readers. This is because understanding the general will requires understanding Rousseau's various commitments to popular sovereignty, legitimacy, democracy, justice, goodness, liberty, equality, and fraternity – along with the nuances of each of those concepts as worked out in his writings. There can be no simple definition of the general will. There can only be excavation. And this excavation ultimately comes from reading the entire *Social Contract*, and further from reading Rousseau's other complementary works on education, culture, the arts, economics, and politics. I have done my best here to impart what I have concluded on the basis of my own such study. But each serious encounter with these materials is bound to generate new insights, so there is good reason for scholars to return to Rousseau's works indefinitely into the future.

On Women in the Social Contract?

Reasonable questions have been raised concerning the role of women in Rousseau's constructive political thought. These questions can and must be asked for at least two reasons. First, Rousseau has a history of making what contemporary readers consider overtly misogynistic observations. Evidence supporting this view is commonly drawn from two of his works from the same period as the *Social Contract*: his *Emile* (1762) and the *Letter to d'Alembert* (1758). It is not especially difficult to find passages in either that would raise suspicions in any fair-minded reader. The *Letter to d'Alembert* admits that it is "possible that there are in the world a few women worthy of being listened to by a decent man," but only to set up the question, "in general, is it from women that he ought to take counsel, and is there no way of honoring their sex without abasing our own?" And in the *Emile*, Rousseau infamously observes that "woman is made specially to please man."[1] Any reconstruction of Rousseau as someone friendly to women, thus, obviously, faces significant obstacles. The second reason why readers must raise the question of women in the *Social Contract* is because Rousseau fails to do so himself. It is odd that a thinker who thought and wrote a great deal about women should never even have raised the female sex in his most celebrated political treatise. In what follows, I sketch Rousseau's understanding of women, largely from the material of Book V of his *Emile*, offer thoughts on the possible role of women in the *Social Contract*, and survey how some contemporary scholars seek to make sense of his conception of women in relation to his politics.

I. SOPHIE

In the nearly five hundred pages of his pedagogical novel, *Emile*, Rousseau outlines a plan of education for a male child from birth to marriage. It is

---

[1] *Letter to d'Alembert*, 47 [V: 44]; *Emile*, 358 [IV: 693].

only in the final chapter that he introduces readers to Emile's future bride, Sophie. Rousseau's treatment of Sophie, however, and of women in general, is not merely fleeting. He dedicates dozens of pages to outlining the faculties and ways of women as he finds them, his ideal standards by which they should be measured, and how these norms might guide Sophie's education. While he begins by acknowledging that men and women are equal on the dimensions where they share physiology and anatomy, such as in their needs for food, drink, and shelter, he also identifies certain foundational differences in physiology and needs that lead to unique roles for each sex. It is naturally this latter set that is of greater interest both to Rousseau in these pages and to contemporary readers.

Rousseau points to what he views as men's greater strength in body and will and to women's lesser strength and passivity to derive his first principle: "that woman is made specially to please man," a principle he repeats in the next paragraph with the notable addition that women are also made to be "subjugated." He continues, however, to note that women will use their unique faculties to "enslave the strong." This is a story of bondage, to be sure, but one with a complex dynamic, to Rousseau's mind. It is one in which both parties in the heterosexual partnership "contribute equally to the common aim, but not in the same way." According to Rousseau, woman's physically smaller stature and, especially, her childbearing role make her dependent on men. This physical dependence requires that she must make men like her. That is, she requires a degree of *amour propre*. This is how she is able to get men to perform the tasks she requires but cannot do for herself. Although Rousseau often writes of the dangers of *amour propre*, he also importantly on occasion points to its necessity – nowhere so much as in the *Emile*. So a woman, for Rousseau, "must make herself agreeable to man instead of provoking him." From a position of physical weakness, one cannot coerce. But in winning the approval of others one can achieve the same effect. So a woman's power, he comments, is "in her charms."[2] Insofar as she can charm men, she can exercise her will and influence others.

Because women differ in this way from men, Rousseau infers, their education must likewise differ. He divides this education into that of the exterior and that of the interior of the pupil. Externally, physical education plays an important role. As with men, he wants girls to be physically fit – although not for all the same reasons as men. Following the model of the Spartan mother, he promotes physical vigor among females so that they

[2] *Emile*, 358 [IV: 693–4].

might bear strong boys, who can presumably defend the republic. Within the exterior realm, however, Rousseau gives greater attention to attire and fashion. For him, this interest in adornment is closely related to the powerful workings of *amour propre* in women. Since, as he assumes from the beginning, women depend on men, they must please them. And the most immediate way in which they please men, according to Rousseau, is by their appearance. So, the logic goes, "Not satisfied with being pretty, they want people to think they are pretty."[3] Yet this is a potentially dangerous path. Women can be misled down the path of passing and foolish fashions in the quest for recognition and affection. Along these lines, he goes out of his way to condemn the corset, or the "gothic shackles," which he finds not only unnecessarily inhumane to the wearer, but also aesthetically displeasing: "It is not pleasant to see a woman cut in two like a wasp."[4] Beyond this, he expressly condemns opulent attire and trinkets, which are aimed more at satisfying an unhealthy vanity than at expressing true beauty. He prefers to let nature shine through, for women's appearance to be true to their age and natural body types, and to limit ornamentation to simple items, such as ribbons and flowers. An interest in dolls and attire will inevitably lead, Rousseau suggests, to taking up the useful arts of sewing, embroidery, lace-making, and the like. Rousseau, however, ultimately gives far greater attention to the education of the interior. Girls must be taught religion, virtue, and morality, although he does not mean by this to impose the sharp moralism of his fellow Genevan, Jean Calvin. The Calvinists were renowned for legislating away fun, and Rousseau would have none of that. Sophie must be permitted to "be lively, playful, frolicsome, to sing and dance as much as she pleases, and to taste all the innocent pleasures of her age."[5]

Girls are to learn religion, but with as little attention as possible to the metaphysics and various rites that came to be associated with the dominant strands of Christianity in the eighteenth century. Rousseau discourages mothers from teaching their daughters about the virgin birth, Christ's divinity, and the metaphysics of the Holy Trinity. Not only are these abstractions with which presumably, on Rousseau's logic, women typically struggle to grasp. They are also unhelpful in making Sophie happy as a subject of the republic. The same goes generally for religious rites, which

[3] *Emile*, 365 [IV: 703].
[4] *Emile*, 367 [IV: 705].
[5] *Emile*, 374 [IV: 716].

are diverse and of little real consequence. It should be added, however, that he places no emphasis on these matters in Emile's education, either.

What really matters in religious education is imparting the moral lessons of Jesus Christ: that

an arbiter of the fate of human beings exists and that we are all His children; that He prescribes that we all be just, love one another, be beneficent and merciful, and keep our promises to everyone – even to our enemies and His; that the apparent happiness of this life is nothing; that there is another life after it in which this Supreme Being will be the rewarder of the good and the judge of the wicked.[6]

Readers of the *Social Contract* immediately recognize the parallels here to his program for a civil religion (*SC*, 4.8.33) with their parallel emphases on civic justice, as well as divine rewards and punishment. Further paralleling the *Social Contract*'s civil religion is a precept of tolerance – namely, that the only negative dogma mothers should teach their daughters are those that seek to impose other, more specific, religious beliefs than those stated earlier should be punished for being sacrilegious and intolerant. In these respects, Sophie's religious outlook differs little, if at all, from what Rousseau desires of all citizens in the *Social Contract*.

Beyond the expressly religious dimensions of morality, Rousseau stresses that women should be virtuous. He defines virtue elsewhere in his work as the capacity to overcome the passions.[7] This ability to conquer the passions is most obvious in the specific virtue of self-control or self-mastery. This virtue is by no means demanded only of Rousseau's women. He stresses its importance to men repeatedly throughout his writings. But it is clearly the most important virtue for women. Rousseau writes of what he acknowledges to be a corrupt society, "Amidst our senseless arrangements a decent woman's life is a perpetual combat against herself." She must fight off all temptations that persistently threaten to cast her from society. Any letting down of her guard carries enormous personal consequences. To this end, Rousseau counsels that girls develop a healthy sense of shame. But more than that they should fear shame, he is above all eager that women should love virtue:

Sophie loves virtue. This love has become her dominant passion. She loves it because there is nothing so fine as virtue. She loves it because virtue constitutes a woman's glory and because to her a virtuous woman appears almost equal to the angels. She loves it as the only route of true happiness, and because she sees

---

[6] *Emile*, 381 [IV: 729].
[7] "Letter to Franquières," 281 [IV: 1143].

only misery, abandonment, unhappiness and ignominy in the life of a shameless woman.[8]

Here one finds the various modes of moral psychology at work. A woman is to be motivated by the love of what is good in itself, by a sense of her own dignity as a woman, by fear of social consequences, and by desire for her own happiness. One finds Rousseau variously appealing to these various motives – for both men and women – throughout his works.

While it is obvious that for Rousseau morality is the most important part of religion, the trick is to teach students to make the right moral decisions in practice. To explain how this might come to pass, he sketches out a tri-partite moral psychology. All individuals – men and women – have three sources of moral ideas: inner sentiment (or "conscience"), opinion, and reason. The differences between men and women reside in the degree to which each exercises influence over their moral judgments and choices. Rousseau elsewhere sketches out what he means by conscience and opinion. The conscience is an "innate principle of justice."[9] It is fixed, innate, and eternal. Opinion, by contrast, consists in the norms of others (whether it be a husband, the coterie at a local salon, the neighborhood, the city, or France itself), and is subject to whim and change. Navigating life successfully requires sensitivity to both conscience and opinion. One who fails to heed opinion is in danger of alienating one's compatriots; one who fails to heed the conscience is in danger of becoming a monster.

Since the conscience is fixed and opinion flexible, these two voices can and often do conflict. The question is how to mediate on those occasions. Choosing requires the faculty of reason. Since apparently this was an open question among many in the eighteenth century, Rousseau forthrightly asks, "Are women capable of solid reasoning?"[10] His answer is a definite "yes," although he does not advise that women employ it precisely as men do. Since women are more dependent on others than men, they should be especially sensitive to opinion. He does not apparently require the same of men, who should feel free to disregard opinion, even where it does not expressly contradict conscience. But in instances where opinion conflicts with conscience, both women and men must choose conscience. He describes the process thus:

[8] *Emile*, 369 [IV: 709], 397 [IV: 751]. See Okin 1979, 161–2.
[9] *Emile*, 289 [IV: 598]. See Appendix A, A.4.1.
[10] *Emile*, 382 [IV: 730].

As soon as she depends on both her own conscience and the opinion of others, she has to learn to compare these two rules, to reconcile them, and to prefer the former only when the two are in contradiction. She becomes the judge of her judges; she decides when she ought to subject herself to them and when she ought to take exception to them. Before rejecting or accepting their prejudices, she weighs them. She learns to go back to their source, to anticipate them, to use them to her advantage. She is careful never to attract blame to herself when her duty permits her to avoid it. None of this can be done well without cultivating her mind and her reason.[11]

So Rousseau dissents from those who reject women's capacity to reason. Women weigh the moral value of various maxims and are fully capable of choosing well quite on their own.

While he grants the capacity of women to reason, however, he insists that their talents for reasoning differ from men's. Although Rousseau does not explain his basis for arriving at this judgment, he finds men to have a greater facility for abstract thinking – the ability to observe nature and hone in on the general principles and axioms that explain scientific phenomena. The discoveries of a Newton or Descartes are for him, presumably, possible by virtue of their distinctly masculine minds. Lacking this ability, women, by contrast, have a superior skill in the mechanical sciences. They have a natural talent for observation and detail lacking in men. As in the natural, so in the human sciences as well: "Men will about the human heart philosophize better than she does; but she will read in men's hearts better than they do."[12] To be sure, he associates the former activity with "genius"; the latter he simply attributes to the power of "observation." As he does elsewhere in this chapter of the *Emile*, Rousseau holds these typically male and typically female attributes to be complementary. But it is worth noting before pushing forward that he identifies the role of the lawgiver as significantly mechanical. The lawgiver is "the mechanic who invents the machine" of the body politic (*SC*, 2.7.2, 69 [III: 381]). It is doubtful that Rousseau imagines the lawgiver as a woman, since he employs specifically masculine pronouns throughout the discussion and cites only masculine examples, such as Lycurgus, Moses, Numa, and Solon. Nevertheless, if one were inclined to hold Rousseau to the standards of internal consistency, it would seem that lawgiving would at least partly be properly the task of women, as he describes them in his discussion of Sophie.

---

[11] *Emile*, 383 [IV: 731–2].
[12] *Emile*, 387 [IV: 737].

2. WOMEN IN ROUSSEAU'S REPUBLIC?

While his thought on women is developed extensively in the *Emile*, it is somewhat remarkable that, as one recent commentator has remarked, "Women and domestic life are completely absent from Rousseau's most well known political philosophy, most notably, *On the Social Contract*."[13] This has led most readers interested in these questions to focus, reasonably, on his works that do consider women, especially the *Emile*. But since Rousseau himself often connects the *Social Contract* to the *Emile* and published them at the same time, it is worth speculating what the role of women in his republic might be. In doing so, I will focus on a small handful of questions. Are women citizens in Rousseau's republic? Can they hold public office? What other roles might be available to women in a distinctly Rousseauean republic?

Are women citizens in Rousseau's republic? Although there is no text in the *Social Contract* denying women citizenship, it is virtually certain that he had no intention of extending them the full rights of citizens. When Rousseau speaks of citizens in the *Social Contract* and elsewhere, he consistently employs masculine pronouns. This is not merely linguistic convention, but at least occasionally reflects his thoughts on citizenship. Rousseau often presents the republic as a particularly demanding political system. Far more for him than most, the republic insists that all citizens be actively involved. At a minimum, they must be available for frequent meetings of the assembly, have access to information pertaining to the issues of the day, and absorb that information. All of this takes time, and it is far from clear that women – who have extensive domestic duties throughout the day – have this, even if for Rousseau they have the requisite intellectual capacity.

One can find, however, another strain in Rousseau that runs counter to this vision of the citizen as someone with extensive spare time. In none of his writings does he suggest that citizens should have considerable leisure time. In fact, his strong preference is that citizens be kept busy with work – perhaps farming above all. In his constitutional proposal for Corsica, he strongly cautions against cultivating idle citizens, which in Switzerland at least, "introduced corruption and multiplied pensioners of the powers." Here he insists on his citizens being hard at work most of the time. Yet even here, he is specific that one condition of citizenship is to

---

[13] Lange 2002, 19.

have an "estate of his own independently of his wife's dowry."[14] So while citizenship may or may not demand extensive leisure time, it persistently demands masculinity.

What role, then, do women play in Rousseau's state? It is clear enough that they are required in their procreative role. But this would be true of any state. So it is necessary to make the question more precise: what role do women play in a distinctively Rousseauean republic? Most immediately, women effectively run the households. Not in the sense that they command husband and children. But they guide them by winning the esteem of their husbands and respect of their children. As he expressly warns, "Woe to the age in which women lose their ascendency, and in which their judgment no longer have an effect on men!"[15]

The posited influence of men and women here is par excellence a working of "opinion," Rousseau's sense of which we have briefly considered already. Although Rousseau demands that men acquire a stronger immunity to others' norms than women, he is clear that both men and women are subject to its force. When Rousseau announces in his *Letter to d'Alembert* that "Opinion is the queen of the world," he does not hold half the world to be outside her realm. In fact, he identifies kings as the first slaves of opinion.[16] Establishing sound opinion is presented, moreover, as one of the grand achievements of Rousseau's lawgiver, and he institutes a censor to maintain good mores in Book IV. Along these lines, it is quite possible Rousseau understands women as playing a crucial role in the maintenance of opinion generally. Rousseau's citizen-husbands know that they must earn the respect of their wives. And in order to do this they must be virtuous. Indeed, Sophie's parents offer Fénelon's Telemachus as a model of virtue for her future husband. Maintaining a wife's respect presumably, then, means approximating that model as far as possible.

Another distinctively Rousseauean role for women is in the formation of the general will, the very core of Rousseau's political program. It is the general will that seeks to promote the common good over any particular faction within the state. The general will, further, demands that citizens *want* the common good – that the common good not be a happy accident resulting spontaneously from the pursuit of private pleasures. Subjecting citizens to the constant judgment of their neighbors and wives is one way to bring them back to the general will. But in his treatment of

[14] *Corsica*, 136 [IV: 916], 139 [IV: 919].
[15] *Emile*, 390 [IV: 742].
[16] *Letter to d'Alembert*, 73 [V: 67].

Sophie, Rousseau offers another intriguing way in which citizens might be prompted to think beyond their own self-interest: love. It is worth excerpting several sentences to understand how he means for this to happen.

In love everything is an illusion. I admit it. But what is real are the sentiments for the truly beautiful with which love animates us and which it makes us love. This beauty is not in the object one loves; it is the work of our errors. So, what of it? Does the lover any the less sacrifice all of his low sentiments to this imaginary model? Does he any the less suffuse his heart with the virtues he attributes to what he holds dear? Does he detach himself any the less from the baseness of the human *I*?[17]

Rousseau candidly admits that much of love is illusory. Love's object is never so perfect as imagined. But the sensations inspired by love are very real. While a lover is never so beautiful as imagined, that idea of beauty awakened in the process is real indeed. Real also are actions and deeds love inspires. It inspires lovers to be virtuous. And it inspires lovers to ascend in interest from the singular "I" to the common "we," just as he demands in *Emile's* Book I:

Good social institutions are those that best know how to denature man, to take his absolute existence from him in order to give him a relative one and transport the *I* into the common unity, with the result that each individual believes himself no longer one but a part of the unity and no longer feels except within the whole.[18]

It seems that the institution of marriage constitutes just such a mechanism for this essential process of making Rousseauean citizens. In the most sincere way possible, Rousseau imagines, lovers inspired by their beloved can no longer act on purely selfish impulses (not even in the *amour de soi* sense). They want what is best for the both of them. If this can be true for a couple, presumably, then one can imagine that this broadening of the "I" to the "we" might be extended to the broader political community. This kind of extension is ultimately necessary for a successful republic ruled by the general will, and one can argue that romantic relationships can generate some of the energy useful in establishing that will. In this spirit, it is worth observing here that in his *Corsica*, he expressly lists marriage as required for citizenship. While there might be other reasons for this, it is suggestive that a loving relationship, such as a marriage, is virtually a prerequisite for cultivating a conception of the general will.[19]

[17] *Emile*, 391 [IV: 743].
[18] *Emile*, 40 [IV: 249].
[19] *Corsica*, 139 [III: 919].

3. EVALUATIONS?

What I have said about the role of women in Rousseau's politics makes him nothing approaching a champion of women's rights. His view of women's place has been characterized most charitably as "traditional" and less so as amounting to "a public sexual order which is little short of despotism."[20] Again, there is no concealing Rousseau's decidedly antiquated remarks on the nature and role of women as he understood them. Further, it must be acknowledged that others in his milieu did not echo the dominant view of women in the eighteenth century.[21] In some instances, these were not merely representatives of his epoch – they were acquaintances and even, sometimes, close friends. In formulating his thoughts, Rousseau had opportunity to weigh, and so can be considered to have rejected, alternatives that actively embraced female citizenship.

All this being said, many contemporary readers and even advocates of feminist philosophy find his politics less than appalling and even, in some instances, appealing. Helena Rosenblatt, for example, has argued that many of Rousseau's most damning statements about women come in a particular context of bourgeois women advocating bourgeois values at the expense of virtue as he understood it. Since Rousseau likewise holds nothing back similarly in his rants against bourgeois men, Rousseau's fight, we might say, is with the vapid bourgeois class – not specifically women. Mary Jo Marso, while finding Rousseau's masculine political project a failure in its explicit aims, points to his own unmanly model of democratic citizenship, where protest, sacrifice, resistance to opinion, and the capacity to value the dignity of others are uniquely feminine traits in Rousseau's conception of women. Melissa Butler finds in Rousseau's *Social Contract* at least a partial solution to the problem of "care ethics," where the work of caring for children, the elderly, and the disabled has traditionally and disproportionately fallen to women, insofar as Rousseau's republic promises to provide resources for this essential social function. Defending this view, she points to the fact that women do not appear in the *Social Contract* because the bulk of their traditional duties have been assumed by the state. And most recently, Rosanne Terese Kennedy points to textual evidence in the *Emile* and elsewhere suggesting Rousseau was far more ambiguous about gender roles than is suggested by focusing on the Sophie storyline. On this rendering, the lines between the sexes are far less demarcated than

---

[20] O'Hagan 1996, 131.
[21] E.g., Condorcet [1790] 2012; Holbach 1774; and Helvétius [1772] 1810.

the scholarship tends to draw them.[22] Of course, as with all texts – especially Rousseau's – there is no universality of opinion. Readers must grapple with his words, silences, and contexts to make the best sense they can of an admittedly complex figure.

---

[22] See Rosenblatt 2002; Marso 1999; Butler 2002; and Kennedy 2012.

References

Aquinas, St. Thomas. 2003. *Summa Theologicae*. In *On Law, Morality, and Politics*, 2nd ed. Edited by William P. Baumgarth and Richard Regan, S.J. Indianapolis: Hackett Publishing.

Aristotle. 1984. *The Complete Works of Aristotle: The Revised Oxford Translation*. Princeton: Princeton University Press.

Augustine. 1994. *Political Writings*. Trans. Michael W. Tkacz and Douglas Kries. Indianapolis, IN: Hackett Publishing.

Bacon, Francis. [1620] 1999. *New Organon* in *Selected Philosophical Essays*. Edited by Rose-Marie Sargent. Indianpolis, IN: Hackett Publishing.

Ball, Terence. 1995. *Reappraising Political Theory: Revisionist Studies in the History of Political Thought*. Oxford: Oxford University Press.

Barry, Brian. [1965] 1990. *Political Argument*. Berkeley: University of California Press.

Barzun, Jacques. 2000. *From Dawn to Decadence: 500 Yeas of Cultural Life, 1500 to the Present*. New York: Harper Collins.

Bayle, Pierre. [1681] 2000. *Various Thoughts on the Occasion of a Comet*. Translated by Robert C. Bartlett. Albany: SUNY Press.

Bell, Daniel. 1976. *The Coming of Post-Industrial Society: A Venture in Social Forecasting*. New York: Basic Books.

Benner, Erica. 2009. *Machiavelli's Ethics*. Princeton: Princeton University Press.

Berlin, Isaiah. 1969. "Two Concepts of Liberty." In *Four Essays on Liberty*. Oxford: Oxford University Press.

———. 2002. *Freedom and Its Betrayal: Six Enemies of Human Liberty*. Edited by Henry Hardy. Princeton: Princeton University Press.

Bertram, Christopher. 2004. *Routledge Philosophy Guidebook to Rousseau and the "Social Contract."* London: Routledge.

———. 2012. "Rousseau's Legacy in Two Conceptions of the General Will: Democratic and Transcendent." *Review of Politics*, 74 (2): 403–19.

Blum, Carol. 1986. *Rousseau and the Republic of Virtue: The Language of Politics in the French Revolution*. Ithaca, NY: Cornell University Press.

Boatwright, Mary T., Daniel J. Gargola, and Richard A. Talbert. 2004. *The Romans: From Village to Empire*. Oxford: Oxford University Press.

Bossuet, Jacques. [1709] 1990. *Politics Drawn from the Holy Scripture*. Edited by Patrick Riley. Cambridge: Cambridge University Press.

Boswell, James. [1764] 1953. *Boswell on the Grand Tour: Germany and Switzerland, 1764*. Edited by Frederick A. Pottle. New York: McGraw-Hill.

Boyd, Richard. 2004. "Pity's Pathologies Portrayed: Rousseau and the Limits of Democratic Compassion." *Political Theory*, 32 (4): 519–46.

Braybrooke, David. 2001. *Natural Law Modernized*. Toronto: University of Toronto Press.

Brest, Paul, Sanford Levinson, J. M. Balkin, and Akhil Reed Amar. 2000. *Processes of Constitutional Decisionmaking*, 4th ed. Gaithersburg: Aspen Publishers.

Burke, Edmund. [1790] 1987. *Reflections on the Revolution in France*. Edited by J. G. A. Pocock. Indianapolis, IN: Hackett Publishing.

Burlamaqui, Jean-Jacques. [1747] 2006. *The Principles of Natural Law and Politic Law*. Edited by Peter Korkman. Indianapolis, IN: Liberty Fund.

Butler, Melissa. 2002. "Rousseau and the Politics of Care." In *Feminist Interpretations of Rousseau*, ed. Lynda Lange. University Park: Pennsylvania State University Press.

Butterworth, Charles E. 1992. "Interpretive Essay," in *Reveries of the Solitary Walker*. Indianapolis, IN: Hackett Publishing.

Calvin, Jean. [1536] 1991. *Institution of the Christian Religion*, in *Luther and Calvin on Secular Authority*, ed. Harro Höpfl. Cambridge: Cambridge University Press.

———. [1945] 1963. *Rousseau, Kant, and Goethe*, trans. Peter Gay. New York: Harper Books.

Cassirer, Ernst. [1954] 1963. *The Question of Jean-Jacques Rousseau*, trans. Peter Gay. Bloomington: Indiana University Press.

Church, Jeffrey. 2010. "The Freedom of Desire: Hegel's Response to Rousseau on the Problem of Civil Society." *American Journal of Political Science*, 54 (1): 125–39.

Cicero, Marcus Tullius. 1994. *On Duties*. Cambridge: Cambridge University Press.

———. 1999. *On the Commonwealth and On the Laws*. Cambridge: Cambridge University Press.

Cladis, Mark Sydney. 2006. *Public Visions, Private Lives: Rousseau, Religion, and 21st-Century Democracy*. New York: Columbia University Press.

Cobban, Alfred. 1968. *Rousseau and the Modern State*. Hamden, CT: Archon Books.

Cohen, Joshua. 2010. *Rousseau*. Oxford: Oxford University Press.

Condorcet, Marquis de. [1790] 2012. "On the Emancipation of Women. On Giving Women the Right of Citizenship." In *Condorcet: Political Writings*, ed. Steven Lukes and Nadia Urbanati. Cambridge: Cambridge University Press.

Constant, Benjamin. [1814] 1988. *The Spirit of Conquest and Usurpation and Their Relation to European Civilization*. In *Political Writings*, ed. Biancamaria Fontana. Cambridge: Cambridge University Press.

———. [1815] 2003. *Principles of Politics Applicable to All Governments*. Indianapolis, IN: Liberty Fund.

———. [1819] 1988. "The Liberty of the Ancients Compared with that of the Moderns." In *Constant: Political Writings*, ed. Biancamaria Fontana. Cambridge: Cambridge University Press.

Cooper, Laurence D. 1999. *Rousseau, Nature, and the Problem of the Good Life*. University Park: Pennsylvania State University Press.

———. 2002. "Human Nature and the Love of Wisdom: Rousseau's Hidden (and Modified) Platonism." *Journal of Politics*, 64 (1): 108–25.

———. 2008. *Eros in Plato, Rousseau, and Nietzsche: The Politics of Infinity*. University Park: Pennsylvania State University Press.

Coulter, Ann. 2011. *Demonic*. New York: Crown Forum.

Cranston, Maurice. 1982. *Jean-Jacques: The Early Life and Work of Jean-Jacques Rousseau, 1712–1754*. Chicago: University of Chicago Press.

———. 1991. *The Noble Savage: Jean-Jacques Rousseau, 1754–1762*. Chicago: University of Chicago Press.

Crocker, Lester G. 1968. *Rousseau's Social Contract: An Interpretive Essay*. Cleveland: Press of Case Western Reserve University.

Cusher, Brent Edwin. 2010. "Rousseau and Plato on the Legislator and the Limits of Law." PhD dissertation, University of Toronto.

Dagger, Richard. 1981. "Understanding the General Will." *Western Political Quarterly*, 34 (4): 359–71.

Dahl, Robert A. 1991. *Democracy and Its Critics*. New Haven, CT: Yale University Press.

Damrosch, Leo. 2005. *Jean-Jacques Rousseau: Restless Genius*. Boston: Houghton Mifflin.

Dent, N. J. H. 1988. *Rousseau: An Introduction to His Psychological, Social, and Political Theory*. Oxford: Basil Blackwell.

———. 1992. *A Rousseau Dictionary*. Oxford: Blackwell.

Dent, Nicholas. 2005. *Rousseau*. London: Routledge.

Derathé, Robert. 1964. "Introduction and Editorial Notes." In *OEuvres complètes*, ed. Robert Derathé, vol. 3. Paris: Pléiade.

———. 1970. *Jean-Jacques Rousseau et la science politique de son temps*. Paris: Presses Universitaries de France.

Derrida, Jacques. [1967] 1976. *Of Grammatology*. Translated by Gayatri Chakravotry Spivak. Baltimore: Johns Hopkins University Press.

Diderot, Denis. 1992. *Droit Naturel*. In *Diderot: Political Writings*, ed. John Hope Mason and Robert Wokler. Cambridge: Cambridge University Press.

Dietz, Mary G. 1986. "Trapping the Prince: Machiavelli and the Politics of Deception." *American Political Science Review*, 80 (3): 777–99.

Dufour, Theophile. 1925. *Recherches bibliographiques sur les oeuvres imprimes de J.-J. Rousseau*, Vol. I. New York: Burt Franklin.

Dworkin, Ronald. 1985. *A Matter of Principle*. Cambridge, MA: Harvard University Press.

———. 1986. *Law's Empire*. Cambridge, MA: Harvard University Press.

———. 2011. *Justice for Hedgehogs*. Cambridge, MA: Harvard University Press.

Engels, Friedrich. [1878] 1939. *Herr Eugen Dühring's Revolution in Science (Anti-Dühring)*. New York: International Publishers.

d'Entrèves, Alexander Passerin. [1951] 1994. *Natural Law: An Introduction to Legal Philosophy*. New Brunswick, NJ: Transaction Publishers.

Estlund, David. 1989. "Democratic Theory and the Public Interest: Condorcet and Rousseau Revisited." *American Political Science Review*, 83 (4): 1317–40.

Fénelon, François de. [1699] 1994. *Telemachus*. Edited by Patrick Riley. Cambridge: Cambridge University Press.

Fichte, J. G.. [1795–96] 2000. *Foundations of Natural Right*. Edited by Frederick Neuhouser. Cambridge: Cambridge University Press.

Filmer, Sir Robert. [1680] 1991. *Patriarcha and Other Writings*. Edited by Johann P. Sommerville. Cambridge: Cambridge University Press.

Fischer, David Hackett. 2004. *Liberty and Freedom: A Visual History of America's Founding Ideas*. Oxford: Oxford University Press.

Fish, Stanley. 1989. *Doing What Comes Naturally: Change Rhetoric, and the Practice of Theory in Literary and Legal Studies*. Durham, NC: Duke University Press.

Foucault, Michel. [1961] 1988. *Madness and Civilization: A History of Insanity in the Age of Reason*. New York: Vintage Books.

Fralin, Richard. 1978. *Rousseau and Representation: A Study of the Development of His Concept of Political Institutions*. New York: Columbia University Press.

Gouhier, Henri. 2005. *Les Méditations Métaphysiques de Jean-Jacques Rousseau*. Paris: Librarie Philosophique.

Gourevitch, Victor. 1994. "Rousseau and Lying." *Berkshire Review*, 15: 93–107.

———. 1997. "Editorial Notes." *The Social Contract and Other Later Writings*. Cambridge: Cambridge University Press.

Grant, Ruth W. 1997. *Hypocrisy and Integrity: Machiavelli, Rousseau, and the Ethics of Politics*. Chicago: University of Chicago Press.

Grimsley, Ronald. 1968. *Rousseau and the Religious Quest*. Oxford: Oxford University Press.

———. 1972. "Introduction" to *Du Contrat Social*. Edited by Ronald Grimsley. Oxford: Oxford University Press.

Grotius, Hugo. [1625] 2005. *Rights of War and Peace*. Edited by Richard Tuck. Indianapolis, IN: Liberty Fund.

Habermas, Jürgen. [1962] 1989. *Structural Transformation of the Public Sphere: An Inquiry into a Category of Bourgeois Society*. Translated by Thomas Burger. Cambridge, MA: MIT Press.

———. 1997. "Popular Sovereignty as Procedure." *Deliberative Democracy: Essays on Reason and Politics*, ed. James Bohman and William Rehg. Cambridge, MA: MIT Press.

Hall, R. W. 1982. "Plato and Rousseau." *Apeiron*, 16 (1): 12–20.

Hanley, Ryan Patrick. 2008a. "Commerce and Corruption: Rousseau's Diagnosis and Adam Smith's Cure." *European Journal of Political Theory*, 7 (2): 137–58.

———. 2008b. "Enlightened Nation Building: The 'Science of the Legislator' in Adam Smith and Rousseau." *American Journal of Political Science*, 52 (2): 219–34.

————. 2011. "Love's Enlightenment: Fenelon and the Ethics of Other-Directedness." Presented at the annual meeting of the Association for Political Theory, October 14, 2011.

————. 2012. "Rousseau's Virtue Epistemology." *Journal of the History of Philosophy*, 50 (2): 239–63.

Hegel, G. W. F. [1802–03] 1999. *On the Scientific Ways of Treating Natural Law, on Its Place in Practical Philosophy, and Its Relation to the Positive Sciences of Right*. In *Hegel: Political Writings*. Cambridge: Cambridge University Press.

————. [1807] 1977. *Phenomenology of Spirit*. Translated by A. V. Miller. Oxford: Oxford University Press.

————. [1821] 1991. *Elements of the Philosophy of Right*. Edited by Allen W. Wood. Cambridge: Cambridge University Press.

————. [1830–31] 1988. *Introduction to the Philosophy of History*. Translated by Leo Rauch. Indianapolis, IN: Hackett Publishing.

Helvétius, Claude. [1772] 1810. *A Treatise on Man; His Intellectual Faculties and His Education*. Translated by W. Hooper. London: M. D. Albion Press.

Hendel, Charles. 1934. *Jean-Jacques Rousseau: Moralist*. London: Oxford University Press.

Hobbes, Thomas. [1651] 2002. *Leviathan*. Edited by A. P. Martinich. Peterborough, ON: Broadview Press.

Hoffmann, Stanley. 1963. "Rousseau on War and Peace." *American Political Science Review*, 57 (2): 317–33.

Hoffmann, Stanley and David P. Fidler, eds. 1991. *Rousseau on International Relations*. Oxford: Oxford University Press.

Holbach, Paul Henri Thiry baron. [1772] 2006. *Good Sense*. Stockbridge, MA: Hard Press.

————. [1774]. *Système sociale, ou principes naturels de la morale et del politique avec un examen de l'influence du gouvernment*. London.

Hulliung, Mark. 1994. *Autocritique of the Enlightenment: Rousseau and the Philosophes*. Cambridge, MA: Harvard University Press.

Hume, David. [1741] 1994. "Of Parties in General." In *Hume: Political Essays*, ed. Knud Haakonssen. Cambridge: Cambridge University Press.

————. [1748] 1994. "Of the Social Contract." In *David Hume: Political Essays*, ed. Knud Haakonsen. Cambridge: Cambridge University Press.

————. [1752a] 1994. "Of Commerce." In *Hume: Political Essays*, ed. Knud Haakonssen. Cambridge: Cambridge University Press.

————. [1752b] 1994. "On the Balance of Trade." In *Hume: Political Essays*, ed. Knud Haakonssen. Cambridge: Cambridge University Press.

————. [1754] 1994. "Idea of a Perfect Commonwealth." In *Hume: Political Essays*, ed. Knud Haakonssen. Cambridge: Cambridge University Press.

Inston, Kevin. 2010. *Rousseau and Radical Democracy*. London: Continuum Publishing.

Israel, Jonathan. 2010. *A Revolution of the Mind: Radical Enlightenment and the Intellectual Origins of Modern Democracy*. Princeton: Princeton University Press.

———. 2011. *Democratic Enlightenment: Philosophy, Revolution, and Human Rights 1750–1790*. Oxford: Oxford University Press.

de Jouvenel, Bernard. 1972. "Rousseau's Theory of the Forms of Government." In *Hobbes and Rousseau: A Collection of Critical Essays*, ed. Maurice Cranston and Richard S. Peters. Garden City, NY: Anchor Books.

Kant, Immanuel. [1764–65] 2005. "Selections from the Notes on the *Observations on the Feeling of the Beautiful and Sublime*." In *Notes and Fragments*, ed. Paul Guyer. Cambridge: Cambridge University Press.

———. [1766] 2002. *Dreams of a Spirit-Seer* In *Kant on Swedenborg: Dreams of a Spirit-Seer and Other Writings*, ed. Gregory R. Johnson. West Chester, PA: Swedenborg Foundation.

———. [1781/87] 1965. *Critique of Pure Reason*. Translated by Norman Kemp Smith. New York: St. Martin's Press.

———. [1784] 1991. "Idea for a Universal History with a Cosmopolitan Purpose." In *Kant: Political Writings*, ed. Hans Reiss. Cambridge: Cambridge University Press.

———. [1785] 1996. *Groundwork of the Metaphysics of Morals* in *Practical Philosophy*, ed. Mary J. Gregor. Cambridge: Cambridge University Press.

———. [1793] 1996. *On the Common Saying: That May Be True in Theory but It Is of No Use in Practice*. In *Practical Philosophy*, ed. Mary Gregor. Cambridge: Cambridge University Press.

———. [1795] 1996. "Toward a Perpetual Peace." In *Practical Philosophy*, trans. Mary Gregor. Cambridge: Cambridge University Press.

———. [1797] 1996. *Metaphysics of Morals*. In *Practical Philosophy*, ed. Mary Gregor. Cambridge: Cambridge University Press.

———. [1798] 1991. *The Contest of the Faculties*. In *Kant's Political Writings*, ed. Hans Reiss. Cambridge: Cambridge University Press.

Kapust, Daniel J. 2011. "The Problem of Flattery and Hobbes's Institutional Defense of Monarchy." *Journal of Politics*, 73 (3): 680–91.

Kateb, George. 1980. "Comments on Gourevitch." *Berkshire Review*, 15: 122–8.

Kelly, Christopher. 1987. "To Persuade without Convincing: The Language of Rousseau's Legislator." *American Journal of Political Science*, 31 (2): 321–35.

———. 2010. "Introduction and Notes." In *Emile or On Education*, Collected Writings of Rousseau, Vol. 13, ed. Christopher Kelly. Hanover, NH: University Press of New England.

Kelly, Christopher and Eve Grace. 2001. "Introduction." In *Letter to Beaumont, Letters Written from the Mountain, and Related Writings*. Hanover, NH: University Press of New England.

Kelly, Christopher and Roger Masters. 1994. "Introduction and Notes." In *Social Contract, Discourse on the Virtue Most Necessary for a Hero, Political Fragments, and Geneva Manuscript*, Collected Writings of Rousseau, Vol. 4, ed. Roger D. Masters and Christopher Kelly. Hanover, NH: University Press of New England.

Kennedy, Rosanne Terese. 2012. *Rousseau in Drag: Reconstructing Gender*. London: Palgrave.

Kitto, H. D. F. [1952] 1991. *The Greeks*. London: Penguin Books.

Klausen, Jimmy Casas. 2014. *Fugitive Rousseau: Slavery, Primitivism, and Political Freedom*. New York: Fordham University Press.

Klosko, George. 1986. *The Development of Plato's Political Theory*. New York: Methuen.

Koons, Robert C. 2011. "Dark Satanic Mills of Mis-Education: Some Proposals for Reform." *Humanitas*, 34 (1 & 2): 134–50.

Krause, Sharon. 2014. "Freedom, Sovereignty, and the General Will in Montesquieu." In *The General Will: the Evolution of a Concept*, ed. James Farr and David Lay Williams. Cambridge: Cambridge University Press.

Kuehn, Manfred. 2001. *Kant: A Biography*. Cambridge: Cambridge University Press.

Lane, Frederic Chapin. 1973. *Venice: A Maritime Republic*. Baltimore: Johns Hopkins University Press.

Lang, Lynda. 2002. "Introduction" to *Feminist Interpretations of Jean-Jacques Rousseau*, ed. Lynda Lange. University Park: Pennsylvania State University Press.

Leibniz, G. W. [1693] 1972. *Codex Iuris Gentium (Praefatio)*. In *Leibniz: Political Writings*, ed. Patrick Riley. Cambridge: Cambridge University Press.

Levine, Andrew. 1976. *Politics of Autonomy: A Kantian Reading of Rousseau's 'Social Contract.'* Amherst: University of Massachusetts Press.

Lintott, Andrew. 1999. *The Constitution of the Roman Republic*. Oxford: Oxford University Press.

Livy. 2002. *Early History of Rome: Books I–V of The History of Rome from Its Foundations*. Trans. Aubrey de Sélincourt. London: Penguin Books.

Locke, John. [1663–64] 1997. *Essays on the Law of Nature*. In *Political Essays*, ed. Mark Goldie. Cambridge: Cambridge University Press.

———. [1690] 1988. *Second Treatise of Government*. In *Two Treatises of Government*, ed. Peter Laslett. Cambridge: Cambridge University Press.

Lomonaco, Jeffrey. 2002. "Adam Smith's 'Letter to the Authors of the *Edinburgh Review*.'" *Journal of the History of Ideas*, 64 (3): 659–76.

Loewenstein, Karl. 1973. *The Governance of Rome*. The Hague: Martinus Nijhoff.

Luther, Martin. [1520] 1958. "The Freedom of a Christian." In *Martin Luther: Selections from His Writings*. New York: Anchor Books.

Machiavelli, Niccolò. [1513] 1995. *The Prince*. Translated by David Wooten. Indianapolis, IN.

———. [1531] 1998. *Discourses on Livy*. Translated by Harvey C. Mansfield and Nathan Tarcov. Chicago: University of Chicago Press.

MacKay, Christopher S. 2004. *Ancient Rome: A Military and Political History*. Cambridge: Cambridge University Press.

MacPherson, C. B. 1962. *The Political Theory of Possessive Individualism: Hobbes to Locke*. Oxford: Oxford University Press.

Madison, James. 1999. "Universal Peace." In *James Madison: Writings*, ed. Jack N. Rakove. New York: Library of America.

Madison, James, Alexander Hamilton, and John Jay. [1787–88] 1999. *The Federalist Papers*. Edited by Clinton Rossiter. New York: Mentor Books.

Maguire, Matthew W. 2006. *The Conversion of the Imagination: From Pascal through Rousseau to Tocqueville.* Cambridge, MA: Harvard University Press.

Malebranche, Nicholas. [1680] 1992. *Treatise on Nature and Grace.* Trans. Patrick Riley. Oxford: Oxford University Press.

Maloy, J. S. 2005. "The Very Order of Things: Rousseau's Tutorial Republic." *Polity* 37 (2): 235–61.

Mandeville, Bernard. [1705] 1997. *Fable of the Bees* in *Fable of the Bees and Other Writings,* ed., E. J. Hundert. Indianapolis, IN: Hackett Publishing.

Manin, Bernard. 1987. "On Legitimacy and Political Deliberation." *Political Theory,* 15 (3): 338–68.

Marso, Lori Jo. 1999. *(Un)Manly Citizens: Jean-Jacques Rousseau's and Germaine de Staël's Subversive Women.* Baltimore, MD: Johns Hopkins University Press.

Martinich, A. P. 1992. *The Two Gods of Leviathan: Thomas Hobbes on Religion and Politics.* Cambridge: Cambridge University Press.

———. 1995. *A Hobbes Dictionary.* Oxford: Blackwell.

Marks, Jonathan. 2005. *Perfection and Disharmony in the Thought of Jean-Jacques Rousseau.* Cambridge: Cambridge University Press.

———. 2006. "The Divine Instinct? Rousseau and Conscience." *Review of Politics,* 68 (4): 564–85.

Marx, Karl and Friedrich Engels. [1848] 1994. *Communist Manifesto.* In *Selected Political Writings,* ed. Lawrence Simon. Indianapolis, IN: Hackett Publishing.

Mason, John Hope. 1995. "Forced to Be Free." In *Rousseau and Liberty,* ed. Robert Wokler. Manchester: Manchester University Press.

Masters, Roger D. 1968. *The Political Philosophy of Rousseau.* Princeton: Princeton University Press.

———. 1978. "Introduction." In *On the Social Contract with Geneva Manuscript and Political Economy.* New York: St. Martin's Press.

McCormick, John P. 2007. "Rousseau's Rome and Repudiation of Populist Republicanism." *Critical Review of International Social and Political Philosophy,* 10 (1): 3–27.

McLendon, Michael Locke. 2009. "Rousseau, Amour Propre, and Intellectual Celebrity." *Journal of Politics,* 71 (2): 506–19.

Melzer, Arthur M. 1983. "Rousseau's Moral Realism: Replacing Natural Law with the General Will." *American Political Science Review,* 77 (3): 633–51.

———. 1990. *The Natural Goodness of Man.* Chicago: University of Chicago Press.

Mill, John Stuart. [1859] 1989. *On Liberty.* Edited by Stefan Collini. Cambridge: Cambridge University Press.

Miller, Fred J. 1995. *Nature, Justice, and Rights in Aristotle's Politics.* Oxford: Oxford University Press.

Miller, James. 1984. *Rousseau: Dreamer of Democracy.* New Haven: Yale University Press.

Millet, Louis. 1967. "Le Platonisme de Rousseau." *Revue de l'enseignement philosophique.* June/July.

Montesquieu, Charles de Secondat. [1721] 1964. *The Persian Letters.* Trans. George R. Healy. Indianapolis, IN: Bobbs-Merrill.

———. [1734] 1999. *Considerations on the Causes of the Greatness of the Romans and Their Decline*. Trans. David Lowelthal. Indianapolis, IN: Hackett.

———. [1748] 1989. *The Spirit of the Laws*. Trans. and ed. Anne R. Cohler, Basia Carolyn Miller, and Harold Samuel Stone. Cambridge: Cambridge University Press.

Morgenstern, Mira. 1996. *Rousseau and the Politics of Ambiguity: Self, Culture, and Society*. University Park: Pennsylvania State University Press.

———. 2008. "Strangeness, Violence, and the Establishment of Nationhood in Rousseau." *Eighteenth-Century Studies*, 41 (3): 359–81.

Mowbray, Miranda and Dieter Gollmann. 2007. "Electing the Doge of Venice: Analysis of a 13th Century Protocol." http://www.hpl.hp.com/techreports/2007/HPL-2007–28R1.pdf (accessed 1/11/11).

Murray, Christopher John, ed. 2004. *The Encyclopedia of the Romantic Era, 1760–1850*. New York: Fitzroy Dearborn.

Nadler, Steven. 1992. *Malebranche and Ideas*. New York: Oxford University Press.

———. 2010. *The Best of All Possible Worlds*. Princeton: Princeton University Press.

Nederman, Cary J. [2005] 2009. "Niccolò Machiavelli." *Stanford Encyclopedia of Philosophy*, http://plato.stanford.edu/entries/machiavelli/, accessed 12/14/11.

———. 2009. *Machiavelli*. Oxford: One World.

Neidleman, Jason. 2012. "Rousseau's Rediscovered *Communion des Coeurs*: Cosmopolitanism in the *Reveries of the Solitary Walker*." *Political Studies*, 60 (1): 76–94.

Neuhouser, Frederick. 1993. "Freedom, Dependence, and the General Will." *Philosophical Review*, 102 (3): 363–95.

———. 2008. *Rousseau's Theodicy of Self-Love: Evil, Rationality, and the Drive for Recognition*. Oxford: Oxford University Press.

Nicolet, Claude. 1980. *The World of the Citizen in Republican Rome*. Translated by P. S. Falla. Berkeley: University of California Press.

Nietzsche, Friedrich. [1887] 1966. *Beyond Good and Evil*. Translated by Walter Kaufmann. New York: Vintage Books.

———. [1887] 1994. *On the Genealogy of Morality*. Edited by Keith Ansell-Pearson. Cambridge: Cambridge University Press.

Noone, John B. 1972. "Rousseau's Theory of Natural Law as Conditional." *Journal of the History of Ideas*, 33 (1): 23–42.

Norwich, John Julius. 1989. *A History of Venice*. New York: Vintage Books.

Nuzzo, Angelica. 2011. "Arbitrariness and Freedom: Hegel on Rousseau and Revolution." In *Rousseau and Revolution*, ed. Holger Ross Lauritsen and Mikkel Thorup. London: Continuum.

Oakeshott, Michael. 1991. "On Being Conservative." In *Rational in Politics and Other Essays*. Indianapolis, IN: Liberty Fund.

O'Hagan, Timothy. 1996. "Rousseau and Wollstonecraft on Sexual Equality." In *A Textual Introduction to Social and Political Theory*, ed. Richard Bellamy and Angus Ross. Manchester: Manchester University Press.

———. 1999. *Rousseau*. London: Routledge.

————. 2004. "Taking Rousseau Seriously." *History of Political Thought*, 25 (1): 73–85.

Okin, Susan Moller. 1979. *Women in Western Political Thought*. Princeton: Princeton University Press.

Pangle, Thomas L. 1999. *Justice among Nations: On the Moral Basis of Power and Peace*. Lawrence: University of Kansas Press.

Pascal, Blaise. [1660] 1996. *Pensées*. Translated by A. J. Krailsheimer. New York: Penguin Books.

Piff, Paul K., Daniel M. Stancato, Stéphane Côte, Rodolfo Mendoza-Denton, and Dacher Keltner. 2012. "Higher Social Class Predicts Increased Unethical Behavior." *Proceedings of the National Academy of Sciences of the United States*, 109 (11), 4086–91.

Pinkard, Terry. 2001. *Hegel: A Biography*. Cambridge: Cambridge University Press.

Plamenatz, John. [1963] 1992. *Man and Society: Political and Social Theories from Machiavelli to Marx, Volume Two: From Montesquieu to the Early Socialists*, rev. ed. London: Longman.

Plato. 1961. *The Collected Dialogues of Plato*. Edited by Edith Hamilton and Huntington Cairns. Princeton: Princeton University Press.

Plutarch. 2001. *Plutarch's Lives*. Edited by Arthur Hugh Clough. New York: Modern Library.

Pocock, J. G. A. 1975. *The Machiavellian Moment: Florentine Political Thought and the Atlantic Republican Tradition*. Princeton, NJ: Princeton University Press.

Pomeroy, Sarah B. 1998. *Ancient Greece: A Political, Social, and Cultural History*. Oxford: Oxford University Press.

Popper, Karl. [1945] 1971. *The Open Society and Its Enemies, Volume I: The Spell of Plato*. Princeton: Princeton University Press.

Proudhon, Pierre-Joseph. [1851] 2007. *General Idea of Revolution in the Nineteenth Century*. New York: Cosimo Classics.

Pufendorf, Samuel. [1672] 1994. *Of the Law of Nature and of Nations*. In *The Political Writings of Samuel Pufendorf*. Translated by Michael J. Seidler. Oxford: Oxford University Press.

————. [1673] 1991. *On the Duty of Man and Citizen*. Edited by James Tully. Cambridge: Cambridge University Press.

Putterman, Ethan. 2010. *Rousseau, Law, and the Sovereignty of the People*. Cambridge: Cambridge University Press.

Rasmussen, Dennis C. 2008. *The Problems and Promise of Commercial Society: Adam Smith's Response to Rousseau*. University Park: Pennsylvania State University Press.

Rawls, John. 1971. *A Theory of Justice*. Cambridge, MA: Harvard University Press.

————. [1985] 1999. "Justice as Fairness: Political, Not Metaphysical." In *Collected Papers*, ed. Samuel Freeman. Cambridge, MA: Harvard University Press.

————. [1993] 2005. *Political Liberalism*, expanded edition. New York: Columbia University Press.

————. 2007. *Lectures on the History of Political Philosophy*. Edited by. Samuel Freeman. Cambridge, MA: Harvard University Press.

Riley, Patrick. 1970. "A Possible Explanation of the General Will." *American Political Science Review* 64 (1): 86–97.

———. 1982. *Will and Legitimacy: A Critical Exposition of Social Contract Theory in Hobbes, Locke, Rousseau, Kant, and Hegel.* Cambridge, MA: Harvard University Press.

———. 1986. *The General Will Before Rousseau: The Transformation of the Divine into the Civic.* Princeton: Princeton University Press.

———. 1993. "The Elements of Kant's Practical Philosophy." In *Kant and Political Philosophy: The Contemporary Legacy,* ed. Ronald Beiner and William James Booth. New Haven: Yale University Press.

———. 1994. Introduction and notes to *Telemachus, Son of Ulysses,* by François de Fénelon. Edited by Patrick Riley. Cambridge: Cambridge University Press.

———. 1996. *Leibniz' Universal Jurisprudence: Justice as Charity of the Wise.* Cambridge, MA: Harvard University Press.

———. 2001a. "Rousseau, Fénelon, and the Quarrel Between the Ancients and the Moderns." In *The Cambridge Companion to Rousseau,* ed. Patrick Riley. Cambridge: Cambridge University Press.

———. 2001b. "Rousseau's General Will." In *The Cambridge Companion to Rousseau,* ed. Patrick Riley. Cambridge: Cambridge University Press.

Ripstein, Arthur. 1994. "Universal and General Wills: Hegel and Rousseau." *Political Theory,* 22 (3): 444–67.

Roosevelt, Grace G. 1987. "A Reconstruction of Rousseau's Fragments on the State of War." *History of Political Thought,* 8 (2): 225–44.

———. 1990. *Reading Rousseau in the Nuclear Age.* Philadelphia: Temple University Press.

Rosenblatt, Helena. 1997. *Rousseau and Geneva: From the 'First Discourse' to the 'Social Contract,' 1749–1762.* Cambridge: Cambridge University Press.

———. 2002. "On the 'Misogyny' of Jean-Jacques Rousseau: The *Letter to d'Alembert* in Historical Context." *French Historical Studies,* 25 (1): 91–114.

Rossiter, Clinton. 1948. *Constitutional Dictatorship.* Princeton: Princeton University Press.

Rousseau, Jean-Jacques. [1739] 1964. "La Verger de Madame la Baronne deWarens." In *OEuvres complètes,* ed. B. Gagnebin and M. Raymond, vol. 2. Paris: Pléiade.

———. [1744–45] 1998. "Letter on Italian and French Opera." In *Essay on the Origin of Languages and Writings Related to Music,* The Collected Writings of Rousseau, Vol. 7, ed. John T. Scott. Hanover, NH: University of New England Press.

———. [1749] 2006. "The Banterer." In *Autobiographical, Scientific, Religious, Moral, and Literary Writings,* The Collected Writings of Rousseau, Vol. 12, ed. Christopher Kelly. Hanover, NH: University of New England Press.

———. [1749–56] 2005. "On Wealth and Fragments on Taste." In *The Plan for Perpetual Peace, On the Government of Poland, and Other Writings on History and Politics,* The Collected Writings of Rousseau, Vol. 11, ed. Christopher Kelly. Hanover, NH: University Press of New England.

———. [1751] 1997. *Discourse on the Arts and Sciences*. In *The Discourses and Other Early Political Writings*, ed. Victor Gourevitch. Cambridge: Cambridge University Press.

———. [1751] 1997. "Last Reply by Jean-Jacques Rousseau of Geneva." In *The Discourses and Other Early Political Writings*, ed. Victor Gourevitch. Cambridge: Cambridge University Press.

———. [1751] 1997. "Observations by Jean-Jacques Rousseau of Geneva on the Answer Made to His Discourse." In *The Discourses and Other Early Political Writings*, ed. Victor Gourevitch. Cambridge: Cambridge University Press.

———. [1752–53] 1997. "Preface to Narcissus." In *The Discourses and Other Early Political Writings*, ed. Victor Gourevitch. Cambridge: Cambridge University Press.

———. [1755] 1997. *Discourse on Political Economy*. In *The Social Contract and Other Later Political Writings*, ed. Victor Gourevitch. Cambridge: Cambridge University Press.

———. [1755] 1997. *Discourse on the Origin and the Foundations of Inequality Among Men*. In *The Discourses and Other Early Political Writings*, ed. Victor Gourevitch. Cambridge: Cambridge University Press.

———. [1756] 1978. *The Geneva Manuscript*. In *On the Social Contract with Geneva Manuscript and Political Economy*, ed. Roger D. Masters. New York: St. Martin's Press.

———. [1756] 1997. "Letter from J. J. Rousseau to M. de Voltaire, 18 August 1756." In *The Social Contract and Other Later Political Writings*, ed. Victor Gourevitch. Cambridge: Cambridge University Press.

———. [1756] 2010. *Favre Manuscript of Emile*. In *Emile, or On Education*, *The Collected Writings of Rousseau*, Vol. 13, ed. Christopher Kelly and Allan Bloom.. Hanover, NH: University Press of New England.

———. [1757] 2006. *Moral Letters* in *Autobiographical, Scientific, Religious, Moral, and Literary Writings*, The Collected Writings of Rousseau, Vol. 12, ed. Christopher Kelly. Dartmouth College Press.

———. [1758] 1960. *Letter to M. d'Alembert on the Theater*. Translated by Allan Bloom. Ithaca, NY: Cornell University Press.

———. [1758] 1967. "Letter to Deleyre." In *Correspondance complète de Jean-Jacques Rousseau*, ed. R. A. Leigh. Geneva: Institut et Musée Voltaire.

———. [1758] 1997. "The State of War." In *The Social Contract and Other Later Political Writings*, ed. Victor Gourevitch. Cambridge: Cambridge University Press.

———. [1761] 1997. *Julie; Or, the New Heloise: Letters of Two Lovers Who Live in a Small Town at the Foot of the Alps*. Translated by Philip Stewart and Jean Vaché. The Collected Writings of Rousseau,Vol. 6.Hanover, NH: University Press of New England.

———. [1761] 1997. "Letter to d'Offerville." In *The Social Contract and Other Later Political Writings*, ed. Victor Gourevitch. Cambridge: Cambridge University Press.

———. [1762] 1979. *Emile, or On Education*. Translated by Allan Bloom. New York: Basic Books.

———. [1762] 1997. *Of the Social Contract*. Edited by Victor Gourevitch. Cambridge: Cambridge University Press.

———. [1762] 1995. "Letters to Malesherbes." In *The Confessions and Correspondence, Including the Letters to Malesherbes*, ed. Christopher Kelly, Roger D. Masters, and Peter G. Stillman. *The Collected Writings of Rousseau*. Vol. 5. Hanover, NH: University Press of New England.

———. [1763] 2001. *Letter to Beaumont*. In *Letter to Beaumont, Letters Written from the Mountain, and Related Writings*, The Collected Writings of Rousseau, Vol. 9, ed. Christopher Kelly and Eve Grace.. Hanover, NH: University Press of New England.

———. [1763] 1997. "Letter to Usteri." In *The Social Contract and Other Later Political Writings*, ed. Victor Gourevitch. Cambridge: Cambridge University Press.

———. [1764] 2001. *Letters Written from the Mountain*. In *Letter to Beaumont, Letters Written from the Mountain, and Related Writings, The Collected Writings of Rousseau*, Vol. 9, ed. Christopher Kelly and Eve Grace. Hanover, NH: University Press of New England.

———. [1764] 1997. "On Theatrical Imitation: An Essay Drawn from Plato's Dialogues." In *Essay on the Origin of Languages and Writings Related to Music, The Collected Writings of Rousseau*, Vol. 7, ed. John T. Scott. Hanover, NH University Press of New England.

———. [1764] 1937. "Letter to M. l'Abbé de Carondelet." In *Citizen of Geneva: Selections from the Letters of Jean-Jacques Rousseau*, ed. Charles W. Hendel. Oxford: Oxford University Press.

———. [1764] 2005. *Judgment of the Plan for Perpetual Peace*. In *The Plan for Perpetual Peace, On the Government of Poland, and Other Writings on History and Politics*, The Collected Writings of Rousseau, Vol. 11, ed. Christopher Kelly. Hanover, NH: University Press of New England.

———. [1765] 2005. *Plan for a Constitution for Corsica*. In *The Plan for Perpetual Peace, On the Government of Poland, and Other Writings on History and Politics*, The Collected Writings of Rousseau, Vol. 11, ed. Christopher Kelly. Hanover, NH: University Press of New England.

———. [1767] 1997. "Letter to Mirabeau." In *The Social Contract and Other Later Political Writings*, ed. Victor Gourevitch. Cambridge: Cambridge University Press.

———. [1768] 1997. *Discourse on This Question: What Is the Virtue a Hero Most Needs and Who Are the Heroes Who Have Lacked This Virtue?* In *The Discourses and Other Early Political Writings*, ed. Victor Gourevitch. Cambridge: Cambridge University Press.

———. [1769] 1997. "Letter from J. J. Rousseau to M. de Franquie`res, 25 March 1769. " In *The Social Contract and Other Later Political Writings*, ed. Victor Gourevitch. Cambridge: Cambridge University Press.

————. [1771] 1995. *The Confessions and Correspondence, Including the Letters to Malesherbes*, The Collected Writings of Rousseau, Vol. 5, ed. Christopher Kelly, Roger D. Masters, and Peter G. Stillman.. Hanover, NH: University Press of New England.

————. [1772] 1997. *Considerations on the Government of Poland.* In *The Social Contract and Other Later Political Writings*, ed. Victor Gourevitch. Cambridge: Cambridge University Press.

————. [1776] 1990. *Rousseau, Judge of Jean-Jacques: Dialogues*, The Collected Writings of Rousseau, Vol. 1, ed. Roger D. Masters and Christopher Kelly.. Hanover, NH: University Press of New England.

————. [1778] 2000. *Reveries of the Solitary Walker.* Translated by Charles E. Butterworth. Indianapolis: Hackett Publishing.

————. 1959–95. *Œuvres complèt.* Edited by B. Gagnebin and M. Raymond. Paris: Pléiade.

————. 1994a. "Political Fragments." In *Social Contract, Discourse on the Virtue Most Necessary for a Hero, Political Fragments, and Geneva Manuscript*, The Collected Writings of Rousseau, Vol. 4, ed. Roger D. Masters and Christopher Kelly.. Hanover, NH: University Press of New England.

————. 1994b. "Fragment on Freedom." In *Social Contract, Discourse on the Virtue Most Necessary for a Hero, Political Fragments, and Geneva Manuscript*, The Collected Writings of Rousseau, Vol. 4, ed. Roger D. Masters and Christopher Kelly.. Hanover, NH: University Press of New England.

————. 1997. *Essay on the Origin of Languages in Which Something Is Said About Melody and Musical Imitation.* In *The Discourses and Other Early Political Writings*, ed. Victor Gourevitch. Cambridge: Cambridge University Press.

————. 2001. *History of the Government of Geneva.* In *Letter to Beaumont, Letters Written from the Mountain, and Related Writings*, The Collected Writings of Rousseau, Vol. 9, ed. Christopher Kelly and Eve Grace.. Hanover, NH: University Press of New England.

————. 2005a. "Response to the Anonymous Letter Written by Members of the Legal Profession." In *Letter to d'Alembert and Writings for the Theater*, The Collected Writings of Rousseau, Vol. 10, ed. Allan Bloom, Charles Butterworth, and Christopher Kelly.. Hanover, NH: University Press of New England.

————. 2005b. "Separate Fragments." In *The Plan for Perpetual Peace, On the Government of Poland, and Other Writings on History and Politics*, The Collected Writings of Rousseau, Vol. 11, ed. Christopher Kelly. Hanover, NH: University Press of New England.

————. 2005c. "Fragments on the *Polysynody.*" In *The Plan for Perpetual Peace, On the Government of Poland, and Other Writings on History and Politics*, The Collected Writings of Rousseau, Vol. 11, ed. Christopher Kelly. Hanover, NH: University Press of New England.

————. 2007. "Various Fragments." In *Autobiographical, Scientific, Religious, Moral, and Literary Writings*, The Collected Writings of Rousseau, Vol. 12, trans. and ed. Christopher Kelly. Hanover, NH: University Press of New England.

Russell, Bertrand. [1945] 1972]. *A History of Western Philosophy* [New York: Simon & Schuster.

Sandel, Michael. 1996. *Democracy's Discontent: America in the Search of a Public Philosophy*. Cambridge, MA: Harvard University Press.

Schmitt, Carl. [1932] 2007. *The Concept of the Political*, expanded edition. Trans. George Schwab. Chicago: University of Chicago Press.

Schwartzberg, Melissa. 2003. "Rousseau on Fundamental Law." *Political Studies*, 51 (2): 387–403.

———. 2008. "Voting the General Will: Rousseau on Decision Rules." *Political Theory*, 36 (3): 403–23.

Scott, John T. 1994. "Politics as an Imitation of the Divine in Rousseau's *Social Contract*." *Polity*, 26 (3): 473–501.

Seung, T. K. 1976. *Cultural Thematics: The Formation of the Faustian Ethos*. New Haven, CT: Yale University Press.

———. 1993. *Intuition and Construction: the Foundation of Normative Theory*. New Haven: Yale University Press.

———. 1996. *Plato Rediscovered: Human Value and Social Order*. Lanham, MD: Rowman and Littlefield.

———. 2005. *Nietzsche's Epic of the Soul: Thus Spoke Zarathustra*. Lanham, MD: Lexington Books.

———. 2006. *Goethe, Nietzsche, and Wagner: Their Spinozan Epics of Love and Power*. Lanham, MD: Lexington Books.

———. 2007. *The Cultural Background of Western Philosophy*. Seoul, Korea: Korean Academic Research Council.

Shklar, Judith N. 1969. *Men and Citizens: A Study of Rousseau's Social Theory*. Cambridge: Cambridge University Press.

Scholz, Sally. 2013. "Rousseau on Poverty." *Economic Justice Philosophical and Legal Perspectives*, ed. Helen M. Stacy and Win Chiat Lee. Berlin: Springer.

Silverthorne, J. M. 1973. "Rousseau's Plato." *Studies on Voltaire and the Eighteenth Century*, 116: 235–49.

Simpson, Matthew. 2006a. "A Paradox of Sovereignty in the *Social Contract*." *Journal of Moral Philosophy*, 3 (1): 47–58.

———. 2006b. *Rousseau's Theory of Freedom*. London: Continuum.

———. 2007. *Rousseau: A Guide for the Perplexed*. London: Continuum Books.

Skinner, Quentin. [1981] 2000. *Machiavelli: A Very Short Introduction*. Oxford: Oxford University Press.

———. 2002. *Visions of Politics, Volume II: Renaissance Virtues*. Cambridge: Cambridge University Press.

———. 2008. *Hobbes and Republican Liberty*. Cambridge: Cambridge University Press.

Smith, Adam. [1759] 2009. *Theory of Moral Sentiments*. Edited by Ryan Patrick Hanley. London: Penguin Books.

Smith, Steven B. 1989. *Hegel's Critique of Liberalism: Rights in Context*. Chicago: University of Chicago Press.

———. 2011. "Strauss's Rousseau and the Second Wave of Modernity." In *The Art of Theory*, http://www.artoftheory.com/strauss's-rousseau-and-the-second-wave-of-modernity-steven-b-smith/, accessed October 9, 2012.

Spinoza, Benedict. [1670] 2001. *Theological-Political Treatise*. Translated by Samuel Shirley. in Spinoza: Complete Works. Indianapolis, IN: Hackett Publishing.

———. 2000. *Political Treatise*. Translated by Samuel Shirley. Indianapolis, IN: Hackett Publishing.

Sreenivasan, Gopal. 2000. "What is the General Will?" *Philosophical Review*, 109 (4): 545–81.

Steinberger, Peter J. 2008. "Hobbes, Rousseau and the Modern Conception of the State." *Journal of Politics*, 70 (3): 595–611

Stephens, James Fitzjames. [1873] 1993. *Liberty, Equality, Fraternity*, ed. Stuart D. Warner. Indianapolis, IN: Liberty Fund.

Strauss, Leo. [1953] 1965. *Natural Right and History*. Chicago: University of Chicago Press.

———. 1975. "Three Waves of Modernity." In *Political Philosophy: Six Essays by Leo Strauss*, ed. Hilail Gildin. Indianapolis: Pegasus.

Strong, Tracy B. [1994] 2002. *Jean-Jacques Rousseau: The Politics of the Ordinary*. Lanham, MD: Rowman and Littlefield.

Talmon, J. L. 1955. *The Origins of Totalitarian Democracy*. London: Secker and Warburg.

Taylor, Charles. 1992. *Sources of the Self: The Making of the Modern Identity*. Cambridge, MA: Harvard University Press.

———. 2007. *A Secular Age*. Cambridge, MA: Harvard University Press.

Trachtenberg, Zev M. 1993. *Making Citizens: Rousseau's Political Theory of Culture*. London: Routledge.

———. 2001. "Rousseau's Platonic Rejection of Politics." In *Rousseau and the Ancients/Rousseau et les Anciens*, ed. Ruth Grant and Phillip Stewart. Montreal: Pensée Libre.

Tuck, Richard. 2004. "The Utopianism of *Leviathan*." In *'Leviathan' after 350 Years*, ed. Tom Sorell and Luc Foisneau. Oxford: Oxford University Press.

Vaughan, C. E. [1915] 1962. "Introduction" and "Editorial Notes" to *The Political Writings of Jean-Jacques Rousseau*. New York: John Wiley and Sons.

Vaughan, Sharon K. 2008. *Poverty and Western Political Thought*. Lanham, MD: Lexington Books.

Vico, Giambattisa. [1725] 2000. *The New Science*. Translated by David Marsh. New York: Penguin Books.

Viroli, Maurizio. 1988. *Jean-Jacques Rousseau and the 'Well-Ordered Society.'* Translated by Derek Hanson Cambridge: Cambridge University Press.

Waltz, Kenneth N. 1959. *Man, the State, and War: A Theoretical Analysis*. New York: Columbia University Press.

Warburton, William. [1738] 1846. *The Divine Legation of Moses Demonstrated*, 10th edition. London: Thomas Tegg.

Wiker, Benjamin. 2008. *Ten Books that Screwed up the World: And Five Others that Didn't Help*. Washington, DC: Regnery Publishing.

Williams, David Lay. 2007a. *Rousseau's Platonic Enlightenment*. University Park: Pennsylvania State University Press.

———. 2007b. "Ideas and Actuality in the Social Contract: Kant & Rousseau." *History of Political Thought*, 28 (3): 471–97.

———. 2010a. "Political Ontology and Institutional Design in Montesquieu and Rousseau." *American Journal of Political Science*, 54 (2): 525–42.

———. 2010b. "Spinoza and the General Will." *Journal of Politics*, 72 (2): 341–356.

———. 2012. "The Platonic Soul of the *Reveries*: the Role of Solitude in Rousseau's Democratic Politics." *History of Political Thought*, 33 (1): 87–123.

Williamson, Kevin D. 2011. *The Politically Incorrect Guide to Socialism*. New York: Regnery Publishing.

Wingrove, Elizabeth Rose. 2000. *Rousseau's Republican Romance*. Princeton: Princeton University Press.

Wokler, Robert. 2001. *Rousseau: A Very Short Introduction*. Oxford: Oxford University Press.

Wolin, Sheldon S. 2006. *Politics and Vision*, revised edition. Princeton, NJ: Princeton University Press.

Index

active obedience, 67
Aeneid (Virgil), 26, 30–2
Alliance between Church and State
    (Warburton), 95
amour de-soi, 17
amour propre, 18–19, 75
    artificiality of, 206–7
    dangers of, 23–4
    development of, 19
    doux commerce and, 209
    egoism and, 24
    in *Emile*, 273–4
    free will and, 249–50
    general will and, 24
    slavery and, 21
    social esteem and, 19
    sovereignty and, 74
    wealth and, 19–20
ancient laws, 141
Anti-Dühring (Engels), 238
apathy, political, 148–9
Aquinas, Thomas, 33–4
aristocracies, 121–7
    definition of, 116
    economic inequality under, 124–6
    elective, 123–4
    in Geneva, Switzerland, 123
    hereditary, 122–3
    history of, 122
    magistrates within, 169
    natural, 122
    oligarchy from, 136
    size of state for, 116, 124
    varieties of, 122–4
Aristotle, 116
    on natural slavery, 40–1
Arouet, François-Marie. *See* Voltaire
atheism, 192
    as civil threat, 193
    for Holbach, 192
    intolerance and, 201
    Rousseau on dangers of, 192–3
authority. *See* political authority

Bacon, Francis, 9
Baybeyrac, Jean, 5
Bayle, Pierre, 195
Beaumont, Christophe de, 191–2
Bell, Daniel, 2
Bentham, Jeremy, 239
Berlin, Isaiah, 1, 55, 100, 216
Bertram, Christopher, 60, 258
birds, imagery of, 29–30
Boiley, Charles-Ange, 26
Bolomey, Benjamin Samuel, 26
Borgia, Cesare, 128, 222
Bossuet, Jacques Bénigne, 130
Boswell, James, 29
Buddhism. *See* Tibetan Buddhism
Burlamaqui, Jean-Jacques, 5, 15–16, 69
    on government as social contract, 150
    politics of, 39
Butler, Melissa, 281

Caesar, Julius, 184
Calvin, Jean, 4, 260, 274
capitalism. *See also* wealth
    development of, 6
Catiline Affair, 183–4
cats, imagery of, 28–9
censors
    in Comitia Centuriata, 186
    function of, 186–7
    as moral judges, 187
    public opinion as influence on, 187–8
    virtue of, 190
censorship, 186–91
    Constant on, 190, 191
charity, 231–2
Christianity, 83, 95–6, 214, 260, 274
    civil religion and, 194
    political virtues of, 197–9
    as religion of man, 197
    social virtues of, 197–9
    tyranny and, 198
Cicero (Emperor), 183–4
    moral philosophy of, 221